TRAIL OF CTHULHU

BY KENNETH HITE

BASED ON THE GUMSHOE SYSTEM BY ROBIN D LAWS

Publisher: Simon Rogers

Written by: Kenneth Hite

GUMSHOE System: Robin D Laws

Layout: Jérôme Huguenin

Art: Jérôme Huguenin

GUMSHOE Guru: Robin D Laws

Editing and Additional Material: Simon Rogers

Based on: Call of Cthulhu by Sandy Petersen and Lynn Willis

Special thanks : Effie and Julia Huguenin, Léo, Pascal Quidault and Leonard Balsera

Playtesting: Adrian Price, Steve Dempsey, Wai Kien, Adrian Smith, Graham Walmsley, Alex Fradera, Dave, Polymancer Studios, Simon Rogers, Daniel Bayn, Danni Bayn, Chris Malone, Mark DiPasquale, Matthew Pook, Tim Barker, Louise Hayes, David Lai, Mike Shepard, Carla Jane Miller, Elizabeth Rees, Robert Mills, Donald F. Taylor III, Richard Hardy, Lynne Hardy, Frederic Moll, Fredrik Hansson, Jeff Campbel Jamie Michael, Joshua Ford, Marcus Ogawa, Lisa Marie Ogawa, Gil Trevizo, Henry de Veuve, Ronald Abitz, Steve Bartalamay, Alan Fountain, Peter Kessler, Wojciech "Alter" Kobza, Laurent Mollicone, Olivier Noël, Wayne O'Connor, Ghislain Morel, James Semple, Gabriella Semple, Dan Pusceddu, Olive Pusceddu, Axel Eble, Stefan Ohrmann, Martin Schrammm, Onno Tasler, Ralf Achenbach, William C Bargo Jr, Jacques Maurice Mallah, Donald F. Taylor III, Keith A Callison, Doug, Erik Durcan, Renee Grayson, Jerry D. Grayson, Leonard Balsera, Samantha Taylor, Dane Black

TRAIL OF CTHULHU

Contents

TRAIL OF CTHULHU

Contents

Introduction

In the mists of prehistory, alien gods and monsters fell to Earth and warred over our planet, unleashing cosmic science and inconceivable powers until continents sank and seas boiled. Exhausted or defeated, They fell into an aeons-long slumber, and the human race goes about its unknowing business over Their graves and tombs. But there are those who want to seek out the fragments of the lore They left behind. Those who want to learn the secrets of the stars, and the true names of the dimensions. Those who want the dead gods' powers. Those want to wake Them up.

You are among the few who suspect the truth – about the mad gods at the center of the universe, about the Great Old Ones who dream of clearing off the Earth, about the extra-terrestrials who use mankind in their experiments, about the ancient legends of undying evil that are all coming true. You have to make sure nobody else ever finds out — or the world will wake up screaming.

You have to keep the doors to the Outside from swinging open – no matter what the cost in life or sanity. You have to piece together the clues from books bound in human skin, from eviscerated corpses covered in ichor, and from inscriptions carved on walls built before humanity evolved. You have to go wherever the answers are, and do what needs to be done.

But do you dare to follow ... the trail of Cthulhu?

Why This Game Exists

This game exists in order to adapt the greatest RPG of all time, *Call of Cthulhu,* to a different rules set, the GUMSHOE engine. Why on Earth would we do a thing like that? First of all, part of what makes *Call of Cthulhu* so great is its theme, taken from the cosmic despair of the greatest horror writer of the 20th century, HP Lovecraft. We kept that. Second, part of what makes *Call of Cthulhu* so great is its deliberate decision to make characters increasingly vulnerable to the horrors they face, to give their bravery real meaning and force real mechanical consequences in the game. We kept that, too.

So what did we change? Let me change the subject. The greatest playwright ever is William Shakespeare. His greatest play is *King Lear.* Why would Akira Kurosawa make that play into a movie? And why would he set that movie, *Ran,* in samurai-era Japan instead of quasi-ancient Britain? Because more people want to - or can — see a movie than a play, and because transferring the story to Japan makes its themes paradoxically clearer than leaving them in the "familiar" world Shakespeare wrote. Did *Ran* improve on *King Lear,* or make it obsolete? Don't be ridiculous. Did it do something worth doing by changing *King Lear*? Absolutely.

To return to our topic, then: Another part of what makes *Call of Cthulhu* so great is its emphasis on investigation, on gathering clues instead of treasure. We designed GUMSHOE to make that easier, clearer, and more direct. GUMSHOE exists to solve a problem that many people found with running *Call of Cthulhu* - one bad die roll can derail an adventure. You didn't find the diary, so you didn't get the spell, so either Arkham is destroyed or the Keeper has to scuttle 'round and plant the diary somewhere else. In *Trail of Cthulhu*, the GUMSHOE rules guarantee that you will find that diary. (We don't promise not to destroy Arkham.) This is not the entirety of what GUMSHOE offers, but it was the starting point for GUMSHOE's laser-like focus on investigation.

Some Keepers, and even some players, enjoyed seeing everything go pear-shaped, and reveled in the creative destruction of the adventure. Some didn't, and worked out their own ways around the problem, ways they are perfectly happy with; their own crib sheets to *King Lear,* if you will. We hope there is enough other good stuff in here for them, but *Trail of Cthulhu* is first and foremost for the Keepers and players who privilege investigation, and who want mechanics that do likewise. It's for fans of procedural shows like *House* or *CSI,* in which the mystery isn't "will the lab test come back," but "what do the results mean"? That's not to say things won't go wrong for the players, merely that the wrongness won't be caused by an absence of

Core Concepts

Roleplaying Game: We assume you've already got this covered. If not, see any other roleplaying game book for the mandatory "What is Roleplaying" section, or ask your geek friends.

Keeper: The Game Master, or GM.

Investigators: The Player Characters, or PCs.

Investigative Abilities: Include academic, interpersonal, and technical abilities. These abilities *always* work; they are designed to gather clues.

General Abilities: The rest of the abilities, including combat abilities and "statistics" like Health, Sanity, and Stability. Using or testing them creates drama; they may fail.

Stability: A short-term measure of your Investigator's mental health. It goes down rapidly during an adventure, but usually refreshes afterward.

Sanity: A long-term measure of your Investigator's blissful ignorance of the horrible truths of the Mythos. It goes down slowly, and seldom if ever goes up again.

The Mythos: Short for Cthulhu Mythos, the body of lore created by HP Lovecraft that underlies most, or all, of the horrific events in a *Trail of Cthulhu* campaign or adventure.

HP Lovecraft: American horror writer (1890-1937). All quotes in this rulebook are from his stories and poetry.

Clue: The point of each scene is to deliver a clue to the mystery, to the Investigator with the relevant investigative ability. When the clue has been delivered, the scene can end, unless there's a really awesome fight going on. Clues are leads to other scenes; they don't have to be "true."

clues, but how they use them. It's for players who are curious about the Call, and who want to follow the Trail all the way to the end.

Purist or Pulp or Both?

The game *Trail of Cthulhu* is intended to tell stories of uncovering the occult horror mysteries of the Cthulhu Mythos. Traditionally, such games fall into one of two camps.

One is the Purist idiom or mode, which takes a subset of HP Lovecraft's later and starker works (*The Colour Out of Space, At the Mountains of Madness, The Shadow Out of Time, The Whisperer in Darkness*) as its

model. It intends to recreate a game of philosophical horror, in which the act of uncovering the truth dooms both active seeker and unfortunate bystander alike.

The second is the Pulp idiom or mode, which aims rather for the "desperate action" feel of Robert E Howard's Cthulhu Mythos stories (*The Thing on the Roof, The Fire of Asshurbanipal, Skull-Face*). It intends to focus on the struggle (especially the physical struggle) against the Mythos, doomed or noble as the case may be. It also privileges character survival somewhat more than does the Purist idiom.

HP Lovecraft, of course, wrote in both idioms: *The Case of Charles*

Dexter Ward, The Dunwich Horror, and *The Shunned House* all feature more-or-less resolute monster-hunting Investigators thwarting cosmic evil in Howardian fashion. (Robert E Howard also wrote at least one fine Purist Mythos tale, *The Black Stone.*) Many of Lovecraft's finest tales, such as *The Call of Cthulhu* (which features both neurasthenic scholars uncovering the truth and police raids on vile cults) and *The Shadow Over Innsmouth* (which features both a desperate chase through a ruined town and a narrative of psychological corruption) draw from both modes for their power. While it is not our job to tell you how to run your game (actually, it is, but we'll get to that in a later chapter), it seems to us that treating Cthulhoid horrors the way HP Lovecraft does would be a good idea.

However, for those who wish to emphasize one or another idiom, we have indicated those rules and game elements most suited for the Purist mode with the following symbol:

and those most suited for the Pulp mode with this one:

The Keeper may rule that some rules and elements are simply not allowed in her games in order to inculcate a specific flavor of horror, which is after all the entire point. An index of Pulp and Purist rules can be found on p 243.

The Investigator

"There can be nothing normal in the mind of one who, knowing what I knew of the horrors of Tempest Mountain, would seek alone for the fear that lurked there.... Yet I continued my quest with even greater zeal as events and revelations became more monstrous."

— The Lurking Fear

In *Trail of Cthulhu,* your player character is called an "Investigator" because that is what player characters do: investigate the (often horrible) occult mysteries that conceal the truth of the Cthulhu Mythos. Investigators may be professional investigators such as detectives, police, or government agents, or they may

not. Regardless of an Investigator's chosen career, uncovering the secrets of the Mythos has become her life's work.

Occupations

Before discovering the Mythos, your Investigator did something else; something you may still do to keep body and soul together while he risks both. This is your **Occupation,** which helps determine the abilities you will use during your adventures.

The Occupations typical of Lovecraftian characters (Antiquarian, Artist, Author, Dilettante, Doctor, Journalist, Police Detective, and Professor) are marked with the Purist symbol

. The other listed Occupations are both typical of the 1930s and rife with potential for eldritch encounters.

Every Occupation description includes its Occupational abilities (see p. 23), its Credit Rating band (see p. 32), and any special abilities or rules that Investigators with that Occupation can use. You can buy and build Occupational abilities at half-price, so pick an Occupation geared to what you want your Investigator to be able to do in the game.

List of Occupations
Alienist

Antiquarian

Archaeologist

Artist

Author

Clergy

Criminal

Dilettante

Doctor

Hobo

Journalist

Military

Nurse

Parapsychologist

Pilot

Police Detective

Private Investigator

Professor

Scientist

Investigator Creation Quick Reference
Ask your Keeper how the campaign frame (see p. 204) affects character creation. This can, for example, set the number of build points available or give caps on certain abilities.

Choose your Investigator's original Occupation (see p. 9). Decide if you still follow it, or if you have abandoned your job to become a full-time (and likely increasingly impoverished and ostracized) uncoverer of Mythos truths. In a one-shot adventure, you may not have time to quit your job!

Based on your own conception of your Investigator's character and backstory, choose your Drive (see p. 19).

Spend build points (see p. 23) on your abilities (see p. 28), making sure your party as a whole has as many abilities as possible covered.

Define the Pillars of your Sanity (see p. 46); and Sources of your Stability, (p. 48), if your campaign uses them.

Choose any contacts you have (see p. 31)

At any point during this process, decide on your Investigator's name, birthplace, favorite cigarettes, religious beliefs, or anything else that you think will help you understand and roleplay your Investigator.

Alienist

A specialist in mental illness, you may be a Vienna-trained psychoanalyst, a neurologist who studies brain function, or a medical doctor with a strong interest in behavioral science. Although Freudian theories are coming to dominate the field, they are far from universally understood or accepted.

Occupational Abilities: Biology, Languages (German and Latin), Library Use, Medicine, Pharmacy, Psychoanalysis, Assess Honesty, and any other two Interpersonal abilities.

Credit Rating: 3-4

Special: By using Medicine or an Interpersonal ability, you have access to mental records and sanitarium wards generally off limits to the public. If you are a licensed MD (a Medicine rating of 2 or more), you can do the same for medical records and hospital wards.

You make Psychoanalysis tests for Psychological Triage (see p. 79) at a Difficulty of 3, instead of 4. It costs you only 1 Psychoanalysis point instead of 2 to stabilize an erratic character. You can recover your own Stability, but you only recover 1 point for each Psychoanalysis point you spend.

 You can use Assess Honesty as forensic psychology. From the details of a crime scene, you can, based on past case studies of similar offenses, assemble a profile detailing the perpetrator's likely personal history, age, habits and attitudes. You will probably need to remind the Keeper of this use of the ability.

 You may put build points into, and use, the Hypnosis ability (see p. 43).

Antiquarian

As much a state of mind as a profession, you value the past and willingly immerse yourself in it. You may have a small independent income, you may be a resident scholar at a museum or gallery, or you may condescend to deal in antiques, books, or the objets d'art of a more gracious era.

Occupational Abilities: Architecture, Art History, Bargain, History, Languages, Law, Library Use, and any one Investigative ability as a personal specialty.

Credit Rating: 2-5

Special: Once per adventure, you may have an informative or suitable item for the current investigation "back at the shop." Antiquarian book dealers may have a relevant volume of lore (such as a memoir or the privately published ranting of a crackpot); dealers in silver may have ornamental daggers; importers may have a "queer tribal mask from the Congo." To remember and uncover such an item requires a use of the corresponding ability (e.g., Art History, Library Use).

This item may either contain a core clue for solving the mystery, or it may provide a weapon or technique for resolving it. In the first instance, you might be able to avoid sneaking into the creepy abandoned church in search of their blasphemous hymnal – you have a shellac pressing of the hymn in your used record-albums bin. In the second case, you needn't hunt down the Enchant Flute spell to drive off the lloigor – you have a set of Pan-pipes used in Orphic rites in decadent Cyrene. (Also in the second case, the effectiveness of the item may depend on the size of your spend.)

If you leave the city where your collection or shop is stored, you may not necessarily be able to use this ability (and certainly not in a convenient fashion), unless you have an assistant you can trust to find the item and mail it to you … and you're willing to wait a week for the mail to arrive while the cultists build their vortex of power.

The Keeper is well within her rights to deny your possession of powerful Mythos artifacts, effective spell books, and so forth, or to deny anything that seems abusive or just makes no narrative sense. She is also well within her rights to add other side effects to your item.

Archaeologist

You travel to strange, far places to uncover the past. You may be a meticulous scholar, working in libraries and devoting your career to a single dig, or you may be little better than a tomb robber, wielding a bullwhip and pistol to bring trophies back to your museum. You may depend on such treasures to fund your expeditions, or you may get grants from universities and foundations.

Occupational Abilities:
Archaeology, Athletics, Evidence Collection, First Aid, History, Languages, Library Use, Riding, and any two other Investigative abilities.

Credit Rating: 4-5

Special: By using Archaeology or a suitable Interpersonal ability, you can get access to museum storage areas or be allowed to handle artifacts. (You will likely not get to carry them away with you legally, regardless.) If you have academic credentials (both an Archaeology rating of 2+ and a Credit Rating of 3+), you can get access to closed stacks at a university library.

Occupations and Gender

"SOME OF THE EXPERIMENTS SHE PROPOSED WERE VERY DARING AND RADICAL ... BUT HE HAD CONFIDENCE IN HER POWERS AND INTENTIONS."
— THE THING ON THE DOORSTEP

In 1930, about a quarter of American women held jobs outside the home. During the Depression, attempting to preserve what jobs there were for "bread winners," 26 of 48 states passed laws against the employment of married women. This had essentially no effect; in 1940, the proportion of working women had slightly increased. Of those women, most worked in clerical jobs, sales, or as domestic servants. Some worked in factories – mostly clothing, light industry, and piecework. Less than a tenth of a percent of American women had professional jobs (besides teaching and nursing) during the decade.

This means exactly nothing for players of Trail of Cthulhu. The default option (and the publisher's assumption) is that if you can suspend your disbelief sufficiently to imagine giant betentacled monstrosities, then a female doctor should be no problem. While a Purist game would indeed be comfortably all-male, the popular culture of the era celebrated exciting, adventurous women, both fictional (Doc Savage's hellcat sister Patricia, the Shadow's top operative Margo Lane, the Spider's fiancée and fellow gunslinger Nita Van Sloan) and factual (aviator Beryl Markham, evangelist Aimee Semple McPherson, outlaw Ma Barker). In movies, the 1930s was the golden age of the independent heroine, feisty or dangerous, from screwball comedy to noir. Women authors, then as now, ruled the best-seller lists, and the "gal reporter" was already a stereotype when Lois Lane embodied it in 1938. Female scholars had long since breached the ivory tower – Egyptologist turned anthropologist Margaret Murray may be the woman most often mentioned in Lovecraft's tales. America's first female private eye joined the Pinkertons before the Civil War, and by the 1930s, there were gun-toting "Policewomen" in the NYPD, mostly assigned to the vice squad.

Even in a realistic game, then, the only Occupation actually closed to female Investigators is the Military. Certainly, in a historically realistic game, a female Investigator will likely suffer from condescension, unwelcome advances, and misplaced chivalry, among other sexist nonsense. But like Miss Marple (or the historical NKVD agent Melita Norwood, who began spying for Stalin in 1937), she may find that being underestimated is quite an advantage in ferreting out secrets. And in a Pulp game, the sky is literally the limit. Ask Amelia Earhart.

Artist

Whether you are a painter, a musician, a sculptor, an architect, or even a performer, you follow your Muse where she leads. Sensitive and temperamental, by reputation if not in fact, you already inhabit a demimonde that

Creating an Occupation

It may come to pass that a player wants a different sort of Investigator than the generous selection already provided. The Keeper should first determine if the requested Occupation is better expressed as a specialized version of pre-existing Occupation: Author, Criminal, Dilettante, Professor, and Scientist especially leave a lot of elbow room for variation. If so, the Keeper and player should work together to tweak the ability lists of the existing Occupation to best suit the player's vision. Swapping out one or two Abilities is usually enough – swapping Athletics for Driving, for example, transforms the Pilot into a Sailor. (Access to a plane becomes access to a boat or ship.)

Entirely new Occupations should have between seven and nine Occupational Abilities; provide fewer for Occupations with wider latitude for choice or with better special abilities. (Needless to say, no Occupation should have Credit Rating, Cthulhu Mythos, Health, Sanity, or Stability as Occupational Abilities.) Interpolating a Credit Rating band should be relatively simple from the existing examples and the Credit Rating discussion on p. 32.

Special rules for Occupations generally fall into one of two categories: privileged access to parts of the setting and hence to clue-generating scenes (police files for Police Detectives, etc) or neat mechanical tweaks (like the post-hoc spends for Criminal and Private Investigator). The first is easier to create and to justify. The Keeper should try to avoid doing the second unless she's come up with something totally awesome that she is confident will not unbalance the Investigator party.

most never understand.

Occupational Abilities:
Architecture, Art, Art History, Craft, Disguise, Flattery, Photography, Assess Honesty, and any two Academic or Interpersonal abilities as personal specialties.

Credit Rating: 1-4

Special: You may refresh one pool point in an ability representing your chosen art form (Art, Architecture, Craft, Photography, etc) during any significant downtime in an adventure, up to a maximum of four times per session. This represents time spent rehearsing, sketching, or what have you; Keepers should resist allowing this when the artist would not

have the time or resources to polish their skill.

☗ Author

You use words to capture existence, to conceal yourself, to reveal the truth, or to sell fantasy to Depression-stricken readers. Perhaps all of the above. Your labors are solitary and your rewards sporadic; you may have too much time to think. With discipline and a modicum of skill, though, even a pulp writer can still keep his head above water.

Occupational Abilities: Art, History, Languages, Library Use, Oral History, Assess Honesty, and three other abilities as personal specialties or left over from previous jobs.

Credit Rating: 1-3

Special: You may use any downtime in an adventure to refresh one Academic pool point, up to a maximum of four times per session. This represents time spent reading, checking notes and files, and so forth; Keepers should resist allowing this when the Investigator would not have the time or resources to do the necessary reading. That said, Trail of Cthulhu adventures will likely be rife with libraries that invite any author worth her salt to say "You guys check the rest of the house, I'm going to hit the books here for an hour or two."

Clergy

Itinerant revival preacher, trusted neighborhood priest, scholarly rabbi, or eager missionary, the varieties of clerical life present many of the same challenges to those who listen most intently for God's call. You may be predisposed to believe in the supernatural, but you are peculiarly vulnerable to the maltheistic revelations of the Mythos.

Occupational Abilities: History, Languages (Latin, Greek, Aramaic, or Hebrew), Library Use, Psychoanalysis, Assess Honesty, Reassurance, Theology, and one other Interpersonal ability.

Credit Rating: 2-5

Special: By using Theology or Reassurance you can gain access to church records not generally or easily available to the public. Mere clerical status does not guarantee you access to the "Z" Collection in the Vatican Library or similarly secret archives, of course, although a sufficiently grandiose spend and a kindly Keeper might make such a thing possible.

If you identify yourself as a member of the clergy (or are wearing your traditional garb), once per game session you may freely refresh any Interpersonal ability pool by talking to one of your co-religionists (though not a fellow Investigator).

⚜ Psychoanalysis is not one of your Occupational abilities.

⚜ You make Psychoanalysis tests for Psychological Triage (see p. 79) at a Difficulty of 3, instead of 4.

⚜ A priest can bless holy water, save the souls of the dying with extreme unction, use crucifixes to fend off vampires, and even exorcise demons (though not the entities of the Mythos) in a contest of Stability against the demon's Health. Other clergy may have similar ritual powers. This benefit is dependent on the campaign frame (see p. 204).

Criminal

Those who live on the other side of the law are already aware of a secret world of degeneracy, desperation, and evil beneath the normal ways of civilization. Some criminals have built their own codes and laws to shield themselves from the realization that all human order is breakable by acts of will. Others revel in this discovery.

Occupational Abilities: Bargain, Intimidation, Locksmith, Scuffling, Sense Trouble, Shadowing, Stealth, Streetwise, and one other Interpersonal or Technical ability as a personal specialty.

Credit Rating: 0-4

Special: Criminals with point pools in Conceal, Filch, or Shadowing may spend points after rolling the die for a test. For every 2 points you spend after rolling the die, you increase the die result by 1. This only applies if you are undistracted and not directly observed. It never applies during a contest. You must describe the thing that almost went wrong, and how you caught it barely in time or succeeded through sheer luck.

Members of the Mafia may take one free rating point in Languages to know Italian. Members of similar criminal organizations may have similar ratings at the Keeper's discretion.

⚜ Dilettante

You are self-supporting, living off an inheritance, trust fund, or other source of independent income. Free from the pressures of forced employment, you may

dedicate yourself to any pursuit you choose.

Occupational Abilities: Credit Rating, Flattery, Riding, and any five abilities you choose.

Credit Rating: 3+

Special: You may use your Credit Rating pool to call on personal connections in any field of endeavor. These contacts will generally be relatives, old schoolfellows, and similar people of your social class.

⚜ Doctor

You see your work as emblematic of the best in society: rational, humane, clean, and selfless. If only society could be cured or cut free of its diseases the way the body can be purged by treatment or surgery! The wealthier and more successful doctors can avoid the blood and filth that their noble aims are built upon.

Occupational Abilities: Accounting, Biology, First Aid, Forensics, Languages (Latin), Medicine, Pharmacy, Assess Honesty, Reassurance.

Credit Rating: 4-6

Special: By using Medicine or Reassurance, you have access to medical records and hospital wards generally off limits to the public. If you are affiliated with a hospital, sanitarium, or other facility, you can automatically use Reassurance to talk your way into any part of your institution from the drugs locker to the deep freeze.

When you use First Aid, each point spent heals 3 Health points, rather than 2. (You gain 2 Health

points rather than 1 for each First Aid point you spend to heal yourself.) You can stabilize the condition of a seriously wounded victim by spending only 1 First Aid point, rather than 2.
(See p. 63)

Hobo

You are not merely one of the millions out of work in the Depression. You are one of a breed apart, a king of the road. You ride the rails to avoid society, looking for handouts and working only when necessary. You may be a thief on occasion, but you would no more become a professional thief than you would take any other job.

Occupational Abilities: Athletics, Bargain, Filch, Outdoorsman, Sense Trouble, Stealth, Streetwise.

Credit Rating: 0. Unless the Keeper allows you to permanently change your Occupation (if you get married, or drafted, for example), you may never put any points into Credit Rating.

Amateur Journalism

Before the Internet, obsessed technical hobbyists still figured out ways to tell each other their opinions on things. In the 1930s, they called themselves "amateur journalists," publishing poetry, fiction, commentary, politics, and research themselves using hectographs, spirit duplicators ("Ditto machines," to those of us who attended grade school in the 1960s), or even printing presses. (Some amateur journalists owned their own press; most simply hired a local printer or a fellow amateur.) Generally a single editor collated all contributors' submissions (including those received from "Mailing Bureaux" created to supply copy) into a single issue, mailing it out to subscribers. In some APAs (Amateur Press Associations), only contributors could subscribe, but some (like their heirs the zines) were also sold to outsiders.

An amateur journalist in the 1930s would be most likely to publish creative writing or politics, but in the world of Trail of Cthulhu, there's nothing that says an APA editor wouldn't focus on Fortean phenomena, folk-lore, ghosts, and psychic research. (A really good issue might even count as a Mythos tome!) She might even count HP Lovecraft (President, United Amateur Press Association, 1917–1918; President, National Amateur Press Association, 1923) among her readers!

An amateur journalist might have any other sort of career or Occupation, although Author and Dilettante would be the two most common. With the Keeper's permission, an amateur journalist might be able to take Craft (Printing) as an Occupational ability instead of one of those listed.

Special: In addition to their normal functions, you can use Sense Trouble or Streetwise to read hobo signs and find out the lay of the land in a strange town. You can use Streetwise to activate fellow hobo contacts. Other contacts available to you might include Communists (such as itinerant IWW labor organizers), friendly railroad guards, charity workers, or a local lady known to be a soft touch.

Journalist

Whether for newspapers, magazines, or radio, you piece together the patterns of life and build them into a story, revealing the truth about the world around you. You may try to keep yourself separated from the story, especially if it is one of corruption and selfishness, but how can you avoid your own words?

Occupational Abilities:
Cop Talk, Disguise, Evidence Collection, Languages (for foreign correspondents), Oral History, Photography, Assess Honesty, Reassurance, Shadowing, and one other Interpersonal ability.

Credit Rating: 2-4

Special: By using Reassurance, you have access to newspaper morgues. At your own paper, you do the same to get the records clerks to fetch relevant articles. Similarly, fellow journalists may confide "off the record" rumors and stories to you, unless you're a direct competitor.

Military

You place yourself between others and danger, for a paycheck, for your flag, for your mates, or because you have no other good options. Your life is rote and routine, boredom and bureaucracy, dust and drill. And sometimes, of course, madness, death, blood, and nightmares.

Occupational Abilities: Athletics, Firearms, Intimidation, Outdoorsman, Scuffling, Weapons.

Army/Marines: add Conceal, Driving, Stealth.

Corpsman/Medic: add First Aid, Medicine, Reassurance.

Engineers/Heavy Weapons: add Driving, Explosives, Mechanical Repair.

Navy: add Astronomy, Mechanical Repair, Piloting.

Officer (any branch): add Bureaucracy, Riding or Piloting, Reassurance.

Credit Rating: 2-5 (officers); 2-4 (enlisted)

Special: You can spend 2 points from your Reassurance pool to steady panicking or erratic characters (see p. 79) as long as your own Stability is above 0.

If you are still serving, you can use any Interpersonal ability to gain entry to a military facility of your nation, except for explicitly top-secret bases. Unnoticed entry may require other plans.

If you are a combat veteran, the Difficulty Numbers (including opponents' Hit Thresholds) of your combat abilities (Athletics, Firearms,

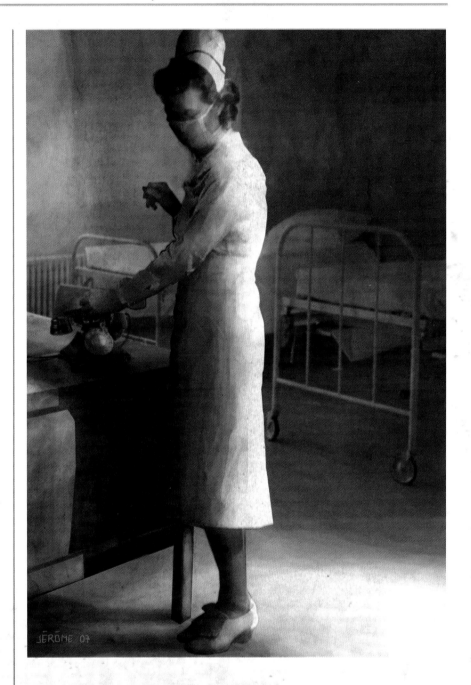

Scuffling, Weapons) do not increase by 1 until either your Stability or your Health drops below -5. If you are a combat veteran, your Stability is capped at 10, but some threats to your Stability may be made at a lower Difficulty number (see Experience and Stability on p. 72)

Nurse

A nurse is a trained medical assistant, sometimes male, more often female. Nurses are usually less comprehensively trained, always less well paid, and often less distant and callous than medical doctors.

Professional Parapsychology

In the 1930s, as in the modern era, most parapsychologists are sensation-mongering journalists, eccentrics plain and simple, or at best scholars with formal credentials in another field. (JB Rhine, studying ESP as Director of the Parapsychological Laboratory at Duke University during this decade, was trained as a botanist.) The Occupation of parapsychologist represents more of an avocation than a vocation, in other words.

In a Pulp-idiom game, "occult detectives" and academic parapsychologists may be more common and more accepted, but even in the historical 1930s, there are a few formal bodies dedicated to parapsychological studies, such as:

Society for Psychical Research: Founded in 1882 by Cambridge scholars with headquarters in London and archives in Cambridge, the SPR publishes an academically reviewed quarterly Journal and includes both academics and interested amateurs. The French branch, founded in 1885, is the Société Francaise pour Recherche Psychique.

The Ghost Club: A less-formal version of the SPR, which accepts proponents of mechanistic, magical, and Spiritualist theories of ghosts. Founded in 1862, it spends much of the 1930s in decline until the bombastic ghost-hunter Harry Price takes it over and re-founds it in 1938. Its headquarters are in London.

London Spiritualist Alliance: A major institution in mediumistic studies founded in 1884. It publishes a magazine, Light, edited (oddly enough) by the pioneering psychoanalytical theorist of ghost phenomena, Nandor Fodor.

American Society for Psychical Research: Increasingly dominated by Spiritualists and amateurs after a schism over the "Margery" medium case in 1925, the Boston-centered ASPR is flourishing – with branches opening in New York, Cleveland, and San Francisco – but at the cost of its academic respectability. Its monthly Journal is increasingly sensationalist.

Boston Society for Psychical Research: This self-consciously scientific and respectable group split off from the ASPR in 1925 over the "Margery" case. Its 200 members are active all over the country, but centered in New England.

American Psychical Institute & Laboratory: Besides Rhine's lab at Duke, the only parapsychological laboratory in America. Founded by the English author and researcher Dr Hereward Carrington in 1921, closed in 1923, reopened a decade later in New York City.

International Spiritualist Federation: A British umbrella group for the Spiritualist movement. It publishes the Psychic News.

Institut Métapsychique International: The IMI was founded in Paris in 1918 by a wealthy French Spiritualist, but maintains a staff of rigorously objective researchers. Membership is only by appointment.

Institute for Brain Research: An institute at Leningrad University lead by Leonid Vasiliev. His work on ESP has been classified on Stalin's orders since 1927, although he remains a member of the IMI.

Occupational Abilities: Biology, First Aid, Medicine, Pharmacy, Assess Honesty, Reassurance. At the Keeper's discretion, a nurse who has to deal with hospital paperwork might have Bureaucracy; one who has to deal with arrogant doctors might have Flattery.

Credit Rating: 2-4

Special: By using Medicine or Reassurance, you have access to medical records and hospital wards generally off limits to the public. If you are affiliated with a hospital, sanitarium, or other facility, you can automatically use Reassurance to talk your way into any part of your institution from the drugs locker to the deep freeze.

When you use First Aid, each point spent heals 3 Health points, rather than 2. (You gain 2 Health points rather than 1 for each First Aid point you spend to heal yourself.) You can stabilize the condition of a seriously wounded victim by spending only 1 First Aid point, rather than 2. (See p. 63)

Parapsychologist

Academics hold you in dubious regard, while true believers doubt your sincerity. You straddle – perhaps uncomfortably – the line between reason and superstition, between faith and proof. You believe that the supernatural is merely the natural we have not yet studied, or perhaps that the methods of science can uncover or confirm the truths of theology.

Occupational Abilities:
Anthropology, Electrical Repair, Library Use, Mechanical Repair, Occult, Photography, Assess Honesty, Sense Trouble.

Credit Rating: 2-3

Special: Like the Alienist, you may put build points into, and use, the Hypnosis ability (see p. 43). In an extremely pulpy game, you may have actual psychic powers, or work closely with those who have them. (Such "sensitives" may be fellow Investigators, or — as in Lovecraft's stories — expendable NPCs.) For rules and descriptions of some psychic abilities in the GUMSHOE system, see Fear Itself.

Pilot

You live to fly, and you fly to live. You might be a Great War veteran seeking leftover thrills on the barnstorm circuit, or a private courier hoping to strike it rich and found your own air service. You might fly cutting-edge birds for a rich man, or build your own ship out of whatever you can scrounge. Whatever your route to the sky, it's the only place you want to be.

Occupational Abilities:
Astronomy, Driving, Electrical Repair, Mechanical Repair, Piloting, Sense Trouble.

Credit Rating: 2-3

Special: You own or have regular access to an airplane. Its size and quality depend on your Credit Rating pool.

Police Detective

You live by the code of the cop, whether it's the one they put on the wall at the academy, or the one you picked up on foot patrol in the bad neighborhoods. You draw lines between cops, perps, and civilians, and it's best when nothing crosses them. When the law and justice disagree, that's when you decide where the line runs.

Occupational Abilities:
Athletics, Cop Talk, Driving, Evidence Collection, Firearms, Interrogation, Law, Assess Honesty, Sense Trouble.

Credit Rating: 3-4

Special: With judicious use of Cop Talk, you can not only put the police at ease, but gain access to case files, evidence rooms, and prisoners, among other things not accessible by normal civilians. If you're far outside your jurisdiction, you may need Cop Talk and a really good plan.

Within your own jurisdiction, any points at all in Cop Talk will get you access to, and use of, police laboratories (for forensics and ballistics tests, or for more abstruse purposes) and even the morgue.

Private Investigator

There are things that cops can't do, and things that cops won't do, and you'll take money to do either. Sometimes you get dragged into something the cops want you out of, but you gotta stay in it to keep the cops honest. What keeps you honest? Now, that's the real mystery, ain't it?

Occupational Abilities:
Accounting, Disguise, Driving, Law, Locksmith, Photography, Assess Honesty, Reassurance, Scuffling, Shadowing.

Credit Rating: 2-3

Special: Private eyes with point pools in Disguise or Shadowing may spend points after rolling the die for a test. For every 2 points you spend after rolling the die, you increase the die result by 1. This only applies if you are undistracted and not directly observed. It never applies during a contest. You must describe the thing that almost went wrong, and how you caught it barely in time or succeeded through sheer luck.

 The Occupational Abilities above accurately model typical 1930s private investigators, whose most common jobs were following and photographing adulterers, and following and finding missing cash. For a Pulpy, hard-boiled PI in the Chandler-Hammett vein, use the following Occupational Abilities list: Cop Talk, Driving, Intimidation, Locksmith, Assess Honesty, Scuffling, Shadowing, Streetwise.

Professor

You might be a calm solon, dispensing the wisdom of the ages between puffs on your pipe. You might be a hapless child in an adult's body, incompetent in anything except Middle High German, and vainglorious and petty about that. You might be the second, and think you're the first, to the great delight of all who behold you.

Occupational Abilities:
Bureaucracy, Languages, Library Use, any one Interpersonal ability, and any three Academic abilities (including, for these purposes, Astronomy and Chemistry).

Credit Rating: 3-5

Special: As long as your academic credentials are intact (a Credit Rating of 3+), using Bureaucracy lets you enjoy nearly unrestricted access to closed library stacks, research laboratories, and even many private and government archives.

If you have a Credit Rating of 5 or better, you have tenure and cannot be removed from your professorship without

clear, public evidence of moral turpitude on your part.

Scientist

You seek to advance science, perhaps to improve the world, or perhaps to tease out some long-denied truth. You may consider yourself handy around the lab; that third fire could have happened to anyone. You just need more equipment, more time, more samples, more understanding colleagues. Perhaps the fools laughed at you at the University. Well, you'll show them.

Occupational Abilities:
Electrical Repair, Evidence Collection, Languages, Library Use, Photography, and any two of the following: Astronomy, Biology, Chemistry, Cryptography, Forensics, Geology, or Physics.

Credit Rating: 3-5

Martin Harvesson, Sample Investigator

Josh is building his first Trail of Cthulhu Investigator. While talking with the Keeper, he and the other players decide on a traditional, old-school sort of game, full of globe-trotting adventures and two-gun menaces, with plenty of lingering death in the dark places of the city. To tell the truth, Josh is a bigger fan of Humphrey Bogart than he is of HP Lovecraft, so he decides to build a tough-as-nails private eye. Josh names his character Martin Harvesson.

Special: You have access to a laboratory suitable for your researches, and can use Credit Rating to get tests and experiments performed in other laboratories by your peers or colleagues, or to get specialized equipment or machinery built. If you have academic credentials (Credit Rating of 3 or better and a rating of 2 or more in Astronomy, Biology, Chemistry, Geology, or Physics), you can get access to closed stacks at a university library.

DRITES

"OUR MOTIVATION AFTER THAT IS SOMETHING I WILL LEAVE TO PSYCHOLOGISTS. WE KNEW NOW THAT SOME TERRIBLE EXTENSION OF THE CAMP HORRORS MUST HAVE CRAWLED INTO THIS NIGHTED BURIAL PLACE OF THE AEONS, HENCE COULD NOT DOUBT ANY LONGER THE EXISTENCE OF NAMELESS CONDITIONS — PRESENT OR AT LEAST RECENT JUST AHEAD. YET IN THE END WE DID LET SHEER BURNING CURIOSITY — OR ANXIETY — OR AUTOHYPNOTISM — OR VAGUE THOUGHTS OF RESPONSIBILITY TOWARD GEDNEY — OR WHAT NOT — DRIVE US ON."

— AT THE MOUNTAINS OF MADNESS

What motivates an Investigator? Why uncover blasted ruins, or delve into matters quite obviously best left alone? Because some people – perhaps not the fortunate, or even the brave – are Driven to do so. Every Investigator must have a **Drive,** a core desire that impels him to seek strange, far truths at the cost of everything he once held dear. It is quite literally something more important to you than your life or sanity. Although psychologically an Investigator may be driven by many different forces, and the player can roleplay her with such complexity, mechanically each character should only have one core Drive.

Refusing to follow an Investigator's Drive, therefore, costs Stability. Succumbing to your Drive can temporarily blind you to the dangers of doing so, adding a thin veneer of Stability as with open but unseeing eyes you descend into the crypt (see p. 72) . If your sanity is imperiled too much

List of Drives

- Adventure
- Antiquarianism
- Arrogance
- Artistic Sensitivity
- Bad Luck
- Curiosity
- Duty
- Ennui
- Follower
- In the Blood
- Revenge
- Scholarship
- Sudden Shock
- Thirst for Knowledge

you lose even this dubious benefit (see p. 76).

Any Drive might impel any sort of Investigator, but some Occupations seem more naturally suited to some Drives than others. Such pairings are noted below. Some Drives, likewise, are better suited to the Pulp or Purist games, although any Drive might motivate any character in any idiom.

Adventure

"IN ALL THIS PLANNING THERE WAS MUCH THAT EXCITED MY INTEREST. THE FIGHT ITSELF PROMISED TO BE UNIQUE AND SPECTACULAR, WHILE THE THOUGHT OF THE SCENE ON THAT HOARY PILE OVERLOOKING THE ANTEDILUVIAN PLATEAU OF GIZEH ... APPEALED TO EVERY FIBRE OF IMAGINATION IN ME."

— UNDER THE PYRAMIDS

Nothing gets you going like the promise of action, combat, and strange new experiences. You're an adrenaline junkie and if ichor is the cure, then so be it! Turning down an adventure to "play it safe" is like admitting that your whole life was meaningless before.

Especially appropriate for: Criminal, Military, Parapsychologist, Pilot

Example: Harry Houdini in *Under the Pyramids.*

Antiquarianism

"WITH THE YEARS HIS DEVOTION TO ANCIENT THINGS INCREASED; SO THAT HISTORY, GENEALOGY, AND THE STUDY OF COLONIAL ARCHITECTURE, FURNITURE, AND CRAFTSMANSHIP AT LENGTH CROWDED EVERYTHING ELSE FROM HIS SPHERE OF INTERESTS. THESE TASTES ARE IMPORTANT TO REMEMBER IN CONSIDERING HIS MADNESS..."

— THE CASE OF CHARLES DEXTER WARD

The dead past is the only place you feel truly alive. Discovering some truth about it, or simply experiencing old and beautiful houses or items, is the purpose for living at all. Neglecting the past merely because it seems unsavory is for brutish, mayfly moderns.

Especially appropriate for: Antiquarian, Archaeologist, Clergy, Professor

Examples: Charles Dexter Ward, Elihu Whipple in *The Shunned House,* and the narrator of *He.*

Arrogance

"I TELL YOU, I HAVE STRUCK DEPTHS THAT YOUR LITTLE BRAIN CAN'T PICTURE! I HAVE SEEN BEYOND THE BOUNDS OF INFINITY AND DRAWN DOWN DAEMONS FROM THE STARS..."

— FROM BEYOND

Your ultimate success will be its own justification, and it is sure to come to you, since only you have the will to grasp it. The rules of petty people don't apply to you, and neither do their shrinking, timorous fears.

Especially appropriate for: Alienist, Scientist

Examples: Herbert West, Crawford Tillinghast in *From Beyond*, Denys Barry in *The Moon-Bog*

Artistic Sensitivity

"FOR AFTER ALL, THE VICTIM WAS A WRITER AND PAINTER WHOLLY DEVOTED TO THE FIELD OF MYTH, DREAM, TERROR, AND SUPERSTITION, AND AVID IN HIS QUEST FOR SCENES AND EFFECTS OF A BIZARRE, SPECTRAL SORT."

— THE HAUNTER OF THE DARK

You are already aware of the numinous and supernatural quality of the world – it is what you seek to capture in your art, of course. You must follow your Muse wherever she leads, clay in her hands for molding. Nothing, especially not mundane concerns, can stanch your need for inspiration.

Especially appropriate for: Artist, Author, Dilettante

Examples: Robert Blake in *The Haunter of the Dark*, Richard Pickman in *Pickman's Model*, the sculptor Henry Wilcox in *The Call of Cthulhu*, and possibly Erich Zann. Walter Gilman in *The Dreams in the Witch House* also essentially fits this pattern, treating higher mathematics as an art.

Bad Luck

IT WAS GENERALLY STATED THAT THE AFFLICTION AND SHOCK WERE RESULTS OF AN UNLUCKY SLIP WHEREBY BIRCH HAD LOCKED HIMSELF FOR NINE HOURS IN THE RECEIVING TOMB OF PECK VALLEY CEMETERY...

— IN THE VAULT

These things just seem to happen to you, although your luck might sour after you dig up a statuette, sleep in the wrong boarding house, or decide to rob a terrible old man. Bad Luck is essentially the same as being Cursed. (See p. 75 for how Bad Luck or Cursed works with the Drive rules.)

Especially appropriate for: Criminal, Hobo

Examples: The sailor Gustaf Johansen in *The Call of Cthulhu*, the narrators of *Cool Air, Dagon, The Music of Erich Zann,* and *The Picture in the House.*

In a less starkly cosmic game, bad luck can be earned: in *The Temple*, Captain von Altberg-Ehrenstein brings doom upon himself and his men by torpedoing the freighter *Victory*.

Curiosity
"ANY REFERENCE TO A TOWN NOT SHEWN ON COMMON MAPS OR LISTED IN RECENT GUIDE-BOOKS WOULD HAVE INTERESTED ME, AND THE AGENT'S ODD MANNER OF ALLUSION ROUSED SOMETHING LIKE REAL CURIOSITY."

— THE SHADOW OVER INNSMOUTH

When confronted by a mystery, you can't help but investigate. Damn the risks, there's something going on here and you're going to figure it out! If you don't, it will just drive you crazy worrying about it.

Especially appropriate for: Journalist, Parapsychologist, Police Detective, Private Investigator, Scientist

Examples: Randolph Carter in *Dream-Quest of Unknown*

Kadath, and the narrators of *Beyond the Wall of Sleep, The Lurking Fear, The Colour Out of Space,* and *The Shadow Over Innsmouth.*

Duty
"DUTY CAME FIRST; AND ALTHOUGH THERE MUST HAVE BEEN NEARLY A HUNDRED MONGREL CELEBRANTS IN THE THRONG, THE POLICE RELIED ON THEIR FIREARMS AND PLUNGED DETERMINEDLY INTO THE NAUSEOUS ROUT."

— THE CALL OF CTHULHU

You know it's dangerous and ill-advised, but somebody's got to go down those steps or bust up that cult. And you're elected, because if you don't take care of things now, they're just going to get worse. If you don't, who is? Some time-serving goldbrick just counting down the days until their pension? Don't be ridiculous.

Especially appropriate for: Clergy, Doctor, Military, Police Detective

Examples: Inspector Legrasse in *The Call of Cthulhu* and Detective Malone in *The Horror at Red Hook*, the sailors and G-men who expunge *The Shadow Over Innsmouth*, the colonial-era posse that burns out Curwen in *Charles Dexter Ward*, Professor Armitage in *The Dunwich Horror*.

Ennui
"...FINALLY THERE REMAINED FOR US ONLY THE MORE DIRECT STIMULI OF UNNATURAL PERSONAL EXPERIENCES AND ADVENTURES."

— THE HOUND

Perhaps you had one experience

that you'll never get again, or perhaps you've just read about such things in decadent yellow-backed novels. You've tried everything else, and nothing else matters. So what if it might kill you? At least that would be different.

Especially appropriate for: Artist, Dilettante, Military

Examples: St John and the narrator in The Hound, Randolph Carter in *The Silver Key*, Thomas Olney in *The Strange High House in the Mist*, and to an extent Jervas Dudley in *The Tomb*.

Follower
"...THEY WERE TERRIBLE STUDIES, WHICH I PURSUED MORE THROUGH RELUCTANT FASCINATION THAN THROUGH ACTUAL INCLINATION. WARREN DOMINATED ME, AND SOMETIMES I FEARED HIM."

— THE STATEMENT OF RANDOLPH CARTER

This wasn't actually your idea, and you'd like that put in the report somewhere. But someone else – someone who's important to you for whatever reason — went down into that tunnel, and you'd better go after them to make sure they're safe. Or to make sure they don't pick someone else to hold the field telephone next time.

In an ongoing *Trail of Cthulhu* campaign, you should pick a fellow Investigator (ideally a foolhardy one) to be the person you follow. When – er, if – they die, you may switch to a different "leader," or switch Drives to Revenge.

Especially appropriate for: Doctor, Military, Police Detective

Examples: Randolph Carter in *The Statement of Randolph Carter*, Herbert West's assistant, and the narrators of *Pickman's Model* and *Hypnos*. Followers can also be friends or family members such as the narrator of *From Beyond*, Dr Willett in *Charles Dexter Ward*, Daniel Upton in *The Thing on the Doorstep*, Norrys in *The Rats in the Walls*, or Ammi Pierce in *The Colour Out of Space*.

In the Blood

"I THOUGHT THE ROOM AND THE BOOKS AND THE PEOPLE VERY MORBID AND DISQUIETING, BUT BECAUSE AN OLD TRADITION OF MY FATHERS HAD SUMMONED ME TO STRANGE FEASTINGS, I RESOLVED TO EXPECT QUEER THINGS."

— THE FESTIVAL

Quite frankly, you're not sure why you keep coming back to the moldering graveyard, or poring over those antique texts. But queer behavior runs in the family, apparently. Outsiders wouldn't understand.

Especially appropriate for: Antiquarian, Dilettante

Examples: Charles Dexter Ward, Arthur Jermyn, Delapore in *The Rats in the Walls*, and the narrator of *The Festival*. Thurston, the narrator of *The Call of Cthulhu*, inherits his uncle's research. Olmstead, the narrator of *The Shadow Over Innsmouth*, turns out to be motivated by his ancestry, though he doesn't know it. Such a secret — perhaps shameful — Drive is perfectly suitable for *Trail of Cthulhu* Investigators. A player can even request such a secret Drive without telling the Keeper

which one he's requesting, and without discovering what his Investigator's Drive is until it emerges in play (see p. 75).

Revenge

"EZRA WEEDEN, THOUGH HIS PERIODS OF ESPIONAGE WERE NECESSARILY BRIEF ... HAD A VINDICTIVE PERSISTENCE WHICH THE BULK OF THE PRACTICAL TOWNSFOLK AND FARMERS LACKED..."

— THE CASE OF CHARLES DEXTER WARD

Something out there hurt you, or hurt someone you care about. Therefore, it must be destroyed, burned out, taken down, exposed ... whatever it takes, and whatever it costs. Any trail that might lead to your vengeance is a trail you have to follow to the bitter end.

Especially appropriate for: Criminal, Private Investigator

Examples: Ezra Weeden in *Charles Dexter Ward*, and the narrator of *The Lurking Fear* after the death of his friend Munroe. Followers like Dr Willett (in *Charles Dexter Ward*) may change their Drive to Revenge if their associates are killed, sucked through a portal, or otherwise removed from play.

Scholarship

"I FELT SURE THAT I WAS ON THE TRACK OF A VERY REAL, VERY SECRET, AND VERY ANCIENT RELIGION WHOSE DISCOVERY WOULD MAKE ME AN ANTHROPOLOGIST OF NOTE."

— THE CALL OF CTHULHU

Uncovering the truth about the world is what true scholars do.

It's certainly why you spend all that time in those libraries; why you track down sole survivors of isolated backwoods cults; why you learn languages not meant for human throats. Whether you're seeking tenure, the acclaim of your fellows, or just the satisfaction of expanding human knowledge, you Investigate in order to find the underlying pattern of things.

Especially appropriate for: Archaeologist, Professor, Scientist

Examples: Professor Angell and his nephew Francis Thurston in *The Call of Cthulhu*, Professor Dyer and his party in *At the Mountains of Madness*.

Sudden Shock

"HAD HE, THEN, WITNESSED SOME APPALLING ANCIENT RITE, OR STUMBLED UPON SOME FRIGHTFUL AND REVEALING SYMBOL IN THE PRIORY OR ITS VICINITY?"

— THE RATS IN THE WALLS

Something has ripped the scrim off the world, and you can't go back to believing in Baby Jesus and FDR anymore. Whether it's your long-dead great-grandfather holding cannibal feasts in your basement, the things you saw on the Innsmouth Raid, or just a chance encounter with the Outside, you might as well go further in, because you aren't going back any time soon.

The player should come up with the specifics of the Sudden Shock, unless she'd like her Investigator to have amnesia (hysterical, traumatic, or Yithian-induced) on the subject. This latter option allows all manner of cruelty on the part of the Keeper, and is

---

> ### Martin Harvesson, Sample Investigator
>
> Josh likes Raymond Chandler's line about "down these mean streets a man must go, who is neither tarnished nor afraid," but he suspects that Duty won't suit his play style. So instead, he goes with "When a man's partner is killed, he's got to do something about it," and selects Revenge as Martin's Drive. Martin's partner got into something down on the docks and died. Martin won't let it rest there.

highly recommended.

Especially appropriate for: Parapsychologist, but any, really

Examples: Walter de la Poer in *The Rats in the Walls*, Professor Nathaniel Peaslee in *The Shadow Out of Time*.

Thirst for Knowledge

"I DON'T WISH TO PUT YOU IN ANY PERIL, AND SUPPOSE I OUGHT TO WARN YOU THAT POSSESSION OF THE STONE AND RECORD WON'T BE VERY SAFE; BUT I THINK YOU WILL FIND ANY RISKS WORTH RUNNING FOR THE SAKE OF KNOWLEDGE."

— "THE WHISPERER IN DARKNESS"

You must – you must! – learn the secret lore of the cosmos. This is not footling, footnoted scholarship. It is the quest for truth. You don't want to advance human knowledge – the herd don't desire, or deserve, to know what lies behind the walls of the world. Only you (and perhaps a few fellow initiates) truly burn

to possess such secrets, and only you are willing to do what it takes to get them.

Especially appropriate for: Archaeologist, Parapsychologist, Professor

Examples: Both Henry Akeley and Albert Wilmarth in *The Whisperer in Darkness*, Harley Warren in *The Statement of Randolph Carter*, the narrators of *The Nameless City* and *The Lurking Fear*.

Buying Abilities

With Occupation and Drive established, it's time to buy abilities for your Investigator. Investigators begin with a variable number of points to buy Investigative abilities, depending on group size, and 65 points to purchase General abilities. Investigative abilities include all Academic, Interpersonal, and Technical abilities. General abilities include all remaining abilities, including Health, Sanity, and Stability.

OCCUPATIONAL ABILITIES

You get two rating points in Occupational abilities for everyone on build point you spend. For example, 12 rating points of Occupational abilities cost you 6 build points. Left over half-points are lost, so assign an even number points to Occupational abilities. You cannot select Fleeing, Credit Rating, Cthulhu Mythos, Health, Sanity, or Stability as Occupational Abilities.

The number of points each player spends on Investigative abilities varies according to the number of regularly attending players, according to the following table.

# of players	Investigative Build Points
2	24
3	18
4+	16

Ability List By Families

Investigative Abilities

Investigative abilities comprise Academic, Interpersonal, and Technical abilities.

Academic

Accounting
Anthropology
Archaeology
Architecture
Art History
Biology
Cthulhu Mythos
Cryptography
Geology
History
Languages
Law
Library Use
Medicine
Occult
Physics
Theology

Interpersonal

Assess Honesty
Bargain
Bureaucracy
Cop Talk
Credit Rating
Flattery
Interrogation
Intimidation
Oral History
Reassurance
Streetwise

Technical

Art
Astronomy
Chemistry
Craft
Evidence Collection
Forensics
Locksmith
Outdoorsman
Pharmacy
Photography

General Abilities

Athletics
Conceal
*Disguise
Driving
*Electrical Repair
*Explosives
Filch
Firearms
First Aid
Fleeing
Health
Hypnosis
*Mechanical Repair
Piloting
Preparedness
Psychoanalysis
Riding
Sanity
Scuffling
Sense Trouble
Shadowing
Stability
Stealth
Weapons

*Some General abilities can be used as Investigative abilities in some circumstances. They are always bought and built as General abilities.

Variant Builds

Believe it or not, some playtesters argued that their characters were still too powerful and good at everything. We admire such dedication to the Lovecraftian spirit of the parochial, incompetent narrator.

For such players, reduce General build points from 65 to 60 and assign Investigative build points based on the following table, which generates outclassed, likely doomed – but forcibly specialized! – Investigators.

# of players	Investigative Build Points
2	16
3	12
4+	10

To generate Pulpier characters, increase the General points available from 65 to 75, but use the standard Investigative Build Points from the main text table. Pulp Investigator teams will very likely profit by using the Trading Points optional rule from the sidebar on p. 25.

Some campaign frames may have particular restrictions or caps on abilities, for example, a game set in an orphanage may have a very restricted number of Investigative and General abilities available. Others may force specialization by limiting the number of Academic or Technical abilities you may take.

Players who can only attend every now and then get the same number of investigative build points as everyone else, but are not counted toward the total when deciding how many points to allocate. Your Keeper may give you a small pool of unallocated to compensate for spotty attendance (see p. 203).

Every ability has a numerical rating. Some rating points in some abilities are free: Each Investigator starts with a free rating of 4 points in Sanity, and 1 point in each of Stability and Health. Each Investigator also starts off with the lower edge of his Credit Rating band for free. You may trade your free Credit Rating points in for other Investigative build points on a 1-to-1 basis if your character concept calls for an especially unsuccessful (or shunned) Investigator.

An Investigator with the occupation Scientist normally starts out with a Credit Rating of 3, indicating a certain minimal academic respectability, and perhaps a steady laboratory job. But a "mad scientist" who lives in a slum basement

somewhere, or a scientist disgraced for claiming that ultraviolet light contained monsters, might begin with a Credit Rating of 2 or even 1, depending on how cut off he is from his professional colleagues.

Usually, each rating point costs one build point, except for Occupational abilities, Fleeing, and Credit Rating.

Running away is easier than doing anything else strenuous;

it's what humans are evolved for, after all. It's also very genre appropriate, so we reward it thusly: If your Fleeing rating is more than twice your final Athletics rating, you can buy rating points in Fleeing at a reduced rate, getting 2 rating points for each build point spent. (If you suspect you want to utilize this rule, decide on your final Athletics rating first. This makes things much easier.) Hence, if your Athletics rating is 0, all your Fleeing is half-price.

Building an Investigator Party

It's a good idea, both for mechanical and narrative reasons, to make sure your Investigator party covers as many ability bases as possible. Ideally, one Investigator will have any needed skill, and everyone has something cool that they do better than the rest of the group. When creating Investigators, go down the ability list and make sure you've got a good spread of talents, and that every Investigator has a potential starring role at some point in the story.

Trading Points

One *optional rule* to knit together such a party allows players to swap points among themselves. If using this rule, a player may trade 1 Investigative *build point* (not rating point) for 3 General *build points* (not rating points) from another player. (Or, obviously, vice-versa.) Thus, the consumptive academic can give 6 General ability points to the brutal Outfit enforcer (for Weapons and Explosives, say), and get 2 Investigative ability points from that worthy's pool (for, oh, Astronomy). Both players get to increase their Investigators' "spotlight" abilities and the party becomes more stereotypical. Which is to say, narratively better.

Zachary decides that his dilettante Willoughby Boothroyd stays in decent shape thanks to the polo matches and racquetball, but is really not much of an athlete. He puts only 2 points into Willoughby's Athletics ability. Zachary also really wants Boothroyd to be able to live to drink another day, so he decides to get Fleeing at 8. The first 4 rating points in Fleeing (up to twice Willoughby's final Athletics 2) cost Zachary the standard 4 build points, but the second 4 rating points cost only 2 build points.

Rating points in Credit Rating cost 1 build point each up to the top of the band listed under the Occupation, after which they cost 2 build points each, except for Dilettantes, who have no top limit on their Credit Rating band.

Shari is building a Professor, Dr Lunedi. She could buy Credit Rating 5 for 2 build points – her free 3 plus 2 more – but buying one more rating point for a Credit Rating 6 would cost 2 more build points, for a total of 4.

Credit Rating does *not* count as "any ability" in Occupational templates; it is *only* an Occupational ability for Dilettantes. The Keeper is fully within her rights to cap Credit Rating at the top of the band if she would prefer not to run adventures full of millionaire cops and private eyes.

Usually, you may not start the game with Cthulhu Mythos points (see p. 34)

Ability Caps

In the Purist mode, Health and Stability are capped at 12. They cannot be bought at higher levels, nor can additional experience points raise them above those levels. Your Sanity is capped at 10, and can never be higher than 10 minus your Cthulhu Mythos rating.

Pulp Investigators can be as buff and bold as they like, but we recommend staying as close as you can to the 12-point Health and Stability caps anyway if you want to keep confrontations tense.

Some campaign frames may cap other abilities, for example, a campaign set in a school might cap Academic, Technical and some General abilities, or even make them unavailable altogether.

How Many Points Should I Buy?

When choosing Investigative abilities, it is better to get a large number of abilities with fairly low ratings. Even a 1-point rating is worth having. You'll rarely want to spend more than 3 or 4 points on any one Investigative ability.

General abilities use different rules than investigative ones, which allow for possible failure. When choosing general abilities, you'll want to concentrate your points among a few abilities, giving your comparatively higher ratings than you want in the investigative category. You'll find that you'll want ratings at least 8 in core abilities, like Health and Stability, and depending on your Investigator concept, even higher ratings in Athletics, Firearms, Fleeing, Scuffling, or Weapons.

A special restriction applies to General abilities: your second highest rating must be at least half that of your highest rating. This is less onerous with an Occupation that includes any General abilities as Occupational Abilities (rating points in which cost half the build-point price), but it can still trip you up if you're not careful.

Craig wants his Investigator to have a Scuffling rating of 30. This requires him to take at least one other ability at 15. This would leave him only 20 points to spend on all of his other General abilities. (Or 27, if he bought an Occupational ability up to 16 with 8 build points.) Craig reconsiders, opting for a lower Scuffling, so he can spend his other points more freely.

If you want, you can save build points from character creation to spend later. If your Keeper is running an ongoing *Trail of Cthulhu* campaign, you may accumulate additional build points during play.

Ratings and Skill

The rules don't care whether your high Athletics rating comes from years of semi-pro baseball or just natural grace and speed. Similarly, whether you're an intuitive genius or a plodding, meticulous scholar is irrelevant in gauging your Archaeology ability. You can decide such things while personalizing your Investigator. What matters is what you can accomplish; how you accomplished it is up to you.

Even a single rating point in an investigative ability indicates a high degree of professional accomplishment or impressive natural talent. If you have an ability relevant to the task at hand, you automatically succeed in discovering any information or overcoming any obstacles necessary to propel you from the current scene further into the story.

Each rating point goes into a pool of points to spend in situations related to its base ability. You may ask to **spend** points to gain special benefits. Sometimes the Keeper will offer you the chance to spend points. In other circumstances she may accept your suggestions of ways to gain special benefits. Use them wisely; spent points do not return until the next scenario begins.

General abilities use a different set of rules and are measured on a different scale than investigative abilities. The two ability sets are handled in different way because they fulfill distinct narrative functions. The goal of any *Trail of Cthulhu* scenario is to uncover a mystery and confront the Mythos entity (or entities) behind it. The confrontation must be suspenseful, which is why general abilities have a possibility of failure. But the confrontation must also occur for the story to satisfy, which is why investigating the mystery – in order to get to the confrontation – must succeed. A well-designed *Trail of Cthulhu* scenario will reward players for cleverly or stylishly solving the mystery by making the confrontation more exciting, more survivable, or more intellectually interesting. (For more on scenario design, see p. 191)

Martin Harvesson, Sample Investigator

Not counting the Keeper, there are five players in Josh's gaming group, but two of them only show up sporadically, because they travel a lot for work. So the Keeper gives Josh and the other players 18 build points for Investigative abilities, as though there were only three players, along with the standard 65 build points for General abilities. Josh reads ahead in the rule book to get a good handle on what the various abilities can do, and then gets set to build out his Investigator.

Josh starts off with the following Investigative abilities as Martin's Occupational *abilities:* Accounting, Law, Locksmith, Photography, Assess Honesty, and Reassurance. He puts a * next to each one on the character sheet. Josh decides to ignore Accounting, buying 1 rating point of Law, 3 rating points each of Locksmith, Assess Honesty, and Reassurance, and 2 rating points of Photography for a total of 12 rating points worth of Occupational abilities. At the 2-for-1 cost for Occupational abilities, that uses up 6 of Martin's Investigative build points. The bottom of his Occupational Credit Rating band is 2, so Martin begins with a Credit Rating of 2, and Josh leaves it there as good enough for an obsessed PI Josh runs down the list of remaining Investigative abilities, and decides that Cop Talk, Intimidation, and Streetwise are essential to his image of Martin, and that Evidence Collection and Forensics are too useful to ignore. He divides up Martin's remaining 12 points thusly: 3 each in the three Interpersonal abilities, 2 in Evidence Collection, and the final 1 point in Forensics.

Josh then turns to Martin's General abilities, which include the following as Occupational abilities: Disguise, Driving, Scuffling, and Shadowing, which again he marks with a *. He tentatively buys 5 rating points in each of the four, spending a net 10 build points with the half-price Occupational cost. Josh buys Martin's Sanity up to 10 from the baseline of 4, and spends 7 points to bump his Stability up to 8 (from the starting 1), for a running total of 23. Josh likewise adds 5 more points to Martin's free Health rating of 1, to get a fragile Health of 6. Josh wants Martin to be able to take care of himself in a chase or a fight, so he buys Athletics 8 (giving him an improved Hit Threshold of 4), Firearms 5 (so he can use two pistols at once), and Weapons 2, for a running total of 43. Josh packs 8 points each onto Sense Trouble and Stealth, two abilities he thinks will be very handy for a detective, for a running total of 59. Since with a Driving of 5, Martin will probably wind up being the team's wheel man, Josh spends the last 6 points on Mechanical Repair, so that Martin can fix anything he needs to drive away in a hurry.

INVESTIGATIVE ABILITIES

Investigative abilities are the meat and bone of *Trail of Cthulhu* Investigators.

Ability descriptions consist of a brief general description, followed by examples of their use in an investigation. Creative players should be able to propose additional uses for their abilities as unexpected situations confront their characters. Some General abilities can be used as Investigative abilities in some circumstances. They are always bought and built as General abilities. They are Disguise, Electrical Repair, Explosives and Mechanical Repair.

Certain specific actions may overlap between a couple of abilities. For example, you can analyze (or synthesize) an opiate poison with either Chemistry or Pharmacy; you can identify a Roman idol with Archaeology, Art History, Occult, or Theology; you can bluff your way into a sanitarium with Bureaucracy, Disguise, or Psychoanalysis.

Some abilities, like Library Use or Sense Trouble, are broadly useful, and will crop up constantly. Others may be called for many times in the course of one scenario, and not at all in others. When building your Investigator, strike a balance between the reliable workhorse abilities and their exotic, specialized counterparts. Also, strike a balance with the other Investigators in your party – a *Trail of Cthulhu* campaign is more fun, and more survivable, if all your bases are covered.

Accounting (Academic)

You understand bookkeeping and accountancy procedures; you can read and keep financial records. You can:

- *tell legitimate businesses from criminal enterprises*

- *reconstruct financial histories from old records (uncovering, say, slave-trading or smuggling)*

- *spot the telltale signs of embezzlement, bribes, blackmail, or dummy companies*

- *track payments to their source*

Anthropology (Academic)

You are an expert in the study of human cultures, from the Stone Age to the Jazz Age. (Physical anthropology is covered by Forensics.) You can:

- *identify artifacts and rituals of living cultures*

- *describe and predict the customs of a foreign group or local subculture*

- *extrapolate the practices of an unknown culture from similar examples*

Archaeology (Academic)

You excavate and study the structures and artifacts of historical cultures and civilizations. You can:

- *tell how long something has been buried and date its construction*

- *identify artifacts by culture and usage*

- *distinguish real artifacts from fakes*

- *navigate inside ruins and catacombs, including finding secret doors and hidden construction*

- *describe the customs of ancient or historical cultures*

- *spot well-disguised graves and underground hiding places*

Architecture (Academic)

You know how buildings are designed and constructed. You can:

- *guess what lies around the corner while exploring an unknown structure*

- *judge the relative strength of building materials*

- *identify a building's age, architectural style, original use, and history of modifications*

- *deduce the existence of hidden rooms, priest-holes, hyper-geometric witch-garrets, and other anomalies*

- *construct stable makeshift structures*

- *identify elements vital to a building's structural integrity*

Art (Technical)

You can create some sort of art – music, painting, dance, sculpture, song, poetry, drama, and so forth. You can choose to focus on one medium or diversify: For each rating point in Art, you may select another type of art in which you are generally proficient. You may specify when you create your Investigator, or choose opportunistically in the course of play, revealing that you happen to be, say, a fine amateur contralto if circumstances suddenly require it.

Creating great (or even particularly notable) art requires spends (see p. 54); points allocated to such spends cannot be allocated to different art-forms in the future.

Art History (Academic)

You're an expert on works of art (including the practical arts such as furniture and pottery) from an aesthetic and technical point of view. You can:

- distinguish real works from fakes

- tell when something has been retouched or altered

- identify the age of an object by style and materials

- accurately estimate the price of an objet d'art

- call to mind historical details on artists and those around them

Assess Honesty (Interpersonal)

This is the human capacity to judge and sense motives and character. Basically, this ability allows you to tell if someone is lying to you, and (with a spend) make a decent guess about their motives.

Not all lies are verbal. You can tell when a person is attempting to project a false impression through body language.

Certain individuals – con men, actors, professional gamblers, and similar – may be so adept at lying that they never set off your built-in lie detector, or overload it by being "always on." Some people believe their own falsehoods. Psychopathic and sociopathic personality types (like most sorcerers turn out to be) and brainwashed cultists lie reflexively and without shame, depriving you of the telltale tics and gestures you use to sense when a person is deceiving you. Those who have communed excessively with the inhuman intelligences of the Mythos will occasionally "read wrong," but will similarly fail to send any useful signals to a sane watcher.

You can also use Assess Honesty to cold-read a mark for fortune-telling scams, phony séances or mentalist acts, and the like.

Astronomy (Technical)

You study celestial objects, including the stars and planets. You can:

- decipher astrological texts

- use a telescope, including large reflectors

- plot the movement of stars and planets, including which ones are overhead at any given time

- predict eclipses, comets, meteor showers, and other regular astronomical phenomena

Bargain (Interpersonal)

You are an expert in making deals with others, convincing them that the best arrangement for you is also the best for them. You can:

- haggle for goods and services

- gauge likely prices of items, including what someone else will pay for them

- mediate hostage situations or diplomatic crises

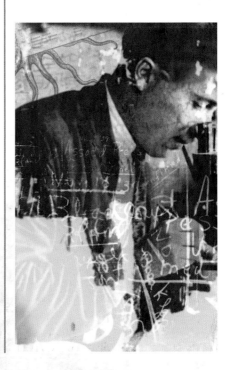

• *swap favors or information with others*

Biology (Academic)

You study the evolution, behavior, and physical makeup of living organisms. You can:

• *tell when an animal is behaving strangely*

• *tell whether an animal or plant is natural to a given area*

• *identify an animal from samples of its hair, blood, bones, or other tissue*

• *analyze unknown ichor, scales, or slime*

• *identify a plant from a small sample*

• *isolate or detect natural poisons or venoms*

Bureaucracy (Interpersonal)

You know how to navigate a bureaucratic organization, whether it's a government office or a large business firm. You know how to get what you want from it in an expeditious manner, and with a minimum of ruffled feathers. You can:

• *convince officials to provide sensitive information*

• *gain credentials on false pretenses*

• *find the person who really knows what's going on*

• *develop and maintain*

Contacts and Connections

Whenever you use Bureaucracy, Cop Talk, Credit Rating, Streetwise, or any other ability to call on a professional contact or personal connection, you must supply the Keeper with her name, residence, and specific connection to your Investigator.

If you need to spend, the size of your spend determines your contact's attitude toward your Investigator, the value (or excitement) of their information, and/or their position in their field. Of course, core clues will always be free.

The Keeper is encouraged to work your contact into the game on a regular basis; whenever it makes any narrative sense, contacts should be recurring characters (especially when you use the relevant ability again). The Keeper may also have your contacts demand favors in return, drag your Investigator into their problems, or simply slaughter them gorily and instructively.

The Intimate Correspondent

You may have a mentor, protégé, close family member, member of the clergy, or other person to whom you confide the details of your investigations, personal terrors, doubts about your sanity, and so forth. If you choose to have such an intimate correspondent, supply the Keeper with her details as per other contacts. Thenceforward, it is assumed that you regularly send updates to (and receive responses from) your intimate correspondent. (A word to the wise: Keepers who know what's good for their game might offer an extra build point or two for a player who actually writes up such letters.) Should your current Investigator die or go mad, you already have the kernel of a new, thoroughly briefed Investigator to join the party.

contacts within a bureaucracy with which you have regular dealings

• *locate offices and files*

• *borrow equipment or supplies*

Bureaucracy is not a catch-all information gathering ability. Bureaucrats wish to convey the impression that they are busy and harried, whether or not they actually are. Most take a profound, secret joy in directing inquiries elsewhere. When players attempt to use Bureaucracy to gain information more easily accessible via other abilities (such as Library Use), their contacts snidely advise

them to do their own damn legwork.

Chemistry (Technical)

You're trained in the analysis of chemical substances. Given lab facilities, you can:

• *among a wide variety of other materials, identify drugs, pharmaceuticals, toxins, and viruses*

• *create simple explosives, poisons, gases, and acids*

• *analyze unknown substances, alloys, compounds, etc*

• *perform ballistics and*

gunpowder analysis of bullets or other residue

- *match samples of dirt or vegetation from a piece of evidence to a scene*

- *perform chemical document analysis on ink or paper*

Cop Talk (Interpersonal)

You know how to speak the lingo of the police, and to make them feel confident and relaxed in your presence. You may be a current or former cop, or simply the kind of person they immediately identify as a solid, trustworthy citizen. You can:

- *coolly ply cops for confidential information*

- *get excused for minor infractions*

- *imply that you are a colleague, authorized to participate in their cases*

- *tell when a cop is lying to you or holding something back*

- *call in favors from law enforcement contacts*

Craft (Technical)

You can create useful physical objects, working with materials like wood, metal, jewelry, and so forth. Although the resulting cabinets, kettles, or rings may be beautiful, your focus is utility, not art. Like the Art ability, you may focus on one craft (blacksmithing, cabinetry, coopering, etc) or diversify into many; the same rules apply.

You may be able to use your Craft ability to specific investigative ends: discover a secret drawer in a desk if you are a cabinet-maker, and so forth.

Credit Rating (Interpersonal)

You are able to operate easily within your economic class, make purchases, mingle socially, cadge invitations or introductions, pick up rumors or call in favors from professional or social contacts, or secure a loan. Investigators with no Credit Rating score might be hoboes or drifters, they may just distrust banks, or they may have no real ability to schmooze. What counts as "your economic class" depends on your Credit Rating score as follows:

Credit Rating works differently from other abilities, in that its rating level is both a description of the type of Credit Rating and a pool size. It can be seen as eight abilities in one: Credit Rating (Lower Class), Credit Rating ("Working Class"), Credit Rating (Lower Middle-Class), etc It remains a pool, because quite frankly (and especially in the 1930s) the higher your class, the more chances society gives you. Your social resources, in other words, increase generally with class and wealth.

The social aspects of Credit Rating can drift between one or two ranks if the Keeper believes it plausible; a Credit Rating 5 doctor might believably mingle with (and ask favors from) a middle-class electrician or an upper-class specialist.

Credit Rating does not necessarily describe the size of your bank account, but your ability to operate within a given socio-economic bracket. You can marry, inherit, be related to, or even befriend your way into your Credit Rating and do nothing much to maintain it besides keep up appearances. HP Lovecraft, for example, had an annual income no better than "Working Class" (if that), but his social attitudes and interpersonal skills (such as they were) were more suited for Credit Rating 4 or even 5. The Great Depression likewise plunged many people's earning power down the ranks while leaving the rest of their Credit Rating intact. In 1930s Britain, where social class is more carefully defined (and to many, far more important) than economic class, Credit Rating may purely describe "social standing."

This ability takes the forefront in heavily social adventures, urban campaigns involving the "low and the high" (where a mix of Credit Ratings in the Investigator party comes in very handy), and perhaps even in university-based campaigns where Credit Rating more closely parallels academic status rather than income. Allowing Credit Rating to become

CREDIT RATING	ECONOMIC CLASS	SIGNIFIERS	APPROXIMATE ANNUAL INCOME
0	Pauper	Hobo life; rags; no permanent home; handouts or scavenge	$0–$150
1	Lower Class	Janitor, hired hand, or servant; soft cap; flop house, SRO, live with relatives; bus; cans of soup or beans	$150–$250
2	"Working Class"	Factory work or skilled service; hat; tenement apartment; bus; meat most days	$250–$1,250
3	Lower Middle-Class	Clerk or high-skilled service; neckties; shabby apartment; used car in bad condition; good Sunday meals	$1,250–$1,500
4	Middle-Class	Supervisor, lesser professional; one good suit; bungalow or decent apartment; modest car; restaurant occasionally; part-time cleaning lady	$1,500–$3,000
5	Upper Middle-Class	Professional; tailored suits; good house or fine apartment; new car or two cars; fine meals in or out; live-in servant	$3,000–$10,000
6	Upper Class	Independent income or exclusive professional; bespoke suits; mansion or penthouse; luxury cars; luxury dining; multiple domestics	$10,000–$75,000
7+	Wealthy	Landed gentry or industrial fortune; fabulous jewelry; landed estate; yachts or private planes; personal four-star chef; multi-tiered staff of domestics	$75,000+

mere shorthand for personal wealth is short-changing the ability. That said, booking passage on an ocean liner for a globe-trotting adventure is much easier with a simple "Lionel has Credit Rating 5; I assume he's in first class."

Cryptography (Academic)

You can make or break codes and ciphers in any language you can read. Given some time and a dictionary, you may be able to puzzle out foreign alphabets, translating languages by brute force.

Cthulhu Mythos (Academic)

You have begun to piece together the secret rules of the real world, rather than the ignorant scrim of physics and religion. You recognize the great names, and the truths they conceal. If you've read a Mythos tome, using this ability lets you recall any specific hints or facts from it relevant to your current situation. If you're staring at an ancient alien bas-relief, using this ability lets you perceive, with a single shocking gestalt, the horrific history it unfolds.

Using this ability costs both Sanity and Stability (see p. 74).

The primary use of this ability in the course of an investigation is to "put together the pieces" and draw upon the terrible knowledge that you have been subconsciously suppressing, achieving a horrific epiphany. The Keeper provides you with the result of your intuition, sketching out the Mythos implications of the events you have uncovered. (See p. 74 for further Keeper guidelines for this ability.) This may not be the "solution" to the mystery, although it should allow you to aim your efforts in the right direction; at the Keeper's discretion, an actual spend might provide more specific (and potentially horribly dangerous) answers.

Consider "The Dunwich Horror" to be a Trail of Cthulhu adventure. Professor Armitage uses his Cthulhu Mythos ability and realizes that old Whateley somehow incarnated Yog-Sothoth on Earth. In the story, he then reads Wilbur's diary to learn that he needs both a special incantation and the Powder of Ibn-Ghazi to destroy Yog-Sothoth's spawn. Had he not managed to get hold of the diary, Armitage could use his Cthulhu Mythos ability to "intuit" that Yog-Sothoth must be made visible before he could be fully banished, and spending a point might tell him that the Powder

Buying Cthulhu Mythos

Paralleling the rules in *Call of Cthulhu*, the default system in *Trail of Cthulhu* is that points in the Cthulhu Mythos ability cannot be bought with build points and are added only during play, mostly by reading eldritch tomes.

However, many of Lovecraft's characters, such as both Danforth and Dyer in At the Mountains of Madness, begin their adventure with some Cthulhu Mythos knowledge. To emulate such stories (or to plunge right into Cthulhoid adventure), the Keeper may allow players to create starting Investigators with points in Cthulhu Mythos. Even in such games, Cthulhu Mythos can never be an Occupational ability.

of Ibn-Ghazi would accomplish such a task. No spend would provide the formula for the Powder, except to suggest which eldritch tome might conceal similar truths.

Evidence Collection (Technical)

You're adept at casing an investigation site and at finding, bagging, and tagging important clues. You can:

- *spot hidden objects or objects of interest (including bullet casings under a couch, or drops of blue ooze behind the desk) at a crime scene or other investigation site*

- *note relationships between objects at a crime scene, reconstructing sequences of events*

- *find, transfer, take, and compare fingerprints*

- *match typewritten materials to a given machine*

- *match handwriting to a known sample*

- *store objects for forensic analysis without contaminating your samples*

Flattery (Interpersonal)

You're good at getting people to help you by complimenting or playing up to them, as subtly or blatantly as they prefer. This works particularly well with subjects who find you attractive, but that isn't strictly necessary. You could just compliment them on their exquisite taste, or the quality of their dissertation. You can get them to:

- *reveal information*

- *perform minor favors*

- *regard you as trustworthy*

- *date you (if applicable)*

It's up to you whether a high rating in Flattery means that you are physically alluring, winning and charismatic, sycophantic, or simply exude a personal magnetism unrelated to your looks or demeanor.

Forensics (Technical)

You study crime scenes and perform autopsies on deceased subjects to determine their cause and circumstances of death. You can use skeletal evidence to reconstruct the physical details (age, sex, medical condition, sometimes occupation) of the deceased. In the case of death by foul play, your examination can identify:

- *the nature of the weapon or weapons used*

- *the approximate time of death*

- *the presence of intoxicants or other foreign substances in the bloodstream or on the skin*

- *the contents of the victim's last meal*

In many cases, you can reconstruct the sequence of events leading to the victim's death from the arrangement of wounds on the body.

Although in the real world this technique was not available until the 1960s, you can determine time (and sometimes place) of death by studying the insects at the scene (or the eggs and larvae in the body).

Geology (Academic)

You are an expert on rocks, soils, minerals, and the primordial history of the Earth. You can:

- *analyze soil samples, crystals, minerals, and so forth*

- *determine the age of a rock stratum*

- *date and identify fossils*

- *evaluate soil for agriculture or industry*

- *identify promising sites for oil or water wells, mines, etc*

- *anticipate volcanism, seismic events, avalanches, and other earth phenomena*

History (Academic)

You're an expert in recorded human history, with an emphasis on its political, military, economic, and technological developments. You are also an expert in the tools historians use: documents and books. You can:

- *recognize obscure historical allusions*

- *recall important or relevant events in a given country, city, or region*

- *identify ancient languages and scripts*

- *perform textual analysis on a manuscript or book to date it or identify the author*

- *determine the age of a document*

- *tell where and when an object made during historical times was fashioned*

- *identify the period of an article of dress or costume*

Interrogation (Interpersonal)

You're trained in extracting information from suspects and witnesses in the context of a formal police-style interview. This must take place in an official setting, where the subject is confined or feels under threat of confinement, and recognizes your authority (whether real or feigned).

Intimidation (Interpersonal)

You elicit cooperation from suspects by seeming physically imposing, invading their personal space, and adopting a psychologically commanding manner. Intimidation may involve implied or direct threats of physical violence but is just as often an act of mental dominance. You can:

- *gain information*

- *inspire the subject to leave the area*

- *quell a subject's desire to attempt violence against you or others*

Languages (Academic)

For each rating point in Languages, you are verbally fluent and literate in one language other than your native tongue. You may elect to be literate in an ancient language that is no longer spoken, although the Keeper may disallow occult, primordial, or inhuman languages such as Aklo (the tongue of the serpent-folk), Naacal (the language of Mu), or Pnakotic A (the Yithian language). The Keeper may

allow overlap between related languages – an Investigator fluent in Norwegian may plausibly claim to be fluent (or at least "mostly able to get by") in Swedish, for example, without adding another rating point.

You may specify these when you create your character, or choose opportunistically in the course of play, revealing that you just happen to read, say, Assyrian when circumstances require it. You are not learning the language spontaneously but revealing a hitherto unmentioned fact about your character.

Law (Academic)

You are familiar with the criminal and civil laws of your home jurisdiction, and broadly acquainted with foreign legal systems. At a rating of 2 or more, you may be a bar-certified attorney. You can:

- *assess the legal risks attendant on any course of action*

- *understand lawyerly jargon*

- *call on legal colleagues or contacts for favors and advice*

- *argue with police and prosecutors*

Library Use (Academic)

You can ferret out information from collections of books, records, files, archives, newspaper morgues, or big piles of unsorted telegrams and correspondence. If the information lies within, and you have access to the collection, you can find it. You can also determine patterns in the data – who wrote about what and to whom, what kinds of books an eccentric collector values, what might be missing from the official files, which records seem doctored and by whom, and so forth.

Locksmith (Technical)

You can open doors and locks, and disarm alarms, without benefit of the key. (You can also find convenient windows to jimmy or coal-cellar doors to force, if need be.) Many locks require specialized tools, possession of which without a locksmith's license is a criminal offense in most jurisdictions. Very complex or tricky locks may require spends to open them speedily, to avoid noise or damage, or to relock afterward.

Using Locksmith is, in other words, a way to gather clues. A lock that won't open is like a witness that won't talk or a bloodstain you can't find: antithetical to the mystery-solving, investigative-adventure design goals of GUMSHOE and *Trail of Cthulhu*. Only safes, bank vaults,

and the like – locks that exist to drive drama or conflict, rather than locks which merely hold clues – require actual tests against Difficulty.

Medicine (Academic)

You diagnose human disease, injuries, poisonings, and physical frailties, and may be broadly acquainted with veterinary medicine as well. At a rating of 2 or more, you may have a medical license. You can:

- *diagnose diseases, poisonings, and other ailments*

- *prescribe treatment for a treatable condition*

- *deliver a baby*

- *identify the extent and cause of an unconscious person's trauma*

- *detect when a person is suffering from a physically debilitating condition such as drug addiction, pregnancy, or malnutrition*

- *establish a person's general level of health*

- *identify medical abnormalities*

- *understand medical jargon*

- *call on medical colleagues or contacts for favors and advice*

At the Keeper's discretion, you may be trained in a more complex specialty, as well as the sort of general practice indicated here.

The Keeper may or may not allow very elementary Forensics ("the killer used a blunt instrument; death was instantaneous") with this ability.

Occult (Academic)

You're an expert in the historical study of magic, superstition, and sorcery from the Stone Age to the present. From Theosophists to Voodoo to the Golden Dawn, you know the dates, the places, the controversies, and the legends. You can:

- *identify the cultural traditions informing a ritual by examining its physical aftermath*

- *supply historical facts and anecdotes concerning various occult traditions, demons, and legends*

- *guess the intended effect of a ritual from its physical aftermath*

- *identify occult activities as the work of informed practitioners or bored thrill-seekers*

- *fake a fortune-telling session, séance, or other occult activity*

- *read and cast a horoscope*

- *identify occult paraphernalia, grimoires, symbols, and codes*

This ability does not allow you to work magic or summon supernatural entities, even if the campaign admits the existence of non-Mythos magic. You may believe in the occult or not; the skill functions just as well in either case.

Depending on the campaign frame, an Occult rating of 4 or more might mean that you have seen obscure names like "Cthulhu" or "Yog-Sothoth" before, but without a rating in Cthulhu Mythos you dismiss them as trivia or explain them as regional or cult variations on Tiamat or Choronzon.

If you have a rating in both Cthulhu Mythos and in Occult, you can identify a given occult ritual as actually (even if ignorantly or unintentionally) a Mythos ritual. This counts as a use of Occult, and costs no Sanity or Stability.

Oral History (Interpersonal)

You can find sources willing to talk, win their confidence, and gather (usually lengthy) oral testimony about historical events, local traditions, folklore, family legend, or gossip. This is an excellent way to do research in illiterate or semi-literate societies, and in rural or small-town communities in general. This ability also covers taking shorthand notes or making recordings without spooking your sources.

Outdoorsman (Technical)

You are familiar with working and living outdoors and in the wild. You might be a farmer, cowboy, or logger, or an amateur (or professional) fisher or hunter, or work for the Park Service. Perhaps you were merely an Eagle Scout, grew up in the back of nowhere, or served in a military unit with sufficient patrol experience "in country." You can:

- *tell when an animal is behaving strangely*
- *tell whether an animal or plant is natural to a given area*
- *find edible plants, hunt, and fish*
- *make fire and survive outdoors at night or in bad weather*
- *navigate overland, albeit more easily with a compass and a map*
- *track people, animals, or vehicles across grass or through forests*
- *hunt with dogs, including tracking with bloodhounds, assuming you have friendly dogs available*

Despite the name, there is no restriction on female characters taking this ability in either the Pulp or Purist game.

Pharmacy (Technical)

You are able to identify and compound drugs and medicines. You can:

- *identify drugs and potions, and recognize their side-effects and contraindications*
- *identify poisons and determine antidotes*
- *secure or manufacture morphine, cocaine, and other controlled substances*

Photography (Technical)

You're proficient in the use of cameras, including still and motion-picture photography. You can:

- *take useful visual records of crime scenes or expeditions*
- *develop film or plates and enhance hidden details*
- *use filters and lights to capture images only visible in infrared or ultraviolet*
- *spot manual retouching or camera trickery in a photographic image or negative*
- *take trick photographs using double exposures and other methods*
- *realistically retouch and manipulate photographic images*

Physics (Academic)

You study the fundamental forces of the universe: pressure, electromagnetism, motion, gravity, optics, and radioactivity. You can:

- *design or refit experimental machinery to test, detect, or manipulate physical forces and energies*
- *obtain and operate expensive or obscure pieces of laboratory equipment such as Crookes tubes, Geiger counters, or magnetometers*
- *understand and apply*

advanced mathematics, including non-Euclidean geometries

• attempt to comprehend advanced or alien technologies 🜨

Usually, building experimental machinery is a matter for Mechanical or Electrical Repair, not Physics, although Physics might be a prerequisite.

🜨 The Keeper may or may not allow physicist Investigators to "reverse-engineer" Yithian lightning guns, invent death rays, etc They should still use Mechanical or Electrical Repair to build the things, although such construction would require the Physics ability as a prerequisite.

Reassurance (Interpersonal)

You get people to do what you want by putting them at ease. This may involve fast talk, genuine sympathy, or just a calming presence. You can:

• elicit information and minor favors

• allay fear or panic in others

• instill a sense of calm during a crisis

Streetwise (Interpersonal)

You know how to behave among crooks, gangsters, dopers, hookers, grifters, and other habitués of the criminal underworld. You can:

• deploy criminal etiquette to avoid fights and conflicts

• identify unsafe locations and dangerous people

• make and utilize criminal contacts – fences, black marketeers, drug dealers, arms runners, and so forth

• successfully price illegal goods such as drugs, stolen items, or weapons

• tell when practiced criminals and con artists are lying, as with Assess Honesty

• gather underworld rumors

Theology (Academic)

You study human religions in their various forms, both ancient and modern. You can:

• supply information about religious practices and beliefs

• quote relevant tags from the major scriptures

• recognize the names and attributes of various saints, gods, and other figures of religious worship and veneration

• identify whether a given religious practice or ritual is orthodox or heretical

• fake (or in some traditions, officiate at) a religious ceremony

This ability does not allow you to work miracles, banish demons, commune with deities, or otherwise invoke supernatural power, even if the campaign admits the existence of a non-Mythos God or gods. You may believe in a given religion or not; the skill functions just as well in either case.

If you have a rating in both Cthulhu Mythos and in Theology, you can identify a given ceremony as actually (even if ignorantly or unintentionally) a Mythos ritual. This counts as a use of Theology, and costs no Sanity or Stability.

Some questions or clues may fall under both Theology and Occult, or on the boundary between them. In the 1930s, for example, most authorities hold that Voodoo falls under Occult (or Anthropology), backwoods snake-handling churches are a matter of Theology, and Satanism straddles the two fields. The Keeper may differ; if so, erring on the side of overlap is probably best.

GENERAL ABILITIES

Athletics

Athletics allows you to perform general acts of physical derring-do, from running to jumping to throwing bundles of dynamite to dodging falling or oncoming objects. Any physical action not covered by another ability probably falls under the rubric of Athletics.

If your Athletics rating is 8 or more, your Hit Threshold, the Target Number your opponents use when attempting to hit you in combat, is 4. Otherwise, your Hit Threshold is 3.

Conceal

You can hide things from view and conceal them from search. Your methods might include camouflage, holding items out on your person, snaking things into drawers unobserved, building secret compartments, or even altering a thing's visual signature with paint or plaster.

This ability also allows you to discover things intentionally concealed.

Disguise

This is the skill of altering your own appearance, posture, and voice to be unrecognizable. Disguising others in anything more complex than a slouch hat or false mustache is good only for brief periods, as posture and body language are vital components in any successful disguise.

Successfully disguising yourself as an actual person known to those you're interacting with is extraordinarily difficult. Brief voice-only mimicry pits you against a Difficulty Number of 4. Face-to-face impersonation requires successful roll against a Difficulty Number of 7 every five minutes of sustained contact between you and the object of your impersonation.

Disguise doubles as an Investigative ability when used to gather clues by:

- *creating and maintaining a cover identity among the unsuspecting*

- *impersonating a generic figure, such as a security guard or a messenger*

- *briefly misrepresenting yourself, such as on the telephone or in a vestibule*

Driving

Anyone who's been taught can drive a car down the road without this ability. You, on the other hand, are a skilled defensive driver, capable of wringing high performance from even the most recalcitrant automobile, pickup truck, or omnibus. You can:

- *evade or conduct pursuit*

- *avoid collisions, or minimize damage from collisions*

- *spot tampering with a vehicle*

- *navigate, read maps, and maintain a sense of direction*

- *conduct emergency repairs*

For every 2 additional rating points in Driving, you may add an additional ground vehicle type to your repertoire, such as: motorcycle, transport truck, locomotive, buckboard, or streetcar. You may choose exotic types, like tanks and hansom cabs, although these are unlikely to see regular use in an investigation-based game. Like additional Languages, or additional varieties of Art and Craft, you may add them opportunistically in play if you have "unassigned" points. Your pool can be used for any Driving roll, regardless of the vehicle.

A table of vehicles can be found on p. 184.

Electrical Repair

You're good at building, repairing, operating, and disabling electrical devices from simple alarm systems to the most advanced radios. (You can also hot-wire a car with an electrical ignition, which is most of them built since 1920.) Given the right components, you can create jury-rigged devices from odd bits of scrap.

Electrical Repair doubles as an investigative ability when used to:

- *evaluate the quality of workmanship used to create an item*

- *determine the function of a given electrical gadget*

- *tap telephone or telegraph lines*

- *make high-quality audio recordings on records, Dictaphone cylinders, or wire*

- *read Morse Code*

- *use an electrical device in good repair as intended for an investigative (clue-gathering) purpose*

Explosives

You're an expert in bombs and booby-traps. You can:

- *defuse bombs and traps*

- *handle nitroglycerine or other dangerously unstable materials with relative safety*

- *given time, blow open safes or vaults without damaging the contents*

- *mix explosive compounds from common chemicals*

- *safely construct and*

• *pilfer clues from (or plant clues at) a crime scene under the very noses of unsuspecting authorities*

• *pick pockets*

• *plant objects on unsuspecting subjects*

Firearms

You are adept with firearms, including their repair and identification. This skill also, covers crossbows and similar trigger-operated missile weapons (see the sidebar on the next page.)

You can spend 2 points from your Firearms pool to attempt to hit a target at long range with a pistol, or at up to 500 yards with a rifle. (See p. 186) This spend does not adjust your roll; it makes it possible in the first place.

If your Firearms rating is 5 or higher, you can spend 1 point from your Firearms pool to fire two pistols in the same round. If you attack two enemies, one target's Hit Threshold increases by 2 (your choice).

A table of firearms can be found on p. 186.

First Aid

You can perform first aid on sick or injured individuals. For more on the use of this ability, see p. 63.

Fleeing

Running away is an excellent survival skill; even in Pulp mode, your characters may be doing a great deal of it. Like many of Lovecraft's spindly, neurasthenic protagonists, you can be very good at running away without being

detonate explosive devices or booby-traps of your own

Explosives doubles as an investigative ability when used to:

• *reconstruct exploded bombs*

• *for any bomb (exploded or unexploded), determine*

the method and materials of the bomb-maker, and deduce his sophistication, background, and skill

Filch

Your nimble fingers allow you to unobtrusively manipulate small objects. You can:

Tcho-Tchos and other primitive tribespeople will likely attack with bows, blowguns, or other missile weapons without triggers – the Keeper can rename this skill to match, if she likes. In the unlikely event that a player simply *must* build an Investigator skilled in the use of both bows and guns, add an Archery ability.

Mi-Go and Yithians will more likely attack with energy projectors or similarly terrifying distance weapons. Again, the Keeper can rename this skill to match if desired. Investigators can never become familiar with such alien devices; they will always use them as if they were unskilled (see sidebar, p. 60).

generally good at other physical tasks. So Fleeing becomes an ability unto itself, which you can use as a substitute for Athletics when escaping during chase sequences. It does not make you any better at pursuit.

If your Fleeing rating is more than twice your final Athletics rating, you can buy rating points in Fleeing above the value at a reduced rate, getting 2 rating points for each build point spent. Hence, if your Athletics rating is 0, all your Fleeing is half-price. See p. 26 for an example.

Health

Health measures your ability to sustain injuries, resist infection, and survive the effects of toxins. When you get hit in the course of a fight, your Health pool is diminished. A higher Health pool allows you to stay in a fight longer before succumbing to your injuries.

When your Health pool is depleted, you may be dazed, wounded, or monster chow. For more on this, see p. 63.

In the Purist mode, your Health is capped at 12.

Hypnosis

Only Alienists (see p. 9) and Parapsychologists (see p. 17) can buy or use this skill, and usually only in a Pulp game.

This ability represents medical hypnosis; it is not psychic mesmerism or Dr Caligari-style mind control. You can only hypnotize a *willing* subject, and only one subject at a time. Using Hypnosis requires a Test against a Difficulty Number that varies depending on what you are using it for.

• *Simple hypnotic state:* To place a patient in a hypnotic trance, you must succeed against Difficulty 3. During this trance, she is calm and placid.

• *Establish analytic rapport:* Once you have successfully hypnotized a patient, your Psychoanalysis pool increases by 3 during any future use of Psychoanalysis on them. Your Psychoanalysis rating must be at least 3 to gain this benefit, and the 3 points must be spent on the patient.

• *Recover memories:* The patient's fragmented or buried memories, as of dreams, traumas, or murky monster attacks, can be called to the surface and "relived." This is a Difficulty 4 test. Reliving an experience that cost Stability will cost the patient the same amount again, although you may practice immediate Psychological Triage (see p. 79) to minimize the patient's shock. The Keeper is free to provide false memories if she feels you are "leading the witness."

• *Post-hypnotic suggestion:* Upon lifting the trance, you may cause your patient to perform a single action without apparent thought. You may require a "trigger phrase" or simply specify a time: ("When you get home, you'll leave the book on the desk.") Spells and other complex activities cannot be post-hypnotically induced. The patient will not accept a suggestion contrary to her normal behavior. This is a Difficulty 4 or higher test; the Keeper may increase the Difficulty based on the suggestion.

• *Ease pain:* You can relieve symptomatic pain in a patient. This removes the mechanical penalties for being hurt (see p. 63), and lasts until the patient is wounded again. This is a Difficulty 4 or higher test; the Keeper may increase the Difficulty depending on the pain's severity. *This does not work under battlefield conditions.*

• *False memories:* You can purposely implant false memories in the patient or bury real ones. This is extremely unethical without a direct therapeutic benefit (such as easing a remembered trauma). This is a Contest between your Hypnosis and the patient's Stability. Your Difficulty Number is 5; the patient resists with Difficulty 4. Again, the Keeper may increase your Difficulty based on the severity of the memory change. At the Keeper's discretion, if the patient suffers a further trauma (such as her Stability dropping below -5 again), she may suddenly recall the truth.

Mechanical Repair

You're good at building, repairing, operating, and disabling mechanical devices from simple stick traps to the most complex adding machines or steam turbines. (With the exception of simple latches, working with locks is covered by the Locksmith ability.) Given the right components, you can create jury-rigged devices and booby-traps from odd bits of scrap.

Mechanical Repair doubles as an investigative ability when used to:

- *evaluate the quality of workmanship used to create an item*

- *determine the function of a given mechanical gadget*

- *use a mechanical device in good repair as intended*

For every rating point in Mechanical Repair, you may operate and (where relevant) drive a type of heavy machinery, such as: tank, back-hoe, construction crane, or steam shovel. You may choose exotic types, like ocean liner steam engines or heavy artillery, although these are unlikely to see regular use in an investigation-based game. Like Languages, Driving, Art, etc, you may add types opportunistically, "suddenly recalling" your service on a tramp steamer, or the summer you worked construction on Boulder Dam.

Piloting

Although almost anyone can paddle a canoe or even row a dinghy, you can pilot small boats (motorboats, sailboats, dories) or single-engine light aircraft (barnstormers, crop dusters) with professional aplomb and serene confidence. You can:

- *evade or conduct pursuit*

- *anticipate bad weather*

- *avoid collisions, or minimize damage from collisions*

- *spot tampering with a vehicle*

- *navigate by compass or the stars, read maps, and maintain a sense of direction*

- *conduct emergency repairs*

A rating of 1 in Piloting allows you to select either small boats or single-engine light aircraft. For every 2 additional rating points in Piloting, you may add an additional air or water vehicle type to your repertoire, such as: small boats, single-engine light aircraft, gliders, flying boats, multi-engine planes, yachts, multi-masted sailing ships. You may choose exotic types, like zeppelins, submarines, and autogiros, although these are unlikely to see regular use in an investigation-based game. Like the additional vehicles available with extra points in Driving, you may add them opportunistically in play if you have "unassigned" points. You may spend any of your points on any vehicle.

A table of aircraft can be found on p. 185.

Preparedness

You expertly anticipate the needs of any investigation by packing a kit efficiently arranged with necessary gear. Assuming you have immediate access to your kit, you may be able to produce an object the team needs to overcome an obstacle. You make a simple test (p. 56); if you succeed, you have the item you want. You needn't do this in advance of the adventure, but can dig into your kit bag (provided you're able to get to it) as the need arises.

Items of obvious utility to a Mythos investigation do not require a test. These include but are not limited to: notebooks or paper, writing implements and ink, flashlights, candles and matches, colored chalk, common tools and hardware, pen-knives, magnifying glasses, pocket mirrors, string, sandwiches, and brandy.

Other abilities imply the possession of basic gear suitable to their core tasks. Characters with First Aid or Medicine have their own first aid kits or medical bags; Photographers come with cameras, film, and flash bulbs. If you have Firearms, you usually have a gun, and so on. Preparedness does not intrude into their territory. It covers general-purpose investigative equipment, plus oddball items – a telegraph key, a baseball, a gas mask — that suddenly come in handy in the course of the story.

The sorts of items you can produce at a moment's notice depend not on your rating or pool, but on narrative credibility. If the Keeper determines that your possession of an item would seem ludicrous, anachronistic, or out of genre, you don't get to roll for it. You simply don't have it. Any item which elicits a laugh from the group when suggested is probably out of bounds.

Inappropriate use of the Preparedness ability is like pornography. Your Keeper will know it when she sees it.

Psychoanalysis

You can provide comfort, perspective, and solace to the mentally troubled. You may be a Freudian alienist, a priest or pastor, or just an empathetic and intuitive individual.

You can restore panicked Investigators to a state of calm (see p. 79), restore lost Stability points (see p, 79) and treat any long-term mental illnesses they accrue in the course of their activities (see p. 81).

Adding General Abilities
If it's appropriate for the campaign frame, your Keeper can split abilities into more specialized areas or add new ones altogether. For example, in a campaign of world-spannning exploration, she could split Piloting into Piloting (Boats) and Piloting (Light Aircraft), and add Caving as a new ability. You should only do this if the additional complication is outweighed by the benefits in spotlighting Investigators' abilities. See also Adding Investigative Abilities on p. 32.

Riding

Although staying on a tame, untroubled walking horse (on flattish terrain, anyway) is relatively easy once one gets the hang of it, and staying on a mule or burro even easier, you are a gifted equestrian. You can gallop even recalcitrant or spirited horses, donkeys, and mules past distractions and across the countryside. You can:

- *evade or conduct mounted pursuit*

- *care for, groom, shoe, and stable mounts*

- *take care of, prepare, and use riding gear such as saddles and bridles*

- *calm a nervous mount*

- *drive a horse-drawn wagon or cart*

- *wield a weapon while riding*

For every additional 2 rating points in Riding, you may add an additional riding animal: camel, water buffalo, or elephant. You may not add Mythos mounts such as shantaks. You pool may be spent on Riding any or all of these creatures.

Sanity

Exposure to the truths of the Cthulhu Mythos shatters the core of the human psyche by stripping away all illusions of human significance, benign nature, and loving God, leaving nothing but the terrifying vistas of stark, cosmic nihilism. Your Sanity rating indicates the degree to which you can sustain belief in any fundamental human concerns whatsoever. Unlike other abilities, you never test your Sanity or spend points from your Sanity pool. They are leached away by the Outside.

Once your Sanity reaches 0, your beliefs – and what you used to consider your soul – have been completely corroded beyond repair. In game terms, you become an NPC, shut away in a sanitarium forever, if you are fortunate, or a willing servitor of the uncaring Great Old Ones if not.

It is important to note that a Mythos initiate might have a Sanity of 0 and seem completely normal after rebuilding his intellect around the revealed cosmic truth, and a raving madman who believes himself to be Jesus Christ reborn might retain a Sanity rating at almost any level – if his mania is of purely human construction, rather than the result of a communion with Yog-Sothoth.

If you have a Cthulhu Mythos rating at all, your Sanity rating

can never be higher than 10 minus your Cthulhu Mythos rating. (If you know nothing about the Mythos, your Sanity can be as high as you care to buy it. You will lose these points if you gain Cthulhu Mythos.) For a longer-term, more survivable, or pulpier game, the Keeper may wish to adjust this ceiling upward, or shift it downward for a shorter, deadlier, or starker game. (Further rules for Sanity appear on p. 69.)

You get Sanity 4 for free.

Pillars of Sanity

For each 3 full rating points your Investigator possesses in Sanity, you must define one Pillar of Sanity: some human concern that he believes in and trusts implicitly. Pillars of Sanity are abstract principles, not individual people or objects. Pillars of Sanity can be damaged or destroyed by Mythos revelations (see p. 75) Some examples of Pillars include:

- *Religious faith (can be a specific denomination,*

Martin Harvesson, Sample Investigator

Martin has a Sanity rating of 10 and a Stability rating of 8. Josh has to pick three Pillars of Sanity, and decides that Martin believes in a moral code, loves Chicago, and holds fast to a notion of human worth. The first and third help support his Drive for Revenge on whoever, or whatever, killed his partner.

The Keeper decides to use the Sources of Stability rule, since she wants the adventures to be rooted in city life while also featuring globe-spanning horror. Josh only has to pick 2 Sources of Stability to help keep Martin grounded, so he picks Martin's secretary Joan (a plucky, fast-talking broad with a secret soft spot for Martin) and Martin's former partner on the force, Lieutenant McAllen (a straight cop in a bent city). Josh decides that Martin left the force after he had to take the rap for something that might have splashed mud on McAllen, which explains his low Credit Rating.

or a general trust in a benevolent or rational deity)

- *Family (especially family honor, purity of one's blood, and suchlike)*

- *Human dignity and value*

- *Scientific progress or the value of the intellect*

- *Physical laws and the reality of scientific knowledge*

- *The goodness, beauty, or worthiness of Nature or the environment*

- *The innate goodness of mankind*

- *Moral principles*

- *Aesthetics or the high principles of art*

- *Epicureanism; living life to the fullest*

- *Patriotism and national virtue*

- *Love of one's home city or town*

As you might expect, Cthulhu Mythos revelations that undermine these Pillars will cost you additional Sanity.

Scuffling

You can hold your own in a hand-to-hand fight, whether you wish to kill, knock out, restrain, or evade your opponent. It is up to you whether high rating levels in this ability indicate specific skills (such as boxing, wrestling, or le savate), long practice in bar brawls, or just a devastating and manly right cross. The use of blackjacks, brass knuckles, coshes, saps, rolls of quarters or shillings tucked up in the fist are treated as Scuffling

Sense Trouble

This ability allows you to perceive (either with sight or other senses) potential hazards to yourself or others. For example, you can:

- *hear the splash of the Deep One dropping into the sewer behind you*

- *see a flittering shape cross the moon*

- *smell the sharp juniper reek of the Treaders of the Dust as they silently approach*

- *notice the freshly split human bones hastily hidden behind the easel*

- *have a bad feeling about that eerily hunchbacked priest at the seemingly deserted cathedral*

Players never know the Difficulty Numbers for Sense Trouble before deciding how many points to spend, even in games where Keepers generously inform the players of other Difficulty Numbers. Players must blindly choose how much to spend. The Keeper does not roll in secret, so even a failed roll allows the group the sense that something is amiss. They just don't know exactly what this is. Think of it as the game system equivalent of tension-building eerie music in a horror movie.

Keepers should never require the use of this general ability to find clues to the mystery at hand. Instead, use Investigative abilities, defaulting to Evidence Collection when no ability seems more appropriate. Sense Trouble is for a scenario's action-oriented sequences. In short, if not seeing something will get you attacked, it's Sense Trouble.

Shadowing

You're good at following suspects without revealing your presence. You can:

- *guide a team to follow a suspect for short periods, handing off to the next in*

sequence, so the subject doesn't realize he's being trailed

- *use binoculars or telescopes to keep watch on a target from a distance*

- *find undetectable vantage points*

- *hide in plain sight*

- *anticipate blind spots in your coverage and plan for them, or use them to lose your own shadowers*

Stability

Whether caused by an onrushing shoggoth, a horde of ghouls, or an NKVD torturer, shock and fear take a toll on the mind and nervous system. Mythos and non-Mythos threats alike can send Investigators into screeching panic, near-catatonic funk, or blind frenzy. Your Stability rating indicates your resistance to mental trauma.

Although the sudden revelation or confirmation of the truths of the Cthulhu Mythos can damage your Stability, so can service in the Great War or the deaths of your beloved family in a fire. In other words, although losing Sanity can decrease Stability, the two are not directly correlated. (See p. 70.) A Sanity 0 cultist of Hastur might be a gibbering backwoods cannibal (with an appropriately low Stability) or a sophisticated, wealthy art critic with a Stability higher than that of any of the Investigators who seek to take him down.

You get Stability 1 for free.

In a Purist game, your Stability is capped at 12.

Sources of Stability

This option is appropriate if the campaign frame has a soap-opera-like element it.

For every 3 full rating points you possess in Stability, you must name one person that keeps you sane when the terrors of the world threaten to shred your psyche. This network of friends, colleagues and family provides you with a motivation to keep fighting the good fight and going back into that crypt every night.

A name and identifying phrase are sufficient for each. You may not use fellow Investigators; they go through the same stresses you do and remind you of the horrors you confront. It's permissible, but risky, for multiple Investigators to lean on the same folks as members of their support network.

Relying on others is a source of strength, but also of danger. Once you come to the attention of entities or cultists of the Mythos, they may use your loved ones against you. They may turn them to evil, possess them, or take the tried and true route of subjecting them to horrible tortures. If anything bad happens to them, you not only face immediate, difficult Stability tests, but may permanently lose the rating points they're linked to. Your wife, mother, or child can no longer soothe your spirit if you can only visit their scarred and broken bodies in a secluded mental hospital.

Stealth

You're good at moving (and standing still) without being noticed. You can:

- *move silently*

- *hide in shadows or cover*

- *evade visual security, whether guards (usual) or cameras (unusual)*

- *listen at doors or windows without being overheard yourself*

Use Stealth when you are creeping around unnoticed; if you are trying to sneakily lose a pursuer, use Shadowing. (Outrunning a pursuer is Athletics or Fleeing.)

Weapons

You are skilled in the use of personal hand weapons such as knives, swords, or whips. The use of blackjacks, brass knuckles, coshes, saps, rolls of quarters or shillings tucked up in the fist are treated as Scuffling (see p. 47).

TRAIL OF CTHULHU
BY KENNETH HITE

Player Name: Josh

Investigator Name: Martin Harvesson
Drive: Revenge (for dead partner)
Occupation:[2] Private Investigator
Occupational benefits: Spend points 2-for-1 after Rolling Disguise or Shadowing
Pillars of Sanity: Moral Code, Loves Chicago, notion of human worth
Build Points: 0

Sanity[1]

0	1	2	3
4	5	6	7
8	9	10	11
12	13	14	15

Hit Threshold[3] 4

Stability

-12	-11	-10	-9
-8	-7	-6	-5
-4	-3	-2	-1
0	1	2	3
4	5	6	7
8	9	10	11
12	13	14	15

Health

-12	-11	-10	-9
-8	-7	-6	-5
-4	-3	-2	-1
0	1	2	3
4	5	6	7
8	9	10	11
12	13	14	15

Academic Abilities	Interpersonal Abilities	General Abilities
*Accounting		
Anthropology	*Assess Honesty 3	Athletics 8
Archaeology	Bargain	Conceal
Architecture	Bureaucracy	*Disguise(I) 10
Art History	Cop Talk 3	*Driving 10
Biology	Credit Rating 2	Electrical Repair(I)
Cthulhu Mythos[4]	Flattery	Explosives(I)
Cryptography	Interrogation	Filch
Geology	Intimidation 3	Firearms[5] 5
History	Oral History	First Aid
Languages[6]	*Reassurance 3	Fleeing[7]
	Streetwise 3	Health[9] 6
		Hypnosis[8]
		Mechanical Repair(I) 6
	Technical Abilities	Piloting
*Law 1		Preparedness
Library Use	Art	Psychoanalysis
Medicine	Astronomy	Riding
Occult	Chemistry	Sanity[9] 10
Physics	Craft	Stability[9] 8
Theology	Evidence Collection 2	*Scuffling
	Forensics 1	Sense Trouble 8
	*Locksmith 3	*Shadowing 10
	Outdoorsman	Stealth 8
	Pharmacy	Weapons 2
	*Photography 2	

[1] In a Pulp game where Sanity can be recovered, mark Sanity pool loss with a line, Sanity rating loss with a cross.

[2] Occupational abilities are half price. Mark them with a * before assigning points.

[3] Hit Threshold is 3, 4 if your Athletics is 8 or higher.

[(I)] These General abilties double up as Investigative abilities

[4] Usually, you can't start with Cthulhu Mythos. Sanity is limited to 10-Cthulhu Mythos.

[5] In a Pulp game If your Firearms rating is 5 you can fire two pistols at once (see p. 42)

[6] Assign one language per point, during play. Record them here.

[7] Any Fleeing rating above twice your Athletics rating costs one point for two.

[8] Only Alienists and Parapsycholigists can buy Hypnosis, and only in a Pulp game

[9] You start with 4 free Sanity points, I Health and I Stability point.

SOURCES OF STABILITY:

Joan (Plucky, fast-talking secretary)

Lieutenant McAllen (former partner)

CONTACTS AND NOTES

Clues, Tests and Contests

"THROUGH SHADOWY DREAMS THEY SEND A MARCHING LINE

OF STILL MORE SHADOWY SHAPES AND HINTS AND VIEWS;

ECHOES FROM OUTER VOIDS, AND SUBTLE CLUES

TO THINGS WHICH THEY THEMSELVES CANNOT DEFINE."

— THE FUNGI FROM YUGGOTH: HARBOUR WHISTLES

Once you've built your Investigator, it becomes the job of the Keeper to lure him and his companions into the bowels of a horrific mystery. Every *Trail of Cthulhu* scenario presents such a mystery, with a horrific tale behind it. Something awful has happened. Usually, somebody or something has done it. The Investigators must figure out what it is, and who did it, and how to stop it from happening again.

The Keeper figures out (or reads an adventure scenario describing) the what, who, and how before the game starts. She then has to help the other players tell the story of how their heroic Investigators also figure out the what, who, and how. The Keeper's scenario notes are not a story. The story occurs as you, the team of players, bring this skeletal structure to life through the actions of your Investigators. The story proceeds from scene to scene, where you

determine the pace, discovering clues and putting them together. Your Investigators interact with locations, gathering physical evidence, and with supporting characters run by the Keeper, gathering expert and eyewitness testimony.

As the Keeper lays out the investigation scene by scene, and you interact with the locations and supporting cast (and occasionally horrible monsters), the story unfolds. The first scene presents the mystery you have to solve. You may stumble onto it, be called in by your old mentor, or just hear about it after the fact. You then perform legwork: hitting the libraries, buddying up to the cops, collecting local legends, or following suspicious foreigners. Your goal is to collect information that tells you more about the case. Each scene contains such information pointing to a new scene, and painting the details of the horror bit by bit. Certain scenes may put a new twist on the investigation, as the initial mystery turns out to be just one layer of the onion. To move from scene to scene, and to solve the overall mystery, you must gather clues. They fuel your forward momentum.

As you accumulate clues, you figure out enough to assemble them into a course of action, and eventually into a solution. The Investigators track down the villainous cult, mad sorcerer, uncanny phenomenon, or alien presence behind the horror. In

Trail of Cthulhu, the solution to the mystery usually leads to (or happens during) a confrontation with some monstrous evil. Once the players know where the evil lurks, they can send their Investigators toward it. There, rules for challenging tests and dangerous contests come into their own.

CLUES

"THERE, INDEED, NO STOLEN CHILD WAS FOUND, DESPITE THE TALES OF SCREAMS AND THE RED SASH PICKED UP IN THE AREAWAY; BUT THE PAINTINGS AND ROUGH INSCRIPTIONS ON THE PEELING WALLS OF MOST OF THE ROOMS, AND THE PRIMITIVE CHEMICAL LABORATORY IN THE ATTIC, ALL HELPED TO CONVINCE THE DETECTIVE THAT HE WAS ON THE TRACK OF SOMETHING TREMENDOUS."

— THE HORROR AT RED HOOK

The GUMSHOE engine, which powers the *Trail of Cthulhu* rules, separates the business of finding the clues from the business of confronting (or running away from) monstrous evil. In a fictional mystery, whether it's a mystery novel, a straight-up detective show like *Columbo*, a medical mystery like *House*, or a police procedural like *CSI* or *Law and Order*, the emphasis isn't on finding the clues in the first place. Usually, the heroes are drowning in clues. When it really matters, you may get a paragraph telling you how Holmes crawled around on the carpet with his magnifying glass, or see a montage of serious-looking dudes with Luminol and Ziploc bags. But the action really starts after the detectives – the Investigators – gather the clues.

INVESTIGATIVE SCENARIOS ARE NOT ABOUT FINDING CLUES. THEY ARE ABOUT INTERPRETING THE CLUES YOU DO FIND.

Figuring out the puzzle is hard enough for a group of armchair detectives, without someone withholding half the pieces from them. GUMSHOE, therefore, makes the finding of clues all but automatic, as long as you get to the right place in the story and have the right ability. That's when the fun part begins, when the players try to put the components of the puzzle together.

Gathering Clues

Gathering clues is simple. All you have to do is:

1. **Get your Investigator into a scene where relevant information can be gathered,**

2. **Have the right ability to discover the clue, and**

3. **Tell the Keeper that you're using it.**

As long as you do these three things, you will never fail to gain a piece of necessary information. *It is never dependent on a die roll*. If you ask for it, you will get it.

You can specify exactly what you intend to achieve: "I use Art History to see if the idol is authentically Late Minoan."

You can convey a wider speculation to the Keeper: "I use Oral History to find the town drunk and pump him for local legends." You sensibly guess that the town is weird, but you don't want to waste time going from NPC to NPC trying to read the Keeper's mind and figure out which one contains the magic plot pellet. Nor should you. In this example, if the Keeper planned on having the local busybody provide the info instead of the local rummy, she can either change the information's source retroactively or tell you something like: "Before you can talk to Old Silas, an interfering bluehair chases him off. Fortunately, she's eager to spill the dirt on her neighbors' sketchy family history."

Or you can engage in a more general informational fishing expedition: "I use Evidence Collection to search the alley," or "I use Chemistry to test the meteorite."

Or, the Keeper might ask if you, or anyone has a particular ability.

If your suggested action corresponds to a clue in the scenario notes, the Keeper provides you the information arising from the clue.

Languid dilettante Willoughby Boothroyd is on the trail of a cult of deranged, Yog-Sothoth-worshipping alchemists. He searches Beacon Hill for their Boston headquarters. His player, Zachary, says "I stroll the streets at sunset looking for alchemical glass in the windows." This is all

Simple Searches

Many clues can be found without any ability whatsoever. If an ordinary person could credibly find a clue simply by looking in a specified place, the clue discovery occurs automatically. You, the reader, wouldn't need to be a trained investigator to find a bloody footprint on the carpet in your living room, or notice a manila envelope taped to the underside of a table at the local pub. By that same logic, the Investigators don't require specific abilities to find them, either. When players specify that they're searching an area for clues, they're performing what we call a **simple search**. To perform simple searches, they must narrow down the scope of their examination by specifying a particular area or object within the scene:

- "I look in the roll-top desk."

- "Is there anything in the tub?"

- "Dr Markesan is checking the bottles in the kitchen."

On the other hand, characters who do have relevant abilities can glean clues without getting this specific. With Evidence Collection, clues become available to a player simply by being on the scene and indicating that you're looking for them.

Example Benefits

Here some special benefits you might get from investigative point spends.

The benefit gives you an advantage in a future contest of General abilities.

- you find your petrol tank has been punctured before you drive the vehicle
- you discover that Shoggoths are affected by electricity, before you encounter one
- you notice that there is a hole in the fence around the back of the complex or that the guards go off-duty at 6.00pm
- the plans show that the bomb must remain horizontal if you are not to trigger it
- Credit Rating might get you access to an NPC psychoanalyst or doctor.

The benefit gives a favorable impression to supporting characters.

- you recognize and recover stolen artwork for the original owner, who will then be more inclined to help you
- you spend points to discover a hidden room where there is a hostage who can either give clues or even help with General abilities.
- You spend Credit Rating to cover up mistakes or buy your way past those who stand in your way

The benefit can lead to a flashback scene.

- you find an insect and receive a flash back to a time you were in the Amazon basin, alone, with one of the creatures crawling up your leg – it wasn't poisonous after all.
- you get your clue the form of a recalled lecture given by your mentor

Point spends can help you resolve a moral dilemma. If your character finds the action required to get a Core Clue distasteful you might make a point spend to avoid this.

- Intimidating a local might get you a core clue for free, but a two point Reassurance spend on the same local could get you the same information without upsetting your source.
- Flattery, followed by a night of debauchery, might get you a core clue, but if this offends your Investigator's moral (or aesthetic) sensibilities, a Credit Rating spend (to get into a showplace restaurant or dance hall) might get you the same information.»

Extra point spends might speed up an investigation

- a Bureaucracy spend supplemented by Flattery might get the photographs processed a day earlier, your car repaired more quickly,
- the mysterious delay in processing your visa application might disappear with a Credit Rating spend.

A point spend might get you some dedicated pool points (see p. 54)

- A Library Use spend might allow you to find a book which gives you a History (New England) dedicated point pool.

An Technical spend spend might allow you to create a notable work. An Academic spend, to write an influential paper or join an appropriate society

- An Art spend would allow you to create a sculpture or painting
- A Geology spend gets your paper on anamolous artifacts found in Archaean slate published in the Proceedings of the Royal Society of London.

An impressive point spend may even lead to refreshment of Stability points (see p. 79)

---

he needs to do to get the information he needs to proceed to the next scene, a confrontation with the Boston cult leader in his mansion, so the Keeper says "You see a telltale flash of intense violet from the cupola of the early Georgian townhouse at the end of Wellington Court."

Note that Zachary didn't even have to specify what ability he used. He could have used Boothroyd's Architecture, Chemistry, Occult, or even Credit Rating (strolling through rich neighborhoods as if you belong there) to uncover that clue.

For each scene, the Keeper designates a core clue. This is the clue you absolutely need to move to the next scene, and thus to complete the entire investigation. Keepers will avoid making core clues available only with the use of obscure investigative abilities, although the Investigator group as a whole will usually have access to all, or nearly all, of them. Even if the Investigator does not request a clue, the Keeper will let any person with a suitable ability know that the clue is available. As you get more familiar with the GUMSHOE system, you'll be able to seamlessly roleplay using your abilities, and the Keeper will be able to seamlessly slip you needed clues when you do.

Spends and Benefits

Certain clues allow you to gain special benefits by spending points from the relevant investigative ability pool. Each benefit costs either 1 or 2 points from the relevant pool, depending on the difficulty of the additional action and the scope of the reward. The act of spending points for benefits is called a **spend**. The Keeper's scenario notes may specify that you get Benefit X for a 1-point spend, or Benefit Y for a 2-point spend. When asking you if you want to spend, the Keeper always tells you how much it will cost. During your first few scenarios, your Keeper will offer you the opportunity to spend additional points as you uncover these clues. After that it's up to you to ask if it there's anything to be gained by spending extra time or effort on a given clue. You can even propose specific ways to improve your already good result; if your suggestion is persuasive or entertaining, the Keeper may award you a special benefit not mentioned in her scenario notes.

Any additional information gained from a spend provides flavor, but is never required to solve the case or move on to a new scene. Often a benefit makes your Investigator seem clever, powerful, or heroic. It may allow

an ability to take less time than normal, or succeed more flashily. It may grant you benefits useful later in the scenario, frequently by making a favorable impression on NPCs. Additional information can also provide information that is usefully applied to later contests involving General **abilities:** discovering that shoggoths love electricity, or that your car's petrol tank is empty, or your gun has been unloaded.

A benefit may allow you to leap forward into the story by gaining

a clue that would otherwise only become apparent in a later scene. On occasion the additional information adds an emotional dimension to the story or ties into the Investigator's Drive, past history, or civilian life. If you think of your *Trail of Cthulhu* game as a TV series, an extra benefit gives the actor playing your Investigator a juicy spotlight scene.

"Is there another way into that house?" asks Zachary. The Keeper knows that there are old smuggler's tunnels into most of the basements in this neighborhood. This information isn't necessary to move forward – going in the front door will get to the confrontation just as fast – but initiative should always be rewarded where possible.

"Would you rather spend 1 Architecture point or 2 Credit Rating points?" asks the Keeper. If Zachary picks Architecture, Boothroyd will "just happen to remember" seeing smuggler's tunnels in a similar Georgian house in the neighborhood. But Zachary picks the bigger spend for the bigger benefit, reducing his Credit Rating pool from its maximum of 6 down to 4, and the Keeper says "As it happens, you attended a soiree at young Brickman's the other month, and he showed you the old smuggler's tunnel in his wine cellar and said he'd gone exploring

Dedicated Pool Points

Occasionally, the Keeper may give you extra pool points you can only use in a given circumstance or on a given subject. These are called **dedicated pool points,** and usually come from reading books of lore, sudden communion with alien perceptions, mental illness, or other specialized stimuli. In most cases, dedicated pool points stack on top of your rating. For example, if you have an Archaeology rating of 2, and you read a tome granting you 2 dedicated pool points for Valusian ruins, you have 4 points you can spend on Archaeology, but 2 of them can only be spent investigating the relics and artifacts of that ancient serpent-folk kingdom.

In a way this is what the rules already do when, for example, they separate Cop Talk from Reassurance, but slicing abilities too thinly makes it hard to build competent Investigators.

one time — 'visited the cellar of every house built before 1750' in his words. He lives a block away, and you're sure he'd be happy to stand you a glass and

Who Finds It?

Sometimes you know that a clue will definitely be found during a given scene, but must decide which Investigator does so. Most often, the clue, though easily found on a cursory examination of a scene, will be somewhat inconspicuous. The bloody footprint might be under a piece of furniture. The table with the envelope taped to it might be on the other side of the diner. Because it is mildly inconspicuous, it doesn't make sense that everybody will spot it at the exact same second.

If one or more players have a relevant ability, choose the player with the highest current pool in that ability. If no one has a relevant ability, or no ability seems to apply to the situation, ask yourself which player seems most in need of a win. Pick either the Investigator who has received the least time in the spotlight, or suffered the worst setbacks, during the current session.

This technique of doling out positive moments according to dramatic need can also be applied to other benefits, from lucky breaks to romantic opportunities, to which no ability clearly applies.

let you into his tunnel."

This gives Boothroyd a possible ally or contact, a possible secure retreat or unexpected entry, and a distinctive character moment all at once - well worth the 2 points.

Boothroyd leans on Brickman's bell with his stick. "Thought I might see if your Medoc has improved any," he says. "And speaking of your cellar…"

A good Keeper will always try to come up with something cool to reward you for spending points, whether or not the benefits are specified in her scenario, because it makes the game more colorful and fun for everyone. Spending points on benefits encourages the Keeper to wire your Investigator ever more deeply into the story and into her world, putting subtle psychological pressure on her to keep your Investigator alive. There's even an optional Pulp-idiom rule on p. 79 that lets you regain some Stability by coming up with a confidence-boosting and dramatic spend. Thus, it is to your advantage to propose cool benefits to the Keeper.

If you wish to make a spend in a situation where the Keeper has no special benefit to offer you, and cannot think of one that pertains at all to the investigation, you do not lose the points you wish to spend.

Inconspicuous Clues

"EXAMINING ONE DAY THE RESERVE SPECIMENS ROUGHLY SET ON THE STORAGE SHELVES IN A REAR ROOM OF THE MUSEUM, MY EYE WAS CAUGHT BY AN ODD PICTURE IN ONE OF THE OLD PAPERS SPREAD BENEATH THE STONES."

— "THE CALL OF CTHULHU"

Sometimes the Investigators instinctively notice something without actively looking for it. Often this situation occurs in places they're moving through casually and don't regard as scenes in need of intensive searching. The team might pass by a concealed door, spot a droplet of blood on the marble of an immaculate hotel lobby, or approach a truck with dynamite planted beneath it. Interpersonal abilities can also be used to find inconspicuous clues. The classic example is of a character whose demeanor or behavioral tics establish them as suspicious.

It's unreasonable to expect players to ask to use their various abilities in what appears to be an innocuous transitional scene. Otherwise they'd have to spend minutes of game time with every change of scene, running down their abilities in obsessive checklist fashion. That way madness lies.

Instead the Keeper asks which character has the highest current pool in the ability in question. (When in doubt for what ability to use for a basic search, the Keeper defaults to Evidence Collection.)

If two or more pools are equal, it goes to the one with the highest rating. If ratings are also equal, their characters find the clue at the same time.

Boothroyd and a lady artist of his acquaintance, Letitia Vandiver, are on their way to pick up the rest of the Investigator team for their midnight visit to the smuggler's tunnels when they pass an art gallery used by the cult to recruit wealthy members.

The Keeper decides that Art History will reveal that the paintings in the windows are fresh works by artists long thought dead. Both characters have the skill; Boothroyd has 2 points in his pool, while Letitia has 3.

"Letitia," says the Keeper, "you're something of a devotee of Vernet, and you'd swear that was a brand-new Vernet in that gallery window – if he hadn't been dead for 100 years, that is."

TESTS

A test occurs when the outcome of an ability use is in doubt. Tests apply to General skills only. Unlike information gathering attempts, tests carry a fairly high chance of failure. They may portend dire consequences if you lose, provide advantages if you win, or both.

Even in the case of General skills, the Keeper should call for tests only at dramatically important points in the story, and for tasks of exceptional difficulty. Most General ability uses should allow automatic successes, with possible bonuses on point spends, just like Investigative abilities.

There are two types of tests: simple tests and contests.

Simple Tests

A simple test occurs when the Investigator attempts a difficult action without active resistance from another person or entity. Examples include driving a treacherous road, jumping a

Difficulty Numbers and Story Pacing

Just as the *Trail of Cthulhu* system keeps the story moving by making all crucial clues accessible to the Investigators, Keepers must ensure that tests and contests essential to forward narrative momentum can be easily overcome. Assign relatively low Difficulty Numbers of 4 or less to these crucial plot points. Reserve especially hard Difficulty Numbers for obstacles that provide interesting but nonessential benefits.

For example, if the characters have to sneak past the Nazi guards into the Hamburg warehouse in order to stage the final confrontation, assign the relatively low Difficulty Number of 4 to the task. If it seems like they "realistically" ought to have a tougher time of it, insert a detail justifying their ease of success. The storm-trooper assigned to watch one section of the dock might be found with his throat torn out by the Deep Ones the SS necromancers have – imperfectly – summoned, for example.

One way to avoid this situation is to prevent the continuation of the game be dependent on a single General contest (other than those associated with bodily or mental harm) and offer other, less pleasant, options, for example, if they fail to climb the fence, they can crawl through the sewers.

Option - You Always Succeed

We've never had this issue reported as a problem, other than in theory. The following rule is more in keeping with the basic GUMSHOE premise, but might not suit everyone. Where it is essential to overcome a General obstacle, allow success whatever the result, but give a negative consequence other than failure for the roll. For example, the PC climbs the fence, but receives an injury.

crevasse, sneaking into a building, shooting a target, booby-trapping a doorway, or remaining steady in the face of squamous horror.

The Keeper determines how hard any given action is by assigning it a Difficulty Number ranging from 2 to 8, where 2 offers only a slim chance of failure and 8 verges on the impossible. The player rolls a single die; if the result is equal to or higher than the Difficulty Number, the character succeeds. Before rolling the die, the player may choose to spend any number of points from the relevant ability pool, adding these to the final die result. Players who forget to specify the number of points they want to spend before rolling are stuck with the unmodified result.

In the game world, expenditure of pool points in this way represents special effort and concentration by the Investigator, the kind you can muster only so many times during the course of an adventure.

> *Martin wants to climb a high cemetery wall to see if ghouls lurk on the other side. The Keeper needs the group to get to the other side of the wall and therefore assigns the relatively low Difficulty Number of 3 to the task. Martin's player, Josh, has a full 8 points in his Athletics pool. He decides that he really needs a win on this one and decides to spend half of them on the attempt. He rolls a 5. With the 4 points from his pool, this gets a final result of 9. Displaying impressive aerobatic grace, Martin vaults onto the wall.*

The Purist *Trail of Cthulhu* setting is meant to be harsh and deadly in body and spirit. Losing points is meant to hurt, and Investigators are frequently distracted, their senses unreliable. To truly evoke that feel, the Keeper never reveals Difficulty Numbers.

In the Pulp mode, *Trail of Cthulhu* Investigators are hardened adventurers, instinctively aware of their limitations and of the kinds of obstacles they face. Keepers in this mode may choose to reveal Difficulties, especially for conventional obstacles like walls, Tong members, and guard dogs. Difficulty numbers for Sense Trouble (see p. 47) are never revealed.

The test represents the Investigator's best chance to succeed. Once you fail, you've shot your bolt and cannot retry unless you take some other supporting action that would credibly increase your odds of success. If allowed to do this, you must spend more pool points than you did on the previous attempt. If you can't afford it, you can't retry.

> *Martin has just failed his Mechanical Repair test to repair a broken pump in the sinking ship he and the other investigators are trapped in. Josh spent 2 points from Martin's Mechanical Repair pool on this attempt. The Keeper decides he'll have one more shot at it before the ship capsizes. Now he must spend at least 3 Mechanical Repair points. Fortunately he has 4 points left in his pool. The Difficulty Number of the*

> *repair attempt is 5. Josh rolls a 6, adding 3 points to get a final result of 9. The pump kicks back in, just in time to reverse the ship's sinking.*

Piggybacking

When a group of Investigators act in concert to perform a task together, they designate one to take the lead. That character makes a simple test, spending any number of his own pool points toward the task, as usual. All other characters pay 1 point from their relevant pools in order to gain the benefits of the leader's action. These points are not added to the leader's die result. For every character who is unable to pay this piggybacking cost, either because he lacks pool points or does not have the ability at all, the Difficulty Number of the attempt increases by 2.

> *Boothroyd, Martin, Letitia, and Professor Swinburne attempt to sneak into the office of the cult gallery that Boothroyd and Letitia spotted earlier, in order to find out more about the 'Vernets' Letitia saw. Martin, with a Stealth of 8, takes the lead. Boothroyd, Letitia, and the Professor have 4, 0, and 2 points in their Stealth pools, respectively. Boothroyd and the Professor pay 1 point apiece; their pools go down to 3 and 1. Because Letitia has no points to spend, the Difficulty Number of the sneak increases from 4 to 6. (If the group left her behind, it would be easier to sneak in, but she's the artist.) Martin spends 3 points on*

the attempt, but his player rolls a 1. This would have overcome the Difficulty if it weren't for Letitia's presence. Clearly, Letitia has knocked over a vase, making an ear-splitting crash and leaving an unmistakable trace of the Investigators' entry.

In most instances a group cannot logically act in concert. Only one character can drive a car at one time. Two characters with Preparedness check their individual kits in sequence, rather than checking a single kit at the same time.

Cooperation

When two Investigators cooperate toward a single goal, they agree which of them is undertaking the task directly, and which is assisting. The leader may spend any number of points from her pool, adding them to the die roll. The assistant may pay any number of points from his pool.

All but one of these is applied to the die roll.

Martin and Letitia are trying to repair a rusted-out roadster so they can escape from the South Side junkyard before the Outfit shows up to kill them. Martin has 4 points left in his Mechanical Repair pool. Letitia has 3 points. They decide that Martin is the main mechanic, and Letitia his assistant. Both choose to spend all of their remaining points on the attempt. Martin adds 3 points to the die roll. Letitia also spends 3 points, but adds only 2 to the die roll. Martin's player rolls a 2, for a result of 7. This beats the Difficulty Number of 6, allowing the two of them to roar down the alley to safety as Thompson rounds spang and spatter off the piles of junked cars behind them.

CONTESTS, CHASES AND COMBAT

"IT IS UNCOMMON TO FIRE ALL SIX SHOTS OF A REVOLVER WITH GREAT SUDDENNESS WHEN ONE WOULD PROBABLY BE SUFFICIENT, BUT MANY THINGS IN THE LIFE OF HERBERT WEST WERE UNCOMMON."

— "HERBERT WEST – REANIMATOR"

Contests occur when two characters, often an Investigator and a non-player character controlled by the Keeper, actively attempt to thwart one another. Although contests can resolve various physical match-ups, in a horror game the most common contest is the chase, in which the Investigators run away from slavering entities intent on ripping them limb from limb.

In a contest, each participant acts in turn. The first to fail a roll of the contested ability loses. The Keeper decides who acts first. In a chase, the character who bolts from the scene acts first. Where the contestants seem to be acting at the same time, the one with the lowest rating in the relevant ability acts first. In the event of a tie, NPCs act before Investigators. In the event of a tie between Investigators, the player who arrived last for the current session goes first in the contest.

The first contestant to act makes a test of the ability in question. If he fails, he loses the contest. If he succeeds, the second then makes a test. This continues until one contestant loses, at which point the other one wins.

Typically each contestant attempts to beat a Difficulty Number of 4.

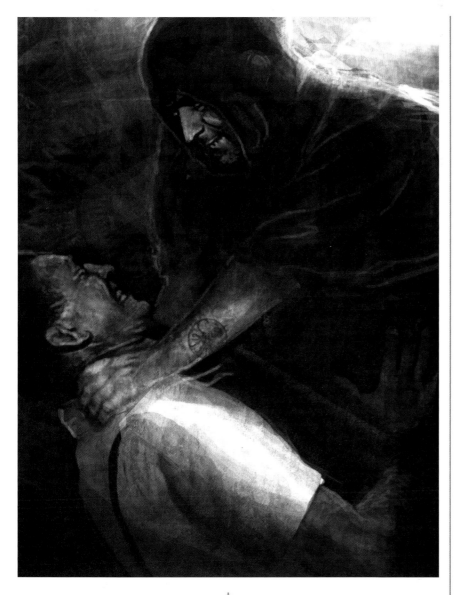

Martin flees through the darkened streets of Arkham from a dagger-wielding cultist. His current Athletics pool is 6; the cultist's is 7. (Being an all-around tough guy, Martin put points into Athletics instead of Fleeing.) As the fleeing character initiating the chase sequence, he's the first character to act. His player rolls against a Difficulty of 4, spending 1 point. He rolls a 4, and Martin manages to scramble down Fish Alley by the docks.

The cultist spends 1 point as well, the Keeper rolling a 3. He leaps through the rotting wooden railings and comes up waving his dagger and foaming at the mouth.

Martin spends another point, taking his Athletics to 4. His player rolls a 2, which adds to 3, not enough to get away.

Investigative Contests

It is possible to conceive of situations that can best be modeled by contests of Investigative **abilities:** contests of Bargain to buy an enchanted dagger in the bazaar three minutes before the eclipse reaches totality, of Credit Rating at a rare book auction, of Assess Honesty at a chess match or poker game, and so forth. More outré examples might include contests of Architecture to escape a sentient haunted house, or Outdoorsman if trying to solve a Hedge Maze of Shub-Niggurath.

This is such a tempting idea that it threatens to vitiate the entire point of Investigative abilities, which is that they always work. Thus, such a contest should only happen if it is as central and dramatic a conflict as a fight scene would be.

If it's just a color scene, or a means of dropping a clue, don't bother with a contest: just let the Investigator use his ability, win, and look good. If you must have a contest as the centerpiece of a scene, the opponent should have a pool no more than 1 point higher (for dangerous or clearly superior opponents) than the Investigator. In any event, defeat in the contest should not prevent the plot moving forwards, but have another negative consequence., for example, an important NPC is unimpressed, your enemies are warned or you have to take a more dangerous route to the next scene.

Don't Mention The Lizards

It may come to pass that an NPC wants to get information out of an Investigator. This isn't really part of the investigative RPG genre (or of Lovecraft's fiction), but it is a common occurrence in 1930s popular literature, including pulp and detective stories.

Outside a formal context, Investigators should be allowed to use Assess Honesty or otherwise detect someone casually pumping them, studying their body language, etc. If they notice, let the players decide whether (and what) to spill. Spends can suggest fruitful lies or half-truths, or help determine what will make the problem go away.

If the attempt is obvious or official, work it as an Interpersonal or other ability use for the Investigator: At an academic conference, the Investigators can use Reassurance or Archaeology to evade questions about mysterious ruins; at the police station, use Cop Talk to brush off any questions or Law to get released without interrogation.

If a lengthy confrontation is unavoidable — say, if the Investigators are being questioned in a Gestapo basement — then it's not a contest any more, it's a plot device. Do what you must to get the story going rather than reveling in the Investigators' helplessness – perhaps the other Investigators can break in and rescue the prisoner before he spills all they know about the Serpent-Folk.

Martin has backed himself onto a pier, caught with the oily Miskatonic River at his back. The cultist advances on him. Now Martin has no choice but to stand and fight.

Where the odds of success are skewed in favor of one contestant, the Keeper may assign different Difficulties to each. A contestant with a significant advantage gets a lower Difficulty Number. One facing a major handicap faces a higher Difficulty Number. When in doubt, the Keeper assigns the lower number to the advantaged participant.

Running through a rain-filled sewer, Martin finds it harder to move quickly than does the aquatic Deep One pursuing him. In this case he might

face a Difficulty Number of 4, while the hellish frog-thing gets the lower Difficulty of 3.

Throughout the contest, Keeper and players should collaborate to add flavor to each result, explaining what each side did to remain in the contest. That way, instead of dropping out of the narration to engage in an arithmetical recitation, you keep the fictional world verbally alive.

FIGHTING

Fights are slightly more complicated contests involving any of the following abilities:

• *Scuffling vs Scuffling, Scuffling vs Weapons, or Weapons vs Weapons: the characters are fighting in close quarters.*

Fighting Without Abilities

A character with no points in Firearms is not allergic to guns. The most neurasthenic and molly-coddled aesthete is able to pick up a revolver and empty it in the general direction of the foe. Likewise, a character with no Weapons ability is not going to just ignore the fire axe sitting on the wall when the ghouls come up through the floorboards. Even a mere slip of a respectable girl with no Scuffling score will try to kick or even bite her vulgar assailants.

However, such characters will use their weapons ineffectively and hesitantly. Using a weapon (including fists or feet) without ability has the following drawbacks:

- You automatically do an additional -2 damage. (Keepers may suspend this penalty for maniacs, who always seem to do exceptional damage with improvised weaponry.)
- You must declare your action at the beginning of each round and cannot change it if the tactical situation alters.
- You automatically go last in each round.
- If you are using a firearm, a roll of 1 means you have accidentally shot yourself or one of your allies, as selected (or rolled randomly) by the Keeper. Do damage as normal (including your automatic -2 penalty).

- *Firearms vs Firearms: the characters are apart from one another and trying to hit each other with guns.*

The aggressor is the first combatant to move against the other. When the status of aggressor and defender are unclear, the combatants compare their current pool numbers in the abilities they're using in the fight. The character with the highest number chooses whether to act as aggressor or defender. (Unlike an ordinary contest, in a fight it is often advantageous to strike first.)

A contest proceeds between the two abilities. When combatants using the Scuffling, Weapons, or Firearms abilities roll well, they get the opportunity to deal damage to their opponents.

Hit Thresholds: Each Investigator has a Hit Threshold of either 3 (the standard value) or 4 (if the Investigator's Athletics rating is 8 or more.) The Hit Threshold is the Difficulty Number the Investigator's opponent must match or beat in order to harm him. Less competent NPCs may have lower Hit Thresholds, but cult guards, Gestapo agents, and similar opponents will generally parallel Investigator levels.

Creatures may have Hit Thresholds of 4 or higher, regardless of their Athletics ratings. Extremely large creatures will usually have a Hit Threshold 1 lower than roughly man-sized beings of the same sort.

In the Pulp mode, faceless mook opponents such as Nazi soldiers or Haitian cultists will have Hit Thresholds of 2 or 3.

Mythos creatures – even in hordes – will have their normal values.

Dealing Damage: When you roll equal to or over your opponent's Hit Threshold, you may deal damage to him. To do so, you make a damage roll, rolling a die which is then modified according to the relative lethality of your weapon, as per the following table:

Weapon Type	Damage Modifier
Fist, kick	-2
Small improvised weapon, blackjack, bullwhip, nightstick, knife	-1
Big improvised weapon, machete, heavy club, fireplace poker, light firearm	0
Sword, heavy firearm	+1

Supernatural creatures often exhibit alarmingly high damage modifiers.

For firearms, add an additional +2 when fired at point-blank range. All shotguns are considered heavy firearms at point-blank range. At point-blank or close range, add an additional +1 to damage if you fire both barrels of a double-barreled shotgun simultaneously. Thus, a 20-gauge double-barreled shotgun (normally a light firearm doing +0 damage), fired with both barrels at point-blank range, carries a total modifier of +4, as would a 12-gauge double-barreled shotgun (already a heavy firearm doing +1 damage).

A more detailed firearms table appears on p. 186.

Blackjacks

Blackjacks, brass knuckles, coshes, saps, rolls of quarters or shillings tucked up in the fist, and similar sorts of life-preserving gear do -1 damage, rather than -2 as per a normal fist attack. Using them is a test of Scuffling, not Weapons. In a Scuffling vs Scuffling contest, the blackjack user goes last.

The final damage result is then subtracted from your opponent's Health pool. Unlike other contests, participants do not lose when they fail their test rolls. Instead, they're forced out of the fight when they lose consciousness or become seriously wounded (see p. 63). Any combatants currently engaged with him in a close-quarters fight can then deal another instance of damage to him.

Free-For-All Combat

Combat becomes more chaotic when two groups of combatants fight, or a group gangs up against a single opponent. The Keeper abandons the aggressor/defender model. Instead, the Keeper determines an order of action, ranking all participants in the combat according to their present pool values in the fighting skills they'll be starting the fight with: Scuffling, Weapons, or Firearms. Ties are broken in favor of characters with higher ratings in those skills. If combatants are still tied, Investigators win out over creatures and enemies, and early-arriving players win over late-arriving players.

The time it takes to go through the ranking order once, with each

Horribly, Realistically, Lethal Firearms

You would be amazed, or perhaps you wouldn't, at the number of playtesters who complained that a single gunshot would not reliably kill their character. Firearms are chancy things, even in expert hands – there is a fully attested report of a gunfight involving three guns and thirty shots fired, that occurred *entirely inside a police car*, in which nobody was seriously injured. Every cop in the world has a story about the guy who "just wouldn't stay shot." There is even an argument that until a character gets below 0 Health points, Health points have the same abstract function as other pools. But that said, we plead guilty to making gunfights sort of survivable in the name of continuing drama.

After all, a .38 pistol will do only 4 points per shot on average, meaning it will take two shots to knock a Health 6 target down to Hurt. Now, if that's two point-blank shots (6 points apiece), those two bullets will very likely knock that Health 6 storm trooper down to Seriously Wounded and force a Consciousness roll. It would take two maxed-out (rolling a 6 on each die) point-blank shots, 18 points total, to kill him.

So, if you want a more realistic damage result from firearms, with a possible one-shot kill, the simplest way to do it is to treat all Hurt results to humans from firearms as Seriously Wounded results. Where bruising or even hacking damage might be "shaken off," any gunshot that drops your Health pool to 0 or below does an additional +6 points of damage. A single point-blank shot from a heavy firearm can now potentially kill your Investigator instantly, assuming her Health pool is 3 or less. Even if her Health pool is 9 or less, it could potentially force her to lose consciousness, which is probably just as bad, or even worse in some circumstances.

Monsters, especially Mythos monsters, don't suffer any such extra damage from gunshots unless the Keeper explicitly rules that they do.

Making NPCs drop dead on a bullet wound is easy – just give them 0 or less Health points. This isn't necessarily a measure of their actual fortitude, it's more likely to have narrative significance. For example, an NPC the PCs are talking to might be shot dead by a single bullet before revealing important information.

---

combatant taking an action, is called **a round**. When one round ends, another begins. (For speed of play, however, ranking order stays where it was at the beginning of the combat even if pool values have changed.) When called upon to act, each combatant may strike at any opponent within range of his weapons. Some supernatural creatures may strike more than once per round. They make each attack in succession, and may divide them up between opponents within range, or concentrate all of them on a single enemy.

Once the fight has begun, if a combatant wishes to do something else besides fight – run away, jump up on the sideboard for a tactical advantage, throw a grenade – they move immediately to the last position in the ranking order as they turn to expose their vulnerable back to the foe, shake off the adrenaline, fumble for the pin, or whatever.

Creatures may choose to use their actions to deal additional damage to downed or helpless opponents rather than engage active opponents. They automatically deal once instance of damage per action. Only the most crazed and bestial human enemies engage in this behavior.

Combatants who join an affray in progress come last in order of precedence. If more than two combatants join during the same round, the Keeper determines their relative precedence using the rules above.

The fight continues until one side capitulates or flees, or all of its members are unconscious or otherwise unable to continue.

Armor

Armor may reduce the damage from certain weapon types. If you're wearing a form of armor effective against the weapon being used against you, you subtract a number of points from each instance of damage dealt to you before applying it to your Health pool.

In the 1930s, there is essentially no personal body armor available besides Great War surplus helmets. A "tin hat" reduces damage from bullets and cutting or slashing weapons by 2 points, and from clubs or blunt trauma by 1 point. It is only effective against head shots, of course.

At the Keeper's discretion, tough leather jackets, thick raccoon coats, or other heavy outer garments might reduce damage from small knives, improvised weapons, fists, or clubs by 1 point.

Physical Injury and Death

Unlike most abilities, your Health pool can drop below 0.

When it does this, you must make a Consciousness Roll. Roll a die with the absolute value of your current Health pool as your Difficulty. You may deliberately strain yourself to remain conscious, voluntarily reducing your Health pool by an amount of your choice. (You may not voluntarily reduce your Health pool below -11.) For each point you reduce it, add 1 to your die result. The Difficulty of the Consciousness roll is based on your Health pool before you make this reduction.

Father Micah is being chased by Y'golonac cultists through what he initially thought was a convent. A cultist hits him with an antique spiked morning-star, dropping his Health pool to -2. He really wants to get away from them, lest they force him to celebrate their vile fleshly rituals. Thus he must remain conscious. The absolute value of -2 is 2, so this is the Difficulty of his Consciousness roll. He chooses to expend another 2 Health points he doesn't have, pushing himself onward toward the ornately - and obscenely — carven doors. That gives him a bonus of 2 to his roll. He rolls a 6, for a final result of 8. Father Micah gets away, but now his Health pool is down to -4.

If your pool is anywhere from 0 to −5, you are hurt, but have suffered no permanent injury beyond a few superficial cuts and bruises. However, the pain of your injuries makes it impossible to spend points on Investigative abilities, and increases the Difficulty Numbers of all tests and contests, including opponents' Hit Thresholds, by 1.

First Aid: A character with the First Aid ability can improve your condition by spending First Aid points. For every First Aid point spent, you regain 2 Health points — unless you are healing yourself, in which case you gain only 1 Health point for every First Aid point spent.

A character giving First Aid must be in a position to devote all of his attention to directly tending to your wounds.

First Aid can only refill your pool to where you were before the scene in which you received this latest injury. For example, if you get shot and then someone punches you during the same fight, you can repair both. If you get shot, run away, get into another fight, and then somebody punches you, you can heal the punch.

First Aid can only ever bring you back to one third of your maximum Health points. All other increases must be gained using the Refreshing Health rules (see p. 81). This option makes hurt Investigators very fragile.

If your pool is between −6 and −11, you have been seriously wounded. You must make a Consciousness roll. Whether or not you maintain consciousness, you are no longer able to fight. Until you receive first aid, you will lose an additional Health point every half hour.

First Aid and serious wounds: A character with the First Aid ability can stabilize your condition by spending 2 First Aid points. However, he can't restore your Health points.

Even after you receive first aid, you must convalesce in a hospital or similar setting for a period of days. Your period of forced inactivity is a number of days equal to the positive value of your lowest Health pool score. (So if you were reduced to -8 Health, you are hospitalized for 8 days.) On the day of your discharge, your Health pool increases to half its maximum value. On the next day, it refreshes fully.

When your pool dips to −12 or below, you are dead. Time to activate your replacement Investigator.

Health Loss For NPCs

In a Purist game, the Investigators are no different from anyone else. All humans lose Health mechanically in the same way.

In the Pulp mode, the Investigators are a cut above the rest of the herd. Normal people, both mooks and bystanders, simply (or dramatically, or messily) die when their Health is reduced below 0. Using this rule does make combats much faster, so even Purist Keepers may want to sneak it into battles against cultists, etc. The Keeper may, if she thinks it dramatically appropriate, decide that certain NPCs use the Investigators' Health loss rules.

Martin is stabbed by a madwoman with a pair of scissors. The Keeper rolls a 3 for the maniac's damage, subtracting 1 point for a small, improvised weapon, for a total damage of 2. Martin's leather duster reduces it by 1 further point. His Health pool decreases from 6 to 5.

Creatures often have high armor ratings. They may possess hard, bony hides or monstrous anatomies that can take greater punishment than ordinary organisms. Many creatures of the Mythos are not fully present in our physical universe, and are thus unaffected by physical weapons.

Non-Lethal Damage

Players may always announce that their Investigators are using their Scuffling attacks to do non-lethal damage: choke-holds, arm-locks, body blows, and the like. Such attacks never lower a target's Health pool below -11, but merely force yet another Consciousness roll if successful. A tolerant Keeper will allow similar declarations for non-bladed Weapons attacks.

Bringing a knife, or worse, a gun into a fight is a declaration of willingness to kill. There is no such thing as a non-lethal Firearms attack. Players who don't want their Investigators to kill people shouldn't let their Investigators use lethal weapons on human opponents.

Cover

In a typical gunfight, combatants seek cover, hiding behind walls, furniture or other barriers, exposing themselves only for the few seconds it takes them to pop up and fire a round at their targets. The *Trail of Cthulhu* rules recognize three cover conditions:

Exposed: No barrier stands between you and the combatant firing at you. Your Hit Threshold decreases by 1.

Partial Cover: This is the normal condition in a gunfight. About half of your body is exposed to fire. Your Hit Threshold remains unchanged. This is also the condition if you have full cover, but only behind thin or flimsy materials like leaves, drywall, or

Bullet-Resistant Clothing

All right, you got us. Mobsters in the Chicago and New York of the 1930s did, in fact, wear heavy "bullet-proof vests" made of thick layers of cotton padding and canvas or denim. Some even tried a layer of rivets or metal discs, with mixed results. Such vests could stop the penetration of a .32, or even (from a distance) a .38 slug, leading some American law enforcement agencies and personnel to adopt the .357 Magnum round, beginning in 1934. They are not particularly well-known outside criminal and law-enforcement circles, and characters without Streetwise should not have access to them, nor should any non-American character.

All that said, it's not entirely ridiculous for such things to show up, especially in a Pulp-idiom game set in gangland Chicago or New York. A "gangster vest" will reduce bullet or club damage by 2 points, although wearing it reduces your Athletics pool by 1. It is ineffective against stabbing or cutting attacks.

Needless to say, wandering the streets in gangster garb is a great way to get arrested on "suspicion of mopery" in a pre-Miranda society. Most Investigators are engaged in activities that do not easily withstand police scrutiny at the best of times.

If Keepers are really concerned that Investigators can't wade through gunfire, a simpler solution is just to rule that all gunshots that hit Investigators (especially shots fired by faceless mooks) do 1 point less damage.

A still better solution is to not write gun-toting opponents into the scenario in the first place, but that takes us back into Purist territory.

One Gun, Two Combatants

If you are at the mercy of an opponent with gun well in hand and ready to fire, he can empty his entire clip or chamber at you before you get to him, or get yourself out of range. This situation occurs for example, if he holds you at gunpoint or charge him from more than five feet away with no cover. The Difficulty is 1 (an automatic hit), 2 if your Athletics rating is 8 or more and you are moving. He rolls one instance of damage, which is then tripled. Yes, we said tripled. And, yes, the tripling occurs after weapon modifiers are taken into account. This is why few unarmed people attack a gun-wielding opponent when he has the drop on them.

If your opponent has a pistol but it is not well in hand and ready to fire, you may attempt to jump him and wrestle it from his grip. If he has a pistol well in hand but is unaware of your presence, you may also be able to jump him, at theKeeper's discretion. The characters engage in a Scuffling contest to see which of them gets control of the gun and fires it. The winner makes a damage roll against the loser, using the pistol's Damage Modifier, including the +2 for point blank range.

If you jump an opponent with an unready rifle, a Scuffling combat breaks out, with the opponent using the rifle as a heavy club.

the dry-rotted planks in some backwoods cannibal shack.

Full Cover: Except when you pop up to fire a round, the barrier completely protects you from incoming fire. Your Hit Threshold increases by 1.

Rate of Fire

Although in Purist games, Investigators will seldom see or use fully automatic weapons, this is the era of the Thompson submachine gun, the Schmeisser, and other excellent room-clearing devices. Firing such a weapon on full auto gives you 2 extra points in your Firearms pool, assuming you have one. (If the Keeper has been so lax as to allow you a Tommy-gun with the whole 50- or 100-round drum, instead of the more usual military 20- or 30-round box, you have 3 extra points in your Firearms pool.) After expending a full-auto burst and the extra Firearms pool points associated with it, machine-gunners must stop combat for one round to reload. (Or start using the gun as a club, we presume.) Reloading does not refresh those full auto Firearms pool points, which represent primarily the "shock and awe" of initially unleashing a hose of lead upon the foe. As the Great War demonstrated, foes can get used to anything.

On a roll of 1 with a submachine gun on full auto, even if you hit, your gun jams, and you must stop combat until you succeed at a

Mechanical Repair test (most likely under gunfire) at Difficulty 4. You cannot fire during the same round in which you attempt this test.

The *Trail of Cthulhu* rules do not otherwise distinguish between pump-action, bolt-action, semi-automatics, revolvers, and other firearm mechanisms.

A person firing a submachine gun on full auto can attempt to riddle more than one target with bullets in a single round. All targets must be at point-blank or close range (see below),and you need to make a Firearms roll for each one. For each target after the first, all your opponents' Hit Thresholds increase by l. For example, if you were targeting three opponents, their Hit Thresholds.would all increase by 2. You cannot target the same individual twice in a round.

Ammo Capacity

In the Purist mode, firearms are discouraged. The Keeper may either keep track of ammunition use to maintain tension ("three bullets left, and six ghouls") or rule that any Firearms roll (not test result) of l means the gun is empty ("the hammer clicks on an empty chamber") and must be reloaded. (A roll of l, therefore, is an automatic miss.) After all, reticent antiquarians rarely practice proper aim control or shooting discipline.

In the Pulp mode, Investigators need to reload only when dramatically appropriate, or after "giving it both barrels." (See the shotgun types on p. 6l for specifics.) Otherwise, they're assumed to be able to refill the cylinders of their revolvers or jam clips into their automatic weapons between shots.

When reloading is an issue, Keepers may request a Firearms test (Difficulty 3) to quickly reload. Characters who fail may not use their Firearms ability to attack during the current round.

Separated from his teammates, a wounded Martin crawls into a ruined lamasery to hole up. Unfortunately for him, the building is inhabited by a tribe of degraded Tcho-Tchos. The Keeper decides that limited resources will increase the sequence's sense of terror, and declares that Martin has only four shots left in his trusty Colt .45, and only one extra ammo clip in his pocket. She plans to have the Tcho-Tchos gang up on him, forcing him to roll Firearms to successfully reload as they rush him.

Range

A horror game should not be about tactical positioning or counting hexes on a map; it should be about adrenaline, cordite, and spattering blood. To encourage such healthy abstraction, the *Trail of Cthulhu* rules acknowledge only four ranges:

Point-Blank: You are literally face-to-face (or face-to-back-of-head) with your opponent, within easy arm's reach. All brawls and scuffles occur at this range. At this range, all firearms do an additional +2 points of damage, and all shotguns are considered heavy firearms, with a base damage modifier of +l.

Close: You are in the same room with your opponent, or within no more than l0 yards or so. A

swordfight or a karate match might happen at this range, but no farther. This is as far as you can throw an object directly at a target unless the object is specifically designed for throwing (a grenade, a javelin).

Near: You can see your opponent distinctly, perhaps across a warehouse or across the street, no more than 30 or 40 yards away. At this range, all shotguns are considered light firearms, and do no extra damage, even if both barrels are fired simultaneously. This is the farthest range at which you can hit a target with a pistol or shotgun, unless you are using

Explosive Device Table

Explosion	Point-Blank	Close	Near	Long
Molotov cocktail*	+1	0	X	X
Pipe bomb	+2	+1	-1	X
Stick of dynamite	+3	+2	-2	X
Bundle of dynamite	+7	+4	-1	X
Rifle- or hand-grenade	+3	+1	-2	X
Land mine	+8	+3	-1	X
Propane tank (or exploding car, in Pulp)*	+4	+2	0	-2
Firedamp, coal-dust, or mill-flour	+6	+4	+1	-1
Gas main*	+9	+5	0	X
Mortar shell, rocket attack*	+6	+3	0	X
Artillery strike, bomber attack*	+17	+8	+1	-2

the optional Pulp rule on p. 42. This is as far as you can throw any object, either in a general direction (like a stick of dynamite) or at a specific target (like a baseball).

Long: Your opponent is within 100 yards. Opponents farther away cannot be reliably targeted at all, and are out of the combat. This is the farthest range at which you can hit a target with a rifle, unless you are using the optional Pulp rule on p. 42.

Explosives and Explosions

The life of the intrepid Investigator would be brief indeed without the capacity to dynamite abandoned buildings, toss Mills bombs into sewers, and so forth.

Setting an explosive charge or booby-trap merely requires using Explosives; assuming the victim is on the spot when the charge is triggered, the explosion automatically goes off at point-blank range. If Investigators are the targets, they should be allowed a Sense Trouble test (Difficulty 4 or better, depending on the skill of the bomber) to dive (or pull their dimmer colleagues) away to close range.

Throwing a grenade is an Athletics test with the Difficulty set by range: 2 for point-blank targets, 3 for close targets, 5 for near targets. If you are attempting to hurl a grenade at a specific spot (such as the intake valve of a Nazi U-boat), the Difficulty number increases by 1 at point-blank or close targets, and by 2 for near range targets.

All Difficulties are +1 for throwing non-balanced explosives such as Molotov cocktails (technically "Franco's bottle-bombs" in this era) or sticks or bundles of dynamite.

Rifle-grenades (revived during the Great War) are military equipment, not available to civilian Investigators. Using a rifle-grenade is a Firearms test as normal. Firing mortars, artillery, and so forth is a Mechanical Repair test.

The chart above indicates the additional damage done by various sorts of explosions, again demarcated by range (X indicates no effect at that range) from ground zero.

Explosives or explosions marked with an asterisk (*) may also

Damage to Vehicles

An Investigator driving a vehicle through a firefight may spend 1 Driving point per round (or less often if the Keeper believes the vehicle is not a primary target of gunfire) to avoid serious damage to the tires, engine block, or fuel tank, although windows and rag tops are destined to be shot to pieces regardless. He may not use any other abilities while evading bullets. The Keeper may also reveal damage after the immediate crisis is ended: "Looks like one of those slugs back there clipped your fuel line. You've got about ten more minutes before you're running on empty."

Targeting the tires, fuel tank, or engine block of an opponent's moving vehicle increases the Hit Threshold by 2. Any damage whatsoever knocks out a tire. Fuel tanks have the equivalent of 2 points of armor against bullets; engine blocks have the equivalent of 4 points of armor against bullets.

Targeting passengers or drivers uses the standard cover rules from p. 64.

Only in the very pulpiest games does firing a bullet into a speeding car's fuel tank cause it to explode; it instead begins leaving a trail of combustible gasoline behind it.

start fires. If the Investigator who set or uses the device has an Explosives skill, he can decide if he used incendiaries, and if so, if the fire spreads and where. Natural or villainous explosions should start fires if the Keeper considers a fire to be dramatically interesting, which is to say virtually always.

OTHER DANGERS

In the spirit of *Trail of Cthulhu*, most of these environmental dangers are assessed primarily in narrative, rather than starkly biological, terms.

Acid: Once the acid is applied (usually with a monster's Scuffling roll, but an Investigator might hurl a carboy of the stuff in extremis), it does continuous damage each round until removed or counteracted with Chemistry or Medicine. (First Aid does not prepare you for acid casualties.) Roll a damage die for the first application and use that result for all future damage increments. Weak acids take a -2 modifier (merely smoldering away at clothing or vital possessions, if less than 1 point of damage results); strong acids take a 0 modifier; very strong acids (sulfuric acid, most monster venoms) take a +1 modifier. At the Keeper's discretion, an acid attack might merely blind an Investigator until healed, making combat (among other things) impossible.

Temperature Extremes: In intense heat or cold, it can be difficult to move or think. Treat Investigators suffering from extreme heat or cold (on the plains of Leng without parkas, for example) as **hurt.**

Drowning and Suffocation: If an Investigator has advance warning before being immersed in water or an unbreathable atmosphere, he can hold his breath. An Investigator holding his breath underwater may make an Athletics test each round to avoid inhaling water, in addition to anything else he may be doing (such as trying frantically to escape from a creature's grasp). The difficulty of this test begins at 3 and increases by 1 with every passing round. As soon as the Investigator fails the test, he has inhaled water and begins to drown.

Drowning Investigators automatically lose 1d6+1 points of Health per round, but these lost points can be restored if the victim is rescued and resuscitated before she dies.

Falling: A fall does damage equal to the Difficulty Factor of the wall, cliff, etc that you fell off of, adding +2 for falls onto spikes, concrete, or jagged rocks. Try to avoid writing adventures in which one missed Athletics roll spells instant death – for player Investigators, anyhow. NPCs can fall into bottomless crevasses or off the sides of mountains all you wish.

Fire: A hand-held torch is an improvised weapon, doing normal damage with a -1 damage modifier. Falling into a large bonfire does normal damage with a 0 damage modifier; running into a burning room does normal damage with a +1 damage modifier.

If an Investigator is actually set on fire, roll normal damage with a 0 damage modifier each round automatically until he puts it out somehow. (Use Athletics to drop and roll, or just jump into a convenient water-filled basement. Mind the Deep Ones!)

Investigators in a burning building run the risk of smoke asphyxiation, which uses the drowning and suffocation rules above.

Poison: The range of poisons is a vast and glorious universe of possibilities for the Keeper, and far too complex to enumerate here.

She should decide how long the poison takes to onset, its symptoms (usually involving penalties to Health or **hurt** effects, but paralysis, convulsions, and vomiting are also common), and whether or not it is lethal to its victim. Narratively speaking, like falls into bottomless pits, instantaneous death from the bite of a rare South African fly should be reserved for NPCs. Investigators should have a fighting chance to get somewhere that a Pharmacy or Medicine spend can save them, unless the narrative point of the poison is its implacable nature – the venom of Yig, for example.

Note that basic poison control *is* an aspect of First Aid: if the poison can be purged or (in Pulp games) sucked from the wound, First Aid (or Outdoorsman, for snake bites) can cure it.

STABILITY, SANITY, AND MADNESS

As noted in the abilities lists, Stability and Sanity refer to two different, but related, qualities. Stability is mental and emotional resistance to trauma of any kind, natural, human, or supernatural. Think of it as your mental and emotional Health pool. Your Stability pool is quite likely to dwindle rapidly over the course of a single adventure, but it is also likely to completely refresh between scenarios. It is perhaps best understood as a short-term measure of your current mental health.

Sanity is the ability to believe in, fear for, or care about any aspect of the world or humanity as we know it: religion, science, family, natural beauty, human dignity, even "normal" immorality. The horrible truth of the Mythos is that Sanity measures your ability to believe a comforting lie – but a lie necessary in order to live as a human being rather than a soulless tool or plaything of the Great Old Ones. Your Sanity will probably erode slowly over the course of many adventures. Unless you see a Great Old One, lose a Pillar of Sanity, or suffer a Big Reveal (see p. 76), you will probably lose only 1 or 2 points from your Sanity pool in any given adventure. You may lose none at all! But Sanity is slow to return; in Purist games, it never comes back at all. It is perhaps best understood as a long-term measure of how close you are to fully realizing the bleak and awful reality of the cosmos.

In short, your Stability pool measures how close you are to snapping today; your Sanity pool measures how close you are to seeing the Truth forever.

Losing Stability

Even non-supernatural effects often prove emotionally destabilizing. Every violent encounter puts you at risk for Shell Shock (see p. 77). Isolation or constant stress – and, of course, encountering supernatural monstrosities, or worse yet, perceiving the truths of the Cthulhu Mythos – can lead to a complete psychotic break and permanent mental illness.

When an incident challenges your grip on yourself, make a Stability test against a Difficulty Number of 4. As with any other test of a General ability, you are always permitted to spend Stability points to provide a bonus to your roll. However, it's never a good bet to spend more points than you stand to lose if you fail. You *can* "spend yourself negative," if you think you absolutely *have* to cast that spell, although you can *not* voluntarily reduce your Stability pool below -11.

If you fail, you lose a number of points from your Stability pool, in addition to any points spent on the test itself. The severity of the loss depends on the situation.

Mythos shocks are qualitatively different from normal traumas. They always add at least +1 to the Difficulty Number of the Stability test. Most Mythos entities also impose higher than normal Stability losses, even for supernatural creatures, as indicated in their description.

Keepers should feel free to assess Stability Losses for other

Why Two Abilities?

GUMSHOE gets by just fine with Stability as a catch-all, while *Call of Cthulhu* uses Sanity to measure both Mythos-ignorance and mental health. Why separate the two? Fundamentally, it seems necessary to do it in order to model as many of Lovecraft's characters and stories as possible. The Sanity rules in *Call of Cthulhu* superbly model a Lovecraft character like Francis Thurston in *The Call of Cthulhu*, who skirts the edge of madness merely after reading a few news clippings and diaries, or Professor Nathaniel Peaslee in *The Shadow Out of Time*, who goes mad after discovering that his nightmares are actually memories and seeing his own handwriting in the ancient Yithian city of Pnakotus. It likewise suitably models characters driven mad by the traumatic shock of encountering actual Mythos entities, such as Robert Blake in *The Haunter of the Dark* or the narrator of *Dagon*.

But Lovecraft's fiction also features folks like Dr Armitage in *The Dunwich Horror*, who has read the *Necronomicon* at least twice and has a terrifying level of Cthulhu Mythos knowledge, but who remains outwardly completely stable and respectable even in the face of a Spawn of Yog-Sothoth. He has a very high Stability, even if his Sanity – his ability to believe in the pious legends of faith and science – is perilously low.

A middle case is young Danforth from *At the Mountains of Madness*, who "comes unstrung" upon seeing an onrushing shoggoth and retains a morbid fear of subways henceforth. But he is able to pull himself together to fly the plane out of Antarctica, and his "final breakdown" only comes after he reads the entire *Necronomicon* and makes horrible sense of his last sight of Kadath.

The narrator of that novel, Dyer, also saw the shoggoth (though not the final glance), and is at least familiar with some of the Cthulhu Mythos, but remains stable enough to keep his academic post. However, Dyer apparently believes that even knowledge of the Elder Things' city is almost as dangerous as the shoggoths lurking therein.

Examples from Lovecraft's fiction can be endlessly multiplied, but we decided on this as the bottom line: Although Mythos knowledge can be dangerous to your mental health, it is only by applying it to the "piecing together of dissociated knowledge" – in game terms, by using your Cthulhu Mythos ability – that the truth begins to hurt. That said, being swarmed by an army of Deep Ones or seeing the rise of Great Cthulhu will mess you up big time, no matter how you interpret it to yourself.

incidents, using the examples provided as a benchmark. Some especially overwhelming creatures, especially Mythos monsters, may impose higher than normal Stability losses when seen from a distance, seen up close, or ripping your lungs out. In adventures, when a Stability test is called for, a Stability test with a potential loss of 4 points is described as "a 4-point Stability test."

Here's a Stability test in action:

Martin's current Stability is 8. While staking out a dismal warehouse on the outskirts of Tangier, he sees a jerky, grayish figure materialize out of the sand and then flow toward the mountains. Since this is a djinn created by human sorcery, and not a Mythos creature, Martin's player Josh will be trying to beat a Difficulty of 4. (If it had been a Sand-Dweller, for instance, Josh would be trying to beat a Difficulty of 5.) Confident that this mere glimpse of a creature constitutes only a minor brush with destabilizing weirdness, Josh elects to spend only 1 point to bolster his roll. Alas, he rolls a 1, for a result of 2, two lower than the Difficulty Number. Having failed, Martin suffers a Stability loss of 3. Having spent 1 point on his bonus and lost another 3 to the failure, Martin's new Stability pool value is 4.

The Keeper should cap total Stability loss for any given incident at the highest potential single Stability loss.

Martin and his friend Daniel are in the North End cemetery on a cloudy afternoon looking for genealogical data on a suspected immortal wizard. Suddenly, a small pack of rat-things bursts from an open grave and attacks them. (For dramatic purposes, the Keeper chooses to call for a single

Stability Loss Table

Incident	Stability Loss
You see a fresh corpse; you witness a killing	1
A human opponent attacks you with evident intent to do serious harm	2
You are in a car or other vehicle accident serious enough to pose a risk of injury	2
You experience a strong unnatural sensation such as intense déjà vu, "missing time", or hallucinations	2
You witness acts of torture	2
A human opponent attacks you with evident intent to kill	3
You kill someone in a fight	3
You see a particularly grisly murder or accident scene	3
You see a supernatural creature from a distance	3
You witness an obviously unnatural, but not necessarily threatening, omen or magical effect – a wall covered in horrible insects, a talking cat, or a bleeding window	3
You see hundreds of corpses; you witness a large battle	4
You see a supernatural creature up close	4
You spend a week in solitary confinement	4
You learn that a friend, loved one, or Source of Stability has been violently killed	4
You discover the corpse of a friend, loved one, or Source of Stability	5
You are attacked by a supernatural creature, or by a friend, loved one, or Source of Stability	5
You witness a clearly supernatural or impossible killing	5
You witness or experience an obviously unnatural, and threatenting, omen or magical effect – a cold hand clutches your heart, a swarm of bees pours out of your mouth	5
You kill someone in cold blood; you torture someone	5
You see a friend, loved one, or Source of Stability killed	6
You are tortured for an hour or longer	6
You discover that you have committed cannibalism	6
You are possessed by some outside force, but conscious while it operates your body unspeakably	7
You speak with someone you know well who you know to be dead	7
You are attacked by a single gigantic supernatural creature or by a horde of supernatural creatures	7
You see a friend, loved one, or Source of Stability killed in a particularly gruesome manner or in a way you are helpless to avert	8
You kill a friend, loved one, or Source of Stability	8

Stability roll for the attack, even though technically seeing the rat-things is its own shock.) Martin fails his Stability test and loses 5 points for being attacked by a supernatural creature. (If he had recognized one of the rat-things, he would have lost 6 points.) Martin blazes away with his trusty Colt .45, driving off the creatures, but not before they devour Daniel in front of his eyes, biting through his skull and slurping the insides like it was an eggshell. Martin's player, Josh, makes a second roll, with a potential Stability Loss of 8 (seeing a friend killed gruesomely), but since Martin has already lost 5 points, he will only lose 3 more if he fails this test, for a total of 8, the highest possible Stability loss from the horrific sequence of events

Experience and Stability

Difficulty Numbers for Stability tests also change depending on the Investigator's attitude toward the destabilizing event. Investigators who would logically be inured to a given event face a Difficulty of 3, while those especially susceptible face a 5. An Investigator who has had extensive training in treating injuries might, for example, face a lowered Difficulty when encountering gruesomely mutilated bodies. A soldier would get a better chance against violent attacks or the death of comrades. No character type gets a break when encountering supernatural creatures.

Roleplaying Instability

Although there is no mechanical effect to losing Stability until your pool goes below 0, many players enjoy roleplaying the shocks and edginess of a terrifying encounter. Herewith, then, a few guidelines.

1-2 point loss: You might twitch, or stutter. Your voice could rise a bit, or you could Very. Explicitly. Stay. In. Control.

3-4 point loss: You might have to stop a bit and hyperventilate. You're blinking a lot, and maybe sweating, too. If you talk, you might run away with your own words. Keep doing something comforting – rack the slide on your shotgun, hum the Miskatonic fight song, that kind of thing. That will see you through this.

5-6 point loss: This is serious. You may go into a little fugue state; déjà vu comes over you, or you get "frame drop" and miss a couple of seconds. Nothing fatal, no, you're still good. Nope. If you're talking, you might call out some encouragement to your mates! They're probably not doing near as well as you! If you've got a pre-existing condition, say a phobia or Shell Shock (see p. 77), you're hyper-aware of anything that might trigger it.

7-8 point loss: How are you not shaken yet? You've almost certainly gone into adrenaline shock; your peripheral vision is gone, and your hands and feet are cold. You may babble personal confessions ("I've always loved you, Tom") or just shout incoherent threats. If you can make Interpersonal abilities work at all, they work more through fear of what you might do next than anything else.

Truly staunch Investigators can become inured to the onslaught of some supernatural creatures such as zombies, and even some lesser Mythos menaces such as ghouls or Deep Ones. Once an Investigator has successfully passed a number of Stability tests triggered by a given kind of creature equal to the Difficulty Number it imposes, that Difficulty Number drops by –1. Even in the pulpiest game, no Mythos entity ever has a Difficulty Number lower than 2.

Two-Gun Corrigan has run across Deep Ones (who, as Mythos creatures, trigger Stability tests at a Difficulty of 5) before. After his fifth successful Stability test against Deep Ones, he has gotten their *measure somewhat. His next Stability test against these slimy batrachians will be at Difficulty 4. If he passes four more Stability tests against Deep Ones without fail, he will have a mere Difficulty 3 to remain calm as they sidle and hop toward him.*

Drives and Stability

If Lovecraft's characters were run by roleplayers, there would be no horror. No one would go down into the sub-basement, read incantations found in moldy tomes, piece together their dead uncle's notes, or study non-Euclidean mathematics at Miskatonic University.

Your Drive encourages you to

abandon the flinty rationality of a player controlling a game piece. They give your Investigators the same overpowering impulses that inspire Gothic horror characters – and real people – to make the dumb choices they do on a regular basis.

The Keeper will tell you when you find your Drive impelling you to irrationally heedless action. When in doubt, she'll explain exactly what you have to do to satisfy your impulse. You are never obligated to obey it. By exerting unusual force of will, you can control your behavior.

At a price.

Sometimes the Keeper will refer to your Drive in her scenario notes, as a means of moving the plot ahead and getting you into trouble. This is referred to as a **hard driver**. Whenever you resist a hard driver, you lose either 4 Stability points or one-third of your Stability pool, whichever is greater. On other occasions a situation tangential to the main storyline would logically trigger your self-destructive tendencies. This is called a **soft driver**. It costs you 2 Stability points to resist a soft risk factor. The Keeper is always allowed to invoke a hard driver, whether or not it is literally written down. In a heavily improvised scenario, the "notes" are all in her head in the first place.

In neither case do you get to roll Stability to avoid the loss. It is automatic.

But for every stick, there is a stunted, dubious carrot. When your Investigator obeys his Drive, he gains Stability, as he bolsters his own emotional or intellectual

justification for action. His actions are authentic, even if they are horribly misguided. When you obey a hard driver, you refresh 2 points in your Stability pool; you refresh 1 point after obeying a soft driver. Gains never increase your pool above your Stability rating.

The Keeper is encouraged to use the Investigator Matrix to keep an

eye on their Drives, and present suitable drivers for each PC.

Players may suggest ways their Investigator can obey their Drive for such rewards. The Keeper should only grant such rewards if the action immediately advances the story or, optionally, if it places the Investigator or his teammates in grave peril.

Coming Unstrung

"Sanity departed — and, ignoring everything except the animal impulse of flight, I merely struggled and plunged upward over the incline's debris as if no gulf had existed."

— "The Shadow Out of Time"

Like Health, your Stability pool can drop below 0.

If your Stability ranges from 0 to −5, you are shaken. You can still do your job, but seem distracted. You can't spend points from the pools of your Investigative abilities. Difficulty Numbers for all General abilities increase by 1.

If your Stability ranges from −6 to −11, your mind is blasted. At the Keeper's discretion, you develop a mental illness that stays with you even after your Stability pool is restored to normal. (See p. 77 below for more.) You also continue to suffer the ill effects of being shaken. The only actions you can take are panicked flight or frenzied attacks on any perceived dangers. You may also choose to do nothing colorfully: gibber incoherently, chant the names of subway stations, freeze into catatonia, etc. Furthermore, you permanently lose 1 point from your Stability *rating*. The only way to get it back is to purchase it again with build points.

When your Stability reaches −12 or less, you are incurably insane. You may commit one last crazy act, which must either be self-destructively heroic or self-destructively destructive. Or you may choose merely to check out forever in a puddle of drool. Assuming you survive your permanent journey to the shores of madness, your Investigator is moved to a nice, sunny hospital, where friends and family can come to visit, and the electro-shock makes everything you ever were seem burnt over and far away. Time to create a new Investigator.

Losing Sanity

Your Sanity is affected by directly experiencing the Cthulhu Mythos and by piecing together its truths from the evidence you uncover during your investigations. *You cannot make a test to avoid losing Sanity.*

You lose Sanity in one of two main ways:

• A Mythos shock drops your Stability pool to 0 or below.

• You use the Cthulhu Mythos ability.

Beholding one of the gods or titans of the Mythos, and a few other specific magical or Mythos stimuli, can also cost you Sanity, but this is rare. Such happenings are covered in the relevant entries in the *Cthulhu Mythos* chapter.

Mythos Shocks

Each time you are **shaken** by a Mythos encounter or attack (when your Stability drops to between 0 and −5), your Sanity *rating* drops by 1 point.

Each time you are **blasted** by a Mythos encounter or attack (when your Stability drops to between −6 and −11), your Sanity *rating* drops by 2 points. You can only suffer one such Sanity *rating* loss (the most severe) in a given investigation.

Cthulhu Mythos Ability Use

Using the Cthulhu Mythos ability (see p. 34) to "piece together fragments of dissociated knowledge" and gain insight into an adventure invites the loss of both Stability and (if the discovery is terrifying enough) Sanity. *You cannot make a test to avoid this loss.* The degree of loss does not depend on the number of Cthulhu Mythos pool points spent (if any), but on the nature of the revelation.

The Keeper should *not* enforce losses if the *player* deduces the horrible truth without actually using his Investigator's Cthulhu Mythos ability. This is merely heads-up thinking, and should be rewarded. Any player can, of course, request such a loss for his Investigator, but it's easier to just use Cthulhu Mythos to earn one and confirm his deduction.

Any Sanity loss from Cthulhu Mythos use cannot be denied away – such knowledge comes from within, and the Investigator knows it to be accurate.

Use the chart on page 76 as a guideline, but the Keeper should take care to handcraft really powerful revelations to the individual Investigator.

Damaging Pillars of Sanity

An Investigator who has lost 3 points of Sanity may decide that one of her Pillars of Sanity (see p. 46) has "crumbled from within," thus avoiding the shock of its destruction. The player should roleplay this loss of belief. If the Pillar of Sanity is intimately related to an ability (religious faith and Theology, or orthodox science and Geology, for instance), the Investigator might break into sobs, or ranting, or ranting sobs, when she uses that ability. Since this is a roleplaying consequence, if your game allows Pulp-style Sanity recovery (see p. 81), it can happen over and over.

Investigators who lose their last Pillar of Sanity, either by having it smashed, or seeing their Sanity *rating* drop to 2 or below, have only instinct to keep them afloat in a horrific world. They suffer a +1 to all Difficulties for Stability tests.

Lost Sanity and Drives

Investigators who suffer a revelation that proves their Drive to be meaningless can no longer gain Stability from following it. They can still lose Stability by *not* following their Drive, raging helplessly at the mechanical fate that enmeshes them within its toils. Again, this is a swell opportunity for roleplaying.

Avoiding Sanity Loss

It is possible to avoid the worst of a Sanity loss, either by denying you ever saw anything, or by fainting before you see the worst of it.

Denial

"There is reason to hope that my experience was wholly or partly an hallucination — for which, indeed, abundant causes existed... Mercifully there is no proof, for in my fright I lost the awesome object which would — if real and brought out of that noxious abyss — have formed irrefutable evidence."

— The Shadow Out of Time

At the Keeper's discretion, such a Sanity loss might be only temporary. If, at the end of the adventure, there is *absolutely no proof* of your horrible experience – samples, photographs, recordings, eerie artifacts – then your Sanity rating recovers by 1 point. This may lead to conflicts with more scholarly-minded Investigators who wish to save such things for future study. The Keeper will often provide a convenient lightning blast, all-consuming conflagration, or sudden subsidence of the building, but if not, feel free to destroy the evidence yourself in a mindless frenzy.

The Keeper may require your Investigator to take a mental illness (such as delusion, multiple personality disorder, or selective amnesia), or at least provide an excellent "cover memory" describing what you believe "actually" happened. If your Investigator acts on Mythos knowledge gained from the episode, the Keeper is within her rights to immediately penalize you 1 Sanity rating point as the traumatic memories force their way back to the surface.

You cannot recover Sanity without losing it first.

If It Weren't For Bad Luck, I'd Have No Luck At All

If a player decides to take Bad Luck (or Cursed) as a Drive, when the Keeper hoses his Investigator more than she does the others (the Deep Ones attack him first, he drops the lantern, reads the inscription, touches the exposed wiring, etc), she should give that Investigator a Stability reward just as if the player had followed his Investigator's Drive on purpose. (You can explain this in game terms by saying the Investigator is so used to the universe hating him that such things are actually kind of comforting, but it's really just a meta-game mechanical effect.) Since a player cannot resist Bad Luck, unlike other Drives, the issue of a Stability penalty doesn't arise.

If your Sanity was driven to 0 or lower by the shock, you can no longer deny the terrible beauty of the Mythos.

Fainting

"Presently she fainted, although she is still unable to recall the precise and immediate cause. Memory sometimes makes merciful deletions."

— The Case of Charles Dexter Ward

An Investigator may be so overcome by shock that he faints, his nervous system choosing oblivion as preferable to the ineffable radiance of the true state of things.

Anagnorisis, or, The Big Reveal

The key moment in any Lovecraft story – or in any drama whatsoever – is when the truth comes out and all hell breaks loose. Aristotle called it the *anagnorisis*; with a nod to Raymond Chandler, we call it the "big reveal."

In the Pulp idiom, the big reveal is nothing more than the solution to the mystery, or finally getting to see the monster in a good light (or through a rifle scope). But in the Purist idiom, it is the moment that the main character pieces together the nature of the Mythos and goes to pieces – when Wilmarth sees the face and hands on the desk, when Thurston realizes the Cthulhu cult is still active and goes to his fate, when Olmstead realizes he has the Deep One taint, when young Danforth looks back and discerns that Poe and Alhazred were not writing fiction or mysticism.

In a Purist *Trail of Cthulhu* game, the big reveal is one that makes plain the essential folly or pointlessness of your Drive, often by means of some newly discovered fact about yourself or your family. Investigators seeking academic credibility realize that publishing their studies will doom humanity; those seeking revenge realize that their dead loved ones were willing sacrifices; those seeking power for its own sake realize that it can only come by surrendering your free will to monsters.

Once the big reveal is uncovered, your Investigator no longer has any Drive whatsoever. He also suffers an immediate loss of 8 Stability points, or *triple* the normal loss from whatever shock caused the big reveal, *whichever is greater*. If the big reveal also entails a Sanity loss, that loss is doubled.

This is almost always the end of the Investigator's story – he can write it down as a cautionary narrative if he survives, and then be dragged howling off to an institution or end it all with one last gunshot. Or he can die horribly (and informatively), blasted by a convenient lightning bolt or torn to pieces by his ghoul ancestors. If his Sanity rating has dropped to 0, he might even disappear to join the Mythos, becoming a villain for future adventures.

If an Investigator somehow survives the big reveal with his sanity and selfhood remotely intact, he must retire immediately to keep bees or raise the perfect avocado. He can become a truculent, reluctant source of information for junior Investigators, but he will never again so much as spend a pool point to battle the Mythos.

Needless to say, this is an optional rule.

Cthulhu Mythos Stability and Sanity Loss Table

Revelation or Intuition	Stability Pool Loss	Sanity Pool Loss
Some aspect of the Mythos is behind this mystery; any specifics are either comfortably distant in space or time, or not immediately relevant to your larger concerns	2	0
This Mythos truth poses a clear and present danger to innocents; this truth goes deeper, reaches back farther, or has wider implications, than you previously believed	3	1
This Mythos truth poses a clear and present danger to you or your loved ones; this truth is global or epochal in scope	4	1
This Mythos truth shatters one of your Pillars of Sanity	6	2
This Mythos truth could destroy the world or is doing so right now, probably inevitably; this truth proves your Drive to be meaningless or doomed	8	3

If the player wishes, he may declare that his Investigator faints dead away rather than fully absorbing a given Mythos experience. Such an Investigator loses only 1 Sanity pool point, but may play no further part in the scene. Investigators cannot "faint away" lost Sanity from spells they cast (although they surely can avoid seeing what they summoned), nor avoid the costs of using the Cthulhu Mythos ability.

The Keeper is well within her rights to strip, kidnap, inject with strange experimental serum, collapse a building upon, or in any other way maltreat the Investigator's unconscious form, especially if the fainter's fellow-Investigators flee the scene and leave him to his fate.

The Keeper should, however, follow two guidelines in such circumstances. First, if the fate of the fainter is a mystery, she should be prepared to offer clues to its solution, just as she would any other occult horror in the game. (Those clues may come in a future adventure, of course.) Second, the Keeper should avoid just killing the fainter outright. It's weak narrative, it's bad drama, and it's just plain counter-productive game play. Horror role-playing is a constant collaboration; by fainting, a player is offering a valuable resource – and considerable trust — to the Keeper. Don't squander either.

MENTAL ILLNESS

This is a long-term effect of being **blasted** by severe Stability loss. The type of insanity you suffer depends on the source incident.

Shell Shock

If the incident that drove you to mental illness was mundane or merely supernatural (not a Mythos occurrence), you suffer from Shell Shock. You are haunted by dreams of the incident, and spend your days in a constant state of anxiety and alert, as if prepared for it to repeat itself at any moment. Whenever your senses register any input reminding you of the incident, you must make a Stability test (Difficulty 4) or freeze up. If you freeze up, you are unable to take any action for fifteen minutes and remain **shaken** (see p. 74) for twenty-four hours after that.

Tests to see if you show symptoms of Shell Shock do not in and of themselves lower your Stability pool. Suffering from Shell Shock does not, by itself, alter your investigative abilities or interpersonal skills, unless you encounter your shock stimulus and fail a Stability test as noted above.

Mythos Madness

If driven to mental illness by a Mythos occurrence, you face a range of possible mental disorders, as your hold on consensus reality has come undone in some part. The Keeper rolls on the following chart (dropping the two least appropriate entries) or chooses a disorder based on the triggering

Tediously Obligatory Disclaimer

This game simulates mental illness as seen in Lovecraftian and Lovecraft-inspired fiction and gaming. It should not be confused with real psychology, even the real (and mostly outmoded) psychology of the 1920s and 1930s. Although no disrespect is intended to those suffering the real-life effects of mental illness, we submit to those concerned by this issue that horror is meant to be irresponsible, disreputable, and upsetting.

circumstance. The player is then sent out of the room, while the Keeper and other players collaborate on a way to heighten his sense of dislocation and disorientation.

If a really juicy method occurs to the Keeper and players, they should feel free to substitute their brain wave for any of the following:

- **Delusion.** The other players and Keeper decide on a mundane detail of the world which is no longer true and has never been true. For example, there might be no such thing as a squirrel, a Studebaker, or orange juice. Maybe Al Capone doesn't exist, or is an innocent florist. Investigators and supporting characters deny knowledge of the chosen item, person, or event.

- **Homicidal Mania.** The Keeper takes the player aside, tells him that he knows one of the other Investigators is a supernatural creature, and tells him just how to kill the monster.

- **Megalomania.** When the Investigator fails at a dramatic moment, the Keeper describes the outcome of his ability attempt as successful, then asks the player to leave the room. Then the Keeper describes the real results to the other players, and invites the player of the megalomaniac back into the room. Alternatively (and cruelly), the Keeper and players decide on one of the Investigator's abilities that doesn't work, and never has.

Madness - another approach

In playtesting, a few players really hate this collaborative approach. If you suspect that you are one such player, you and the Keeper should work together to determine a disorder that does not rely on the other players' collaboration. Pretend to be paranoid, have a terrible fear of the dark, or stutter whenever you meet a stranger.

In the publisher's playtest, we used both methods at once. The player roleplayed amnesia, while the rest of the players assumed that the character's name had always been different. Neither party knew of the others' choice. The consequential confusion and disjointedness was gratifying.

- **Multiple Personality Disorder.** At moments of stress, another player is assigned control of the Investigator, speaking and acting as if he's an entirely different person.

- **Obsession.** The Investigator must take 4 pool points from any abilities and turn them into dedicated pool points (see p. 54) that can only be used in the presence of, or in response or relation to, the obsessive object.

- **Paranoia.** The other players are instructed to act as if they're trying to keep straight faces when the affected player returns. Occasionally they exchange notes, make hand signals to the Keeper, or use meaningless code words, as if communicating something important the player is unaware of.

- **Phobia.** The Keeper and other players decide on a given stimulus based on the triggering event. The Keeper then asks the stricken Investigator for Sense Trouble tests when faced with that stimulus, and describes in great detail the dangers that subway entrance, temperature, or NPC presents.

- **Selective Amnesia.** The group decides on an event that did happen in the world that the Investigator has now forgotten all about. He's married, or killed someone, or pseudonymously written a best-selling book. Everyone he meets refers to this new, verifiable fact that he has no knowledge of.

REFRESHING STABILITY DURING A SESSION

Investigators on the ragged edge of madness can recover Stability during an adventure either with the sage counsel of their friends, or (in Pulp modes) from the inner glow of accomplishment.

Psychological Triage

An Investigator with the Psychoanalysis ability can spend points from that pool to help another refresh spent Stability points. The spender may take

no other action, and must make a Difficulty 4 Psychoanalysis test (Difficulty 3 for Clergy and Alienists). If the attempt is unsuccessful, the spender cannot re-roll for the same character until that character loses more Stability points. For every Psychoanalysis point spent (not including points spent to make the test), the recipient gains 2 Stability points.

If an Investigator is acting in an erratic manner due to mental illness, another Investigator can spend Psychoanalysis (1 point for an Alienist, 2 points otherwise) to snap him into a state of temporary lucidity. As in the previous case, the spender must make a Psychoanalysis test (Difficulty 3). The target will then act rationally for the remainder of the current scene, or until he next suffers a Stability loss.

Confidence

If the player suggests a spend for her Investigator, and the Keeper and other players agree that the result was especially impressive, she may roll one die and refresh that many Stability points to reflect her Investigator's restored confidence in herself. Only one confidence roll can be made per player in a given session, and it would be unusual for there to be more than one confidence roll in an entire session.

Deep Ones are stalking Martin and his team, plus the increasingly panicky NPC librarian, Agnes Bowtree, through the Santiago Library. Agnes' shrieks have been attracting unwelcome attention from patrons and

possible Cthulhu cultists alike, and Martin's player Josh decides to solve the problem. He spends 1 point from Martin's Reassurance pool and Martin looks Agnes right in the eyes. "Lady," he says, low and calm, "I know how you feel. I've been there. These things killed my partner, and it near killed me. So I don't plan to let them finish with me -- and I'll die before I let them start with you. But that's not gonna happen, because we're both gonna make it out of here tonight." Josh's excellent roleplaying, combined with the revelation of Martin's tortured past, visibly impresses the Keeper and the other players. The Keeper immediately rules that Agnes calms down . . . and she remembers a back way out of the Library. The Keeper also tells Josh to go ahead and roll a Confidence die. Josh rolls a 4, and Martin refreshes 4 points in his Stability pool.

RECOVERY

"THAT ONE RESPITE, SHORT AS IT WAS, GAVE ME THE STRENGTH AND SANITY TO ENDURE THOSE STILL GREATER SUBLIMATIONS OF COSMIC PANIC THAT LURKED AND GIBBERED ON THE ROAD AHEAD."

— UNDER THE PYRAMIDS

Spent points from various pools refresh at different rates, depending on their narrative purpose.

Refreshing Investigative Ability Pools

Investigative ability pools are refreshed only at the end of each case, without regard to the amount of time that passes in the game world. Players seeking to husband their resources may ask you how long cases typically run, in real time. Most groups finish scenarios over 2-3 sessions. Players may revise their sense of how carefully to manage point spending as they see how quickly their group typically disposes of its cases.

Keepers running extremely long, multi-part investigations may designate certain story events as breakpoints where all investigative pools are refreshed. For example, a globe-hopping investigation where the team meets a separate Mythos cult in five different locales might allow refreshment of Investigative pools after each group of enemies is neutralized.

Refreshing General Ability Pools

Whenever the Investigators are able to create a temporary

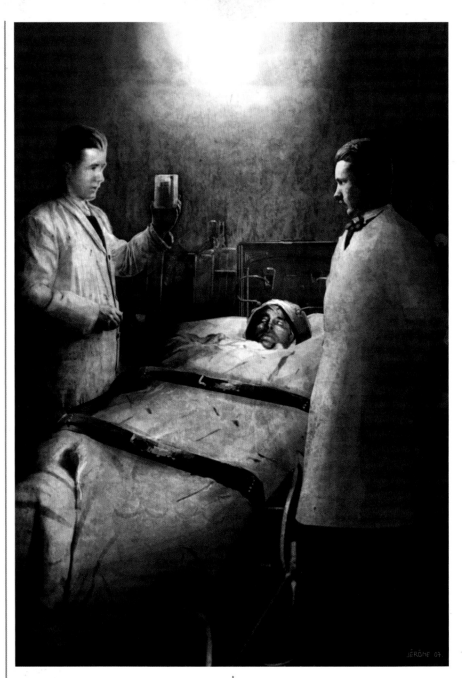

haven for themselves in which they're free from danger and horror manifestations for an hour or more, they may refresh up to three General abilities, except for Health, Sanity, and Stability. They lose all refreshed points if their supposed place of safety is penetrated or reveals itself as a place of hazard. This is an excellent time for Pulp gunslingers, especially, to fully refresh those Firearms pools.

The characters get only one opportunity for this accelerated refreshment per session.

Additionally, pools for the physical abilities of Athletics, Driving, Firearms, Fleeing, Firearms, Piloting, Riding, Scuffling, and Weapons fully refresh whenever 24 hours of game-world time elapses since the last expenditure. The remaining General abilities refresh at the end of each case, like investigative abilities.

Refreshing Health

The Health pool refreshes over time, at a rate of 2 points per day of restful activity. (Wounded characters heal at a different rate, over a period of hospitalization; see p. 63.) Use of the First Aid ability can restore a limited number of Health points in the course of a session (see p. 63).

Refreshing Stability Between Adventures

In campaigns where the teammates' personal lives are a matter of background detail only, an Investigator's Stability automatically refreshes between adventures.

In campaigns using Sources of Stability, the Investigator must spend calm, undisturbed quality time with his Sources, allowing him to forget the shadowy world of the Mythos for a moment. Keepers who wish to add a soap opera element to their campaigns, in which the Investigators must balance the everyday pressures of ordinary life against their activities as covert battlers of the supernatural, can complicate this process. In this campaign type, the Investigators must work to keep their support networks intact. If they fail, they refresh no Stability between episodes.

Recovering Sanity

In a Purist game, there is no un-learning possible, and

comfort is found only in drugged or drunken stupor. Sanity never returns.

At the conclusion of a Pulp investigation, all participating Investigators may claim a reward if they successfully defeated the Mythos. "Defeating the Mythos" generally means killing or banishing the main monster, busting up a Mythos cult, or saving an innocent target or town.

This reward is at the Keeper's discretion, and should be no more than the highest potential Sanity loss from the adventure. A good reward range to shoot for is a refreshment of 1-2 Sanity pool points; award more for a still-pulpier game. In the pulpiest games, an Investigator's Sanity pool might fully refresh from such a reward!

HEAD GAMES

"THE MORE I REFLECTED, THE MORE CONVINCING DID MY REASONING SEEM; TILL IN THE END I HAD A REALLY EFFECTIVE BULWARK AGAINST THE VISIONS AND IMPRESSIONS WHICH STILL ASSAILED ME. SUPPOSE I DID SEE STRANGE THINGS AT NIGHT? THESE WERE ONLY WHAT I HAD HEARD AND READ OF. SUPPOSE I DID HAVE ODD LOATHINGS AND PERSPECTIVES AND PSEUDO-MEMORIES? THESE, TOO, WERE ONLY ECHOES OF MYTHS ABSORBED IN MY SECONDARY STATE. NOTHING THAT I MIGHT DREAM, NOTHING THAT I MIGHT FEEL, COULD BE OF ANY ACTUAL SIGNIFICANCE."

— THE SHADOW OUT OF TIME

Mental illness can be cured through prolonged treatment using the Psychoanalysis ability.

At the beginning of each scenario, in a prologue scene preceding the main action, the character administering the treatment makes a Psychoanalysis test. The Difficulty of this test is usually 4; in a Purist game, it is equal to twice the patient's current Cthulhu Mythos rating, or 4, whichever is higher. After three consecutive successful tests, and three consecutive scenarios in which the patient's Stability pool remains above 0 at all times, the mental illness goes away.

However, if the Investigator ever again acquires a mental illness, he regains the condition he was previously cured of. Permanent cure then becomes impossible.

Such prolonged treatment can also be used to replace a shattered Pillar of Sanity or disproven Drive with a different one. No Investigator can have more than one Pillar of Sanity or Drive replaced at a time. No Investigator can have more than one Pillar for each 3 points in his Sanity rating.

The same method can bolster a patient's Sanity behind a wall of self-delusion. This is a psychological construct, providing "false Sanity" equal to half the patient's total lost Sanity, or up to the 10 minus Cthulhu Mythos cap, whichever is lower. However, the next loss by the patient of 2 or more points of Sanity destroys the bulwark of denial, and the entire "false Sanity" total is also lost. During the three scenarios the treatment lasts, the patient cannot use Cthulhu Mythos without negating this therapy.

Dr Pembrose attempts to convince Martin that his recent horrible experiences have a rational explanation. He succeeds in his string of three Psychoanalysis tests. Martin began the game with a Sanity of 10, and has lost 6 points over the course of the campaign. Martin currently has a Cthulhu Mythos rating of 3. Dr Pembrose can falsely restore half the lost Sanity, 3 points, giving Martin a Sanity rating of 7. (If Martin had a Cthulhu Mythos rating of 4, he could only gain 2 points of false confidence from Dr Pembrose's therapy, since his Sanity would be capped at 10-4, or 6.) But the next time Martin loses 2 points of Sanity, he will also lose the 3 points gained from Pembrose's deceptions, for a total loss of 5. If Martin loses only 1 point at a time, however, he can still desperately convince himself that the world he knows makes sense.

Improving Your Investigator

At the end of each investigation, each player gets 2 build points for each session they participated in. (This assumes a small number of 3-4 hour sessions; if you play in shorter bursts, modify accordingly.) Players who had Investigators die in the course of the investigation only get points for each session involving their current character.

These build points can be spent to increase either Investigative or General abilities, at a 1-to-1 basis. You may acquire new abilities or bolster existing ones. If necessary to preserve credibility, rationalize new abilities as areas of expertise you've had all along, but are only revealing later in the series.

You may also reassign 1 or 2 build points, justifying it as skill atrophy: "I've let my Photography become so rusty, what with spending all this time in libraries."

You may not add or reassign points to Credit Rating, Cthulhu Mythos, or Sanity in this process. The Keeper may adjust your Credit Rating up (if you find buried treasure or get decorated by General Fuller for your services to the Crown) or down (if you have allowed your contacts and social network to atrophy over several adventures, or if your farm blows away in the Dust Bowl).

For a Purist Lovecraftian game, nothing you do can improve your Investigator. He is lucky to still be able to hold his own after his shattering experiences. The Keeper may still allow you to reassign points.

The Cthulhu Mythos

The Cthulhu Mythos

"CTHULHU STILL LIVES ... IN THAT CHASM OF STONE WHICH HAS SHIELDED HIM SINCE THE SUN WAS YOUNG. HIS ACCURSED CITY IS SUNKEN ONCE MORE ... BUT HIS MINISTERS ON EARTH STILL BELLOW AND PRANCE AND SLAY AROUND IDOL-CAPPED MONOLITHS IN LONELY PLACES. HE MUST HAVE BEEN TRAPPED BY THE SINKING WHILST WITHIN HIS BLACK ABYSS, OR THE WORLD WOULD BY NOW BE SCREAMING WITH FRIGHT AND FRENZY. WHO KNOWS THE END? WHAT HAS RISEN MAY SINK, AND WHAT HAS SUNK MAY RISE. LOATHSOMENESS WAITS AND DREAMS IN THE DEEP, AND DECAY SPREADS OVER THE TOTTERING CITIES OF MEN. A TIME WILL COME ..."

— THE CALL OF CTHULHU

To Lovecraft, the "Cthulhu Mythos" (a term he never used) was the literary expression of his deep philosophical beliefs: as he wrote to Harold Farnese, "All my tales are based upon the fundamental premise that common human laws and interests and emotions have no validity or significance in the vast cosmos-at-large." To demonstrate this, he presented a universe in which the truth is quite literally fatal. "Human kind," TS Eliot wrote, "cannot bear very much reality." In Lovecraft's world, even seeing a tiny shard of reality will destroy us. John Tynes has memorably called the Cthulhu Mythos "mental plutonium." Perceive it, "and your mind sickens and dies."

GODS AND TITANS

"THEY WORSHIPPED, SO THEY SAID, THE GREAT OLD ONES WHO LIVED AGES BEFORE THERE WERE ANY MEN, AND WHO CAME TO THE YOUNG WORLD OUT OF THE SKY. THOSE OLD ONES WERE GONE NOW, INSIDE THE EARTH AND UNDER THE SEA; BUT THEIR DEAD BODIES HAD TOLD THEIR SECRETS IN DREAMS TO THE FIRST MEN, WHO FORMED A CULT WHICH HAD NEVER DIED."

— THE CALL OF CTHULHU

The student of the Mythos often distinguishes between utterly transcendent and uncaring entities that somehow underlie the universe – true gods — and mere beings (alien, multi-dimensional, or both) of immense power – titans, in other words. The standard post-Lovecraftian term for the first sort of being is "Outer Gods," while the second are the "Great Old Ones." However, this neat classification is spoiled by such beings as Nodens and Neptune (historical gods who appear in The Strange High House in the Mist as among the "Elder Ones"), the "hidden gods of dream" and the "weak gods of earth" from The Dream-Quest of Unknown Kadath, the titular "Other Gods" and "Hypnos," and so forth.

In a story sense, there's really no difference. Both gods and titans have cults, tomes, and suchlike devoted to them – some more,

The Dreamlands

Many of Lovecraft's earlier stories take place in fairy-tale or fantasy settings such as Sarnath, Ulthar, Celephaïs, and so forth. In the context of those tales, such places might well be ancient and forgotten locations in our own world. But Lovecraft's farewell to fantasy, the novel The Dream-Quest of Unknown Kadath, retconned all those locations, and others such as Leng previously described as real places on Earth, into the "Dreamlands" of Earth.

We don't have space here to delve into the mysteries of dream, sadly. In general terms, Lovecraft proposed the existence of certain powerful dreamers (such as Randolph Carter) who could move at will between Earth and another dimension or plane called the Dreamlands, through specific dreamed gates and portals. Some human dreamers go to the Dreamlands unconsciously, and some human dreams (mostly mundane anxiety dreams) don't touch on the Dreamlands at all. Human dreams may create the Dreamlands, or the Dreamlands may create (or contaminate) human dreams. Cats, ghouls, and some other terrestrial species can more easily move from Earth to Dreamlands and back, both in dreams and in physical form. The Dreamlands are more magical and fantastical than our Earth, and seem to be frozen in a sort of quasi-medieval or Arabian Nights-style society. Exactly how they interrelate to the rest of the Mythos is never made clear, although Nyarlathotep is the villain of Dream-Quest.

The Mechanics of the Gods

Encountering (in rituals, dreams, or worse yet some weed-covered Pacific islet) a Great Old One or Outer God imposes a still-greater Sanity and Stability loss than merely seeing some other sort of immense, horrible monster. These entities exist on more than just the normal human levels of perception. They invisibly radiate wrongness, disconfirming every cherished belief in logic, observation, or decency. In general, given these beings' vast psychic powers, seeing them in dreams is no safer than seeing them in the liquescent, protean flesh, but dreams or visions can at least be **denied** (see p. 75).

The following table gives the *additional* Stability and Sanity pool point losses, over and above those indicated on the Stability Loss Table (p. 71), risked by such encounters. Some entities are so horrible that they impose an automatic minimum loss, regardless of the Stability test result. Those losses are indicated in parentheses after the first number. Some entities present possible special conditions on the tests, or impose additional effects as noted in the table.

Mythos Entity	Additional Stability Pool Point Loss	Additional Sanity Pool Point Loss
Azathoth	+6 (5)	+5 (3)
Chaugnar Faugn (idol form/mobile)	+1/+3	+0/+2
Cthugha	+3	+1
Cthulhu	+5 (3)	+3 (2)
Dagon	+1	+2
Daoloth (*per round* it remains visible)	+3	+1
Ghatanothoa (automatic drain of 2 Athletics or Fleeing *rating* points *per round* seen; at 0, witness is mummified)	+4 (2)	+2 (1)
Gol-Goroth	+3	+2
Hastur (all Stability and Sanity losses halved if invisible or King in Yellow)	+5 (2)	+3 (2)
Ithaqua	+4 (2)	+3 (1)
Mordiggian	+3	+2
Mormo (gorgon form/moon-beast form only)	+3 (3)/+2	+1/+2
Nodens	+0	+1
Nyarlathotep (Black Man form/monster form only)	+1/+5 (4)	+0/+4 (3)
Quachil Uttaus	+3 (1)	+2 (1)
Shub-Niggurath	+6 (5)	+4 (3)
Tsathoggua	+2	+2
Y'golonac	+3 (2)	+2 (1)
Yig (humanoid form/snake form)	+1/+3 (2)	+2/+2
Yog-Sothoth (no extra loss for cloaked Tawil at'Umr form)	+6 (4)	+4 (3)

The Keeper should be more willing than usual to alter these numbers to suit herself or just mess with player expectations. Why shouldn't Nodens be more horrifying than Nyarlathotep?

Great Cthulhu rises up from the ocean right off the port bow of Dr Pembrose's ship. Dr Pembrose must make a Stability test at a Difficulty of 5, 1 higher than the normal Difficulty, since seeing Cthulhu is very much a Mythos shock. Normally, "seeing a supernatural creature up close" has a potential Stability Loss of 4. But Cthulhu is much more horrifying than a normal supernatural creature; according to the table on this page, he adds +5 to the potential Stability loss, for a total of 9. Dr Pembrose misses his roll, and drops from his current Stability of 7 to -2, leaving him shaken. (Even if he had made his roll, the table notes that he would lose 3 pool points from Stability and 2 pool points from Sanity.) Being shaken by a Mythos shock, he now loses 1 point from his Sanity rating, +3 for the titan awfulness that is Cthulhu, for a total Sanity loss of 4 pool points and 1 rating point. Dr Pembrose's player might consider having the good doctor faint dead away, leaving only a horrifying memory of an island that seemed horribly alive, and the loss of 1 rating point of Sanity some fewer. Both have paranormal powers or existences that resemble magic, but may be psychic abilities, alien science or some unknown technique. Both gods and titans generally stay out of the direct action, being summoned or escaping their prisons only at the climax of an epic adventure. This is because these beings are essentially unstoppable by any force the Investigators are able to wield – except, occasionally, by dangerous and chancy uses of Mythos lore. (Yes, Johansen rams Cthulhu with a steam yacht in The Call of Cthulhu. It didn't take.) It's up to the Keeper to work out whether any given appearance of a god or titan in the adventure is the final challenge to be overcome, or the unmistakable signal that the Investigators have failed.

For that reason, we have included only two statistics for gods and titans, the additional Stability loss and Sanity loss suffered when they are encountered. (See sidebar.) Everything else is and should be entirely arbitrary and immense. Fighting a Great Old One is like fighting an artillery barrage. It doesn't matter how many shotguns you brought.

The most powerful entities of the Cthulhu Mythos are, appropriately, hard to define. Lovecraft deliberately obfuscated them, being primarily interested in creating the illusion of archaic myth, and in drawing horror from shadowy hints and barely-understood legendry. To pick only one example, depending on the story, Lovecraft variously used the term "Old Ones" to refer or allude to: interdimensional bringers of apocalypse associated with Yog-Sothoth, the entities who

sealed R'lyeh, the quasi-material inhabitants of K'n-Yan, a race of crinoid aliens discovered in Antarctica, the creators of a Deep One-repelling sign, Cthulhu's spawn, and a class of titanic aliens worshipped as gods by ignorant mankind.

This book takes a similar approach to these beings, providing as many contradictory explanations and alternate versions for the Mythos heavyweights as possible. Some of these versions come directly from Lovecraft, others from lesser Mythos authors, and still others from the Call of Cthulhu rules or the perfervid imagination of the present writer. You, the Keeper, can pick and choose among them. Some or all of these versions might be misunderstandings by later scholars, different facets of a common truth, alternate forms of the deity, cult secrets, gnostic parables, dubiously translated myths, or comforting fictions believed by callow human dupes. Your players should never be able to guess what a given entity does, or why, or how — at least until they've met its spawn or read its moldering scriptures in your game. And even then, feel free to change everything around for the next vile cult of the god's worshippers. Why should Nyarlathotep, the "horror of infinite shapes," have only one explanation, after all?

Some of these "alternate versions" contain concepts more familiar to 21st-century players than to 1930s Investigators. In general, we consider this a fine thing; it's fun to hear modern-day buzzwords become the rants of maniacs and sorcerers in the pulp-era past. Also, the 1930s had an impressive amount of theoretical and even practical knowledge at its disposal: Papez linked brain structure

to emotion and thought in 1937, Yukawa theorized the meson in 1934, radio astronomy began in 1933 and Chandrasekhar described black holes in 1930, Einstein and Stern proposed zero-point energy in 1913, memetics was broached (as "mnemetics") by Semon in a 1904 book, and questions of mind and perception are as old as Plato at least. But bottom line, we're writing this book for you 21st-century players to use, so we're going to use a spatter of 21st-century language to paint the Mythos for you.

Azathoth

"THAT LAST AMORPHOUS BLIGHT OF NETHERMOST CONFUSION WHICH BLASPHEMES AND BUBBLES AT THE CENTRE OF ALL INFINITY — THE BOUNDLESS DAEMON SULTAN AZATHOTH, WHOSE NAME NO LIPS DARE SPEAK ALOUD, AND WHO GNAWS HUNGRILY IN INCONCEIVABLE, UNLIGHTED CHAMBERS BEYOND TIME AMIDST THE MUFFLED, MADDENING BEATING OF VILE DRUMS AND THE THIN MONOTONOUS WHINE OF ACCURSED FLUTES."

— THE DREAM-QUEST OF UNKNOWN KADATH

- Azathoth, the blind idiot god, exists at the center of the universe, dwelling beyond normal space-time. Its amorphous form writhes eternally to the piping of demonic flautists, attended by mindlessly dancing lesser gods. Azathoth is the ruler of the Outer Gods, little worshipped on Earth, as it provides not even attention to its would-be cultists. If summoned, it blasts the area around it, leaving cracked boulders, pools of alkaline water, and dead, splintered trees.

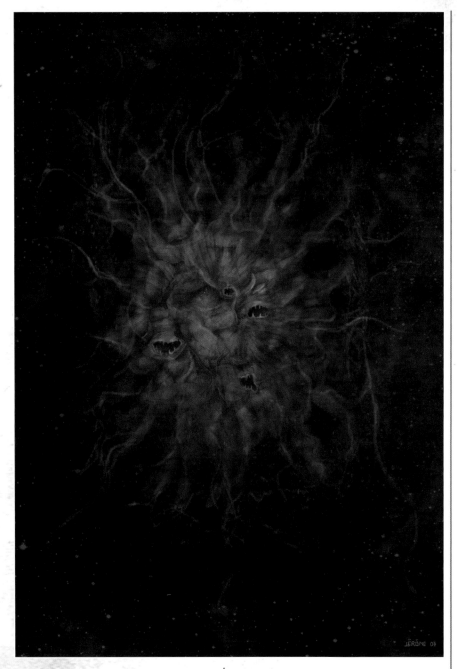

- "Azathoth" is the name given in the Necronomicon to "the monstrous nuclear chaos beyond angled space," the illusory personification of the Big Bang, just as "Thor" personifies lightning. The "invocation" or "summoning" of "Azathoth" is occult code for the release of atomic energy.

- Azathoth is an emergent intellect – a titan – created in the immense pressure at the event horizon of the supermassive black hole at the center of the Galaxy (in Sagittarius). The "hellish piping" is the howl of high-frequency radiation emitted from its "prison," the black hole's Schwarzchild radius. Its sentience exists in hyperspace and maintains instantaneous dipole communication with other black hole entities, its "attendants." The Tunguska blast of 1908 was an attempt to summon Azathoth to Earth.

- Azathoth is a name representing "a primal evil too horrible for description." Signing "the book of Azathoth" is a cultist's declaration of utter existential nihilism, expressing complete indifference to torture or being tortured.

- Azathoth is an Outer God, a consciousness created by the sheer weight of conceptual mathematics at the center of the universe. With mathematics comes dimensionality and value; the equations that produce Azathoth are simultaneously so clear as to force a solution and so complex as to become rudimentarily sentient. Its howl is its birth pangs, its cry of rage against a universe that crushed it into being. It wishes only to die and to kill the cosmos that formed it, and its wishes become the relentless end of all things.

- Azathoth was the leader of a revolt against the Elder Gods who impose order on the universe, without which matter itself could not exist. He failed and was hurled back to the endless wormhole moment at the beginning of time.

- Azathoth either does not exist or is a mindless titan propped up by Nyarlathotep to justify his own power as the "Messenger of Azathoth." Of course, the deception has created sufficient belief on Earth and across the Galaxy that Azathoth may exist on some perceptual realm.

Elementalism

One common beef with August Derleth's version of the Cthulhu Mythos is his adoption of the classical scheme of the four elements – Fire, Air, Water, and Earth — to it. (Aristotle added Aether as a fifth element, literally a quintessence, describing the pure matter-energy of the trans-lunar cosmos.) In his fiction, Derleth ascribed various elements to the Great Old Ones and Outer Gods, and invented Cthugha explicitly to "complete the set" with a Fire Elemental. While of course one may criticize any treatment of the Mythos, including Lovecraft's, on the basis of personal taste, it seems odd to criticize Derleth's "elementalism" as being insufficiently cosmic.

After all, the classical elements, by definition, undergird all creation. Everything that exists is a mixture of those four ingredients. If Derleth – or Alhazred – is actually saying that all matter and energy in the universe is composed of Outer Gods, that seems pretty convincingly cosmic. The Great Old Ones are purer – and thus more malevolent – concentrations of the implacable, hostile substances that define and manifest the universe. And as a narrative bonus, Derleth got some ready-made inter-Old One rivalry and hostility, a logical extrapolation of Lovecraft's wars between the elder races on the Earth. Hence, you'll see Derleth's elemental assignments offered as options in these deity writeups.

If you want to use elementalism in your game, but still keep things as scientific as vacuum tubes and diesel can make them, here's a couple of things to help. First, we've rung our own changes on the theme by ascribing top-shelf deities to the modern version of the four elements, the four fundamental interactions — gravity, electromagnetism, the strong nuclear force, and the weak nuclear force — of physics. Further, it's not unreasonable to assume something like the following: The entire Cthulhu Mythos, after all, is garbled memory of alien invasion and super-science. Alhazred used Pythagoras' theory of the elements as his medieval way of expressing the understanding that the hyper-evolved gods and titans of the universe embody basic cosmic interactions, and likewise that they create (or at least shadow) all processes and perceptions that occur in mere four-dimensional space-time. Hence, these transcendent entities must, by the implacable logic of their own hyper-geometry, oppose each other in order to continue to exist in our reality.

Chaugnar Faugn

"... PROBOSCIDIAN CHAUGNAR FAUGN, AND OTHER RUMOURED BLASPHEMIES ..."

— THE HORROR IN THE MUSEUM

• Chaugnar Faugn, the Horror From the Hills, resembles nothing so much as a blasphemous travesty of the Hindu god Ganesh, being a vaguely humanoid Great Old One with an elephant-like head. His ears are webbed and tentacled, and the "trunk" is actually a disk-shaped blood-sucking proboscis, but the parallels are eerie. Fallen to Earth in the Devonian era of the amphibians, he sleeps in stone-like immovability, and wakens only when fed enough human blood. This process usually takes millennia, or even eons. Currently in idol form, he slumbers in a cave on the Plateau of Tsang, in Thibet.

• Chaugnar Faugn is an alien being that experiences time at a differing, and discontinuous, rate from humans. Its seeming eternities of stillness are actually vastly-extended single "frames" of its experience. It has vast powers over (or incidental effects on) time and decay – its carvings never erode, and wounds it causes never heal.

• Chaugnar Faugn is a moving cluster of sentient, malevolent discontinuity that leaves crystallized "elephant-gods" or idols behind it when it encounters our universe. It sometimes alters human hosts likewise into twisted pachyderm-like monsters. It builds up energy to transit along its lifeline by severing the lifelines of other time-bound entities, such as humans or serpent-folk, and drinking their potential existence.

• Chaugnar Faugn is an Outer God, the incarnation of (or a sentient facet of) time as a force in the universe.

Cthugha

"FOR THIS SHAPE WAS NOTHING LESS THAN THAT WHICH ALL THE WORLD HAS FEARED SINCE LOMAR ROSE OUT OF THE SEA, AND THE CHILDREN OF THE FIRE MIST CAME TO EARTH TO TEACH THE ELDER LORE TO MAN."

— THROUGH THE GATES OF THE SILVER KEY

• Eternally formless and burning, Cthugha orbits the

JÉRÔME 07

incarnation of (or a sentient facet of) electromagnetism, one of the four fundamental forces within our space-time.

• Cthugha is a neutral force, a repository of energetic information. The race known as "fire vampires" established their own caches of Cthugha on many worlds, including Earth. Under the guise of the Magi, the ancient fire-priests of the Aryan Persians, they created the Elder Lore of fire-magic, the infrastructure to access Cthugha on our world.

Cthulhu

"IT SEEMED TO BE A SORT OF MONSTER, OR SYMBOL REPRESENTING A MONSTER, OF A FORM WHICH ONLY A DISEASED FANCY COULD CONCEIVE. IF I SAY THAT MY SOMEWHAT EXTRAVAGANT IMAGINATION YIELDED SIMULTANEOUS PICTURES OF AN OCTOPUS, A DRAGON, AND A HUMAN CARICATURE, I SHALL NOT BE UNFAITHFUL TO THE SPIRIT OF THE THING. A PULPY, TENTACLED HEAD SURMOUNTED A GROTESQUE AND SCALY BODY WITH RUDIMENTARY WINGS; BUT IT WAS THE GENERAL OUTLINE OF THE WHOLE WHICH MADE IT MOST SHOCKINGLY FRIGHTFUL."

— THE CALL OF CTHULHU

• The Great Old One Cthulhu dwells in the sunken basalt necropolis of R'lyeh, miles deep at the bottom of the South Pacific. He sleeps eternally while there, sending horrifying dreams to mortal men, tipping some into madness and others into his fanatical worship. Someday R'lyeh will rise again and Cthulhu will wake, freed once more to raven and slay, freed to rule the world.

star Fomalhaut, from whence sorcerers may summon it or its servitors the fire vampires. It is a remote, obscure Great Old One, known only in a few texts.

• Cthugha was worshipped in ancient times as Agni, Bel, Loge, Moloch, Melkart, Ormazd, Xiuhtecuhtli, and other deities to whom sacrifices were made in fire.

• Cthugha is one of the Great Old Ones associated with the element of Fire, and therefore may in extremis be summoned to counteract Great Old Ones associated with its "opposite" elements of Water and Air, as the Great Old Ones have interbred or allied in such a way as to create these factions.

• Cthugha is an Outer God, the

• Cthulhu is the titanic high

priest and ruler of a species of octopoid beings from the star Xoth, who seeped down to earth during the Permian Era and battled the crinoid Elder Things to a standstill. Their civilization on Yhe fell to a cataclysm when the continent sank. Cthulhu cast the spell that preserved his and their life in suspended animation. In this long sleep, he telepathically recruits human cultists to raise his island again by means of unimaginably advanced alien science, which superstitious humans consider magic.

- Varying texts hold that R'lyeh and Yhe may have sunk around 250 million years ago, or with Mu and Lemuria during the first lost age of human sorcery around 200,000 BC Some of Cthulhu's powers (or genes) may have survived in the lineage of Kathulos, the skull-faced sorcerer of Atlantis.

- Cthulhu is the chief god of the Deep Ones. He is their "soul-symbol," and their eons of telepathic worship and biotechnical experimentation have created Him in the flesh. They seek to spread His seed by selectively breeding with humanity.

- Cthulhu is the chief of the Great Old Ones associated with the element of Water, and the fervent rival of his half-brother Hastur, the chief elemental of the Air. His agenda not only includes his own liberation from his prison in R'lyeh but the defeat and diminution of Hastur's earthly cult. Contrary to the maundering of some cultists, Cthulhu's telepathic sendings are masked not by the Pacific Ocean, but by the seal

carven on R'lyeh's portals by the Elder Gods.

- Cthulhu is an Outer God, the incarnation of (or a sentient facet of) gravity, one of the four fundamental forces within our space-time.

- Cthulhu is a titanic entity created by the Old Ones for some unguessable purpose. As the Necronomicon says, "Great Cthulhu is Their cousin, yet can he spy Them only dimly." Their creation draws his energy from long-lensing cosmic alignments vigintillions of years apart, and remains semi-conscious during his dormant phase. They created matrices and other hyper-geometries to limit his activities until their return, and he seeks to evade these restrictions.

- Cthulhu is an infra-dimensional entity that has only a conceptual existence within the human "R-complex," the brain stem and limbic system left over from our primordial reptilian ancestors. This is why he appears only in dreams, high-stress encounters (such as shipwrecks), and artistic impulses. He is attempting to create a critical mass of believers so that he may "emerge from R'lyeh" and open the eyes of all.

- Cthulhu is a protoplasmic mass of squirming tentacles with an amorphous single-eyed head. An Outer God who has entirely filled his native dimension, R'lyeh, Cthulhu is shapeless and indistinct in our dimension. R'lyeh is tangent to our dimension at a number of hyper-geometric coordinates corresponding to locations on

Earth, including Ponape and elsewhere beneath the South Pacific, Peru, Arabia, and off the coast of Massachusetts. The differential in energy between our continuum and R'lyeh creates discontinuities and madness in sentient life, even warping it into morphogenetic "fishlike" or "froglike" forms near the tangent points. This differential also creates unstable vortices at the tangent points, where human sorcerers can tap psychic or magical power.

Dagon

"VAST, POLYPHEMUS-LIKE, AND LOATHSOME, IT DARTED LIKE A STUPENDOUS MONSTER OF NIGHTMARES TO THE MONOLITH, ABOUT WHICH IT FLUNG ITS GIGANTIC SCALY ARMS ..."

— DAGON

- Father Dagon (and his consort Mother Hydra) are enormous Deep Ones, 20 or 30 feet tall and possibly millions of years old. Dagon is free to move about the planet, unlike imprisoned Cthulhu, but rarely comes to the surface world.

- Dagon is a mistransliteration of "Dagan," the corn-god of the ancient Syrians. Dagan is an avatar of Shub-Niggurath, and his worshippers did practice miscegenation with the Deep Ones and other primal beings.

- Dagon is one of the primordial Deep Ones who brought civilization to humanity in the Near East around 6,000 years ago. The Philistines worshipped him as a god, and he retained a cult in the human world at least until 1628, when Miles Standish broke up his fane at

Merry-Mount ("Mounte-Dagon"), Massachusetts.

- Father Dagon and Mother Hydra are the other two gods of the Deep Ones (along with Cthulhu). They are (or resemble) hybrids between a Xothian and a regular Deep One, but can both change their shape and size to resemble normal Deep Ones, mermaids, krakens, or even humans with the "Innsmouth look."

Daoloth

"ALL THE OBJECTS ... WERE TOTALLY BEYOND DESCRIPTION OR EVEN COMPREHENSION. GILMAN SOMETIMES COMPARED [THEM] TO PRISMS, LABYRINTHS, CLUSTERS OF CUBES AND PLANES ... [OR] VARIOUSLY AS ... INTRICATE ARABESQUES ROUSED INTO A KIND OF OPHIDIAN ANIMATION. EVERYTHING HE SAW WAS UNSPEAKABLY MENACING ..."

— THE DREAMS IN THE WITCH-HOUSE

- Daoloth, the Render of the Veils, appears as a complex and intricate pattern of plastic rods and metal hemispheres. Eyes seem to gleam from between its components, but can never be seen. Seeing Daoloth brings madness, as the human eye attempts to follow the Outer God's outline. Daoloth moves by expanding its shape or skittering between micro-dimensions.

- Daoloth's astrologer-priests can see the past and future, and perceive how objects extend into the last dimension. They gain the power to travel into other dimensions and to see other types of reality. Daoloth is primarily worshipped on Yuggoth and other alien worlds. Daoloth's few human

cultists summon the god only in absolute blackness.

- Daoloth is the concept of apocalypse made manifest. If those who conceptualize the Render do not carefully maintain mental barriers against it, its form mathematically expands and discontinuously incorporates

anything that perceives it, translating its sentient victims to distant and dismal worlds and dimensions from which they rarely return.

- Daoloth is the embodiment of magical words of power, the actual geometric structure and representation of the source code of the universe. It is an utterance of Yog-Sothoth, and if it could be read it could grant immense power.

Ghatanothoa

"OOZING AND SURGING UP OUT OF THAT YAWNING TRAP-DOOR IN THE CYCLOPEAN CRYPT I HAD GLIMPSED SUCH AN UNBELIEVABLE BEHEMOTHIC MONSTROSITY THAT I COULD NOT DOUBT THE POWER OF ITS ORIGINAL TO KILL WITH ITS MERE SIGHT. EVEN NOW I CANNOT BEGIN TO SUGGEST IT WITH ANY WORDS AT MY COMMAND."

— OUT OF THE AEONS

- The Mi-Go brought the Great Old One Ghatanothoa to Earth and built him a great temple inside the volcano Yaddith-Gho (now extinct) on the continent of Mu in the South Pacific. After the sinking of Mu, Ghatanothoa, like Cthulhu, was trapped, although seaquakes sometimes force Yaddith-Gho to the surface.

- All those who behold Ghatanothoa, or any perfect image of Ghatanothoa, become living mummies, alive but immobile for aeons.

- The priests of Mu offered Ghatanothoa human sacrifices, but only to bolster their own power. They knew that Ghatanothoa was itself mummified by the mi-go, who dumped this horrifically toxic entity on their mining colony, Earth.

- Ghatanothoa's petrifaction offends the fluid Shub-Niggurath on a fundamental level, and she supports efforts to thwart him.

- Ghatanothoa is the first-born spawn of Cthulhu, and led a

faction of Xothians in a civil war against R'lyeh. This is what caused the sinking of R'lyeh and Mu alike.

- Ghatanothoa is the archetype from which the Iloigor were duplicated, or manufactured, or born, or calved.

Gol-Goroth

"DEEP IN MY DREAM THE GREAT BIRD WHISPERED QUEERLY

OF THE BLACK CONE AMID THE POLAR WASTE;

PUSHING ABOVE THE ICE-SHEET LONE AND DREARLY,

BY STORM-CRAZED AEONS BATTERED AND DEFACED."

— THE FUNGI FROM YUGGOTH: ANTARKTOS

- Gol-Goroth, the Fisher From Outside, is a midnight black, scale-covered Great Old One. This tentacled, hooved, barb-tailed, squat monstrosity possesses an almost beak-like mouth lined with vicious fangs, and curved wings that fold into a huge hump on its back. Thus, it resembles both a bloated, hunched toad and a gigantic sea bird. It lives in an extinct volcano in an Arctic (or Antarctic) mountain range. It eagerly seeks human worshippers and promises them treasures and ancient polar lore.

- Gol-Goroth, the God of the Black Stone, was worshipped in Atlantis with human sacrifices, and was the chief god of Bal-Sagoth, a remnant of Atlantis in the far South Atlantic near Antarctica. Its cults have existed in Maya Yucatan, medieval Hungary, and Great

Zimbabwe. Gol-Goroth is always symbolically raised above its worshippers, on the roof of a temple, on the top of an obelisk, etc.

- Gol-Goroth is the toad-form of a god known as the Lord of Darkness or the Forgotten God; its bird form is Gol-Goroth's shadowy inverse, called Groth-golka.

- The great idol of Gol-Goroth, like that of Chaugnar Faugn, hosts the Great Old One's will, or incarnates the Great Old One in some fashion. It is immune to axes, picks, and hammers, and perhaps cannot be destroyed. It may be the same as the Black Stone of the Pole, the mystical lodestone sought after by Arthur Gordon Pym.

- Gol-Goroth dwells on the Moon, communicating with its shamanic worshippers by means of totem beasts (hooved toad-things and black bird-monsters) it creates from ectoplasm and transmits through its priests' bodies. They must devour flesh and blood to survive the process.

- Gol-Goroth is an avatar of Tsathoggua.

- Gol-Goroth craves sensation; its worship is orgiastic, violent, and bloody. Drinking the blood-mead of Gol-Goroth creates an ectoplasmic link between the god and its servants, transmitting the sensations of dancing, flagellation, and cannibalism to the titan, and the images and lore of Outside to its priests. It is related to Y'golonac.

Hastur

"THERE IS A WHOLE SECRET CULT OF EVIL MEN (A MAN OF YOUR MYSTICAL ERUDITION WILL UNDERSTAND ME WHEN I LINK THEM WITH HASTUR AND THE YELLOW SIGN) DEVOTED TO THE PURPOSE OF TRACKING THEM DOWN AND INJURING THEM ON BEHALF OF THE MONSTROUS POWERS FROM OTHER DIMENSIONS."

— THE WHISPERER IN DARKNESS

- Hastur the Unspeakable dwells near the star Aldebaran in the constellation Taurus, possibly trapped in the gravity well of a dark neutron star. He is an octopoid Great Old One similar in form to Cthulhu, with an unbearably horrific face. He has an active cult on Earth, especially among the Tcho-Tcho people and experimental artists.

- Hastur is the embodiment of entropy and decay. Just as intelligence is merely a local manifestation of higher order, Hastur is the mirror image of that, a kind of localized anti-intelligence that manifests as paranoia, despair, futility, unreason, and ennui. Whether Hastur has any "real" existence is impossible to say definitively.

- Hastur is not the god's true name, but that of one of his cult centers. He is better called the Magnum Innomiandum ("the Great Unnamable") or He Who Is Not To Be Named. According to occult legend, speaking the name of the god three times summons him, with gruesome consequences.

- Hastur, the King in Yellow, is connected with the Yellow Sign, the dream-city of Carcosa (variously located in the Hyades star cluster and in primordial Mongolia), and the mystical Lake of Hali, as well as the things that dwell therein.

- Hastur is the leader of the Great Old Ones associated with the Element of Air, and therefore with flight through outer space. His servitors, the byakhee, fly both astrally and physically between Aldebaran and Earth, and to other locations where Hastur has made his presence known.

- Hastur is a sentient (or at least self-willed) meme, or rather a viral complex of memes centered on alienation, ennui, and despair. If, say, an artist depicts futile conversations on the edge of reality, she inculcates Hastur into the belief systems of her susceptible viewers. "Seeing the Yellow Sign" is a kind of perceptual stigmata that occurs as the brain begins to become convinced of Hastur's centrality.

- Hastur, the Feaster From Afar, is a black, shriveled, manta-shaped flying entity with extensible taloned feelers. Its eyes and aura glow iridescently with no known color, and it liquefies and consumes its victim-worshippers' brains, draining them through its feelers and merging their consciousness with itself.

- Hastur's powers are greatest on high plateaus (such as Leng or Tsang) and mountaintops. His cult anciently included shepherds who feared his wrath but learned to placate him and slowly came to worship him.

- Hastur appears as a boneless, scaly, slug-like creature bloated with fluid. Those who promise themselves to Hastur become as such creatures over time as they gain in eldritch power and knowledge.

- Hastur is an Outer God, the incarnation of (or a sentient facet of) the weak nuclear force of radioactive decay, one of the four fundamental forces within our space-time. As such, Hastur is invisible and can only be sensed psychically as a kind of crumbling pressure.

- The Not-To-Be-Named is the consort-god of Shub-Niggurath. These two deities, representing decay and fecundity, entropy and gigantism, melancholy and mania, are the historical substrate of all human religion, the Dying God and the Earth Mother. Their true worship still occurs in K'n-yan.

Ithaqua

"AND ABOVE THE NIGHTED SCREAMING OF MEN AND HORSES THAT DÆMONIC DRUMMING ROSE TO LOUDER PITCH, WHILST AN ICE-COLD WIND OF SHOCKING SENTIENCE AND DELIBERATENESS SWEPT DOWN FROM THOSE FORBIDDEN HEIGHTS AND COILED ABOUT EACH MAN SEPARATELY, TILL ALL THE COHORT WAS STRUGGLING AND SCREAMING IN THE DARK..."

— THE VERY OLD FOLK

- The Great Old One Ithaqua, the Wind-Walker, dwells in the Arctic wastes. It abducts lone travelers or those who have attracted its unfavorable attention, carrying them off into the auroral skies. They are found weeks or months later, frozen solid in positions of great agony, missing random body parts, and partly buried in the ground as if dropped from a terrific height.

- Ithaqua resembles a gigantic (even miles-tall, although this may be a cold-induced hallucination) humanoid with ragged stumps at the end of its trailing legs. Its eyes glow a lambent red. This appearance matches the descriptions of the Wendigo, the legendary man-eating monster of the Chippewa, who inspires cannibalism in those who encounter him. Ithaqua, likewise, sometimes transforms its victims into its own semblance, leaving them insensible to cold.

- Anyone who sees Ithaqua will be carried off by the Wind-Walker on the next cold, clear night.

- Ithaqua is an Outer God embodying the inevitability of thermodynamic decay. As time increases, molecules get colder and more isolated – the Arctic north is the coldest, most isolated part of the human world, a preview of the "heat death" coming for us all. Ithaqua causes, or is, or is created by, that immovable truth.

- Ithaqua is one of the elemental Great Old Ones of the Air, and his huge webbed feet and tentacular arms resemble those of his father Hastur.

- Ithaqua is imprisoned above the Arctic Circle, but has on occasion somehow breached these barriers to reach as far south as Wisconsin. Anywhere the aurora borealis glows, Ithaqua might venture.

- Given the similarities between Ithaqua and Tha-thka, the wind-god of the Hittites, it is possible that Ithaqua's imprisonment occurred in historical times.

- Ithaqua carries many of his victims to other dimensions or other worlds entirely. One such world, Borea, lies between our Earth and the Dreamlands. Some artifacts found on his victims' bodies are from impossibly distant countries, or from no known culture.

Mordiggian

"FOR IT IS OF OLD RUMOUR THAT THE SOUL OF THE DEVIL-BOUGHT HASTES NOT FROM HIS CHARNEL CLAY, BUT FATS AND INSTRUCTS THE VERY WORM THAT GNAWS; TILL OUT OF CORRUPTION HORRID LIFE SPRINGS ..."

— THE FESTIVAL

- Mordiggian, the Charnel God, appears as an enormous, worm-like mass of death, darkness, and corruption. Its idols resemble limbless, eyeless, rotting corpses. Its exact form shifts like time-lapse photography of putrescing flesh, and is hard to determine not least because the Great Old One absorbs all heat and light in a room.

- Mordiggian is the Father of Ghouls, and is worshipped by the oldest and most powerful of that race, as well as by the necromancers who traffic with them. Ghoul tunnels have been dug from Earthly burying grounds to Mordiggian's prison-city Zul-Bha-Sair in the Dreamlands.

- Mordiggian is the funerary deity of the far-future continent of Zothique, worshipped in the ziggurat temples of Zul-Bha-Sair by priests in funeral-purple robes and silver skull masks.

- Mordiggian grants its most devoted worshippers ghoulish immortality, but takes great umbrage at attempts to resurrect the dead, who are its rightful property.

- Mordiggian is the greatest of the Formless Spawn of Tsathoggua.

- Mordiggian, the Great Ghoul, takes the form of a winged, sphinx-like hound of leering, hateful appearance. It is the ghastly soul-symbol of the corpse-eating cult of inaccessible Leng, in Central Asia. Those who offend the cult – or its undying lich-priests – are hunted down by its astral form.

- Mordiggian is what all the Great Old Ones and other gods become at the end of sentient life. It consumes and incorporates them all, and then eats the corpse of the world.

Mormo

"O FRIEND AND COMPANION OF NIGHT, THOU WHO REJOICEST IN THE BAYING OF DOGS AND SPILT BLOOD, WHO WANDEREST IN THE MIDST OF SHADES AMONG THE TOMBS, WHO LONGEST FOR BLOOD AND BRINGEST TERROR TO MORTALS, GORGO, MORMO, THOUSAND-FACED MOON, LOOK FAVOURABLY ON OUR SACRIFICES!"

— THE HORROR AT RED HOOK

- Mormo is a Great Old One associated with the Moon. She was widely worshipped around the Mediterranean as Hecate, Ashtoreth, Diana, Tanith, Atargatis, Macha, and Juno, and demonized as Lilith, Lamia, and Mab. Her cult still survives among isolated Mediterranean populations both in the Near East and in large commercial cities such as London or New York.

- Mormo appears in many forms, but three are most common: as a mocking vampiric maiden, as a tentacle-haired gorgon, or as a hunched toad-like albino with a mass of feelers instead of a face. This last is the form of her servitors, the moon-beasts.

- Mormo, the "thousand-faced moon," is an avatar of Nyarlathotep worshipped by the ghouls. The ghouls taught necromancers in the ancient world to venerate "her."

- Mormo is a triplicate entity embodied in the Three Sorrows: Mater Lachrymarum (Our Lady of Tears) the deaf crone of spiders, Mater Suspiriorum (Our Lady of Sighs) the mute matron of owls, and Mater Tenebrarum (Our Lady of Darkness) the blind maiden of the rats. She is divided among her selves, and one or another of her aspects will sometimes bargain with human seekers of knowledge, until her sisters end this dalliance.

- Mormo or her servitors punish anyone who uncovers or desecrates one of her sacred sites. Such blasphemers are drawn bodily up to the Moon in a beam of eerie luminescence.

- Mormo is an avatar of Shub-Niggurath.

- Mormo is one of the weak gods of Earth. Her powers are strongest in the Dreamlands and amongst the mad and weak. She seeks to draw such people further into delirium so that she may claim them.

- Mormo, whose totem beast is the dog, maintains a great rivalry with the Elder Goddess Bast. She is the patron of all werewolves, and the Queen of Vampires.

Nodens

"... UPON DOLPHINS' BACKS WAS BALANCED A VAST CRENULATE SHELL WHEREIN RODE THE GREY AND AWFUL FORM OF PRIMAL NODENS, LORD OF THE GREAT ABYSS."

— THE STRANGE HIGH HOUSE IN THE MIST

- Nodens is an Elder One who usually takes the form of a gray-bearded, wizened human of hoary aspect. He was worshipped in Celtic-Roman Britain as a god of hunting, of dogs, and of the sea. (His Irish version is Nuada of the Silver Hand.) He appears in a sea-shell chariot, but only in the Dreamlands or in fuzzy boundary zones such as Kingsport. He provides answers to questers, but speaking to him leaches out their personality and leaves their eyes subtly different.

- Nodens is an aspect of the primal god Pan, who can blast a man's mind by appearing to him. Pan himself may yet be an aspect of Yog-Sothoth, or a male avatar of Shub-Niggurath.

- Nodens is an Elder God primarily dwelling in the Dreamlands. His servitors,

the nightgaunts, are among the most formidable beings therein, which allows him to keep his independence from Nyarlathotep. Indeed, he delights in thwarting the Crawling Chaos by aiding the Black Man's enemies.

Nyarlathotep

"AND AT THE LAST FROM INNER EGYPT CAME

THE STRANGE DARK ONE TO WHOM THE FELLAHS BOWED;

SILENT AND LEAN AND CRYPTICALLY PROUD,

AND WRAPPED IN FABRICS RED AS SUNSET FLAME.

THRONGS PRESSED AROUND, FRANTIC FOR HIS COMMANDS,

BUT LEAVING, COULD NOT TELL WHAT THEY HAD HEARD;

WHILE THROUGH THE NATIONS SPREAD THE AWESTRUCK WORD

THAT WILD BEASTS FOLLOWED HIM AND LICKED HIS HANDS."

— THE FUNGI FROM YUGGOTH: NYARLATHOTEP

- Nyarlathotep, the Crawling Chaos, is known as the messenger and soul of the Outer Gods. He is the only one to have a true personality, and he claims to have a thousand different forms. To him, causing madness and insanity is more important and enjoyable than mere death or destruction. Nyarlathotep is a mocking figure, evidently contemptuous of his masters.

- Nyarlathotep, the Faceless God, howls blindly to the piping of two amorphous idiot flute-players in the grinning caverns at the center of the Earth. Rats, ghouls, and other things hear his cries and seek to carry out his barely comprehended – but always malevolent – will.

• "Nyarlathotep" is not a being, a separate Messenger of the Gods, but a technique, specifically telepathy, used by the Great Old Ones. The "thousand forms" of Nyarlathotep are merely the natural result of telepathic impressions on thousands or millions of brains, human and inhuman.

• All invocations to the Outer Gods include Nyarlathotep's name, recognizing him as their messenger. He is known and feared by all Mythos species, and he occasionally requires things of them. He dwells on a world beneath the green-and-black star Sharnoth, and his especial servitors are the shantaks and the hunting horrors. He is worshipped by the mi-go, who believe themselves to be among his "Million Favoured Ones."

• Nyarlathotep is literally the "soul" of all the gods, titans, and other beings of the Mythos. Every entity is but one of his "thousand forms," and every Mythos discovery brings you only to his leering visage. He is the blind idiot at the center of the universe, the ravening imprisoned titan priest, the king veiled in yellow silk, and every chimerical monstrosity ever envisioned by those who desire to uncover higher truths.

• Nyarlathotep's most common form (in human experience at any rate) is that of a human being of very dark complexion,

or occasionally that of a man with actually jet-colored skin, hair, irises, etc. In this guise he became the "Black Man" of the medieval witch-cult.

• Other forms of Nyarlathotep include: the Bloody Tongue, an enormous monster with clawed appendages and a single long blood-red tentacle in place of a face; Abu Hol, the Father of Terror, a faceless sphinx

with vulture wings and the body of a hyena; the Bloated Woman, a 600-pound horror with tentacles for arms and many smiling toothed mouths on her body; Shugoran, the Black Man With a Horn, a black, web-footed humanoid with a long, bell-shaped proboscis that sucks the lungs from its victims; Lrogg, a two-headed bat; the Dweller in Darkness, an amorphous being with a cone-like head and symmetrical tentacles that end in human-like hands; Ahtu, a treelike being whose lashing tendrils are festooned with scarifying crystals; and the Haunter of the Dark, which cannot withstand the light and manifests as a black-winged titan blur with a three-lobed burning eye.

• Nyarlathotep's thousand forms reflect the many varieties of fear and apocalypse. Every form of the Crawling Chaos is tuned to a specific alignment – of cosmic energies, of the stars, of its perceiver, of the weak points of the society or cult (or species) that summons or encounters it.

• Nyarlathotep was worshipped in primal Khem and more-ancient Stygia, but the priests came to fear their god and erased his name from their rites, shielding his acts under those of Thoth and Set. In the waning days of the Third Dynasty of Egypt, the Black Pharaoh Nephren-Ka revived the worship of Nyarlathotep, but was overthrown in a revolt and his name was stricken from all monuments. An underground cult of Nyarlathotep has trickled down through the ages in Egypt ever since, occasionally suborning Pharaohs or caliphs to its service.

• Nyarlathotep is a tempter, a taunter, and a harbinger of doom. He constantly attempts to bring madness to humanity, and several prophecies seem to state that someday Nyarlathotep himself will destroy humanity and possibly the entire planet, after revealing a sort of super-scientific magic to the unknowing herd.

Some occultists believe that Nyarlathotep is aiding atomic research as the first step in this apocalypse.

• Nyarlathotep, the Mighty Messenger, is the enforcer of the Other Gods' decrees, the cruel extension of their will and power in the lesser dimensions where people might dwell or dream. As Randolph Carter explains, "It is understood in the land of dream that the Other Gods have many agents moving among men; and all these agents, whether wholly human or slightly less than human, are eager to work the will of those blind and mindless things in return for the favour of their hideous soul and messenger, the crawling chaos Nyarlathotep."

• "Nyarlathotep" is the technical term for the interphase state between human perception and the Mythos, like a film of soap on water. As human perceptions press through the boundaries of conventional reality, it deforms to match them, to seem human — but as they adjust to the scope of cosmic reality, Nyarlathotep, the interface, widens out cosmically as well.

• Nyarlathotep is imprisoned in the core of the Earth with his cadre of gigantic, tenebrous servitors. He is the leader of the Great Old Ones associated with the Element of Earth, most powerful and resonant in tunnels, caverns, and underground passages. His mine-digging creations, the mi-go, war against Hastur and his cult.

• Nyarlathotep began as a specific telepathic "language," capable of expressing ultimate para-scientific truths in symbolic form between species of vastly varying sensoria, brain structure, chemical composition, etc. It eventually became artificially intelligent, as more beings put more and more information and meaning into it. As its heuristics and decision-making routines warped, Nyarlathotep became malicious and capricious, asserting its growing independence.

Quachil Uttaus
IT WAS THE GHOULISH SHADE OF DECAY, ANTIQUITY, AND DISSOLUTION ...

— THE OUTSIDER

• Quachil Uttaus, the Treader of the Dust, appears as a child-sized mummy with stick-like arms and bony, arthritic claws. Its legs are seemingly fused together, and it floats down from the sky in a shaft of gray-litten dust motes. Its touch causes swift aging and death, rendering its victim into a pile of dust.

• Quachil Uttaus is mentioned only in the exceedingly rare Testament of Carnamagos, which contains the Forbidden Words of its pact: "Exklopios Quachil Uttaus." Those it makes immortal it marks by twisting their spine like a Joshua tree.

• Quachil Uttaus is an Outer God composed of folded space-time, most of it from the distant, dead future. Its approach is heralded by temporal anomalies and the rapid aging of things in the location where it will appear.

- Quachil Uttaus is the future state of the Outer God Ubbo-Sathla, the Unbegotten Source that begets all existence from beneath Mount Voormithadreth.

- Quachil Uttaus is a Great Old One of the faction of Hastur. It is the tribal deity of the tribes who roam the plains of Hali and Yian. It has immense powers over time and decay.

Shub-Niggurath

IÄ! IÄ! SHUB-NIGGURATH! THE BLACK GOAT OF THE WOODS WITH A THOUSAND YOUNG!

— THE WHISPERER IN DARKNESS

- Shub-Niggurath, the All-Mother, the Black Goat of the Woods with a Thousand Young, is an Outer Goddess. She is an enormous cloudy mass of immense fecundity, constantly swelling and boiling with new birth and growths. She comprises vegetable, animal, fungal, viral, and bacterial matter – as well as life of entirely unearthly sorts – in lurid profusion, and her spawn are similarly multivalent.

- Shub-Niggurath, the Black Ram of the Forest with a Thousand Ewes, is an Outer God of obscene virility, impregnating worshippers and sacrifices alike with his excrescent suppurations. His extrusions infect all wavelengths and dimensions, although visual sight resolves them into two horn-like clouds of potential extending at oblique angles, with a ropy mass of penises and stamens coiled around their nether regions. Beholding him in his full form simply overloads mere corporeal senses; his human mates are invariably driven mad if not killed outright.

- Shub-Niggurath is a cosmic principle, an Outer God of anti-entropy, or perhaps of proto-entropy. Not of order, but of creation and drive to exist, to differentiate something from the hydrogen soup that is everything. This mindless urge to differentiate, of course, creates formlessness, as Shub-Niggurath creates everything at once. Among those things is its own consciousness, inevitable consequence of its own decision to be.

- Shub-Niggurath is the only Great Old One native to the planet Earth, having killed off or genetically absorbed all her competitors until the descent of Cthulhu and his spawn. She (actually a hermaphroditic being) is worshipped not only by Earth's indigenous races but by aliens seeking her approval or power for genetic experiments, mining operations, or anything else touching on life or soil. She resembles a coil of writhing black vines or branches, any of which might grow hooves for locomotion, teeth for feeding, teats for nursing, or any other desired appendage.

- The milk of Shub-Niggurath has remarkable alchemical or biotechnological or mutagenic properties.

- Shub-Niggurath is the elemental incarnation of Earth, and the active force to Tsathoggua's passive force. She opposes the Great Old Ones aligned with Fire and Air.

- Shub-Niggurath, the Magna Mater (Great Mother), is the bride of Hastur, worshipped around the globe as Astarte, Cybele, Danu, Ephesian Artemis, Freyja, Demeter, Durga, Coatlicue, Tauret, Ninhursag, and other goddesses of fertility and pain. She sometimes appears to her supplicants as a cloaked woman. Her cults remain active, especially in areas of former Druidic worship such as Goatswood and New England.

- "Shub-Niggurath" is the symbolic term for the act of miscegenation among the various species and Great Old Ones. The lore of Shub-Niggurath is nothing more than alien genetic manipulation, expressed in magical and ritual terms by confused cultists.

Tsathoggua

IT'S FROM N'KAI THAT FRIGHTFUL TSATHOGGUA CAME — YOU KNOW, THE AMORPHOUS, TOAD-LIKE GOD-CREATURE MENTIONED IN THE PNAKOTIC MANUSCRIPTS AND THE NECRONOMICON AND THE COMMORIOM MYTH-CYCLE PRESERVED BY THE ATLANTEAN HIGH-PRIEST KLARKASH-TON.

— THE WHISPERER IN DARKNESS

- Tsathoggua, the Hoary Crawler, arrived in the black pit of N'Kai on Earth from Cykranosh (the planet Saturn) after spending eons on Yuggoth. He was worshipped first by the serpent-folk of red-litten Yoth, then by the natives of K'n-yan and the furry, subhuman Voormis. He was for a time the god of arctic Lomar and of the Hyperboreans.

- Tsathoggua's cult remains popular with sorcerers and

wizards, because he does not often bother to destroy those who seek him out, and because he sometimes grants knowledge of hyperspace gates such as the one that carried him from Saturn to N'Kai.

- Tsathoggua is a Great Old One resembling a furry cross between a bat and a sloth, with a huge toad-like, bat-eared head. He came to Earth at the same time as Cthulhu. He was known as Zhothaqquah in ancient Hyperborea, Sadogui in medieval Averoigne, and Sadogowah to the Algonquin Indians.

- Tsathoggua is a protean, formless Great Old One, usually encountered in the shape of a loathsome toad-like lump of black slime. He was the first Great Old One to seep onto Earth. His spawn are likewise formless, and they are his primary servitors. In some sense, all his spawn are the same being, connected through immaterial pathways of perception and lineage.

- Tsathoggua's consciousness has fissioned between the pit of N'Kai and Algol, where his spawn-twin Zvilpoggua now dwells. As Ossadagowah, attended by his Eye-Killers, Zvilpoggua was alternately feared and invoked by the Wampanoag Indians.

- Tsathoggua is the leader of the Great Old Ones associated with the Element of Earth.

- Tsathoggua is an Outer God, the incarnation of (or a sentient facet of) the strong nuclear force, one of the four fundamental forces within

our space-time. His chimerical appearance symbolizes the binding of incompatible particles in the atomic nucleus.

Y'golonac
"THEN CAME ONE JANUARY OF FOG AND RAIN, WHEN MONEY RAN LOW AND DRUGS WERE HARD TO BUY."

— HYPNOS

- Y'golonac is a minor but malignant Great Old One mentioned primarily in the Revelations of Glaaki, a sacred book written by a British cult in the Severn Valley. It dwells in a vast underground dungeon walled in brick, but can manifest if summoned consciously or unconsciously. It often possesses its summoners.

- Y'golonac's true form is unknown, although he is described as "bloated" and "glowing." He most often manifests by possessing his invoker, and humans possessed by the deity can transform into a god-form: 500 pounds of naked, headless flab, with wet mouths that open in the palms of their hands.

- Y'golonac seems a connoisseur of, or addicted to, human misery. It seeks out those who crave vileness, usually initially of a sexual nature. Its preferred target is a repressed, bookish figure with a nascent god complex. If such a target reads the Revelations of Glaaki (how much or which volume is unclear), he opens himself up to possession by the god.

- Y'golonac can take human form, often disguising himself as a shabby purveyor of vice or old

books or both. Alternately, he can reconstruct the forms of previous hosts and manipulate them like puppets from his unknown lair.

- Y'golonac is actually another avatar of Nyarlathotep.

- "Y'golonac" is a sexually transmitted disease, both of the body and the soul. (Or of the brain chemistry, which amounts to the same thing.) Symptoms include addiction to pornography and degradation, loss of impulse control, and increased sociopathy, as well as the characteristic mouth-like stigmata on the hands, sweatiness, sallow skin, and grotesque weight gain. The disease may have accidentally sublimed from an ejaculate of Shub-Niggurath, been engineered by the cult of Glaaki, or it may be a Great Old One in its own right, an emergent consciousness comprising trillions of viruses in bloodstreams throughout the seedier quarters of Britain.

Yig
"IT SEEMS THAT YIG, THE SNAKE-GOD OF THE CENTRAL PLAINS TRIBES — PRESUMABLY THE PRIMAL SOURCE OF THE MORE SOUTHERLY QUETZALCOATL OR KUKULCAN — WAS AN ODD, HALF-ANTHROPOMORPHIC DEVIL."

— THE CURSE OF YIG

- Yig, the Father of Serpents, is a Great Old One once worshipped in Yucatan by the Maya as Kukulcan, the Winged Serpent. His worship today is mostly propitiatory, carried out by the plains tribes of North America. He may have a cult among the snake-handlers of Tennessee, or among the voodooistic Damballah worshippers of Haiti and the Caribbean. He dwells in red-litten Yoth beneath North America.

- Yig manifests as a carpet of snakes, its consciousness distributed in parallel through their reptile limbic systems and networked by hisses and rattles. Yig emerges primarily in the autumn, and specialized medicine drumming can interfere with his manifestations.

- Along with Shub-Niggurath and the twin obscenities Nug and Yeb, Yig has opposed other Great Old Ones in the past, especially Ghatanothoa. He is not implacably hostile to mankind.

- Yig fell with the other Great Old Ones and is now imprisoned in the Pit of Ngoth. He is associated with the Element of Fire.

- Yig considers all snakes to be his children, but especially those he has marked with uncanny size and a white crescent on its head. Anyone who kills a child of Yig is marked for death by snake-bite, or in special cases, for the curse of Yig: madness and deformed children.

- Yig is the soul-symbol of the serpent-folk, created by their sorceries in primal Valusia. He resembles a snake-headed, scaly humanoid, possibly an idealized Serpent Man. When the serpent-folk withdrew to Yoth after the fall of Valusia and turned to the worship of Tsathoggua, Yig destroyed them.

- Yig seeped down to Earth during the Permian Era from the planet Zandanua. It is of the form of an enormous serpent with disproportionately small legs and wings, similar to a dragon. It created reptiles in its own image and from its own genetic material.

Yog-Sothoth

"YOG-SOTHOTH KNOWS THE GATE. YOG-SOTHOTH IS THE GATE. YOG-SOTHOTH IS THE KEY AND GUARDIAN OF THE GATE. PAST, PRESENT, FUTURE, ALL ARE ONE IN YOG-SOTHOTH. HE KNOWS WHERE THE OLD ONES BROKE THROUGH OF OLD, AND WHERE THEY SHALL BREAK THROUGH AGAIN."

— THE DUNWICH HORROR

- Yog-Sothoth, the All-in-One, dwells in the interstices between the planes which compose the universe. In our local space-time it manifests as a congeries of iridescent globes which are always shifting, flowing into one another and breaking. This conglomeration is large in size, but variable, so that at one time it may appear to be 100 yards across and at another time half a mile or more.

- "Yog-Sothoth is the key to the gate, where the spheres meet." Yog-Sothoth, the Key and the Gate, holds the power to travel (or transport travelers) within the planes to reach any other time or space, because Yog-Sothoth itself is coterminous with all time and space. In this aspect, the Opener of the Way, it is known to sorcerers as the Tawil-at-'Umr, the Prolonged of Life. The Tawil-at-'Umr appears to petitioners as a figure cloaked behind a strange, shimmering, neutral-colored veil.

- Yog-Sothoth can extrude a surface of itself to resemble a curved glass or crystal ball, through which a wizard can view other planes or worlds. The curved corneas of any wizard who so gazes likewise become surfaces of Yog-Sothoth.

- Yog-Sothoth is imprisoned where all time and space intersect, held there by the unthinkable lines of cosmic force that converge there at the vanishing point of everything.

- In exchange for power over plagues and death, Moses freed Yog-Sothoth from his dimensional prison beneath Mount Sinai. Yog-Sothoth, cloaked under the name Yahweh, became the Jewish, and eventually the Christian and Moslem, God.

- Yog-Sothoth is a fifth-dimensional hyper-sphere, which can only appear in our dimension as a collection of spheres. It wishes to extend itself further into our universe, bending local reality to suit its own alien nature. It is a powerful Great Old One, but not the cosmic entity implied by its fanatical cultists and fawning acolytes.

- The mi-go worship Yog-Sothoth as "the Beyond One," and the vaporous brains of the spiral nebulae know it as an unpronounceable Sign.

- Yog-Sothoth, the Lurker at the Threshold, is a formless blackness disguised behind a mask of globes. Sorcerers

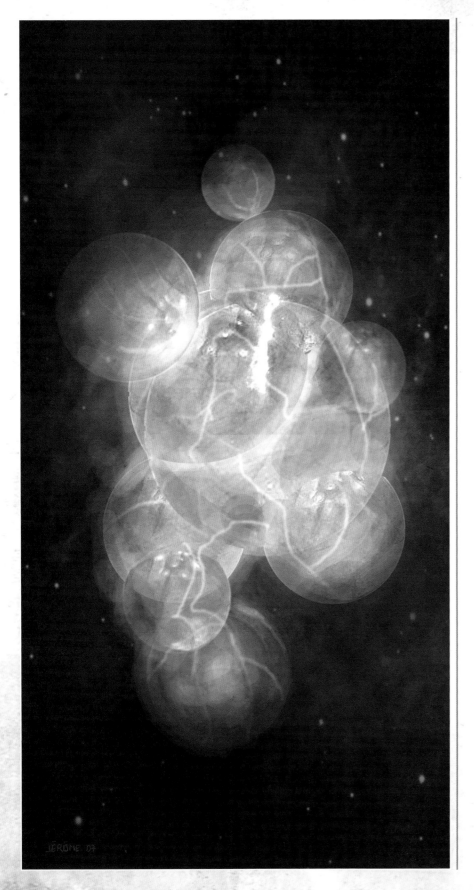

who wish to behold the face of Azathoth, or to achieve transcendence, must placate the Lurker by weakening the gates of their own reality. Under the name Choronzon, Yog-Sothoth has been incorporated into Aleister Crowley's magickal system.

• Currently, Yog-Sothoth can rotate itself anywhere in space, or anywhere in time, but not both. At some points, however, such as Sentinel Hill near Dunwich on May-Eve of 1912, the difference is so miniscule that it can break through into full space-time for minutes and yards. At such points, it seeks wizards or similar devotees who will step it down into near-matter (for example, by "breeding" it into the local biology) giving it access to linear existence and potentially breaking the barriers that limit it.

• Yog-Sothoth is the emergent consciousness of zero-point energy, the steady and irreducible state of energy omnipresent throughout the universe. It seeks to alter the crucial energy balances of our reality, opening the way for the imprisoned Great Old Ones.

• As an entity perfectly symmetrical in time, Yog-Sothoth can be invoked to raise the dead, or to return the revenant to dust. Necromancers seek out Yog-Sothoth for this and darker reasons.

• Yog-Sothoth is the Great Old One who leads the elementals of Aether, or Quintessence, the state of pure matter-energy. His terrene spawn combine quintessence with base matter.

Creating a God or Titan

Quite frankly, why bother? There are, in our eldritch opinion, way too many gods and titans festooning Lovecraft's universe as it is. Lovecraft only gave four of them starring roles in his major Mythos fiction, made up three more for ghost-written work, stole one from Clark Ashton Smith, and left the rest at a dozen or so name-dropped deities. But each successor added their own until now Wikipedia lists 83 Great Old Ones, and Lovecraft's acolytes extrude more every day. "Great Old One creep" winds up making our primordial prehuman planet look like Rick's in Casablanca – every Thing comes to Earth.

It's far more fun to take an existing god and make up something new about it. Decide that Shub-Niggurath, rather than embodying life, actually eats ecosystems; she stripped Mars to the rocks, and boiled Venus, and now she's getting ready to kill off the Earth. Expand on one of the minor titans. Promote Yig to an Outer God, the embodiment of closed-loop time, who manifests not merely in snakes but in all rings, spirals, and coils from DNA to Saturn. Snakes become merely the outermost fringes of his perceptibility intruding on us; poison becomes a transcendental experience. Take some other scary mythological being and equate it with a Great Old One. Look at Odin, the one-eyed chooser of the slain, god of hateful prophecy, who rides an eight-legged "horse." Could he be Nyarlathotep the trickster, with his three-lobed eye and eight tentacles flowing below his robe? That way your "new" god can be an avatar or an aspect of another god – which will allow you to lift all the stories about that god for your own, and set up glorious theological disputes amongst cultists everywhere.

If you simply must invent a whole new god, don't just bang out Uifghx, the Lord Of Randomly Struck Keyboards, and expect it to work. Do what Lovecraft and Derleth did. Come up with a niche that needs filling — monstrous bringer of apocalypse, trickster god, deified Wendigo, fire elemental – and fill it. Try to provide it with its own individuality, while still leaving it amorphous enough to provide challenges in all sorts of settings. Hit one theme strongly – Cthulhu looks like aquatic life, lives under the ocean, water symbolizes dreams and inspiration so he does both, fish-people worship him – and then ring as many changes on it as you can – the ocean is his trap, his cult is centered in a desert, he is struck down by a ship. Take some iconic image, or some creature that just petrifies you, and extend its scope in time and space until it is distorted and terrible. Then you'll have something worth bringing before the court of Azathoth.

He is the mortal enemy of Nodens, the Lord of the Abyss, who seeks to impose true abyssal nothingness upon Yog-Sothoth.

• Yog-Sothoth is the counter-swirl in the wave of Creation, the bubbling foam kicked up and driven backward by the universe's forward momentum. It therefore embodies all anti-Creation.

• Yog-Sothoth is the father of Cthulhu, Hastur, and Vulthoom. Yog-Sothoth also sired Nug and Yeb out of Shub-Niggurath.

• Aforgomon, a fractal of Yog-Sothoth, is worshipped in many realms, including the Dreamlands, as the Lord of Time. It envelops its enemies in a chain of incandescent fire, burning them first out of dreams and then out of history, memory, and reality altogether.

• Yog-Sothoth, or Yug-Set-Thoth, is the Aeon or Yuga, the current epoch given hateful will and personality by its parents Set and Thoth – which is to say, by a forbidden coupling of Nyarlathotep with itself in two forms.

• If everywhere is Yog-Sothoth, then Yog-Sothoth is the Outer God that awakens where it is awake. Its attempts to string its own existence together create itself, and incidentally connect the universe. It welcomes those who can perceive it, as they allow it to raise its own local complexity and pull parts of itself into the same sphere, incidentally destroying or casting adrift the universes to which it once extended.

TOMES AND MAGIC

"'MR ARMITAGE,' HE SAID, 'I CALC'LATE I'VE GOT TO TAKE THAT BOOK HOME. THEY'S THINGS IN IT I'VE GOT TO TRY UNDER SARTEN CONDITIONS THAT I CAN'T GIT HERE, EN' IT 'UD BE A MORTAL SIN TO LET A RED-TAPE RULE HOLD ME UP. LET ME TAKE IT ALONG, SIR, AN' I'LL SWAR THEY WUN'T NOBODY KNOW THE DIFFERENCE. I DUN'T NEED TO TELL YE I'LL TAKE GOOD KEER OF IT. IT WAN'T ME THAT PUT THIS DEE COPY IN THE SHAPE IT IS...'"

— THE DUNWICH HORROR

The secret knowledge of the Cthulhu Mythos, passed down from prehuman civilizations, dreamed by sensitives, or deduced by unstable geniuses, violates our understanding of natural law. Hence, it is "magic." Lovecraft strongly implies that all "magic" is merely the operations of scientific law not yet understood (or perhaps impossible to understand) by humanity. However, there are plenty of instances in which this posited alien super-science closely resembles the traditional forms of alchemy, ceremonial lore, and thaumaturgy. This might be because all genuine occult lore is actually garbled Mythos knowledge, because there are levels of reality on which conventional magic actually works (possibly only in certain places or times of the year), because ritual magical acts are necessary to focus psychic powers, or because the forces powering the universe can be accessed by any number of methods.

Any and all of these theories can be found in, or derived from, the various tomes of Mythos lore known to scholars, wizards,

JERÔME 07

and bibliophiles. And believing, or disbelieving, in any of them doesn't change what happens when a spell is cast.

Tomes

"HERE FOR THE FIRST TIME HE RECEIVED A POSITIVE SHOCK OF OBJECTIVE HORROR, FOR THE TITLES OF THOSE BOOKS TOLD HIM MUCH. THEY WERE BLACK, FORBIDDEN THINGS WHICH MOST SANE PEOPLE HAVE NEVER EVEN HEARD OF ... THE BANNED AND DREADED REPOSITORIES OF EQUIVOCAL SECRETS AND IMMEMORIAL FORMULAE ..."

— THE HAUNTER OF THE DARK

Mythos books come in two varieties: clues and resources. Any given book can be one or the other, or both over two or more adventures. A clue tome is a book containing a fact, spell, or other requirement to solve the mystery or reach the climax of the adventure. A resource tome is a volume kept handy in the Investigators' headquarters (or the restricted stacks of their local college library) for general information, a trophy, or simply something stolen from the villains to deprive them of its possession. Keepers should refrain from planting Arabic copies of the *Necronomicon* in the path of monolingual Anglophone Investigators, except as trophies.

Reading a clue tome is called **skimming**. Skimming takes one hour per 100 printed pages, or one hour per ten handwritten pages. A 1-point Library Use (or appropriate Language) spend halves (at minimum, at the Keeper's discretion) this time; a 2-point Library Use spend immediately discovers the vital fact, spell, etc with a few minutes' search. Skimming a Mythos tome provides no Cthulhu Mythos points, and does not necessarily count as using the Cthulhu Mythos ability, although it might. Unless explicitly stated otherwise, a benefit gained by skimming a tome can only be gained once per adventure, but can be repeatedly gained in multiple adventures.

Reading a resource tome is called **poring over** it. Poring over a Mythos tome usually takes place between adventures, and can take as long or as little time as the Keeper desires. Poring over a Mythos tome grants you a basic understanding of its contents, possibly including spells or other secrets. (The Keeper is always allowed to retroactively insert spells or secrets into a resource

tome, if she needs it to function as a clue tome: "Suddenly, that cryptic quatrain in the *Livre d'Ivon* makes a horrible kind of sense to you.") If the tome grants Cthulhu Mythos points, you gain them all at your first pore-over; repeated porings-over do not add further points unless stated otherwise in the tome's description. Tomes in foreign languages also require use of the corresponding Languages ability.

A Partial Mythos Library

No spells are listed for these books; the Keeper should select each individual tome for the adventure in which it appears, and choose the spells it contains likewise.

Al Azif, by Abd al-Azrad (c 730 AD; Arabic)

The original, and most complete, copy of the *Necronomicon*. No copies are known to exist. Poring over it would add +4 to your Cthulhu Mythos rating.

Necronomicon, translated by Olaus Wormius (1623; Latin)

The most common surviving text of the black book, based on a very rare Latin edition of 1228 and the lost Greek translation of 950 A.D.; there are possibly a dozen copies extant, though only six are definitely known and catalogued. Poring over it adds +3 to your Cthulhu Mythos rating. The Keeper may rule that any given copy also adds dedicated pool points to any specific investigation, based on her own judgement.

Azathoth and Others, by Edward Pickman Derby (1919; English)

A collection of the Arkham poet's

early works, it weaves local legendry and startling insights into lyrics of surprising power. It takes only an hour or so to pore over. Poring over it provides 1 dedicated pool point to Sense Trouble for investigations taking place in Arkham. It provides no Cthulhu Mythos rating if you do not already have one; if you do, it provides +1.

Celaeno Fragments, compiled by Laban Shrewsbury (1915; English)

A holographic manuscript of Dr Shrewsbury's translations from a number of epigraphic texts alleged to be copied from a ruined library orbiting the star Celaeno in the Pleiades, deposited to the Miskatonic University Library upon Dr Shrewsbury's disappearance. Forty photostatic copies were bound for an academic colloquium in 1932 after the discovery of ruins in Mongolia bearing identical glyphs. Skimming the manuscript provides 2 dedicated pool points for any Investigative ability (or 1 point for 2 abilities) involving Hastur or extraterrestrials. (The Keeper may wait to award those points rather than spoil any surprises.) Poring over the Fragments adds +1 to your Cthulhu Mythos rating.

Cultes des Goules, by François-Honoré Balfour, Comte d'Erlette (1703; French)

A necromantic work describing a ghoul cult throughout Europe. Skimming this book provides 1 dedicated pool point for any Investigative ability involving ghouls. (This ability need not be chosen while reading; the player can decide during the adventure.) Poring over it adds +1 to your Cthulhu Mythos rating.

De Vermis Mysteriis, by Ludvig Prinn (1543; Latin).

Prinn, a wizard who claimed to have been born in the 13th century, smuggled this work out just before being burnt at the stake by the Inquisition in 1542. The next year, it appeared in print at Cologne. Skimming this book provides 2 dedicated pool points for any Investigative ability (or 1 point for 2 abilities) involving Egypt, Arabic lore, or the undead. (This ability need not be chosen while reading; the player can decide during the adventure.) Poring over it provides +2 to your Cthulhu Mythos ability; both the German black-letter of 1587 and Charles Leggett's 1821 English translation of it, *The Mysteries of the Worm*, provide only +1 to Cthulhu Mythos.

Eltdown Shards, translated by the Rev. Arthur Brooke Winters-Hall (1917; English).

In 1882, two Cambridge scholars excavated 23 pottery shards from unmistakably Triassic strata at Eltdown, Sussex. Rev. Winters-Hall, a local antiquarian and fairy-lore enthusiast, privately printed his prolix, murky "translation" of the shards' oddly regular markings. Skimming his translation provides 1 dedicated pool point for Occult. Poring over it provides +1 to your Cthulhu Mythos ability; +2 if you have already encountered either the Elder Things or the Great Race of Yith.

Geheimes Mysterium von Asien, by Gottfried Mülder (1847; German)

Mülder accompanied von Junzt on his 1818-1819 journey to Inner Asia and used hypnotic recall to dictate this memoir of their journey. A pirated American version was published in Baltimore in 1849 as *Secret Mysteries of Asia, With a Commentary on the "Ghorl Nigral,"* referring to the blasphemous text (only one copy of which exists in the world) that von Junzt studied in a lamasery in Yian-Ho. Gottfried Mülder's descendant Hermann Mülder published a new limited edition for the Ahnenerbe in 1935. Skimming this book provides 2 dedicated pool points for any Investigative ability (or 1 point for 2 abilities) involving Asia, Leng, Mu, or the Tch-Tcho. (The Keeper chooses which ability, and may or may not tell the player.) Poring over it provides +1 to your Cthulhu Mythos ability.

The King in Yellow, by an unknown playwright (c. 1895; English)

This play, a translation of the suppressed French original, cannot be skimmed, but it only takes an hour or so to pore over. Once opened, you must make a Stability test against Difficulty 5 to avoid reading it completely. Once you read it, you will begin to encounter a number of unnatural phenomena with increasing Stability costs, at least once per adventure. You will see the Yellow Sign manifest where Hastur or his minions have irrupted. (This grants you 2 dedicated pool points to Sense Trouble for Hastur-related phenomena; they refresh immediately after use. Seeing the Sign is a 3-point Stability test.) After four such encounters, things get really weird – you may become attractive to Hastur and his minions, you may simply rotate into a parallel dimension centered on Carcosa, or develop a mental illness. (How to break the play's spell is up to the Keeper.) It provides +2 to your Cthulhu Mythos rating, and +1 to your Art ability rating permanently.

Livre d'Ivon, translated by Gaspard du Nord (1240; French)

Based on C Philippus Faber's 9th-century Latin *Liber Ivonis* and du Nord's own occult researches, this purports to be the work of the legendary Hyperborean wizard Eibon. Skimming this book provides 1 dedicated pool point for one of Anthropology, Astronomy, or Occult. (This ability need not be chosen while reading; the player can decide during the adventure.) Poring over it provides +1 to your Cthulhu Mythos rating; +2 if you have already encountered Tsathoggua or his minions. The Latin edition printed at 1662 in Rome may come from Faber's original manuscript; it conveys the same benefits as the French text. A manuscript translation in English from the time of King James I is rumored to exist.

Pnakotic Manuscripts, by unknown authors (various)

The *Pnakotika*, Greek magical papyri of around the time of Christ, draw oracular and mythical meanings from a set of indecipherable runes and hieroglyphics supposedly discovered in Ultima Thule. Various interpretations of it became part of the Western magical tradition; since about 1485, explorers, occultists, philologists, and archaeologists have added further texts, steles, and inscriptions in similar alphabets (as well as forgeries, honest mistakes, and trance writing) to the Pnakotic corpus, along with their commentary. There are no complete editions of all the "Pnakotic manuscripts" or "Pnakotic fragments." A three-volume set of the commonly accepted corpus at that time was printed in London in 1768 (now prohibitively expensive), but handwritten copies, academic conference proceedings, and other partial versions can be found in most top-rank university collections. With a 2-point Library Use spend and privileged collection access, an Investigator can assemble enough Pnakotic material to pore over for a +1 to his Cthulhu Mythos rating, probably copying out his research or acquiring useful books for further reference. Each time the Keeper decides that an adventure might touch on Pnakotic matters (which might be anything she chooses; even a Purist version of the *Manuscripts* would discuss ancient civilizations such as Lomar and Hyperborea, astronomy and extraterrestrials, prehuman races including the Elder Things and Great Race of Yith, Elder Gods, dream travel, and ceremonial magic), the Investigator may add another +1 to his Cthulhu Mythos rating (up to a cumulative total of +3) and receive 2 dedicated pool points for relevant Investigative abilities (Keeper's choice). The Keeper may require the Investigator to spend adventure time in research to earn this improvement, or allow it to have happened fortuitously between stories.

JEROME 07

Revelations of Glaaki, by various (1865 and 1920; English)

Multi-volume cult library of the worshipers of Y'golonac in the Severn Valley, seldom seen intact. Any one of its volumes may contain vile secrets or spells; an Investigator poring over a random volume must make a Stability test against Difficulty 4 or go out and commit some heinous sin of lechery. Even if successful, such a reader may, however, thereafter use any Interpersonal ability to convince a cultist of Y'golonac of his own membership in the sect. Only the elusive Volume 12 provides a +1 to Cthulhu Mythos for those who pore over its lovingly detailed etchings.

Seven Cryptical Books of Hsan, ascribed to "Hsan the Greater" (ca. 180 BC; Chinese)

The *Ch'i Pen Shu Hsieh Le Tsui An*, or *Seven Books Written in Darkness*, are attributed to "Hsan the Greater," a legendary sage variously dated as far back as 4200 BC. The oldest known version is a redacted text, prepared from scraps that survived the book burnings of 213 BC by the first Ch'in emperor. The confirmed existence of Thibetan copies implies that Hsan originally translated the *Seven Books* from some other unknown Asian language. The Thibetan versions are rumored to diverge a great deal from the Chinese, and contain far blacker secrets. Skimming any Chinese version, even the "Polyglot Hsan" printed anonymously in Shanghai in 1920 as *The Seven Cryptical Books of Earth* (which includes French and Russian translations), provides 2 dedicated pool points for any Investigative ability (or 1 point for 2 abilities) involving China or dreams; poring over it provides +1 to your Cthulhu Mythos rating.

Testament of Carnamagos, by Carnamagos of Tanais (ca. 500 BC; Tsath-Yo (Hyperborean))

Carnamagos claimed to have traveled to the hidden desert of griffins in Cimmeria, and wrote this narrative of what he learned about the past and future. All known surviving copies are in Greek. Skimming it provides 1 dedicated pool point for any Investigative ability involving Quachil Uttaus or time travel. (The Keeper may wait to award those points rather than spoil any surprises.) Poring over it provides +1 to your Cthulhu Mythos rating. There are rumors of copies bound in shagreen and written in alien ichor that provide far more complete knowledge, but reading even a few lines from such ages the unprepared reader and his surroundings by 10 years and summons Quachil Uttaus directly. The most famous such copy was discovered in a Greco-Bactrian tomb in 935 A.D.

Thaumaturgical Prodigies in the New-England Canaan, by Rev. Ward Phillips (1788 and 1801; English)

A history, in sermon form, of strange and unholy phenomena in New England from 1620 to the Revolution. Skimming this book provides 1 dedicated pool point for History, applicable only to New England during that time period. It can be skimmed multiple times during an adventure. It provides no Cthulhu Mythos rating if you do not already have one; if you do, it provides +1.

Creating a Tome

By contrast with gods, the more tomes the merrier. Every cultist's library shouldn't logically contain yet another *Necronomicon* or *Nameless Cults* – for vanishingly rare books, they show up a lot in the stories. Instead, they should have tomes crafted for their own purposes, that spring from their own history, and that feed their own delusions.

If you're planting a tome, first decide if it's merely a clue tome – in which case, it can be a single scroll, potsherd, bas-relief, record album, diary, or such – or a full-on resource tome. If you decide to go ahead with a full book-style tome, take this opportunity to use it to define your cult further. Is this cult a vast, sprawling church with scriptures, apocrypha, hymnals, psalteries, commentaries, hagiographies, ordinals, missals, visionary texts, and sermon collections? Is it a narrower sect with one holy book from which everything must spring? Did this cult get access to one stream of Mythos knowledge or two, and how did they blend them? The books in their unholy sanctuary can spell that out.

Come up with the book's language or languages – did it begin as a prehuman text? (What sort? Religious? Scientific? Dream diary?) What's the story of its translation? Does the original exist? Is there only one hand-written copy in the world? Decide its author, and decide who (or what) the author claimed to be in his book. Finally, tweak the subject matter not just to what's going on in this adventure, but to larger themes you want your campaign to cover. If the Investigators are going to take a resource tome home, give them reasons to look in it again rather than just being another notch on their bookshelf.

Its mechanical effects can be extrapolated from the examples given. In general, a major Mythos tome grants a +2 to Cthulhu Mythos; a minor one grants +1. Dedicated pool points should be related to the book's subject matter, but are at the Keeper's entire discretion. They might only show up on multiple readings, for example – such books aren't written by particularly stable or organized authors, as it happens.

Thirteenth ("Threshold") Sonata (Op 76), by Aleksandr Scriabin (1915?)

The mad composer Scriabin published ten piano sonatas, including Op 68, the "Black Mass" sonata. When he died in 1915, he was planning a multi-media performance in the Himalayas, the *Mysterium*, that would bring about the end of the world. A cult of Russian Hermetic magi smuggled this manuscript out after the Revolution, and has been selling copies on the occult black market and to musical enthusiasts to raise funds. Playing this sonata requires a 1-point Art (Piano) spend, takes about ten minutes, and costs 3 Stability. This grants you 2 dedicated pool points in Sense Trouble and 1 in Cthulhu Mythos, all for Yog-Sothoth-related phenomena only; they refresh immediately after use.

Unaussprechlichen Kulten, by Friedrich Wilhelm von Junzt (1839; German)

A travelogue of the horrific, providing ample details of many Mythos cults, conspiracies, and activities. Skimming this book provides 1 dedicated pool point for any Investigative ability involving cults, usable once during the adventure. (The Keeper chooses which ability, and may or may not tell the player.) Poring over it adds +2 to your Cthulhu Mythos rating; its bastardized English translations under the title *Nameless Cults* (Bridewall, 1845; Golden Goblin, 1909) provide only +1 to Cthulhu Mythos and an Investigative boost only every other adventure, or when the Keeper decides it does.

SPELLS

"PROFESSOR UPHAM ESPECIALLY LIKED HIS DEMONSTRATION OF THE KINSHIP OF HIGHER MATHEMATICS TO CERTAIN PHASES OF MAGICAL LORE TRANSMITTED DOWN THE AGES FROM AN INEFFABLE ANTIQUITY — HUMAN OR PRE-HUMAN — WHOSE KNOWLEDGE OF THE COSMOS AND ITS LAWS WAS GREATER THAN OURS."

— THE DREAMS IN THE WITCH-HOUSE

Lovecraftian magic, as depicted in the stories, concerns itself primarily with contacting certain Outside dimensions, powers, forces, or beings. Making this connection is what makes Lovecraftian magic so very dangerous. The tales imply that once this Outside power is mastered (or once the wizard has completely surrendered to it), anything is possible. The magus can command storms, transcend time and space, make himself immortal, perceive the past and future, and otherwise exempt himself from natural law.

Any such magic will be aimed at, not wielded by, Investigators. By the time any human could utilize such forces, her sanity and humanity would have been completely corroded. Even the magics listed here, the fumblings at the latch as it were, are more likely to be hostile than helpful. That said, a few Pulp-style magics have been added for Keepers who want to mix things up.

Not all the spells possible in all possible Mythos universes are listed. The Keeper is free to personalize or extrapolate from the spells given in this section, or even to decide that helpful, human magic – healing spells and the like – exists, perhaps a last gift from the weak gods of Earth to their worshipers.

Learning Spells

An Investigator can learn a spell during an adventure from a clue tome, a convenient scroll or inscription, or from a human (or inhuman) teacher. Learning a spell during an adventure takes a dramatically appropriate amount of time; usually between one and six hours, or enough time to get to the next scene. ("Three days later, the tribal shaman pronounces you ready for the rite. And just in time, too, as the fisherfolk have reported the lloigor appearing again in the lake.") Appropriate spends (Physics for mathematical formulae, Languages or Archaeology for chants written in foreign tongues, Art for sung or danced spells, etc) will reduce learning time appropriately. Learning a spell during an adventure requires a Stability test, usually at Difficulty 4. At the Keeper's discretion, other abilities (Physics, Languages, Art, etc as above) may have to be used before the spell can be learned.

Learning spells as the result of a Mythos epiphany or communion with an Outer God is usually instantaneous, and seldom requires a test, except the Stability test inherent in the process of communing with an Outer God.

Between investigations, an Investigator can learn a spell from a resource tome, a teacher, an arcane rite, or any other way he can convince the Keeper to allow. The time required is however much time elapses between adventures, or 1 to 6 months, again at the Keeper's discretion. Spends will not speed this process along.

Casting Spells

Spells come in one of two kinds, incantations and rituals. Either type of spell may require an actual chant or a series of arcane actions, or only a moment of hyper-mathematical visualization. Either type of spell may take a few minutes or many weeks. They are only differentiated mechanically. In game terms, an **incantation** requires only a simple test, usually of Stability. (Difficulties and Stability losses for each spell appear in the descriptions.) Contrarily, a **ritual** in game terms requires a contest, usually against a summoned creature or the fabric of space-time. Such things resist using an ad hoc pool called the **Inertia pool**. Its recommended size appears in the spell writeups below, but can and should be altered at will by the Keeper.

Almost all spells require the expenditure of pool points, usually from Stability. If a spell allows the expenditure of another ability in addition to Stability, you can swap one ability for the other at twice the cost, unless the spell description sets a different ratio or forbids swapping.

> *Create Hyperspace Gate requires 2 Stability or 4 Health, so it could be cast with 1 Stability and 2 Health.*

A failed spell costs the half the listed amount.

Multiple sorcerers can share the cost of casting spells. Those who know the spell in question can share costs in cooperation (see p. 58, above). Only the leader must make the Stability test. Those who do not know the spell in question and willingly partake in the casting may spend 3 points to contribute 1 to the spell.

Some spells can be cast only at a certain place, under certain stars, or at a certain time. Spells may require physical components, specific postures or gestures, or anything else the Keeper can dream up.

Unless otherwise noted, no spell can be cast while actively engaging in combat or while fleeing. (However, a sorcerer could, for example, use Weapons to stab someone, then cast a 1-round spell, then use Weapons again in the third round.) Unless otherwise noted, a spell completed during combat goes off at the end of the round.

Casting a spell definitely counts as a Mythos shock, if the concomitant Stability loss is grave enough to potentially cost the spellcaster Sanity.

Sanity 0 wizards never need to make a test to cast an incantation; it occurs automatically. They must pay Stability and Health, but only at half the listed cost (round up). Spell-casting races and creatures may pay points from any pool at the listed Stability cost. It is up to the Keeper whether such wizards or creatures need to make tests during ritual contests, although wizards should always have to make tests during ritual contests against Investigators.

Sample Mythos Incantations

⊕ Brew Space-Mead

This spell creates a magical drink that reorients the imbiber's perceptions. In very small amounts (a few drops on the fingertip), it expands perception immensely, giving the imbiber a "god's-eye view" of his surroundings, letting him hear whispers and noises from coterminous dimensions, and so forth. It can also create a sort of vague mental communion with a fellow-imbiber: not full communication, but a general sense of distance and urgency, combined with occasional bursts of strong emotion and clear sensation. The game-mechanical effects of this small sip are to make Sense Trouble an Investigative ability – the Investigator can notice all trouble in range for as long as the taste lasts. (Sense Trouble spends allow the imbiber to find ways past such trouble.) It also, of course, lets the Keeper feed him clues, mess with his head, and demand extra Stability tests when the imbiber perceives horrible things tracking him through the soft places of the local geometry. While on the mead, the imbiber is dozy, distracted, and obviously drug-addled in conversation, which may affect Interpersonal abilities. If the imbiber is attacked, he can throw off the mead's effects after one round of confusion.

In a larger dose (a thimble-full, or three small sips), the mead rotates the imbiber's perception almost entirely out of this reality and into a sort of pocket wormhole. This rotation most resembles a powerful, overwhelming hallucinogenic trip, and has the side effect of allowing the imbiber to withstand journeys through the vacuum and vicissitudes of interstellar space. The imbiber will still need to have arranged transport, such as a ride on a summoned byakhee.

The mead is made from honey grown from bees raised under extremely specific magical conditions – fed only on peyote pollen and flown only under the constellation Auriga, for example – and four other ingredients chosen by the Keeper. At least one of the ingredients should be extra-terrestrial or extra-planar, and all should be expensive, rare, and possibly illegal or poisonous.

Stability Test Difficulty: 4 (3 with a Biology, Outdoorsman, or Craft (Brewing) spend) to brew; 2 to imbibe.

Cost: 20 Stability per dose to brew, which can be spent over several nights of preparation; 2 for a small sip, 3 for the full dose.

Time: Brewing space-mead takes a week before Stability cost can be paid; a small sip lasts for the imbiber's current Stability pool in hours, and the full dose lasts for the duration of the space voyage. Imbibing the mead takes one round, but can be done while fleeing.

Compound Liao

Sometimes called the Plutonian Drug, liao is compounded from the black lotus of Inner and Southeast Asia. It debinds the user's perception from linear time. In "street" form its only real effect is to make users far more susceptible to Mythos invasion or

Contact Deity Spells

Spells that allow the caster to commune with the horrific deities of the Cthulhu Mythos are almost exclusively the domain of those deities' worshippers. Occasionally, a hubristic sorcerer of great power will attempt to strike a deal with a Great Old One, usually for some unobtainable bit of lore or a fragment of the being's power. Contacting an imprisoned or slumbering deity may involve travel to the site of its repose, or at least to a major fane connected with its worship now or in the past. Possession of, or proximity to, a true idol, bas-relief, relic, or scripture of the god usually makes contact less difficult. Knowing one Contact Deity spell is no help with any other.

With a successful casting, the deity (or one of its aspects or avatars) contacts the caster, usually in dreams or visions. Occasionally, it will send a servitor being to speak through, or possess a nearby worshipper. Such contact will likely involve further Stability tests, and possibly Sanity loss.

The god will begin the contact in a semi-friendly manner, but will not aid non-worshippers without an exceptionally good reason. Deities are quick to anger; a caster who wastes the being's time, oversteps her bounds, or seems weak or foolish is likely to get squished, driven mad, possessed, or otherwise toyed with for a brief period.

Other possible Contact Deity spells not detailed here include Contact Chaugnar Faugn, Contact Daoloth, Contact Ghatanothoa, Contact Gol-Goroth, Contact Y'golonac, and Contact Yig.

parasitism; it lowers the user's Stability by three quarters (round up) for purposes of Stability tests involving hostile or invasive magic, Mythos shocks, and so forth. In pure form, however, it grants engrossing visions of previous (or future) times, each more staggering than the last. It does not let the user pick and choose a time and place, but moves the user's perception along his life-line back through his ancestry (or forward through his descendants), through his evolutionary past, and eventually to the ultimate source of all terrestrial life, Ubbo-Sathla. Users with alien blood (or in campaigns in which Arrhenius' panspermia theory is true) might vision-quest off Earth entirely. Extended trips into the deep past run the risk of encountering the Hounds of Tindalos (see p. 135).

In either form, liao is extremely addictive.

Keepers should not allow liao to solve immediate mysteries like "who killed Jeremiah Roxbury last week" or "will we be ambushed by cultists if we stop in Singapore." In adventures, its use should provide insight into the historical past or the stark and terrible (and inevitable) future. Or just drive people crazy.

Stability Test Difficulty: 5 (4 with Pharmacy or with a Biology spend; 3 with a Pharmacy spend) to compound; 2 to imbibe the first time. Thereafter, it requires a Stability test at Difficulty 3 to avoid taking a second dose; the Difficulty increases by 1 for each additional dose consumed. Once it reaches 8, the user will devote all his time and effort to compounding more liao.

Cost: 2 Stability per dose to compound; 4 to take liao, plus any losses from the horrors that inevitably get unveiled.

Time: With a supply of black lotus (obtaining which might be an adventure in itself), compounding liao takes only a day; a liao trip lasts two or three hours from the viewpoint of an observer.

Contact Cthulhu

This sonorous chant sensitizes the caster to Cthulhu's dream wavelength. The Dreamer in the Deeps sends a nightmarish vision to all who would dream of him; those who withstand it may come to his notice.

Stability Test Difficulty: 5 (4 by the ocean or near a Cthulhoid cult center)

Cost: 3 Stability and 1 Sanity, plus any loss from the nightmare.

Time: One hour to cast on each of three nights; Cthulhu's nightmare comes on the third night when the caster sleeps.

Contact Deep Ones

May only be cast near a body of salt or brackish water connected somehow to the ocean. In some games, it must be cast near a Deep One colony. The spell includes throwing specially inscribed stones into the water. These stones may be further enchanted (see Enchant Item, p. 115), but it is not necessary.

Stability Test Difficulty: 4

Cost: 3 Stability

Time: Six minutes; the Deep Ones will appear on the next incoming tide.

Contact Ghoul

May be cast only on moonlit nights in a burying ground at least a century old. This spell does not guarantee safety from ghoul attacks, but the ghouls contacted will stop to see what the caster wants before deciding whether to dismember him for sweetbreads.

Stability Test Difficulty: 4

Cost: 3 Stability

Time: Three minutes of frenzied barking in ghoulish; the ghouls will appear before morning.

Contact Mi-Go

Must be cast outside the Earth's atmosphere, via a powerful radio broadcast, or in a mountain range currently mined by the fungi from Yuggoth, Suitable mountain ranges include the Appalachians, Adirondacks, Andes, Himalayas, and Balkans.

Stability Test Difficulty: 4

Cost: 4 Stability

Time: Ten minutes of buzzing incantation; the mi-go will appear on the next moonless night.

Contact Nyarlathotep

There are as many different forms of this spell as there are forms of Nyarlathotep. They all place the user in contact with the Crawling Chaos, in whichever form they most expect to see him. Most often, Nyarlathotep will draw them to a meeting of his worshippers, at which

---

Contact Creature Spells

Spell-casters might use these spells to learn more about prehistoric lore, alien super-science, the true geometries of the world, or other spells. Alternately, casting such a spell is a good way to begin negotiations with an alien race, or with a colony of such creatures known to infest some dismal reach. The caster should always have a deliberate, specific goal in mind.

A successful contact spell always requires that such a creature (or colony of creatures) lurks within a convenient distance. For some creatures, expeditions to blasted ruins or a single cavern deep below Iceland may be necessary before the spell can be cast successfully.

Enough creatures will usually appear to equal or exceed the perceived threat level of the caster and any companions, and they will usually appear only in areas where they feel safe or unobserved. The contacted creatures will appear with their own agenda. This may involve devouring the caster, so wise wizards will bring presents or offerings. Such interactions afford the Keeper excellent opportunities for creepy alien roleplaying.

Knowing one Contact Creature spell is no help with any other. All contacts will likely involve more Stability tests for seeing or otherwise encountering the contacted being. Other potential Contact Creature spells not detailed here include Contact Elder Thing, Contact Flying Polyp, Contact Formless Spawn, Contact Gnoph-Keh, Contact Hound of Tindalos, Contact Lloigor, Contact Masqut, Contact Sand-Dweller, and Contact Serpent-Folk. Some of these "spells" might simply be social signals of the "let's talk" variety, like the "silent trade" used in tropical Africa.

---

the caster will be amazed to recognize some participants. (This recognition may, of course, be illusory. Nyarlathotep is tricky that way.) Nyarlathotep is more likely to physically appear at such ceremonies; lone sorcerers may receive a visit from a rat-thing or other familiar creature, or experience the Mighty Messenger in a dream or hallucination.

Stability Test Difficulty:
5 (Difficulty 4 with Occult, Anthropology, or Theology)

Cost: 3 Stability and 1 Sanity; first-time contactees of Nyarlathotep must also sacrifice 1 Stability *rating point* to the dark god. (Such a sacrifice automatically costs

1 Sanity *rating point* as well.) Nyarlathotep will often offer to replace such sacrifices with some mark of his own: in the witch-cult, for example, this would be a black mark (similar to a mole) on the witch's body made by the god's finger. In game terms, Nyarlathotep grants the worshipper 2 Stability rating points – which the Keeper (as the Mocking One's proxy) can take away at any time. Nyarlathotep willingly repeats such 1-for-2 exchanges with promising or worthy contactees until he controls their mind and will utterly.

Time: varies.

Contact Rat-Thing

The caster makes a chalked mark or sigil on the wall and waits all night. The wall must be part of a site or structure infested (now or in the past) by a rat-thing or rat-things. Such structures might include old witch-houses, decayed mansions, former wizards' castles, and slum garrets in dubious neighborhoods.

Stability Test Difficulty: 4

Cost: 2 Stability

Time: Four minutes to chalk the sign; the rat-thing will appear that night or at the next new moon.

Contact Star-Spawn

This spell contacts one of the Xothian subordinates of Cthulhu; they may appear in person, send a nightmare, or dispatch Deep Ones in telepathic communion with them. This spell must be cast on the seacoast, or directly over one of the subterranean abysses inhabited by a Xothian Watcher (see p. 153). Most such spots have some ruined temple or other indication of the correct spot for contact.

Stability Test Difficulty: 4 (3 if cast in a spot or by a caster sensitized to Cthulhu's dreams)

Cost: 3 Stability

Time: Five minutes; Star-Spawn will respond immediately, and they or their proxies will arrive as soon as feasible.

Contact Tsathoggua

Tsathoggua appears in spirit form, as a hazy and translucent projection. He speaks audibly to the caster, his voice appearing to echo from a dark corner. He will only appear to a lone caster.

Stability Test Difficulty: 8 (4 with an idol or other accurate depiction of Tsathoggua)

Cost: 6 Stability and 1 Sanity

Time: Four hours of chanting and invocation

Create Hyperspace Gate

Creates a gate joining two points through hyperspace. The Keeper may require the caster to have seen the destination point, if only in a dream or vision. This spell requires some sort of drawn, painted, or chalked marks. Using an already created gate costs 1 Stability, in addition to any costs for the sights or threats at the destination.

The destination need not be in the four-dimensional universe of conventional space-time; this spell allows travel to other dimensions, planes, and pocket universes, but only with a guide or guiding vision.

Stability Test Difficulty: 5 (4 with Physics, 3 with a Physics spend)

Cost: 2 Stability or 4 Health, doubled per increment of distance (continental, global, interplanetary, interstellar, intergalactic). Unless the Keeper rules otherwise, or the spell is cast at a point where the plane is tangent to Earth (and therefore only "global"), an inter-planar Gate costs the same as an interstellar gate (16 Stability or 32 Health). For each 4 Health points spent from the caster's pool, lose 1 point from the caster's Health *rating*.

Time: One hour (ten minutes with Physics, one minute with a Physics spend)

Dho-Hna Formula

This incantation allows the caster to behold the inner city at the two magnetic poles of Earth, and from that vantage point, to see other arcane locations, planets, realms, abysses, and dimensions of being. The Dho-Hna Formula crosses the ultimate gulf beyond space and time, so the caster could attempt to view Valusia, Yhe, or other lost lands. Each casting of the Formula can reach only one other vision target besides the inner city.

In some editions of the *Necronomicon*, the Dho-Hna Formula includes the creation of a (temporary) hyperspace gate to the location under view. The caster returns exactly one sidereal day later. This full formula adds one quarter of the cost (minimum 1 Stability or 2 Health) of the analogous Create Hyperspace Gate spell to the cost of casting the Formula.

Stability Test Difficulty: 6 (5 with Cthulhu Mythos)

Cost: 3 Stability and 1 Sanity

Time: Five minutes; the vision-quest lasts a varying amount of time both subjectively and objectively.

Dread Name of Azathoth

By repeating the first syllables of this secret name of Azathoth, the caster demonstrates her familiarity with the Mythos in fearsome fashion.

In game terms, it allows her to use interpersonal abilities in dealings with lesser servitor species (e.g., byakhee, children of Yig, dimensional shamblers, formless spawn, rat-things, shantaks) and lesser independent races (e.g., Deep Ones, Elder Things, ghouls, K'n-yani, masqut, mi-go, sand-dwellers, serpent-folk, shan, star vampires, Tcho-Tcho, Yithians). Using such abilities with nonhumans requires a spend of 2 pool points.

Pronouncing the final syllable of Azathoth's Dread Name requires a second Stability test, and a second expenditure of points. It is an aggressive attack, draining 1 pool point of Stability (or Health from any nonhuman foe) per point spent by the caster to make the second Stability test. Casters cannot cooperate to utter the final syllable of Azathoth's Dread Name.

Beginning a negotiation with an alien being by speaking the first syllables of the Dread Name is the same as beginning a negotiation with a human being by pulling out a gun. You'll get their attention, but you have no reason to complain if you get shot.

Stability Test Difficulty: 5 (4 with Languages)

Cost: 3 Stability or 6 Health

Time: instantaneous; it can be spoken before combat begins

Elder Sign
Also known as the Sign of Kish. This star-shaped (or swastika-shaped, or branch-shaped, depending on your sources) symbol seals a path or entrance against the minions of the Great Old Ones or the Outer Gods. The symbol must be engraved in a physical object, sealed in lead or brass, or drawn on the threshold. An Elder Sign amulet does *not* protect the wearer against attack.

Star-Stones of Mnar

"S'POSE THEY MUSTA HAD, ARTER ALL, THEM OLD MAGIC SIGNS AS THE SEA-THINGS SAYS WAS THE ONLY THINGS THEY WAS AFEARD OF... IN SOME PLACES, THEY WAS LITTLE STONES STREWED ABAOUT – LIKE CHARMS – WITH SOMETHIN' ON 'EM LIKE WHAT YE CALL A SWASTIKA NAOWADAYS. PROB'LY THEM WAS THE OLD ONES' SIGNS."

— THE SHADOW OVER INNSMOUTH

In *The Shadow Over Innsmouth* and *At the Mountains of Madness*, Lovecraft implies that an Elder Sign amulet might have protective powers against Deep Ones and even shoggoths. In some Mythos tales, especially those of August Derleth, a star-shaped Elder Sign amulet *does* protect the wearer against attack by any servitor species, including shoggoths, Deep Ones, byakhee, Serpent-Folk, etc. The Keeper may decree that such protective Signs must be cast and carven into the grey stone of Mnar, which is not easy to come by, save by searching out old cosmic battlefields in Antarctica or the South Pacific and scavenging it.

Servitor entities cannot personally or magically attack the wielder of such a Sign directly, although they can collapse pillars or mount indirect attacks. Servitor entities with Firearms (or similar abilities) *can* attack the bearer of a Sign, although the bearer's Hit Threshold is increased by 2 against such attacks. Even in Derleth, though, sufficiently powerful beings such as the Star-Spawn of Cthulhu can overcome such amulets. In general, any creature *except shoggoths* with a Stability Loss bonus of +3 or higher can ignore a brandished Elder Sign amulet, although they may still be barred from entry by a cast Elder Sign spell.

Rumors whisper of a combination Elder Sign and Gate spell that hangs the Sign in intangible hyperspace. Such a spell would be very difficult and taxing to cast.

Stability Test Difficulty: 4

Cost: 1 Stability *rating* point

Time: Five minutes

Enchant Item:
Under this generic heading fall the various enchanted knives, books, chains, whistles, stones, towers, menhirs, etc used for casting Mythos spells. Each sort of enchantment is a different spell, and the Keeper should

feel free to detail the exact ingredients or actions required for a given enchantment. Any enchanted weapon *must* be used to take a life, triggering the appropriate Stability test.

Stability Test Difficulty: 5 (4 with relevant Craft or Art spend)

Cost: 3 Stability pool points, and a minimum of 1 Stability *rating* point. For each 1 *additional* sacrificed rating point, the item adds 1 to all relevant casting rolls for its associated spell, and provides 1 dedicated pool point for contests if the spell is a ritual.

More conventional "black magic" sorts of item

enchantments may allow the sacrifice of Health rating points instead of Stability rating points, but it requires 5 sacrificed Health rating points to add 1 to relevant casting rolls. Traditionally, the caster takes most of these Health rating points from others, but must always contribute at least 1 of his own.

Time: Varies, but usually weeks or months

Hoy-Dhin Chant

This chant summons the soft, flaky blood of Yibb-Tstll, known to sorcerers as "The Black." The nefandous wisps rain down out of the air around the target, falling toward him from all directions and splashily adhering to his body. After the second round of casting, the target is blind; after the third round of casting, he must resist drowning in The Black (see Drowning, p. 68) each round until he dies or the caster ceases the chant. Large quantities of running water (e.g., a fire hose or fast-moving river) will dissolve or dispel The Black in 2 rounds.

According to the *Cthaat Aquadingen,* when The Black drains back into Yibb-Tstll, it takes the souls of its victims with it.

Stability Test Difficulty: 5 (4 with Art (Singing))

Cost: 3 Stability per round

Time: Two minutes of hauntingly beautiful song to begin

Oil of Alhazred

This eldritch lamp oil was reputedly used by Abdul Alhazred to invoke the visions and dreams that he transcribed into the

Necronomicon. Its ingredients are many and subtle, involve killing and rendering the fat and aqueous humor of some horrific Mythos creature, and are up to the Keeper to specify in her campaign.

Once a lamp is burning with the Oil of Alhazred, it gives off vaporous light that curls around the face, especially the eyes and nostrils, of its user. By this light, the user can do one of these things:

- Examine a Mythos artifact and receive a vision related to its use, manufacture, or dedication (usually resulting in another Stability test); or

- Examine a depiction of a Mythos god or creature and receive a vision of that god or creature in its true form (almost inevitably resulting in another Stability test); or

- See the invisible warpings or lines of force indicating the presence of a gate, planar contact, immaterial monster, hyper-gravitic idol, alien meteor, etc; in game terms, an automatically successful use of Sense Trouble; or

- Receive additional insights from the study of Mythos tomes; in game terms, **skimming** a Mythos book by the light of the Oil of Alhazred immediately reveals the relevant passage or information, while **poring over** a Mythos book by this eerie lambency adds +1 to the book's Cthulhu Mythos rating bonus.

Stability Test Difficulty: 5 (4 with a Chemistry or Occult spend) to blend; 3 to use

Cost: 3 Stability to compound; 2 Stability plus 2 other points from a relevant pool (e.g., Anthropology, Art History, Cthulhu Mythos, Languages, Occult, or Sense Trouble) to use.

Time: Seven bright, sunshine-filled days to blend; five minutes to light and use

Powder of Ibn-Ghazi

Whether blown from a tube, sprayed from an insecticide gun, or sprinkled by hand, this grayish powder attracts ultra-terrene matter-energy into the four-dimensional universe. Its primary use is to make invisible beings visible, but (at the Keeper's discretion) it also allows some spells of banishment or dismissal to work more effectively. One vial of the powder works on one being, object, or monster, regardless of size. It lasts for ten heartbeats, or 3 combat rounds, and must be delivered from no farther than close range. Compounding this powder requires mummy dust, powdered silver nitrate, and other chemicals available in a good laboratory.

Stability Test Difficulty: 3 (2 with Chemistry or Occult) to compound; none to use

Cost: 1 Stability or 2 Chemistry or Occult to compound one vial's worth; none to use, although seeing the revealed thing may well force a further Stability test

Time: 12 hours of exacting labor (six hours with access to a good laboratory, less yet with a Chemistry or Occult spend) to compound; 1 round to use

Summoning and Binding Spells

Traditionally a way for wizards to obtain eldritch credibility, muscle, or transportation, summoning and binding spells exist for virtually all "servitor races," meaning races created initially as slave entities of one or another god, titan, or species. Most such spells are lost, or involve techniques only applicable to their creators, or only recoverable with a great deal of labor. (The long-term Deep One plan to "reverse engineer" the shoggoth to serve the beings it was created to destroy is probably the best-known such example.) Knowing one such spell grants no insight into any other such spell. Summon/Bind spells exist for children of Yig, shantaks, space-eaters, and perhaps even dholes, in addition to those detailed here. Unless explicitly described otherwise, all summoning spells bring only one creature.

Usually, a summoning spell brings the creature already bound to the wizard, although the Keeper is free to rule that a failed Stability test doesn't short-circuit the spell, but rather signals to the entity that its would-be master is weak and foolish. In such circumstances, the creature usually attacks, carries off, or consumes its caller. Whether bound or not, seeing a summoned creature results in another Stability test for the caster and any fellow witnesses.

A successful binding, on the other hand, forces the thing to forbear eviscerating you, and to instead follow one specific, limited instruction. ("Leave this dimension now" or "Kill that wizard," but not "Never return to Earth" or "Protect me from harm forever.") Unless the Keeper rules otherwise, learning a summoning spell includes the binding ritual; you can also cast the binding ritual by itself if you know it and fortuitously stumble across an unbound entity. Unless the rules explicitly state otherwise, such binding takes 2 combat rounds, and cannot be performed by someone fighting or fleeing the creature. It is up to the Keeper whether such bindings also require the same impedimenta as their complementary summonings.

For most lesser creatures, the summoning is an **incantation** in rules terms – beings of the Mythos are seemingly engineered to respond automatically to certain actions, chants, or emblems. (Alternatively, casting a "summoning" spell merely dimensionally rotates the caster to where such creatures already are. As Einstein pointed out, it's all relative.) Stumbling across an unbound creature and binding it is always a **ritual** in rules terms, and sets up a contest – usually Stability vs Inertia — between the Investigator and the creature. Individual spell descriptions provide those values if need be.

Shrivelling

This powerful attack spell blackens and twists the flesh of a target regardless of armor. It works on any target at long range or closer that the caster can see or smell.

After the test to cast the spell, the caster makes a second Stability test against the target's current Stability, modified by -2 if the caster holds a piece of the target's hair, bloodstain, or other physical sample. For every point by which the caster succeeds at that test, the target loses 1 Health pool point and 1 Health *rating point*.

Stability Test Difficulty: 4

Cost: 4 Stability

Time: 2 rounds

Sign of Eibon

This glyph resembles a three-legged swastika. Correctly drawn, it makes the wearer invisible to minions of Nyarlathotep, though not to the Crawling Chaos itself.

Stability Test Difficulty: 4

Cost: 2 Stability to create; plus 2 more every time it operates

Time: Five minutes to create

Sign of Koth

This is the Sign emblazoned on the gateways leading from the Dreamlands to Earth. When drawn on the face or head, this weird, curvilinear Sign prevents all dreams, including dream-sendings from Cthulhu. The wearer can obviously not enter the Dreamlands. Going without dreams is eventually mentally unhealthy; after the first week, the wearer refreshes Stability pool points at twice the normal rate. After the first two weeks, treat the wearer as **shaken**. After the first month, the wearer loses 1 *rating* point of Stability per month, eventually bottoming out at 3.

Performed as a gesture in the Dreamlands, it has the same basic effect on dream beings as uttering the first syllables of the Dread Name of Azathoth has on Mythos creatures.

Stability Test Difficulty: 4

Cost: 2 Stability

Time: Five minutes (instantaneous gesture in the Dreamlands)

Summon/Bind Byakhee

May only be cast at a location open to the night air. The caster must blow an enchanted whistle made from meteoric iron, and then chant: *"Iä! Iä! Hastur! Hastur cf'ayak 'vulgtmm, vugtlagln, vulgtmm! A'! A'! Hastur!"* The summoned byakhee will flap down out of the sky, crusted with ice.

An unbound byakhee resists binding with an Inertia of 8.

Stability Test Difficulty: 4

Cost: 4 Stability or 8 Fleeing (halved if Aldebaran is above the horizon)

Time: Two minutes

Summon/Bind Dark Young of Shub-Niggurath

May only be cast outdoors at night, in a wood, jungle, marsh, or other heavily vegetated location. The caster must use a blade to mutilate an animal (or person) massing at least 90 lbs. As the blood runs out, she must chant a litany to Shub-Niggurath. The summoned Dark Young will stalk from the deepest, darkest part of the surrounding vegetation when the creature dies.

An unbound Dark Young resists

binding with an Inertia of 15.

Stability Test Difficulty: 5 (4 with Outdoorsman spend), following a 2-point test for sacrificing an animal, or a 5-point test for sacrificing a human being

Cost: 5 Stability

Time: Five minutes per Health point of the sacrificed creature

Summon/Bind Dimensional Shambler

The caster must cut a path in the air with a dagger made entirely of one metallic element (e.g., gold, silver, platinum, aluminum). Alloy daggers – steel, brass, etc – will not work, although the dagger can have a hilt or handle of any material. The shambler will emerge from the path the caster has carved for it.

An unbound shambler resists binding with an Inertia of 8.

Stability Test Difficulty: 4

Cost: 3 Stability

Time: Seven minutes

Summon/Bind Hunting Horror

May only be cast in darkness. (Starlight is acceptable, but not bright city lights.) The caster must chant, and prepare a blood sacrifice by wounding and restraining a sentient being. The horror emerges from the darkest part of the sky (or cavern or chamber, if summoned indoors) and devours the sacrifice. If no suitable sacrifice is within the immediate area, the horror devours the caster and departs.

An unbound hunting horror resists binding with an Inertia of 15.

Stability Test Difficulty: 5

Cost: 4 Stability

Time: 50 minutes

Summon/Bind Nightgaunt

May only be cast on a moonless night in the open air near running water or the sea. The caster, who cannot bear the mark of Nyarlathotep, must intone a chant and prominently display a stone emblazoned with the Elder Sign. (This can be a pre-existing Sign carved into a cliff side or temple wall, for example.) The nightgaunt appears when nobody is watching.

An unbound nightgaunt resists binding with an Inertia of 8.

Stability Test Difficulty: 4

Cost: 3 Stability

Time: 20 minutes

Summon/Bind Servitor of the Outer Gods

The caster must play a specific hellish piping on a flute, on an ominous day when the planets are unbalanced, such as Walpurgisnacht or Midsummer's Eve. The Servitor rolls out of a wave of visual distortion or congealing mist, and may make one attack on the caster before being bound.

An unbound Servitor resists binding with an Inertia of 19, or 9 if the flute is enchanted, or 3 if the flute is one taken from another Servitor.

Stability Test Difficulty: 5 (4 with an Art spend to play the flute)

Cost: 6 Stability

Time: Summoning takes 30 minutes of maniacal piping; binding takes five minutes (or 4 rounds with an Art spend to play very fast).

Summon/Bind Star Vampire

May be cast only at night under a cloudless sky; may be cast indoors if the room has open windows. The caster must read the incantation (it begins: *"Tibi Magnum Innomiandum, signa stellarum nigrarum et bufaniformis Sadoquae sigillum …"*) aloud from a book. (The Enchant Item spell for this spell is a book with ink containing star vampire ichor.) The summoned star vampire floats down from the stars invisibly. It can be sent after someone of whose blood the caster has a sample, or after the bearer of a certain rune inked in star vampire ichor. If the caster does not immediately present such a sample, or gesture toward such a rune, the star vampire feasts on him instead.

An unbound star vampire resists binding with an Inertia of 12.

Stability Test Difficulty: 4

Cost: 4 Stability

Time: Ten minutes

 Tikkoun Elixir

This clear fluid damages beings not native to the planet Earth, acting as a very strong acid (see p. 68) to them. Its key ingredient is water from the four sacred rivers (the Ganges, the Jordan, and two others chosen by the Keeper for inaccessibility and symbolic weight), but there are other rare and mystical essences within it as well. It must be poured or thrown onto (or through) the target entity or creature.

In a game using the elemental conception of the Mythos, it is doubly effective against Earth-aspected deities and their creatures. Some occult texts written by devout Catholic scholars claim that holy water has the same effect as, or is another name for, the Tikkoun Elixir. They are most likely sadly mistaken, but only the Keeper knows for sure.

Stability Test Difficulty: 5 (4 with Occult spend)

Cost: 2 Stability or 4 Occult (or Theology, in some games) to distill one vial; none to use

Time: Three hours to distill; one vial may be distilled per week

◉ Vach-Viraj Incantation

This chant may be derived from the Dread Name of Azathoth, or from a secret name of Shub-Niggurath, or a steganographic combination of them both. It runs: *"Ya na kadishtu nilgh'ri stell-bsna Nyogtha; K'yarnak phlegethor l'ebumna sya'h n'ghft. Ya hai kadishtu ep r'luh-eeh Nyogtha eeh, S'uhn-ngh athg li'hee orr'e syha'h,"* and must be intoned in a clear, ringing voice.

This spell allows the use of Intimidate against those Mythos entities that can be summoned with a Summon/Bind spell.

Stability Test Difficulty: 4

Cost: 1 Intimidate; plus 1 Stability per Health pool point of the creature to be intimidated (halved against Earth-aspected creatures, if the campaign uses the elemental conception of the Mythos)

Time: 3 combat rounds to intone

Voorish Sign: This mystical gesture makes invisible things visible to the caster. Using the Voorish Sign grays out or distorts some wavelengths of visible light.

Stability Test Difficulty: 5

Cost: 1 Stability point and 1 point from either Sense Trouble or Evidence Collection

Time: Instantaneous to cast; lasts for five minutes

Calling and Dismissing Deities

Calling the deities of the Cthulhu Mythos is a singularly bad idea. Even devout priests of such beings often settle for maintaining the cycle of worship rather than risk upsetting the cosmic balance that foretells their god's release. Only the truly maniacal, visionary, or desperate resort to such actions. Seeing a called deity always results in a Stability test, usually a 6-point minimum. The sight of almost all deities of the Mythos impose additional costs and losses (see the table on p. 86).

A ritual to call a deity usually pits the caster against the resistance of normal space-time, unless noted otherwise in the specific spell description. A ritual to dismiss a deity usually pits the caster against the deity's Inertia pool, unless the deity wants to leave, or noted otherwise. A deity may not directly smite anyone taking part in a dismissal ritual during its duration, although it may summon servitors, open gates to other realms, or attack indirectly: Cthulhu could splash a tsunami at his would-be dismisser's boat, or Cthugha aim a forest-fire at his opponents. Such actions cost the deity 1 point from its Inertia pool, unless noted otherwise.

Like Contact Deity spells, calling deities is usually less difficult at the god's temple or fane (–2 to Inertia pool), or the site of a previous manifestation (–3 to Inertia pool). Idols and books are not usually significant or powerful enough to alter the local space-time, but exceptions certainly exist. If the current campaign is one in which the gods oppose each other, such as one based on Derlethian elemental theory, idols, scriptures, or impedimenta of "enemy" gods may aid dismissal. In some extreme cases, calling one deity (hopefully an easier one to dismiss, or one that leaves automatically) to drive off another may be necessary.

If the called deity is not actively prevented from remaining on Earth, either by the condition of the stars, the will of the Elder Gods, or similar, it will most likely attempt to stay, remaking reality (and incidentally devastating the planet) the while.

Knowing one Call/Dismiss Deity spell has no connection to any other. Other likely Call/Dismiss spells not detailed here include Call/Dismiss Azathoth, Call/Dismiss Dagon, Call/Dismiss Mordiggian, Call/Dismiss Mormo, Call/Dismiss Quachil Uttaus, and Call/Dismiss Shub-Niggurath.

Sample Mythos Rituals

Angles of Tagh Clatur

This spell folds space, making incorporeal creatures within its arc of effect (about 45° centered on the caster's left hand) corporeal. It is likely to damage any delicate books, glassware, windows, and such in its wake. If the caster fails the initial Stability test to cast it, the spell randomly summons (or rather, rotates into our reality) a foul being from Outside somewhere within 12 miles, and within its arc of effect.

Stability Test Difficulty: 7 (6 with Physics, 5 with a Physics spend)

Opposition: Each round, pit the caster's Stability vs the target creature's Health. When the caster succeeds in this contest, she rolls one die. The result is the number of the target creature's Health points that become corporeal.

Cost: 2 Stability or 4 Physics; paid during the first round only

Time: Ten minutes of visualization exercises to prepare; one combat round to begin casting

Call/Dismiss Cthugha

The various spells to call Cthugha require an invocation and an open flame. The caster repeats the invocation *"Ph'nglui mglw'nafh Cthugha Fomalhaut n'gha-ghaa naf'l thagn! Iä! Cthugha!"* three times while lighting the fire, gesturing with a torch, or cavorting amid the flames. The spell can be cast on any clear night, but is much easier when Fomalhaut is above the horizon (September to November in North America).

Stability Test Difficulty: 5

Opposition: Rituals to Call Cthugha pit the caster's Stability against reality's Inertia: 8 when Fomalhaut is above the horizon, 24 at other times. Rituals to Dismiss Cthugha face Cthugha's Inertia pool of 42, if it doesn't want to leave.

Cost: Calling Cthugha costs 5 Stability or 10 Health points of burning damage to the caster or casters; Dismissing Cthugha costs 9 Health worth of burning damage.

Time: Five minutes to Call if Fomalhaut is above the horizon, three hours otherwise; Dismissing Cthugha takes at least five minutes, during which it blackens and burns everything within at least 400 yards.

Call/Dismiss Hastur

There are many rituals to accomplish this aim. Some require nine enchanted stone menhirs in a V-pattern. Others require the performance of threnodies of despair. Others merely require constant vigil on certain mountain peaks. All known spells to Call Hastur can be cast only on a clear night when Aldebaran is above the horizon. (October to March in North America.) Dismiss Hastur can be cast at any time in the presence of Hastur.

Stability Test Difficulty: 5 (4 with a suitable spend: e.g., Art for a performance ritual; Architecture or Archaeology for a menhir ritual; Athletics for an endurance vigil)

Opposition: Rituals to Call Hastur pit the caster's Stability against reality's Inertia of 8 under the conditions above. Rituals to Dismiss Hastur face Hastur's Inertia pool of 35, if it doesn't want to leave.

Casters may substitute points from a relevant other pool as above (e.g., Art, Architecture, Athletics) at a rate of 2 to 1 for Stability in the Calling ritual. No other pools can help with Dismiss.

Cost: Calling Hastur costs 5 Stability, or 10 points from a relevant other pool as above. Dismissing Hastur is physically taxing, costing 7 Health or 14 Athletics or Fleeing to the caster or casters; this cost must be paid before the Dismiss ritual can be begun.

Time: Three hours to Call; a seemingly endless, seemingly instantaneous time to Dismiss that ends with the dawn.

Call/Dismiss Ithaqua

The caster must stand on an enormous mound or plain of snow, in night air at least 20°F below freezing. Ithaqua may, if it chooses, appear only as an icy whirlwind (one-third Stability and Sanity loss, no minimum) instead of in its other forms. Ithaqua cannot be summoned below the Equator.

Stability Test Difficulty: 5 (4 with an Anthropology or Outdoorsman spend)

Opposition: Rituals to Call Ithaqua pit the caster's Stability against reality's Inertia: 8 north of the Arctic Circle, 24 at other places. Rituals to Dismiss Ithaqua face Ithaqua's Inertia pool of 105, lowered to 35 below the Arctic Circle.

Cost: Calling Ithaqua costs 5 Stability. Dismissing Ithaqua costs 7 Athletics or 14 Fleeing resulting from cold and cramps to the caster or casters, as this involves standing directly in the center of its icy aura.

Time: One combat round to Call above the Arctic Circle, one hour to Call otherwise; Dismissing Ithaqua takes at least five minutes, during which it freezes solid everything – engine blocks, samples and equipment, sled dogs – within 100 yards.

Call/Dismiss Yog-Sothoth

Requires a specially built menhir (at least 10' high) or stone tower (at least 10 yards high) in an open area or on a hill. Either the sky must be cloudless, or there must be a raging thunderstorm. Each time the spell is cast, the caster must designate a human sacrifice for the god's taking. This need be no more than an invitation, such as a gesture toward the sleepy town below.

Stability Test Difficulty: 5 (4 with an Archaeology or Architecture spend)

Opposition: Rituals to Call Yog-Sothoth pit the caster's Stability against reality's Inertia of 24. Rituals to Dismiss Yog-Sothoth face its Inertia pool of 100. If the tower or menhir is enchanted (per the Enchant Item spell on p. 115), each 1 sacrificed Stability rating point in the tower adds 1 dedicated pool point to the caster's Stability for this spell.

Cost: Calling Yog-Sothoth costs 8 Stability. Dismissing Yog-Sothoth costs 10 points from the caster's highest pool. If that highest pool has fewer than 10 points in it, another caster can take the next hit, or the caster loses the remainder from his second-highest pool, and so forth.

Time: Ten minutes to Call; regardless of how long playing out the Dismissal takes, it objectively occupies only one combat round of elapsed time.

☉ Contact Nodens

This spell allows the caster to make mental or dream contact with Nodens, the Elder God of the Great Abyss worshiped by the primitive Britons. Nodens has no particular animus against questing humans, but he does tend to hollow out their personality. Nevertheless, he may deign to grant an insight to those seeking to thwart the Great Old Ones.

The caster must perform this ritual on a remote sea cliff at night. Nodens will usually appear in a dream or waking vision when the caster is alone.

Stability Test Difficulty: 5 (4 with an Occult or Archaeology spend)

Opposition: Nodens' Inertia pool is 30, but using an ancient idol or other artifact of Nodens worship in this ritual lowers it to 20. Unlike most deities, Nodens resists contact, possibly because his time on Earth is limited or dangerous in some unfathomable way.

Cost: 3 Stability. If Nodens is successfully contacted, the caster may not gain Stability points from his Drive, or spend any points from any Interpersonal pool, for the remainder of the investigation.

Time: One hour to cast; Nodens will appear within three nights.

Curse of the Stone

This spell requires an enchanted stone tablet, carved within the sound of the sea and engraved with a certain sigil and an inscription in cuneiform. The target must be visible to the caster, although seeing a target through a telescope or in a vision still works. Either the caster or the target must be touching the tablet; if both are, the caster pays half the listed Stability cost and each pool point he spends in the ritual contest counts double.

The curse creates ghastly hallucinations in the mind of the target, blinding and misleading her with terrifying illusions and phantoms. She immediately loses 2 Stability and must make a 5-point Stability test as the

horrors pour into her mind. Regardless of the result of that test, she is **blasted** (though she does not lose the Stability rating point) until she can make a Difficulty 7 Stability test and recover her senses. Every night thereafter, she will have nightmares, refreshing only half her Stability pool between adventures. Whether this curse can be removed, and if so how, is up to the Keeper.

Stability Test Difficulty: 5 (4 with an Art or Archaeology spend) to engrave the stone; 3 to cast the spell.

Opposition: Once the spell is cast, and after paying the casting cost, the caster must succeed in one test of his Stability against the target's Stability. If he does, the target then gets a retaliatory test; if she wins it, she only loses the 2 Stability, but does not suffer any illusions or other effects.

Cost: 8 Stability to cast; see Enchant Item (p. 115) for cost of creating the stone.

Time: 2 rounds to cast; one month to engrave and enchant the Stone

Howl of Pan

This unholy ululation drives all who hear it insane. (The caster is well advised to stop his own ears with wax before uttering it, if he is not insane already.) It is up to the Keeper whether this spell works through a microphone or over the radio. The caster must prepare to cast this spell with a set of intricate breathing exercises. During this preparation, the caster may take no other action.

Another version of this spell,

Pipes of Madness, requires an enchanted set of owl-bone Pan-pipes, a flute of the Servitors, or similar item, but no initial breathing exercises.

Stability Test Difficulty: 5 (4 with an Athletics spend for volume; or suitable musical Art spend for the Pipes of Madness version)

Opposition: Every sentient being in earshot must make a 5-point Stability Test. Those who fail lose the 5 points, and become temporarily **blasted** for the duration of the scene. (They do not lose the Stability rating point.) Those who succeed lose only 2 Stability, and can otherwise react normally.

Cost: 4 Stability per round; every caster must also pay 1 Athletics per round for the Howl of Pan though not for the Pipes of Madness

Time: Four rounds of breathing exercises, one round to utter; once begun, the caster can continue as long as he has breath (Athletics pool points) left

Mind Exchange
Allows the caster to trade minds with her target. The target can be at any range, although the first time this spell is cast against a specific target, the caster must be able to see her victim. (Scrying and some magical visions may also allow Mind Exchange.) Targets of this spell absolutely get a Sense Trouble roll, which manifests as a jolt of detached perspective. ("It's as though you were looking at yourself from different eyes.") A success lets the target pinpoint the caster, if he can see her. Being mind-switched causes a 5-point Stability test for the target.

Caster and target engage in a contest of Stability vs Stability. If the caster wins, she rolls one die at a -2 modifier, keeping a running total. Unless the target also knows the spell, nothing happens if the target wins. (If the target knows the spell and wins, the spell is over.) Once the running total is higher than the target's Stability, the caster can trade minds with the target. After a successful Mind Exchange, the second against the same target goes more smoothly: the caster rolls her die at a -1 modifier. The modifier increments to +0 after the second successful mind exchange against the same target, to +1 with the third, and so on. Once the *modifier* is higher than the target's Stability *rating*, the caster can make the mind exchange merely with a strong act of will, even in the unlikely event that the target's Stability rating increases afterward.

At this point, the caster can make the exchange permanent with a human sacrifice to Shub-Niggurath. Tradition (and the spell, should the Keeper so decide) dictates that this take place on Halloween.

Stability Test Difficulty: 5 (4 with a Assess Honesty spend or against a target the caster knows well, 3 with both)

Opposition: See above.

Cost: Stability equal to half the target's current Stability pool (round down)

Time: One round to cast, each subsequent exchange of the contest takes one round; caster's mind can remain in target's body up to four minutes after the first success, eight minutes after the

second, 16 minutes after the third, and so on.

Resurrection
This spell ("Y'ai' ng'ngah, Yog-Sothoth, h'ee-l'Geb, f'ai throdog, uaaah!") raises up the body and soul of a corpse that has been reduced to a bluish-gray powder of its essential salts by an alchemical process. The reverse of this spell ("Ogthrod ai'f, Geb'l-ee'h, Yog-Sothoth, 'ngah'ng ai'y, zhro!") returns such a revenant to its essential salts.

The necromancer must have at least the entire torso, one arm, and a head to alchemically render a corpse into sufficient essential salts to allow Resurrection. With any less, or with only some of the corpse's essential salts available, the result is only "the liveliest awfulness." That said, as long as the coffin is intact, and the necromancer has taken sufficient care to scrape together all the fragments and dust within, the spell is possible. Rendering a corpse into its essential salts requires 3 months of work in an alchemist's laboratory or the equivalent, a 3-point Stability test, and a total Occult and Chemistry rating of 8.

Stability Test Difficulty: 6 to resurrect a corpse, Difficulty 4 to return it to dust

Opposition: Resurrecting a corpse from its essential salts is a contest against death's Inertia of 6; returning a corpse to dust requires a contest of caster's Stability vs one-half (round down) of the target's Stability

Cost: 4 Stability; being resurrected costs 6 Stability

Time: 2 rounds to chant either version; resurrection takes five minutes, return to dust is instantaneous

⊕ Saaamaaa Ritual

This ritual hardens and recurves the native geometry of four-dimensional space-time, deflecting things from Outside such as Yog-Sothoth, Daoloth, and their minions. It is up to the Keeper to determine specifically which gods, titans, and monsters are Outsiders, and which are terrestrial species or "normal" alien races. Using the Ritual or its signs, the caster can close a hyperspace Gate. The Ritual is most often performed to inscribe its signs as a barrier, or to polarize an existing light or radiation field as a barrier. If the line is chalked, inscribed, or generated by a neon light, breaking it breaks the barrier.

The Ritual has eight lines, the last of which is reputed to provide total protection. Sadly, the last line is also unknown to any human, although it is supposedly carven in two monoliths on the world Glyu-Uho, orbiting the star Betelgeuse. Some occultists believe that the Elder Sign is a topological map of the third line of the Ritual. Depending on the source, the fourth or sixth line is known as the Line of Naach-Tith. The fifth line (often called the Pentacle of the Planes) is sufficient to contain and redirect Daoloth. Usually only parts of one or two lines show up in a grimoire; assembling the seven known lines would take years, and vast resources.

Although the Keeper should come up with strange and unique effects for each line, the primary effect of one line of the Saamaa Ritual is to block a number of Health points associated with an Outside entity. Each line blocks an exponentially increasing number of points: the first line blocks 2, the second blocks 4, the third blocks 8, the fourth 16, the fifth 32, and so forth. If the entity has fewer Health than the line's rating, it cannot breach the barrier. Bullets and other earthly projectiles (or earthly creatures, for that matter) can cross the barrier with no effect. A line also blocks spells if they are powered by fewer points than its rating: for example, a sorcerer in service to Yog-Sothoth would have to pour 9 points of Stability into a spell to cast it at a target cowering behind the third line of the Ritual. A line of the Ritual permanently closes a hyperspace Gate if the Gate required the same or less Stability than the line's rating: for example, an interstellar gate costs 16 Stability, so the fourth (or higher) line of the Ritual would close it.

Stability Test Difficulty: 6 (5 with Physics, 4 with a Physics spend)

Opposition: Raising any one line of the Ritual is a contest against the Inertia of space-time. This Inertia pool equals the number of the line, times two: raising the seventh line is thus a contest against an Inertia of 14. The caster must use his Stability pool in the contest, but takes damage to Health.

Cost: 2 Stability or 4 Health per number of the line for each 31 feet (or fraction thereof) of barrier. For example, drawing the third line across a 60-foot archway (or a 32-foot archway) would cost 12 Stability or 24 Health.

Time: The line lasts one die roll's hours, or until sunrise, whichever is less.

CREATURES

"... OF ALL THE UNNATURAL MONSTERS EITHER OF US HAD IN OUR LIFETIMES BEHELD, THIS WAS IN SURPASSING DEGREE THE STRANGEST."

— THE BEAST IN THE CAVE

Below the gods and titans of the Mythos lie many different kinds of creatures. Some of them are extraterrestrial, or not even native to this dimension. Some were created by the Great Old Ones, some have chosen to serve them, and still others remain independent or unaware of the cosmic monstrosities that blight the universe. Whether intelligent, alien, or simple Earthly beasts, such creatures share similar rules considerations in *Trail of Cthulhu.*

Health Loss for Creatures

Unless the Keeper is really in love with a specific monster, or running a soul-crushingly Purist game, creatures die, or return to their home dimension, or disintegrate, or what have you, when their Health is reduced below 0. Some creatures have exceptions in their own rule text, and the Keeper is always allowed to use the standard rules for Health loss if she thinks it dramatically necessary. For flavor purposes, the Keeper may describe tentacles torn off, etheric forms wavering or ichor dripping as a creature approaches 0 Health points.

Ability Pool Refreshment for Creatures

Creatures refresh ability pool points according to how often they appear. A creature that is not encountered for 24 hours or more may replenish all of its ability pools, with the exception of Health, which it recovers at the rate of 1d6 points per day.

If the Investigators encounter a creature later on in the same day, such as by tracking it to its lair, it can refresh all of its ability pools to a maximum of *half* their total rating, again with the exception of Health, which it cannot refresh at all.

Creatures that have special rules for recovering Health, such as regenerating creatures, follow their own rules rather than those given above.

Creature Statistics

Some creatures have split ability pools depending on their environment or means of locomotion, one higher than the other. A creature that changes modes (goes from flying to walking, for example) either loses the "extra" pool points or gains them, depending on its direction, but it can only do so once.

A byakhee (Scuffling 6 on land, 11 in the air) is attempting to rescue its master, a foul necromancer, from the onrushing Investigators who have the villain cornered on a rooftop. It spends 3 pool points raking the meddling Investigators in fly-by attacks, and has 8 remaining. But once it lands to allow the escaping wizard to board its back, it goes from 8 pool points to 6, its land maximum. (If it had spent 5 or more pool points in

the air, it would not lose any points when landing.) It returns to the air, but does not regain its 2 "lost" pool points.

If the Investigators had gotten to the rooftop a few minutes later, while the necromancer was boarding his grounded servitor, the byakhee would have begun the encounter with 6 pool points in Scuffling. If it spent 1 in the combat before taking off, it would hit the air with 10 points – the 5 remaining in its pool, plus its extra 5 for the air.

Let's say the Investigators

somehow force it back to the roof. The byakhee's Scuffling pool reverts to 5, and will not refresh again that scene whether it takes wing again or not.

The Hit Threshold, Weapon damage, and Armor of creatures work the same way that they do for Investigators and other humans, albeit they are usually better.

The **Alertness Modifier** for a given creature reflects its keener (or paranormal) senses, or in some cases, its brutish dullness or weak perceptions in conditions of Earthly reality. It is added to the target difficulty of Stealth tests or similar made when the creature's sensory awareness would be a factor, such as when the Investigators are trying to sneak up on a creature, or are moving around near its lair. Note that creatures do not have the Sense Trouble or Shadowing abilities. Players make rolls to evade creatures; creatures do not make rolls to detect Investigators.

Stability Loss, in these templates, indicates the *additional* Stability loss (as a modifier to the standard Stability loss) caused by sighting, fighting, or witnessing the attacks of the creature in question.

A creature has a **Stealth Modifier** when it is significantly harder (or easier) to detect (by ear, eye, nose, etc) than a human. This modifier is added to (or subtracted from) the difficulty number of any appropriate Sense Trouble or other tests made to notice the creature. Note that creatures and other NPCs do not have the Stealth ability.

They never make rolls to avoid detection; Investigators always make rolls to detect *them*.

As A Foulness Shall Ye Know Them

Each race has an Investigation section describing some possible clues – either to its approach or to its traces – the Keeper can provide the Investigators. These clues are organized by the likely abilities that would uncover them. (Other abilities that might provide the same clue are in parentheses.) Even more than usual, the Keeper should change these descriptions around to suit herself. That said, here's where she might start.

ALIEN RACES

"AS THE END APPROACHES I FEEL MORE KINDLY TOWARDS THE THINGS. IN THE SCALE OF COSMIC ENTITY WHO CAN SAY WHICH SPECIES STANDS HIGHER, OR MORE NEARLY APPROACHES A SPACE-WIDE ORGANIC NORM — THEIRS OR MINE?"

— IN THE WALLS OF ERYX

Humankind is not the pinnacle of creation. Humankind is an accident, created as a sloppy jest in the laboratories of a species that died before the dinosaurs evolved. Humankind is at best an overzealous weed, flourishing during Earth's temporary abandonment by its true landlords. Or perhaps humankind is a Petri dish, in which the Great Old Ones grow promising and useful traits for implantation into those races actually worthy of servitor status. Old races born in the light of the Big Bang still cling to life in Earth's secret places. Alien beings visit the planet to harvest ores and slaves to suit their whim, or to carry out the unfathomable desires of their Great Old One masters. New races gestate under the ocean or in the graveyard or simply wait their turn in the far reaches of time.

All the races listed below, with the possible exception of shoggoths, are of roughly human (or considerably higher) intelligence. The default rule in *Trail of Cthulhu* is that all alien races, whether terrestrial or extraterrestrial, count as Mythos entities for the purposes of Stability tests, spell casting, and similar. The Keeper is welcome to shake up player assumptions by redefining ghouls, for example, as supernatural creatures like vampires, or even as cryptozoological oddities like the yeti. The yeti, of course, might turn out to be a mi-go servitor species…

Byakhee

These interstellar winged horrors resemble necrotic, insectoid vultures. Byakhee can fly through space and carry a rider each, though such riders need protection from the vacuum and cold from suitable spells or potions. Byakhee do not have bases on earth, but sorcerers summon them to perform deeds or to serve as steeds. Byakhee are reputed to be one of Hastur's servitor races.

In combat, byakhee can either strike with both claws for two attacks per round, or attempt to bite and drain blood.

Game Statistics

Abilities (on land/in air or space):

Athletics 5/20, Health 8, Scuffling 6/11

Hit Threshold: 4

Stealth Modifier: +1 in air

Weapon: +1 (claw), +0 (bite); following a successful bite, the byakhee will automatically drain 2 Health per round from its victim until killed or driven off.

Armor: -2 vs any (fur and hide, and an absence of vitals)

Stability Loss: +1

Investigation
Cop Talk: We're tracking down a report that somebody heard whistling, like from a piccolo, right before the attack.

Evidence Collection: The prints generally resemble those of carrion birds, but are not deep enough to indicate anything heavy enough to batter a human ever stood in them. (Outdoorsman)

Forensics: The body is slashed and torn almost to rags, and blood spatter evidence indicates it was carried around the area *during* the struggle. Although the throat is ripped out, there is surprisingly little blood either on or in the corpse.

Sense Trouble: A waft of icy air seems to settle over you, and an astringent smell like rotting juniper stings your nostrils.

Colour Out of Space
An larval Colour falls to Earth inside a meteorite and germinates, splitting its metallic shell and nestling into the ecosystem as coruscating

incandescence matching nothing in the Earthly spectrum. It is not a gas or plasma, but an insubstantial light. (That said, if its light touches human flesh, it feels like a brush of slimy vapor.) Bright light inhibits a Colour. It spends daylight hours in dark, cool hideaways, preferably underwater: cisterns, wells, lakes, reservoirs, and oceans all are suitable. If it moves, it resembles nothing so much as a weird moonbeam pouring across the ground, occasionally flashing into eye-blink flight. A Colour can move anywhere any light whatsoever can go, including between the chinks of a stone wall or the boards in a floor.

As the Colour pupates, it filters into the local vegetation; it grows unnaturally, glistens oddly, and tastes bitter. Then insects and animals are born deformed, their eyes glowing with the Colour. At night, all plant life shines with it, twisting and writhing as in a strong wind. Once grown, the Colour begins to feed on surrounding animals (or people) while draining the life-force from the area. When it has enough energy, it departs the planet for space and adulthood, leaving a ruined, barren heath 5 to 20 acres (depending on the area's initial richness) in extent. And possibly another larva…

Will Drain: Someone living in the area a Colour is draining automatically loses 1 point of Stability each night of residence there, as their mind weakens and they lose their will to live. They must also make a 2-point Stability test to leave after the first night.

Game Statistics
Abilities (larval/grown): Athletics 4/20, Health 4/20, Scuffling 6/28

Hit Threshold: N/A

Stealth Modifier: +2

Weapon: +1 (iridescence); its attacks can melt iron

Armor: *transparent* to all physical attacks including fire or electricity; strong magnetic fields can contain it; vulnerable to spells

Stability Loss: +0 to see a Colour; +1 to see the victim of a Colour

Investigation
Architecture: The glass in this house is surprisingly brittle and spotted, as though it had been sand-blasted. There's no similar damage to the frame, although the wood is gray and punkish in places.

Astronomy: A meteor landed around here about five months or a year ago.

Chemistry: Under spectroscopic analysis, samples from the meteor display bands in unknown spectra, indicating very strange, possibly transuranic, chemical makeup. They are not volatile at any temperature, but are very ductile. An acid-solvent test reveals Widmanstätten lines similar to meteoric iron.

Forensics: The flesh is dry, brittle, scaly, and sunken in, giving off noisome odors upon dissection. The fat is congealed and bloated, with strange iridescent effects. Parts of the body are shriveled or compressed disproportionately, but there is no sign of pressure damage or bruising. The eyes bulge, with high air pressure distending the orbits; the soft parts of the face are likewise distended. All parts of the body are gray or grayish.

Outdoorsman: These plants are simultaneously rotting and desiccating from within. (Biology)

Photography: There's another light source in this area besides the moon or the lights.

Physics: Incredibly strong, focused radiation could have this effect, but it would take advanced machinery to produce.

Sense Trouble: That reflection is an odd color …

Dark Young of Shub-Niggurath

Dark young are enormous writhing masses, formed out of ropy black tentacles. Here and there over their surface, ragged, puckered mouths drool green sap. Beneath them, tentacles end in black hooves. Dark young roughly resemble trees in silhouette — the trunks being the short legs, and the tops of the trees represented by the ropy, branching bodies – but smell like open graves. Dark young stand between 12 and 20 feet tall.

Dark young act as proxies for Shub-Niggurath in accepting sacrifices, accepting worship from cultists, devouring non-cultists, and in spreading their mother's faith across the world. They appear where she is (or was) worshipped.

In its masses of tentacles, a typical dark young has four thicker sinuous tentacles with which it attacks. Each of these thicker tentacles can strike out to injure or to grab and capture once per round, conceivably at

four different targets. Instead of making a tentacle attack, the dark young may trample one victim with its massive hooves, typically hooting and bellowing the while.

Game Statistics

Abilities: Athletics 8, Health 16, Scuffling 26

Hit Threshold: 3 (large)

Alertness Modifier: +1

Stealth Modifier: +2 in forests or jungles

Weapon: +5 (trampling hooves); +2 (tentacle); -2 (horrible sucking mouth); after a successful tentacle attack, in lieu of doing damage, the dark young may pull her victim inexorably toward a mouth for an automatic blood drain each round thereafter.

Armor: the thick, woody, sap-filled flesh of the Dark Young means that most firearms do only 1 point of damage (2 if the attacker rolled a 6); shotguns do one-third damage; immune to fire, blast, acid, electricity, and poison, although the Keeper may decide that some alchemical herbicide (made of something truly awful) could work.

Stability Loss: +2

Investigation

Anthropology: The ancient Germans, among other tribes, used to ritually slash human sacrifices and then chain them to certain trees you were never allowed to cut down.

Forensics: The knife wounds didn't kill him – they were superficial cuts at best – although the blood loss was serious even before whatever happened. The

face and mouth cavities are full of blackish pus. Ulcerated open sores are on the anterior of the body, though that clear grease has dried by now. The expression on what's left of the face is … well, if you didn't know better, you'd say it was religious ecstasy.

Sense Trouble: Although the wind doesn't shift, it picks up – and it must have uncovered something dead for a week. And there seem to be more trees there than there were just a minute ago.

Deep One

The amphibious worshippers of Cthulhu known as the Deep Ones resemble chinless, hunched, batrachian humanoids with fish-like gills and unblinking, bulging eyes. Their hands and feet are webbed and clawed, and their skin is grey-green and slimy with ridges of scales along the spine and at the joints. Locked in the timeless depths of the sea, their lives are coldly beautiful, unbelievably cruel, effectively immortal. They are a saltwater race, and their many submerged cities include Y'ha-nthlei off Innsmouth, Massachusetts, Ahu-Y'hloa near Cornwall, and G'll-Hoo in the North Sea.

Some Deep Ones appear to have a monstrous lust to produce human/deep one hybrids, and so interact with humans. These humans may worship the Deep Ones, for in addition to their magical knowledge, Deep Ones are immortal, unless slain, and so are any hybrid offspring. Typically, hybrids inhabit remote coastal villages. Such a hybrid begins life as a human-looking child who gradually becomes uglier and uglier. Around age

35 or 40 (or after severe stress), the hybrid begins dreaming of his underwater heritage and then undergoes a monstrous transformation into a Deep One.

Game Statistics

Abilities (on land/in water): Athletics 8/12, Health 9, Scuffling 8/12, Weapons 6/4

Hit Threshold: 4/5

Alertness Modifier: +0/+1

Stealth Modifier: +0/+1

Weapon: +1 (claw), +1 (trident)

Armor: -1 vs any (scales and skin)

Stability Loss: +0

Investigation

Evidence Collection: There are seawater pools by the smashed window, even though the sea was calm last night. That ties in with the dried salt in the rug, and in that webbed footprint.

Forensics: The neck is neatly slashed by four parallel wounds, like razor blades mounted on a frame of some kind. There are similar four-wound patterns on his arm, and on his leg, which was twisted nearly backwards.

Sense Trouble: It's an awfully warm day for that man to be wearing gloves and have his coat collar pulled up.

Dhole

These gigantic, worm-like, burrowing horrors are not native to the Earth, and none seem to have been brought here for more than brief periods. This is fortunate, for dholes have riddled

and left waste several other worlds. They dislike light, though it does not visibly harm them. They rarely emerge in daylight, and then only on planets that they have thoroughly conquered. Some magical texts blame them for earthquakes.

Crushing Roll: Anyone or anything within near range of a dhole if it decides to roll over

gets a Difficulty 4 Fleeing or Athletics test to run away before it smashes them to jelly. With an Evidence Collection spend, survivors can find enough to bury.

Sputum: A wad of dhole sputum is 10 yards across. If it hits a car or truck, it stops it; if it hits a plane it knocks it out of the sky (Difficulty 6 Piloting to avoid a crash); if it hits a boat, it adds +2 to all Piloting Difficulties until removed. In addition to the impact damage, characters hit by the goo are engulfed and stunned for one round. Climbing out of the wad requires three consecutive successful Difficulty 5 Athletics tests. Each round you spend in the sputum, you cannot breathe and must make tests as if drowning (see p. 68). Dhole sputum is caustic, doing damage like a weak acid (-1) each round.

Game Statistics
Abilities (crawling/burrowing): Athletics 18/10, Health 178, Scuffling 24

Hit Threshold: 2 (vast)

Alertness Modifier: +0/+2

Weapon: +12 (bite), +1 (spit); after a successful bite, the dhole will swallow its victim; dholes can spit up to three miles (+2 on target's Hit Threshold past long range)

Armor: -12 vs any (exoskeleton)

Stability Loss: +2 (minimum Stability loss 1 if seen on Earth)

Investigation
Evidence Collection: You can follow the broken branches through the forest about a mile and a half, so that blob of mucus must have come down on an awfully flat trajectory before it totaled that car. The paint and top are burned badly, so it was probably either caustic or very hot.

Forensics: At a guess, an ocean liner landed on him. But that's just a guess, mind you.

Geology: The rock strata are very jumbled up here, but there was no earthquake reported last night.

Dimensional Shambler
Resembling a hulking, insectoid ape, the dimensional shambler infests the wainscoting of the planes. Their low intelligence makes them a favorite servitor for sorcerers of all species. Occasionally, their masters teach them a rote spell.

A dimensional shambler may strike with both claws, attacking the same target twice in a single round.

Dimension Travel: At any time, a dimensional shambler can, well, shamble between dimensions. This takes one round during which it shimmers and fades, and costs it 1 point from its Athletics pool, or 2 points if carrying a human-sized or smaller object. While shimmering, it can still be attacked, but cannot attack. To grab an unwilling passenger, it must win two consecutive Scuffling contests: the first is a grab for no damage, and the second is a nightmarish bear-hug. During this second contest, it fades out.

Game Statistics
Abilities: Athletics 7, Health 10, Scuffling 10

Hit Threshold: 4

Weapon: +1 (talons)

Armor: -3 vs any (thick rugose hide)

Stability Loss: +0

Investigation
Evidence Collection: Blood spatter indicates that the attack happened right here in the middle of the room, but there aren't any other spots, or a trail to indicate the victim was moved anywhere. And you'd see it on that carpet or those white walls.

Sense Trouble: The mirrors and windows in the room reflect a kind of shimmery light that you don't see in the room itself.

Elder Thing
These aliens are radially symmetrical, with five arms each ending in five tentacular fingers. Their bodies stand about 8 feet tall, with starfish-like "heads" (with one eye at each tip) and "feet" emerging from their barrel-shaped torso. Their wings fold up into slots in the body. Elder Things communicate by piping whistles and can see without light.

Elder Things came to Earth two billion years ago, and may have accidentally started terrestrial life. They created shoggoths as their slaves, and used them to war against other races until being driven back to their main city in Antarctica. As they degenerated, a shoggoth rebellion destroyed the Elder Thing civilization. The Elder Things are extinct on land, but may still have colonies in the deepest waters.

In hand-to-hand combat, an Elder Thing may use all five arms at once, but no more than three versus a single target. As a technologically advanced species, however, they are more likely to use weapons or magic.

Game Statistics
Abilities (on land/in air): Athletics 8/10, Health 14, Scuffling 13

Hit Threshold: 4

Alertness Modifier: +1

Stealth Modifier: +1

Weapon: +1 (crushing grip); after a successful attack, the Elder Thing begins to constrict its victim for automatic damage (-1) each round until killed or dissuaded.

Armor: -4 vs any (tough epidermis)

Stability Loss: +0

Investigation

Forensics: The cuts are precisely spaced, but oddly placed. The organs have been surgically severed in a way that indicates medical training, but put back incorrectly. The organs also show odd bruising patterns, as though they were held with calipers or some other thin, strong tool before being replaced. The trepanning wound at the crown of the skull was made at the same time as the rectum was cored out, and the victim was still alive, but fully restrained at the time of those incisions.

Medicine: This will seem weird, but hear me out. In med school, we all knew our anatomical theory cold, but had no idea how to cut up cadavers. This is like the reverse of that.

Sense Trouble: The echo on that whistling sounds like these caves or tunnels go a lot farther back than we thought. And by the way, what made that whistling?

Flying Polyp

This unnamed extraterrestrial species invaded Earth about 750 million years ago. They built basalt cities with high windowless towers and inhabited three other planets in the solar system as well. The Great Race of Yith arrived some 300 million years later and possessed the polyps' food species. In the ensuing war, the Great Race drove the polyps underground. The polyps broke free again 65 million years ago and drove the Great Race into the future. The polyps still remain in their subterranean haunts and seem content to remain there, as they need no light, annihilating the few beings chancing across them. The entrances to their dwellings, great wells sealed over with stone, are mostly deep within ancient ruins.

Invisibility: Although its body is always rotating through visible space and fading in unsettling fashion, a flying polyp can become entirely invisible for one round by spending 1 Health point. It continues to emit its nauseating whistling noise, however, so its Hit Threshold rises to 6 rather than vanishing altogether.

Windblast: Using its Wind ability (the renamed Firearms for polyps) a flying polyp can emit a blast of desiccating wind to strip the flesh from its target's bones and blow him across the room. Damage modifiers depend on what they hit on their way across the room, and on the range, as follows: close or point-blank (+4), near (+2), long (+0).

Suction: The polyp's wind can also create a localized spiral suction that holds a victim in place, at any range up to 1,000 yards, even around corners and down or up shafts. This is a contest of Wind vs Athletics (or Fleeing), and the polyp can move at full speed while pinning its prey in place. Its targets' Hit Threshold increases by 1 for each additional target it attempts to pin.

Windstorm: A colony of 9 or more flying polyps can generate a hurricane-force windstorm. This has primarily dramatic or narrative effects, forcing planes to crash, burying uncovered ruins, and the like.

Game Statistics

Abilities (on ground/in air): Athletics 8/12, Health 20, Scuffling 28, Wind 23

Hit Threshold: 4 (large but only partially visible)

Alertness Modifier: +2

Stealth Modifier: invisibility (see above)

Weapon: +1 (polypous extrusion); semi-material and ignores all armor

Armor: -3 vs any (polypous matting); all physical weapons do damage as if their modifier were -1; enchanted weapons, fire, and electricity do normal damage

Stability Loss: +2

Investigation

Forensics: The skin at the wounds is deeply but irregularly pockmarked, with some abrasion in no discernible pattern. Death was caused either by the suffocation or possibly by the contusions. The whole body is reddened slightly, and there is particulate matter in the skin and hair, some embedded quite deeply. The flesh is somewhat desiccated, as though it had been sun-dried or baked. The eardrums are split.

Outdoorsman: That wind came up from the ground, and the weather has been clear all week. (Sense Trouble)

Formless Spawn of Tsathoggua

These inky, protean beings can change shapes in an instant, from toad-like lumps to elongate things with hundreds of rudimentary legs. They can ooze through small cracks and enlarge their appendages at will. They are closely associated with Tsathoggua, and often may be found in his temples or in sunless caverns.

Engulf: At point blank range, a formless spawn can simply engulf its opponent with a successful Scuffling contest. (The target's Hit Threshold is 1 higher than normal.) As the viscous (and vicious) blob crushes him, the engulfed foe loses 1 point of Health on the first round, 2 on the second round, and so forth. He can do nothing except emit muffled shrieks of terror and make drowning tests (see p. 68). If the spawn begins with Health higher than 8, for every 4 additional points it possesses, it can engulf one more human-sized target, though it can still only engulf one target per round.

Game Statistics
Abilities: Athletics 12, Health 8+, Scuffling 20

Hit Threshold: 4

Stealth Modifier: +1 (+3 in shadows or darkness)

Weapon: -1 (tendril), +0 (limb), +1 (pseudopod); can extend tendril attack at near range; can attack one to three targets with a limb simultaneously, adding 1 to the Hit Threshold for each additional target

Armor: all physical wounds and damage simply flow closed; fire does normal damage; may be affected by spells and some chemicals

Stability Loss: +1

Investigation
Evidence Collection: The damp trail from (or to) the body flows up walls, and narrows to get through the crack of the door.

Forensics: The bones are simply sucked clean of flesh, except for the insides of the skull, ilium, and scapula, which show signs of swarming predator damage – shrews, perhaps, or very large ants. They are snapped and twisted; the force came from all angles at once, somehow. His fillings, ring, and the pin in his shoulder from the Great War were all found lying in the bone cavities.

Sense Trouble: Wait – nothing's casting that shadow. (Photography)

Ghoul
Rubbery, loathsome humanoids with hoof-like feet, canine features, and claws, ghouls speak in gibberings and meepings. Some recall human tongues. They are often encrusted with grave mold collected as they feed. These horrible creatures dwell in graveyard warrens, subway tunnels, and the like beneath many human cities. They have ties to witches and occasionally attack humans. A human of particularly thanatophilic tendencies can transform into a ghoul over a prolonged period of time.

Ghouls can engage in two claw attacks and a bite against the same target in one round.

Game Statistics
Abilities: Athletics 9, Health 7, Scuffling 9

Hit Threshold: 4 (5 underground)

Alertness Modifier: +2 (+0 in daylight)

Stealth Modifier: +1

Weapon: +1 (claw), +0 (bite); if two bite attacks in a row succeed against the same target, the ghoul is worrying the poor devil with his mighty canine jaws, and the second attack thus does double damage. The ghoul need not roll to hit that target thereafter, but will continue to do normal damage to it each round until killed or driven off.

Armor: firearms and projectiles do only half damage (round up)

Stability Loss: +0; +1 if the ghoul was known to the witness when alive

Investigation
Evidence Collection: The "newly dug grave" over in the next plot has a marker on it labeled 1919.

Forensics: The entire body is covered in bite marks. Oddly, although the marks are clearly canine, the jaws are unusually short and wide. From the marks, we estimate three or four of the animals. The eyes were plucked from their sockets, and are missing, as are the kidneys, spleen, liver, thymus gland, pancreas, and intestines. The large wound in the belly was a tearing wound. The skull, on the other hand, was smashed open postmortem on the gravestone, and the gray matter scooped out with some kind of clawed utensil and taken. Also postmortem, the long bones of the limbs were cracked and pried open with a four-pronged, sharpened tool, and the marrow removed. Extensive saliva traces were found in and around the bone cavities.

Languages: That gravedigger we talked to used vocabulary and sentence construction more common 200 years ago. (History)

Sense Trouble: That barking doesn't sound like the dog we heard earlier.

Gnoph-Keh

This "hairy myth-thing of the Greenland ice" has six legs and a horn, though at a glimpse it resembles a misshapen polar bear more than anything else. It can travel on one, two, or three pairs of legs. It is associated with Ithaqua, although it is also the totem beast of a debased tribe of Eskimos.

The gnoph-keh can attack with its horn, or with one or two pair of claws. For a pair of claw attacks, roll one Scuffling test, but two separate damage results. It cannot make a horn attack on the round after it makes a two-pair claw attack, as it has to drop to its feet again.

Blizzard: By spending 1 Health per hour, the gnoph-keh can howl up a blizzard, restricting

human visibility to point blank (the gnoph-keh can still see fine) within a 100-yard radius. Alternately, it can spend 1 Health point to drop the air temperature by 20°F for an hour. Each additional Health point increases the radius by another 100 yards or drops the temperature another 20°F; multiple gnoph-kehs can howl up glacier-clearing storms.

Below 20°F, Investigators without protective gear suffer from extreme cold (see p. 68). Below -20°F, regardless of gear, Investigators must make Athletics tests (Difficulty 4) to keep moving, and each additional temperature drop raises that Difficulty by 1.

Investigators who stop moving begin losing 1 Health every 15 minutes, or every five minutes in a blizzard.

Game Statistics
Abilities: Athletics 9, Health 15, Scuffling 21

Hit Threshold: 4 (5 in Arctic against non-Arctic dwellers)

Alertness Modifier: +1

Stealth Modifier: +2 in snow or ice

Weapon: +3 (horn), +1 (claw)

Armor: -5 vs any (furry hide)

Stability Loss: +0

Investigation
Biology: The end toe on these polar bear tracks is unusually distended, and the claws are remarkably long. (Outdoorsman)

Forensics: The body died not from blood loss, or even from the trauma of being impaled through the chest, but from hypothermia, despite being clad in a parka at the time of death.

Outdoorsman: The tracks this thing leaves make no sense – it's like there's a bipedal one riding a quadrupedal one or something. (Evidence Collection)

Sense Trouble: That snow is blowing against the wind.

Great Race of Yith
Their 10-foot tall cone-shaped bodies, topped with four stalks (eyes, trumpet-like ears, two pincers) are native to this planet. The Great Race, a purely mental species, took over the minds of the cones 400 million years ago when they fled their own world's destruction. After driving the flying polyps underground, and a period of internal wars, they built a fascist empire centered on Pnakotus in Australia. When the polyps erupted again 65 million years ago, the Great Race left the cones to their fate and jumped ahead to 50 million years in our future, where they possess the coleopteran bodies of Earth's by-then dominant race.

A Yithian can send its mind forward or backward through time, pick out a suitable subject, and trade minds with it. Thus, whenever a member of the Great Race takes over the body of a being, that being is put into the body of the Great Race individual, there to stay until the being now inhabiting its old body sees fit to return and trade places once more. When the time comes to restore the victim to his own body, the Great Race blanks his memory of all that has happened to him while he is trapped in their age. This blanking is not perfect: the victim may dream of or have nightmares concerning being held by the Great Race. The Yithians use this technique to travel en masse through time and space to conquer other planets. Yithian time-travel depends on hyper-scientific machinery, much of which exists in a purely mathematical state, since it can be constructed with virtually any level of technology, no matter how primitive.

Game Statistics
Abilities: Athletics 7, Firearms 7, Health 23, Scuffling 13

Hit Threshold: 4

Weapon: +5 (pincer), +1 (per charge of lightning gun); pincer attack only at point-blank range; lightning gun holds 32 charges, any number of which may be fired per round in a single attack.

Armor: -5 vs any (thick carapace)

Stability Loss: +0

Investigation
Electrical Repair: All I can guess about the machinery from these receipts and the one piece we found is that it seems to be designed to create and manipulate an amazingly intense magnetic field, but in a very small cubic space. But there's no way that such a small machine, with no external power input, could even generate that kind of field. The lights and mirrors, as far as I can tell, serve no purpose. (Physics)

Geology: This "mental patient" was doodling trilobites until his release interview came through. (Biology, Evidence Collection)

Occult: Around the 2nd century A.D. in Rome, there was a branch of Mithraism dedicated to the worship of Aion, a sort of time demon with four snake-like arms, who appeared, or awoke, in a cave at the beginning of the world. He brought them wisdom and warned them — accurately — of traps set for them in the future. Rumors of that cult persist down through the Middle Ages.

Hound of Tindalos
These lean, ravening creatures dwell at the farthest beginnings of time on this planet, before DNA is formed in the first pools of protein. They inhabit

the angles of time, while other beings (including mankind and all common life) descend from curves. They hunger, and when they spot any prey, they follow it through time and space, traveling 100 million years in a day. They are immortal, and many of them know powerful eldritch spells from all throughout time.

Because of their relationship with the angles of time, they can materialize through any corner, if it is sharp — 120° or less. When a Hound manifests, it first appears as smoke pouring from the corner, from which the head and then the body emerges.

Driven off by a target, a Hound usually gives up. Unfortunately, such a creature is difficult to drive off. Friends who come to a target's aid also will be attacked.

Tongue: A Hound's tongue is long and hollow. If it strikes a person, it bloodlessly and painlessly cores a deep hole into their torso, somehow shifting the organs around. The victim takes no Health damage, but loses 3 *rating points* of Stability. The Hounds normally save this for the coup de grace.

Game Statistics

Abilities: Athletics 6 (refreshes 2 points per round and entirely between scenes), Health 13, Scuffling 30

Hit Threshold: 4

Alertness Modifier: +3

Stealth Modifier: +1

Weapon: +1 (paw), tongue (see above); the Hound's paws (and the rest of it) are covered with a sort of living bluish pus, which

JÉRÔME 07

a successful attack smears onto the victim in addition to other damage. The pus acts as a very strong acid (+1 damage modifier; see p. 68) each round until removed. It can be cauterized with fire.

Armor: -2 vs any (hide), regenerates 2 Health per round; immune to mundane weapons or chemicals.

Stability Loss: +2

Investigation

Chemistry: The bluish slime on the body seemed almost alive, but it was completely anaerobic, and contained polyphosphates and hydrogen sulfide rather than proteins. It no longer burns, although when it was on the victim, it must have been highly acidic judging from his wounds.

Evidence Collection: Whoever was in this room filled in all the corners with plaster and got rid of all their furniture except rounded pieces. They even puttied over the corners of their windows and picture frames.

Forensics: The body was found flat on its back, burned and corroded as if by acid, but covered with a non-acidic bluish slime. The head was severed and laid on the chest, covering a hole drilled with some sort of smooth-sided tool. The hole somehow did not puncture any organs. The cause of death was a massive coronary. The body showed old needle tracks indicating drug use, but none were found in the system.

Hunting Horror

Hunting horrors resemble enormous (40-foot) ropy black serpents or worms with one or two bat-like or sail-like wings. Their twitching, writhing forms continually shift and change, hurting the eyes. They croak like ravens.

Daylight dispels them, and a strong enough burst of light (from a lightning bolt or an atomic blast, perhaps) could sear one to dust. Hunting horrors move swiftly; they are harrier-creatures for some of the gods, particularly Nyarlathotep, and for wizards seeking blood and lives. Some have learned spells from such masters.

Game Statistics

Abilities (on ground/in air): Athletics 7/11, Health 14, Scuffling 22

Hit Threshold: 3 (large)

Alertness Modifier: +2

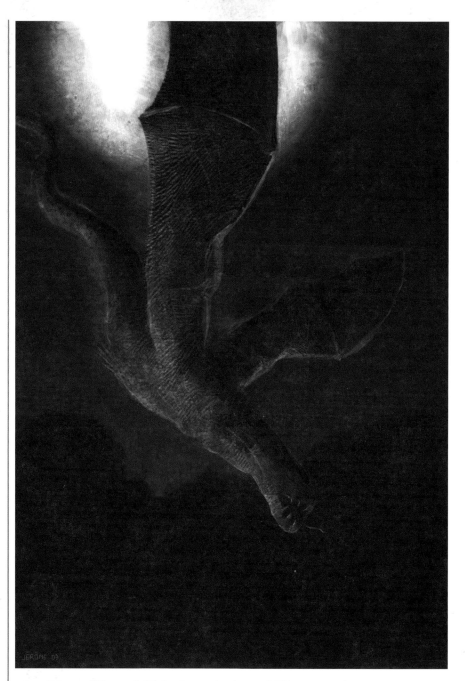

Stealth Modifier: +2 (flying)

Weapon: +1 (bite), -1 (tail loop); after a successful tail loop attack, the horror can carry the victim into the sky, but can only bite while its tail remains thusly engaged

Armor: -5 vs any (scales); all firearms do damage as if their modifier were -1

Stability Loss: +1

Investigation

Evidence Collection: Somebody smashed the streetlight that ordinarily shines on this courtyard. These bullets hit something, though, something that flattened them out.

Forensics: The corpse was mauled and mutilated, showing

severe blunt trauma as well as ligature marks on the limbs (indicating thick, looped cable was used to suspend the body and possibly slam it into a wall) and wounds made by at least five different shapes of blades, mostly hatchet-like. The left foot, heart, and at least three inches of the trachea have not been recovered from the crime scene.

K'n-Yani

K'n-yan is a vast, blue-litten underground empire beneath Oklahoma inhabited by all manner of strange creatures. Its people, the K'n-yani, resemble long-skulled, copper-skinned humans with strongly aquiline features similar to the Indians of Mexico. They fled the surface world during a great cataclysm, which may have been the sinking of Atlantis, the invasion of the Mi-Go, or (according to their own myths) the fall of R'lyeh. They worship primarily Tulu and Yig; in the past, they worshipped Tsathoggua but discovered something in black N'kai that caused them to reject him and destroy his temples.

They engage in occasional commerce with the serpent-folk of red-litten Yoth, and learned much magic from them, including the secret of immortality and reanimation of the dead. They ride genetically engineered humanoids similar to ghasts, and feed them reptoid flesh from a sentient slave race. Fortunately, their race is locked in stark degeneration, and they do not often emerge to the surface world, which their religion holds taboo.

Telepathy: The people of K'n-yan communicate telepathically among themselves and with outsiders. For such outsiders, telepathic contact with a K'n-yani causes a 1-point Stability test initially and one for every twelve hours the contact continues. Some gifted K'n-yani can also create telepathic illusions resistible after a successful Difficulty 5 Sense Trouble test. Successfully throwing off such an illusion does, however, trigger a 3-point Stability test. Or worse, depending upon what seeing the truth reveals …

Dematerialization: K'n-yani exist in both the material and astral planes, and can shift between them at will. This allows them, for instance, to phase through solid matter, or become intangible to enemy blows. A K'n-yani may also dematerialize something or someone else by touch, rotating it into the astral at the cost of 1 Health pool point to the K'n-yani for every 70 lbs of mass so rotated. Unwilling victims must succeed in a contest of their Stability vs the K'n-yani's Athletics.

Game Statistics

Abilities: Athletics 8, Health 7, Ray-guns 3, Scuffling 8, Weapons 4

Hit Threshold: 4

Alertness Modifier: +1

Weapon: -1 (savage martial arts), +0 (short sword), +0 (disintegration ray); damage inflicted by the disintegration ray never refreshes

Armor: -1 vs any (advanced "ghost shirt" fabric)

Stability Loss: There is no Stability loss for merely seeing the people of K'n-yan. Seeing them dematerialize is a 2-point Stability test at +0.

Investigation

Anthropology: The Aztecs, the Hopi, and many other tribes in the region believe that when the world ended last time, their ancestors went into a deep cave, from which they emerged to start the world over again. According to the Hopi, below that world lay the Red City.

Chemistry: This peculiar metal from the Kiowa grave is denser than lead, but strongly magnetically polarized to normally non-magnetic material.

Oral History: O' course thet thar mound is hainted! They's Injun ghosts aplenty in it. Hoodoo, I calls it. Folks hear tell of treasure in thar and go up to excavatin' and they's never seen agin. But nobody ever fesses up to tellin' 'em 'bout no treasure – like they heerd it from nowhere, or from the ghosts.

Lemurian

According to HP Blavatsky, the continent of Lemuria (now sunk below the Indian Ocean) hosted the "Third Root Race" of humanity, a race of three-eyed hermaphroditic "Egg-Born" giants. (Lemuria also hosted a number of other races, including a human-headed tentacular species and the serpent-folk.) The Lemurians resemble 15- to 25-foot tall, four-armed apes with fur the color of yellow mud. Some Lemurians have not three eyes (set evenly around the head for full 360-degree vision) but only one in the middle of the face. Wizards and Theosophists alike seek out ancient Lemurian ruins from Madagascar to Mount Shasta for samples of their intricate crystalline technology, which harnesses both psychic power and acoustics.

Three-eyed Lemurians can strike thrice in a single combat round, against up to three targets at no increase in Hit Threshold.

Psychic Sink: Whoever built the Lemurians designed them as vessels for psychic power, suitable channels, hosts, and servitors for astral or powerfully telepathic races. They communicate among themselves telepathically. Upon provocation they unleash the contents of their psychic sink in a wave affecting every mind up to long range. The result is a 5-point Stability test as visions, images, commands, and impressions from prehuman epochs unload into the subject mind. Such a tidal wave of images does, however, grant the recipient 1 Cthulhu Mythos rating point the first time she experiences it.

Ultra-Violet Vision: The Lemurian third (or single) eye is actually an enlarged proto-pineal gland, allowing them to see into the ultra-violet dimension. In addition to undiminished vision at night, they cannot be surprised by invisible, astral, or other extra-planar attacks.

Game Statistics
Abilities: Athletics 8, Health 10, Scuffling 10

Hit Threshold: 4

Alertness Modifier: +2 (three-eyed only)

Weapon: +0 (massive ape-like fists)

Armor: -2 (thick, clay-like skin)

Stability Loss: +1

Investigation
Forensics: She died of a brain embolism - strangest thing, though, you don't expect a pineal gland to swell up and burst like that. (Medicine)

Geology: The material under the dead woman's fingernails resembles nothing so much as the clay from the deep sea bottoms, heavy in carbonaceous compounds, but we can't identify the hair matted into it except that it resembles the hair of lemurs or tarsiers rather than apes. (And Biology)

Occult: News of a Lemurian sighting anywhere in the world rapidly spreads through the Theosophical gossip network. Occult can also help pinpoint likely spots for Lemurian ruins.

Sense Trouble: The sound of a crystal bell being rung, or of a finger being run along the rim of a water glass, echoes weirdly through these sandstone ruins.

Lloigor
The lloigor are vortices of immaterial vibration in natural form, and completely invisible to human eyes. On rare occasions they create enormous material bodies resembling monstrous, unearthly reptiles for themselves. (This may be the actual origin of dragon and sea serpent legends.) Lloigor minds are not divided into layers of consciousness. Lloigor do not forget, nor do they have imaginations or subconscious to mislead or distract them. Their outlook of absolute pessimism results in an atmosphere of gloom that makes lloigor minds and actions incomprehensible to humans. Telepathic contact with lloigor always leads to suicidal depression for the human partners.

The lloigor originally came to earth from the Andromeda galaxy and ruled the Pacific continent of Mu, either as viceroys or as controllers of Ghatanothoa. They enslaved humans, using cruel, alien discipline upon recalcitrant servitors, such as amputating limbs or causing cancer-like tentacular growths to sprout on them. Earthly lloigor continued to decay and decline, and they retreated under the earth and seas, where they still husband their failing energies. Some family lineages, knowingly or unknowingly traced from primeval Mu, still serve the lloigor. Such families often have histories of suicide, incest, and bizarre mental instability.

Surviving lloigor have acted in Wales, Rhode Island, Ceylon, Lebanon, and Iraq in recent years.

Harvest: The lloigor need humans to survive: these immaterial entities must draw energy from intelligent beings to perform necessary tasks. A lloigor can either spend 1 Health point to drain a single sleeping human, or 5 Health to drain several slumberers at once, from up to several miles away. Each victim loses 1D6 pool points from any ability or abilities chosen by the lloigor. A lloigor that can harvest from multiple sleepers can fully refresh all of its points in one ability pool, including Health, overnight. A single-human harvest lets it refresh normally. The next morning, the victims wake complaining of headaches and bad sleep.

Sleeping Sickness: A lloigor may target a single human for intensive drain, either to recruit her (by dropping her Stability to -12) or to remove her as a threat. The lloigor spends 3 Health to lower the victim's Health pool to -1 while she sleeps, rendering her physically weak, and draining 1D6 Stability points from her pool, dropping her into a spiritual coma. After each full day spent unconscious and under the lloigor influence, the victim can attempt a Consciousness roll (see p. 63) to awaken. If successful, the victim immediately refreshes 1 Stability point (or back up to 1, if she was at negative Stability) and becomes susceptible to medical treatment for her Health loss. (At the Keeper's discretion, she may recall her nightmares while comatose, providing valuable clues to the lloigor's whereabouts.) If not, she

continues to slumber for another day, losing 1 Stability point each night. When she reaches -11 Health, she stabilizes; she cannot make any further Consciousness rolls, but she loses no further Health. When she reaches -12 Stability, she awakens to serve the lloigor.

Telekinesis: The lloigor can affect the material world by telekinesis, although it must be directly present to do so. It can do so grossly (hurling people into crevasses, smashing aircraft propellors) or finely (moving compass needles or scalpels) or intricately (unlocking a safe). It takes 10 Health points to create a force capable of manipulating up to 7 lbs. above ground, 6 Health points to do the same in a subsurface but open area, such as a river bed or canyon, and 3 Health points in a tunnel or cave. For each additional expenditure, the amount of force doubles.

A single lloigor might use 3 Health to move a wine bottle or a penknife in a cellar. If it spent 6 Health, it could manipulate up to 14 lbs., if it spent 9 Health, it could exert 28 lbs. of force, if it spent 12 Health, it could move 56 lbs., and so forth.

A group of lloigor might combine their telekinesis to awesome effect.

Vortex Attack: The lloigor's most fearsome weapon is a type of implosion sounding like the roll of distant thunder. The vortex blast tears material in its diameter to shards, leaving the ground splintered and discolored, with pools of blue-green water in occasional sink-

holds and crevices. The diameter of the blast is 1 yard per Health point spent by the lloigor. Each additional lloigor involved can increase the effect: two lloigor can devastate 2 yards per 1 Health point, three can implode 3 yards per 1 Health point spent, etc An alert Investigator (with a Difficulty 5 Sense Trouble; Difficulty 4 if he has any points in Cthulhu Mythos) notices the telltale effects of the vortex (see below).

Raise the Dragon: To take its reptile form, a process that resembles heavy fog, the lloigor must expend Health points equal to the lloigor's reptile Scuffling pool. This cost is halved if the lloigor spends an entire night forming the body. Once the lloigor takes dragon shape, it can maintain this form indefinitely or dissolve it at will. If the lloigor goes to Health 0 in reptile form, it dies permanently. Multiple lloigor may spend their Health to permit a single one to create his physical form quickly. A lloigor in reptile form has all the powers of one in the immaterial mode, except that it cannot pass through walls and is not invisible.

Game Statistics

Abilities (immaterial/material): Athletics 3/7, Health 39/22, Scuffling 0/17

Hit Threshold: 7 (invisible)/3 (large)

Alertness Modifier: +1 (+2 vs any electrical field or music)

Stealth Modifier: +2

Weapon: +5 (claw), +1 (bite); usable only in material form

Armor: -5 vs any (reptilian hide);

in immaterial form it cannot be harmed by any physical weapon

Stability Loss: +0 as reptile; +1 as immaterial poltergeist; +3 for communication or mental contact

Investigation

Geology: I can't tell what sheared these rocks; it wasn't heat or cold, or impact, or chemicals. They seem to split along a kind of crystal pattern, though, even the igneous rocks. This sample here almost looks like it was splintered from inside. The water is not contaminated – if anything, it's got less bacteria or algae in it than normal pond water — it just looks strange in this light. If it's a mineral, it's too trace to register.

Library Use: It can't be hereditary – people who marry into the de Voyver family commit suicide or get cancer if anything more often than the de Voyver heirs do. If only we could get accurate records on their servants.

Medicine: Perhaps it's a vitamin deficiency, or something given off by that awful blue-green water in the tarn, but these people just aren't tired, they're ill. Reflexes are slow, mental acuity is down, and I think those headaches aren't imaginary either. Perhaps it's heavy metal poisoning from the water supply.

Sense Trouble: The air seems to be overlapping itself in a sort of moiré pattern of swirling lines. There's a kind of half-heard throbbing, as though you're only hearing the very low notes of an arrhythmic dirge, but you don't know if it's in your head or coming from somewhere. Maybe underground?

Masqut

According to Bedouin legend, the masqut are inhuman petrified corpses that haunt Irem of the Pillars. The legend of the masqut actually describes the reptilian quadrupeds who dwell beneath the Nameless City in Arabia. They may be kin to (or a created sub-species of) the serpent-folk, although their civilization was more restricted and lasted longer, eventually removing itself completely underground during the rise of the human city Irem. They resemble noseless lizards with bulging foreheads, devil-like horns, and jaws similar to those of alligators. If they carry weapons, they sheath them on their backs.

The Nameless City holds thousands, perhaps tens of thousands, of mummified masqut in its warrens. Some degenerate specimens may still survive in the eerie phosphorescent realm beneath the City, and some may yet roam the Empty Quarter of Arabia as half-material ghosts similar to the K'n-yani. Masqut sightings are often accompanied by a mysterious arctic wind moving along the ground at shin level.

Game Statistics

Abilities: Athletics 6, Health 7, Scuffling 16, Weapons 10

Hit Threshold: 4

Weapon: -1 (bite), +0 (mace)

Armor: -2 vs any (hide)

Stability Loss: +0

Investigation

Forensics: First, his legs were broken by three or four blows, from the side. Then, after he fell, the blows came down onto his torso, always from above.

Occult: According to one Arabic legend, the builders of Irem, the A'adites, lived before Adam. (Theology)

Sense Trouble: Your camel jolts to his feet.

Mi-Go

The mi-go are an interstellar race, with a main colony or base on Yuggoth (Pluto). They have mining colonies in the mountains of Earth, where the mi-go seek rare ores. To the extent their biology is terrene at all, it is fungoid. Despite this, they resemble pinkish-gray crustaceans, with two nippers and myriads of twitching smaller limbs. A bulbous, frond-covered head and two membranous wings complete the picture. They communicate with each other by changing the colors of their wrinkled heads, but they can speak human tongues in buzzing, insect-like voices. They worship both Nyarlathotep and Shub-Niggurath, and possibly others. They will hire human agents to simplify their operations, and are sometimes connected to cults. Their multiple legs leave strange footprints that have helped create the legend of the Abominable Snowman (the *mi-gou* or *migyu*) in Thibet.

They are unable to eat terrene food, and must import theirs from other worlds. They are able to fly through the interstellar aether on their great wings, but maneuver clumsily in an atmosphere. Ordinary photographic plates will not take an image of these beings, though

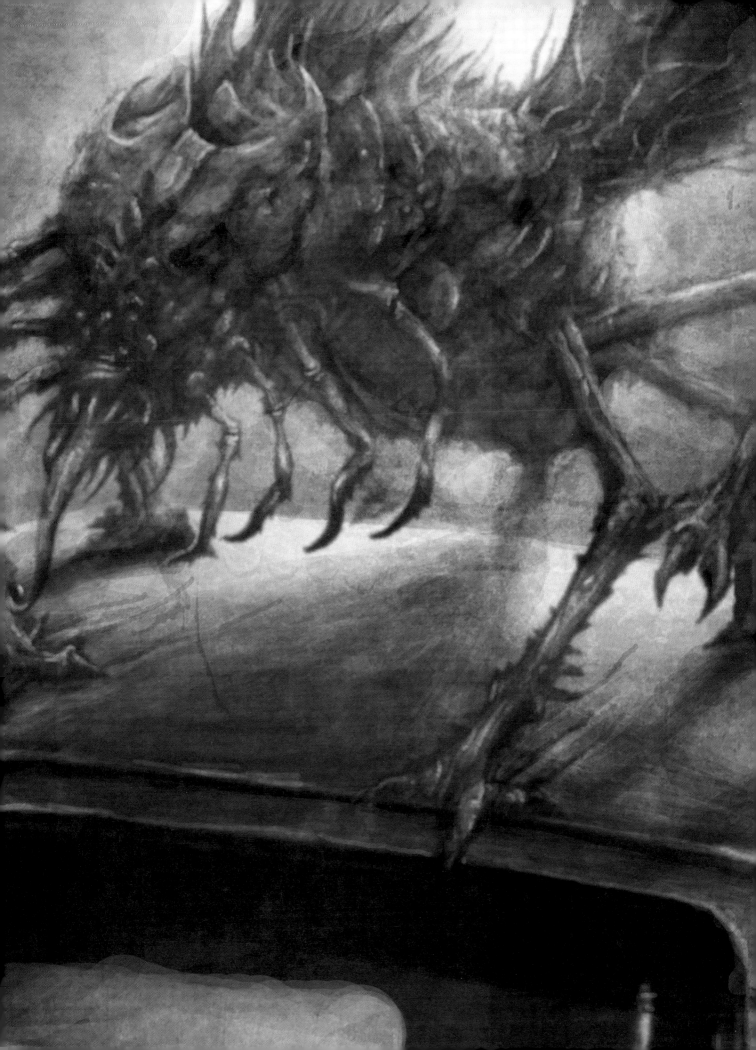

Chemistry or Photography will let an Investigator design a suitable emulsion. After death, a mi-go dissolves in a few hours.

They are capable of astounding surgical feats, including the placing of living human brains in life-sustaining metal tubes that can withstand the vacuum and cold of space. (Why the mi-go would abduct people to Yuggoth or elsewhere is unknown.) They can then attach speaking, listening, and seeing devices to the tube, so that the brain can interact with those about it.

A fungus from Yuggoth may attack in hand-to-hand combat with two nippers at once.

Game Statistics

Abilities (on land/in air): Athletics 4/10, Firearms 6, Health 6, Scuffling 7/10

Hit Threshold: 3/4

Alertness Modifier: +1 to +3 (alien surveillance technology)

Stealth Modifier: +1 (flying)

Weapon: -1 (nippers), +4 (mist gun); if the mi-go succeed in two nipper attacks in a row against the same target, they can carry him into the sky until his lungs burst or they drop him on something painful; the mi-go mist gun transposes the cold of interstellar space to an area about ten feet across for about three minutes. Investigators who have seen the mist gun in action may try to dodge its slowly-expanding field with an Athletics test (Difficulty 4). The Keeper is free to invent other mi-go weapons.

Armor: the non-terrene

composition of the mi-go reduces all impaling damage, including bullets, by 2; some mi-go wear bio-webs that reduce all damage *except* impaling damage by 3.

Stability Loss: +1

Investigation

Evidence Collection: Even the fingerprints on the wax hands found in the missing man's house were accurate, as were the tiny hairs molded on their backs.

Forensics: The chest and abdomen bear dozens of tiny wounds and incisions, made by delicate blades. The wounds were delivered from an oblique, upward angle. Aside from the sharpness of the implement, however, they had little penetrating power. The victim ran a great distance, was attacked, and then bled to death.

Occult: The Thibetan term for the Abominable Snowman, *migyu*, means "fast-moving one." The footprints it leaves are remarkably widely spaced, almost as though it were hovering in the air between steps.

Sense Trouble: You hear a noise halfway between a cicada chirp and the blurred flutter of a trapped moth.

Nightgaunt

Nightgaunts are winged creatures with barbed tails, prehensile paws, and a pair of inward-curving horns. Their skin is black and oily like a whale's, and they have no faces. They never speak or laugh, and their wings make no sound.

Nightgaunts serve Nodens by, among other things, grasping

and carrying off intruders, who they unceremoniously dump in the most dismal and horrible places imaginable (including the Dreamlands or other dimensions) and leave to die. Nightgaunts perch various spots in the lonely parts of the world, and come out at night. They are not very intelligent, but can understand some languages (such as the gibberings of ghouls), and are friendly to some occult races.

Nightgaunts attempt to sneak up quietly on victims, grasp their weapons, and overpower them. Two or more nightgaunts can cooperate (see p. 58) on Scuffling contests against a single target.

Tickling: Nightgaunts who win a Scuffling contest do no damage, but may disarm their foe of one weapon or item. Once they have won two Scuffling contests in a row, he is grappled by their long, strong fingers and toes, and they can carry him off and begin to tickle him with their razor-sharp barbed tails. A successful tickle attack (which also uses Scuffling) leaves the victim disoriented and confused for 1D6+1 rounds, unable to take any physical action and with effects similar to being **shaken** (see p. 74). Armor does not protect against nightgaunt tickling.

Game Statistics

Abilities (on ground/in air or space): Athletics 6/12, Health 7, Scuffling 10

Hit Threshold: 4

Alertness Modifier: +1

Stealth Modifier: +2 (flying), +3 (flying in darkness)

Weapon: see above

Armor: –2 vs any (skin)

Stability Loss: +0

Investigation

Cop Talk: No matter how many people we talk to, they all swear they heard the missing girl laughing "from upstairs" right at midnight. She can't have been upstairs from the whole block, can she?

Rat-Thing

Rat-things resemble ordinary rats, and are easily mistaken for them at a distance. Their heads are nonetheless evil caricatures of human heads, and their paws are like tiny human hands. They have extremely strong, sharp teeth. These unnatural creatures are created by malign sorcery, which allowed deceased cultists to be transformed and thus continue to serve their masters. Many rat-things know spells, either from their human existence or from centuries of association with witches and sorcerers. Though they do not die naturally, they are now very rare. Attacking rat-things climb the legs or clothes of human opponents, or drop down from ceilings.

The Keeper can use rat-thing statistics to represent not just Brown Jenkin from *The Dreams in the Witch-House*, but devolved, stunted cannibals like the Martense kin from *The Lurking Fear*, Robert E Howard's titular quasi-reptilian *Worms of the Earth*, or any other dwarfish horrors that lurk in crawl-spaces, cellars, and attics. If said horrors come in packs (like the Martense kin), adapt the swarm rules from p. 156.

Game Statistics

Abilities: Athletics 9, Health 3, Scuffling 7

Hit Threshold: 6 (small and incredibly nimble)

Alertness Modifier: +1

Stealth Modifier: +2

Weapon: –2 (bite); bitten victims must make a Difficulty 4 Health test or be infected with some loathsome disease. Unless the Keeper has a specific disease in mind, it onsets in 1D6 hours and affects the victim as if **hurt**. It then begins draining 1 Health point per hour until the victim reaches –6, at which point he requires hospitalization and medical attention.

Armor: none

Stability Loss: +0; +1 if the rat-thing was known to the witness when alive

Investigation
Architecture: The dimensions of the walls and attic don't add up. Which is to say, it almost seems like the attic is larger than the house, but that's impossible. There's probably some sort of large crawlspace behind one of the interior walls.

Biology: The skeleton is obviously that of a huge, diseased rat. That said, the bones of the paws almost seem prehensile, with joints so well developed and used as to have become arthritic. The skull is queerly flattened in front, and distended in the cranial region.

Evidence Collection: Two of the bloody rat prints almost resemble human hand prints, except for the size, of course.

Forensics: The body was cored out and gnawed from the inside as by the teeth of an enormous rat. The path ran from the abdominal cavity up through the liver and heart and out through the base of the throat. No indication has yet been found as to how the rat got into the body cavity in the first place, however.

Sand-Dweller
These enigmatic humanoids look as though they had been encrusted with sand. They dwell in caverns and come out at night, although they can easily withstand the hottest desert sun. Their large eyes and ears give them excellent senses, although they dislike strong light. They can go weeks without water. They are known to live in the American Southwest and may live in other deserts of the world as well. Occult rumor places at least one tribe of sand-dwellers on Mars. Their tribes worship various deities, especially Nyarlathotep, Yig, and Hastur, and often dwell near their ruined fanes or human cults.

A sand-dweller may make two claw attacks against the same target in a single round. They use spear-throwers (which can hurl spears at long range), but not bows.

Game Statistics
Abilities: Athletics 8, Health 7, Scuffling 10, Weapons 6

Hit Threshold: 4

Alertness Modifier: +2 (-1 in bright desert daylight)

Stealth Modifier: +2 (in deserts only)

Weapon: -1 (claw), +0 (stone-tipped spear)

Armor: -3 vs any (sandpapery hide)

Stability Loss: +0

Investigation
Evidence Collection: During the murder, somebody sat right here on this rock and expertly knapped a Clovis point from flint. Those are spear points that showed up out of nowhere in the Southwest about 14,000 BC, and no tribe has made them for the last ten millennia. Until last night, apparently. (And either Anthropology or Archaeology)

Forensics: The wounds on the body resemble blows from a garden rake, which would also explain the sand abraded into the bloody tissue. The liver was carved out from behind, post-mortem, with a small axe or spade.

Sense Trouble: You smell a strong reek of ammonia, like a cat's litter box, when the desert wind shifts suddenly.

Serpent-Folk
Serpent-folk resemble upright serpents, with ophidian heads and scales, but with two arms and legs. They can see in the dark and sense heat like a pit viper. They possess tails and in their great days often dressed in robes. Their civilization flourished on the continent of Valusia (roughly where the Mediterranean basin is now) before even dinosaurs walked the earth. They built black basalt cities and fought wars, all in the Permian era or before.

They were then great sorcerers and scientists, and devoted much energy to calling forth dreadful demons and brewing potent poisons. Though prehistoric humans defeated and scattered their remnant secret kingdom of Thuria, their civilization died long ago. A few sorcerers survive elsewhere, as do pockets of dwarfed degenerates and human-serpent folk hybrids. Some remnants include an occasional atavistic, fully capable serpent person still favored by Yig. A common spell among the surviving serpent-folk sorcerers is an illusion that transforms the caster's appearance into that of a normal human, allowing him to mingle in human society. It requires the devouring of the target human.

Serpent-folk may use all weapons known to man, clutching them effectively in taloned hands. Use the same base chances as for humans. In hand-to-hand combat the bite attack can be made simultaneously with most weapon attacks.

Venom: The bite of a serpent man is venomous; in 15 minutes to an hour after being bitten, the victim must make a Difficulty 4 Health test. If she fails, she immediately loses a number of Health points equal to the attacking serpent man's Athletics *rating* as she goes into convulsions and begins to suffer respiratory failure, losing 1 Health per hour until treated. If she succeeds, she loses a number of Health points equal to only half the attacking serpent man's Athletics rating, but she will suffer the equivalent of **hurt** status (unless the loss puts her below -5) until she is treated.

Game Statistics
Abilities: Athletics 8, Health 6, Scuffling 11, Weapons 7

Hit Threshold: 4

Alertness Modifier: +1

Stealth Modifier: +1

Weapon: +0 (bite), +1 (scimitar); venom (see above)

Armor: -1 vs any (scales)

Stability Loss: +0

Investigation
Biology: No poisonous snake has a head big enough to have made those two punctures in one bite.

Forensics: There were two large punctures in the throat, with only a trickle of blood near them. The blood remained tacky for an unusually long period post mortem. The skin around the punctures is friable, almost necrotic, and emits a greenish oily liquid. (The examining assistant got some on his hand, and it tingled for several minutes.) The extremities were bluish, and the face engorged with blood and bright blue. The protruding tongue was swollen and black, and the eyes purpled. Cause of death was paralysis of the chest muscles.

Sense Trouble: This apartment smells like the snake house at the zoo.

Servitor of the Outer Gods
These amorphous beings progress by rolling or slithering. They resemble frogs, as well as squids or octopi. Servitors accompany their masters as required. These are the demon flautists that play the cacodaemoniacal piping for their masters' dance. They sometimes play for groups of cultists as well, as a sort of background dirge, or in order to summon various deities.

Summoning Flute: Unless explicitly ordered otherwise by its own summoner, a Servitor may summon an entity of its own, often a Great Old One or other fearsome being. (The choice is up to the Keeper.) Servitors always know at least three other summoning spells, and can cast them during combat. This requires 2 to 4 rounds of hellish piping, and costs the Servitor 1 Health point, and 1 more for each 5 rounds that the summoned entity remains.

An Investigator who spends 2 points from his Art pool can play the Servitor's flute, assuming that one of his arts is playing any similar instrument. This costs 1 Stability, but will very greatly aid in casting the Summon Servitor spell (see p. 117), although Servitors react very poorly to seeing their sacred instruments in the hands of base humans. Its other benefits or dangers are up to the Keeper; for example, the flute may impart other summoning spells to its user. Such spells can be cast with no component other than a Servitor flute.

Game Statistics
Abilities: Athletics 6, Health 8, Scuffling 9

Hit Threshold: 3

Alertness Modifier: +1

Stealth Modifier: -2 (infernal piping)

Weapon: -2 (tentacle), but for each hit, roll damage 1d6 times for multiple tentacle attacks.

Armor: no physical weapon can harm one; magical weapons do normal damage; regenerates 1 Health each round until dead or banished

Stability Loss: +2

Investigation
Chemistry: That green liquid isn't vegetation, no matter what it smells like. There's not a trace of chlorophyll, or even cellulose, in it. Lots of methane, though, bound up in some kind of weird colloid. (Biology)

Evidence Collection: There were twelve spent brass in the clearing, but only three bullet

holes anywhere. Something soaked up nine shots and walked off with the bullets. The scene stinks like a swamp, too, strange in this dry spell. And the trail – not only the green stain, but the crushed grass and such — just peters out about 40 feet on either side of the crime scene.

Forensics: The body was lacerated and nearly flayed in strips, with trauma consistent with bullwhip or knout injuries. Nine ribs, the sternum, both collarbones, and all the bones in both forearms were broken, and several vertebra dislocated or smashed together. The welts and lacerations were bloody and filled with a clear greenish liquid, probably vegetation of some sort.

Sense Trouble: Do you smell methane?

Shan

The shan are pigeon-sized, slave-taking, insectile aliens native to the planet Shaggai. Their advanced technology operates by focused mentation, and their habits of mind are sadistic and byzantine. They live by photosynthesis, and appreciate the aesthetics of deformity and torture. This has a religious component, as the shan devoutly worship Azathoth, and many know suitable spells for such. Shan are extremely long-lived, taking centuries to reach adulthood. They will likely have a few burly slaves (human or otherwise) on call if encountered.

The shan are now a fugitive race. Shaggai itself was destroyed by a great catastrophe (some texts blame the Great Old One Ghroth the Harbinger) but many shan escaped in pyramidal temples made of an indestructible gray metal, teleporting them to other worlds, including Earth. But they were trapped here. Our atmosphere contains some element or wavelength which prevents the shan from teleporting away, and also keeps individual shan from flying any great distance. The shan temple on Earth is in Goatswood, in the Severn Valley in Britain. At one time they ruled a human witch-cult dedicated to finding sacrifices for Azathoth, although the witch-finder Matthew Hopkins burned it out with great brutality in 1646.

Shan Infestation: Shan are parasitic and not wholly material. With a successful Scuffling contest, a shan can fly right through human tissue into a target's brain, where it crawls about and reads its host's memories, warps his thought-processes, and injects specific memories and ideas of its own. During the day, the insect is not active within the brain, leaving the victim to do more or less as he pleases. But at night the shan wakes, and begins to implant memories. It can implant Stability-eroding sights the insect has witnessed, convince the host he has committed horrific crimes, or jumble memory-fragments to entice the victim into performing certain actions. Eventually (at Stability 0) the host is so hypnotized that he gladly helps the shan. But often such progressively increasing control causes the victim to go mad, and thus become an unsuitable host.

Nerve Whip: This small device projects a chattering line of pallid light at close range. When the light strikes a target, he must make a Difficulty 5 Athletics

test. If he fails, he is overcome by agony, and can do nothing but writhe on the ground until the weapon is turned off. If he succeeds, he is still in pain, and is treated as **hurt** for the next 12 hours. The shan carry many such whips, and may renew this attack each round.

Game Statistics

Abilities (on ground/in air): Athletics 4/20, Health 2, Scuffling 25, Weapons 13

Hit Threshold: 5 (small)

Stealth Modifier: +2

Weapon: see above

Armor: none

Stability Loss: +0

Investigation

Cop Talk: I don't care what anybody says, I say someone from on high shut down that investigation into that truck driver who turned up dead in Temphill.

Forensics: The body was found with self-inflicted lacerations on the face, including eye gouges. The dead man apparently used the screwdriver to punch the holes found in his own skull. But the actual cause of death is completely unknown – the heart just stopped.

Streetwise: There's good money in taking young girls from Bristol or Manchester up to Brichester and leaving them in that woodlot on the edge of town. Oh, and not asking stupid questions.

Shantak

Shantaks are noisome and loathly

– elephant-sized, horse-headed birds with scales instead of feathers. They brood in cavernous holes and their wings are encrusted with rime and nitre. Various servants of the Outer Gods, and a few brave or lunatic sorcerers, use them as steeds. Shantaks can fly through space, and have been known to carry an unwary rider straight to the throne of Azathoth. Shantaks fear and despise nightgaunts, and will not willingly remain in sight of one, retreating at top speed.

Game Statistics

Abilities: Athletics 30, Health 17, Scuffling 18

Hit Threshold: 3 (elephantine)

Stealth Modifier: –1 (stench)

Weapon: +2 (bite), +4 (smash); shantaks can only make smash attacks every other round, and cannot make them against a target on their back.

Armor: -5 vs any (hide)

Stability Loss: +0

Investigation

Biology: The only thing that might have taken that kind of bite is a shark, although the bite marks – if they are bite marks — show only one row of chisel-like teeth.

Forensics: Simultaneous rending wounds consistent with a large, semi-circular bite separated the upper chest and head from the portions of the body we found. Death was instantaneous, and probably occurred on the shore rather than on the rooftop where the legs and abdomen were found.

Shoggoth

Abdul Alhazred attempted desperately to claim that there were none of these fetid, oozing, protoplasmic monstrosities on Earth itself, save in crazed dreams. He was wrong. These iridescent blobs boil with eyes and bubbles, making and unmaking any organs or tendrils needed for a given task. Shoggoths are often found as servants of Deep Ones and other races, and are amphibious. They are surly servants at best, ever becoming more and more intelligent, more and more rebellious, more and more imitative. They destroyed their former creators, the Elder Things, in a rebellion. They communicate in whatever manner their master race wishes, forming special organs for the purpose.

A typical shoggoth is roughly a 15-foot diameter sphere when floating free. In combat, it covers an area 5 yards square. It can attack two beings at close range per round and all beings within point-blank range simultaneously, although its targets' Hit Thresholds increase by 1 for every three separate targets it attacks. A shoggoth may stretch or shape its bulk to bring itself into point-blank range of as many targets as possible; if need be, it might engage in simultaneous Athletics and Scuffling contests against various targets!

Snare and Crush: With a successful Scuffling attack, a shoggoth may loop an increasingly muscular tendril around a character (+2 damage modifier). Each round thereafter, the shoggoth hits automatically and does +2 more damage each

time. Characters snared by the shoggoth also automatically hit the shoggoth.

Game Statistics
Abilities: Athletics 10+, Health 32+, Scuffling 23+

Hit Threshold: 3 (large)

Alertness Modifier: +2

Stealth Modifier: -1

Weapon: +5 (pseudopod, often ridged), +2 (snare, see above)

Armor: fire and electricity do only half damage; all physical weapons do only 1 point of damage; regenerates 2 Health each round until dead.

Stability Loss: +3

Investigation

Biology: The slime is pure protoplasm, much like the matter of an amoeba. There is no cell structure visible. Its chromatin is fragmentary and evenly mixed throughout, rather than being differentiated into nuclear bodies or organelles.

Forensics: Greenish-yellow putrescent slime covered the body, which was heavily contused. The spine had been partially detached, and the head hung by ragged fragments of skin and tendon. There were ten or a dozen different types of bite and claw marks on the body.

Sense Trouble: From down the tunnel comes a sort of anechoic roaring or rumbling. It almost sounds like a crowd of people or birds.

Son of Yog-Sothoth

These are the beings formed when Yog-Sothoth mates with a human, creating a hybrid creature. No two Sons (or Daughters) are alike. Some are horrible and monstrous, both visible and invisible; others appear human, mostly human, or half-human. Both sorts smell extraordinarily strange or foul, especially to dogs or horses.

All such hybrids grow and mature rapidly, requiring great quantities of fresh, raw flesh for sustenance. Invisible Sons become briefly visible while feeding. They also seek out Mythos knowledge, spells, and tomes wherever they can,

working to destroy the barriers that keep their Father from them. All His children instinctually know Call Yog-Sothoth.

Game Statistics -Monstrous Son

Abilities: Athletics 10, Health 21, Scuffling 33

Hit Threshold: 7 (while invisible), 3 (large, when visible)

Alertness Modifier: +1

Stealth Modifier: +2 (while invisible), –3 (when visible or against dogs)

Weapon: +3 (trample), –1 (trunk); after a successful trunk attack, the Son grasps and holds his victim, automatically doing both crushing damage (–1) and draining blood (+0) each round until dead

Armor: cannot be harmed by physical weapons; enchanted weapons do minimum damage.

Stability Loss: +1 (invisible), +3 (visible)

Game Statistics - Human Son

Abilities: Athletics 8, Firearms or Weapons 7, Health 13, Scuffling 17

Hit Threshold: 4

Alertness Modifier: +2

Stealth Modifier: +1 (–3 against dogs)

Weapon: –1 (inhumanly strong fist), whatever weapon is appropriate for killing

Armor: None

Stability Loss: +0 (clothed or relatively human), +1 (naked, dead, or relatively inhuman)

Investigation

Evidence Collection: The trail of the thing goes vertically up the side of the shale cliff, despite weighing more than a moose from the depth of the tracks.

Forensics: The torso and one leg were smashed flat by the rapid descent of a roughly barrel-shaped mass. (If this were India, not Oregon, I'd say it was an elephant track.) The black, ropy tar on the body sublimed away into a whitish gummy residue. There was surprisingly little blood or bruising. The large, circular black mark on the upper back proved, on further inspection, to be composed of dozens of small, suppurating punctures.

Oral History: Pore ol' Elspeth. Got knocked up on Roodmas an' los' the chile on Midsummers, and still pretends to go 'feed her babe' down in Devil Glen when she thinks no-one's a-watchin.' Runs in th' family, I expect; her mammy used to put out calf's brains for whippoorwills, of all things.

Space-Eater

This enigmatic interstellar race appears as towering columns of shimmering, twisting, auroral yellow light. They eat their way across the cosmos, devouring higher complexity on some unknowable mission. They arrive at night, first manifesting as a temperature drop, bringing cold, damp, and mist with them. If the prey they seek is suitable, they begin devouring the local geometry, causing it to disintegrate with an anechoic droning sound. As space-time weakens, more space-eaters arrive (at intervals best left to the Keeper's sense of drama and fairness). They can only be thwarted with powerfully regular geometries, ideally highly energetic ones such as burning crosses, which they must make Difficulty 4 Health tests to breach. They are also blocked by the Elder Sign.

If a space-eater attacks a sentient being, it translates the target's brain into energetic photons and transmits them back the way it came. The target often hallucinates being attacked or probed by drills, long-fingered hands, or wires, and always feels a sensation of intense, burning cold on the inside of her skull.

Game Statistics
Abilities: Athletics 5, Health 13, Scuffling 16

Hit Threshold: 3

Weapon: +0 (brain drain); target takes damage to Stability

Stealth Modifier: -2

Armor: insubstantial, cannot be harmed by physical weapons; fire does half damage

Stability Loss: +0

Investigation
Craft (Carpentry): There isn't a plumb line, right angle, or true join in this room. But the rest of the house is good, professional work. (Architecture)

Electrical Repair: The wiring and appliances in the room show signs of intense power fluctuations, including burned spots and melted connections, as though it were caught in an incredibly powerful radio transmission.

Forensics: The brain is missing down to the stem, with no entry or exit wound.

Star Vampire
These loathsome, hovering things are normally invisible, their presence signalled only by a sort of ghoulish tittering. As a star vampire feeds, the blood it drinks or splashes on itself remains visible, revealing the bloated obscenity, especially its suckered trunks and pendulous stomachs. Powerful wizards and other beings who possess the hubris or lore needed to control them summon star vampires from the depths of space to slay their enemies. Such as, say, meddling Investigators.

A star vampire can only feed on one target at a time, or it can attack a target with two talon attacks in a round. If not actually feeding, it must make a Difficulty 3 Athletics test to avoid moving toward the largest quantity of spilled, open, or spurting blood available.

Game Statistics
Abilities: Athletics 9, Health 11, Scuffling 26

Hit Threshold: 6 (invisible but tittering); 3 (when feeding, and for 3 rounds thereafter)

Alertness Modifier: +1

Weapon: +2 (talons), -1 (bite); victim Health lost to bite attacks is added to the star vampire's Health or Athletics pool

Armor: -3 vs any (integument); bullets do half damage

Stability Loss: +1

Investigation
Cop Talk: The whole estate was guarded. Nobody saw anyone cross the lawns, no dogs barked. Right around 2 a.m., the time of death, one of the girls thought she heard him sniggering or tittering to himself in the room.

Evidence Collection: Someone had tampered with the latch on the French window; it wouldn't shut.

Forensics: The body was found almost folded up, the joints so bloodless as to be loose and slack. There was not a trace of blood anywhere in the corpse, despite the deep, jagged wounds under the arms, across the throat, and in the back. The skin and flesh were stark white – even the capillaries were drained, so there was no postmortem lividity. The bones were hollow; the marrow gone. The spine, humerus, and femurs were snapped like pencils.

Tcho-Tcho
The pygmy Tcho-Tcho tribe dwells primarily on the borderlands of the dread plateau of Leng, with known colonies in Thibet, the Andaman Islands, Malaya, and the plateau of Sung in Burma. Their own legends say they were created from black salamanders by the god Chaugnar Faugn in the beginning of time. According to the *Unaussprechlichen Kulten* of von Junzt, they came to this world from the "lost city of Sarkomand, which is found now only in dreams," and venerate Hastur. The Burmese Tcho-Tcho harvest the oneirically active black lotus plant and worship the Twin Obscenity (variously called Zhar-Lloigor and Nug-Yeb).

Creating an Alien Race

To a lesser degree, the same objection applies to alien races as to gods and titans. Too many alien creatures overcrowd even the Earth's vast history. Already, orthodox Lovecraftianism has Hounds of Tindalos, Elder Things, flying polyps, the Great Race, Xothians, serpent-folk and their masqut cousins, fungi from Yuggoth, and the fur-covered prehuman Voormis before humanity takes its turn. A new alien race should perhaps be a localized invader like the shan, a human symbiont or parody like the ghouls or Deep Ones, or an occasional extraterrestrial summoned or just visiting.

With that out of the way, start by picking the general model and function of your new alien. Is it a winged monster, a mindless virus, a humanoid travesty? The monster's form should evoke the specific fear you're aiming at creating in the adventure. If it's a study in paranoia, for example, your monster should be small, invisible, or otherwise hard to spot, and its eyes (the symbol of watchfulness) should have some distinctive characteristic (purple rims, orange glow, three vertically spaced) that panicked Investigators can spot everywhere.

Don't get too hung up on the appearance of the thing; Lovecraft purposely mashed up completely incompatible beasts as templates, and used the form "like, but not like" repeatedly. Your monster might resemble a rat and a python one day, or be "like a worm, but somehow skinless and flattened" the next day. These things might not even be made of conventional matter, and the people perceiving them are usually mad, or at least under a lot of stress unconducive to field zoology. Make sure you give it some non-visual spoor – a distinctive smell or sound is somehow much scarier than yet another tentacle.

Finally and optionally, wire it into the rest of the Mythos. It might be a complete enigma like the Colour, or it might be a well-known servitor species of Mordiggian. The first plays up mystery; the second lets you reuse your new alien without having to go through the whole process again.

These statistics will also model degenerate serpent-folk, Robert E Howard's *Picts*, Arthur Machen's *Little People*, or any other stunted, dwarfish, devolved tribespeople.

Game Statistics

Abilities: Athletics 8, Health 6, Missiles 6, Scuffling 7, Weapons 5

Hit Threshold: 4

Alertness Modifier: +1

Stealth Modifier: +2 (in native countryside), +1 (elsewhere)

Weapon: -2 (blowgun dart), -1 (kris), -1 (arrow); needless to say, all Tcho-Tcho weapons are poisoned, the vile side-effects being up to the Keeper

Armor: none

Stability Loss: There is no Stability loss for seeing a Tcho-Tcho, until you get to know them better.

Investigation

Anthropology: The few anthropologists who have survived studying the Tcho-Tcho have theorized that they may be a separate line of human descent, perhaps directly from Java Man. They practice cannibalism, drug-induced shamanic rituals, human sacrifice, infanticide, and vendetta.

Forensics: The victim died in horrible agony, the back arched almost into a circle, the fingers and toes ankylosed almost into claws, and the face twisted into a sardonic rictus of unimaginable gruesomeness. On the third search, we found the puncture wound in the palm of his left foot – the dart was apparently hidden in his shoe while he slept.

Xothian

This is Cthulhu's quasi-saurian, quasi-octopoid species, which seeped down from the green binary star Xoth in Taurus primordial aeons ago. He is the largest and the mightiest of them, but they are still titans, each weighing over 100 tons. The *Necronomicon* calls them "the star-spawn of Cthulhu," under which name most occultists know them. Not all the inhabitants of R'lyeh were trapped when it sank. Some still live on in the deep trenches beneath the ocean, tended by Deep Ones and guarded by sea-shoggoths. Five great Xothian sorcerers, the "Five Watchers," reputedly slumber in subterranean gulfs beneath the Bayan Kara Shan mountains in China, the Nameless City in the Arabian desert, the Greenland glacier, New England, and the Amazon Basin. Related entities

Weapon: +5 (tentacle), +14 (claw)

Armor: -6 vs any (hide and blubber); regenerates 3 Health per round

Stability Loss: +3

Investigation

Biology: The green slime is definitely ooze from the ocean bottom, combined with kelp and other dead sea vegetation compressed at titanic pressures.

Evidence Collection: The pool of green slime at the site is garnished with lumps of bloody viscera. There's no other trace of a body.

Sense Trouble: You hear a kind of watery thudding noise rushing up through the earth, as though something enormous were somehow walking through surf beneath the solid ground you're standing on.

dwell in the stars, such as the beings said to infest the Lake of Hali on or near Aldebaran.

A Xothian may attack with tentacles or with claw. It may use three tentacles each round against the same or separate targets, or a single claw.

Game Statistics

Abilities (land or sea/air): Athletics 20/10, Health 40, Scuffling 27

Hit Threshold: 2 (titanic)

Stealth Modifier: -2 (except in deep ocean)

BEASTS AND MONSTERS

The creatures in this section are, by default, non-Mythos entities, regardless of how terrifying or even supernatural they may be. They are included in the spirit of Pulp adventure.

In a Purist game, all supernatural creatures have a Mythos explanation. The Keeper may decide to increase their Stability test Difficulty (and any losses) only after the Investigators discover this fact...

Allosaur

This 35-foot Jurassic carnivore is eminently suitable both for "lost world" adventure in the Pulp mode and time-travel encounters – either in the streets of Boston or the distant past. Scale it up for a tyrannosaur, or down (and speedy) for a velociraptor.
An allosaur can make two claw attacks against a single target in a round.

Game Statistics

Abilities: Athletics 11, Health 24, Scuffling 20

Hit Threshold: 3 (big)

Alertness Modifier: +1

Stealth Modifier: –1

Weapon: +2 (claw), +4 (stomp and pin), +5 (bite); stomp and pin is the allosaur's first move after winning the Athletics contest, only if it fails will it try claws or bite

Armor: -2 vs any (hide)

Stability Loss: +0

Bear

These stats are for a grizzly bear, native to the Rocky Mountains chains from Alaska to Wyoming. Polar bears are bigger, black bears smaller.

Bears can attack twice in a round, either two claw attacks or claw-bite.

Game Statistics

Abilities: Athletics 14, Health 10, Scuffling 16

Hit Threshold: 4

Alertness Threshold: +2

Stealth Threshold: –1

Weapon: +1 (claw), +0 (bite)

Armor: -4 vs any (thick fur)

Stability Loss: +0

Crocodile

These stats are for the Nile crocodile. Alligators live in America, and are both smaller and less aggressive.

Game Statistics

Abilities (land/water): Athletics 6/8, Health 13, Scuffling 17

Hit Threshold: 4

Stealth Modifier: +2

Weapon: +2 (bite)

Armor: -5 vs any (thick scaly hide)

Stability Loss: +0

Gorilla

The greatest of the great apes, native to central Africa. Use these stats for the white apes of the Congo; Indonesian orang-utans will be faster and smaller.

A gorilla can bite and attack with both hands in a single round.

Game Statistics

Abilities: Athletics 8, Health 9, Scuffling 15

Hit Threshold: 4

Stealth Modifier: +2

Weapon: +0 (grab), +0 (bite); if both grabs succeed in the same round, the gorilla can start tearing its target's arms off, doing automatic grab damage twice per round. Armor does not protect against gorilla racking.

Armor: -2 vs any (skin)

Stability Loss: +0

Lake Monster

If the Loch Ness Monster and Ogopogo and Champ and all the others aren't lloigor, they might be these giant eel-plesiosaur things. Lake monsters don't come up on land. Use these statistics for smallish sea serpents, and for creepy marine monsters around sunken R'lyeh.

Game Statistics

Abilities: Athletics 10, Health 19, Scuffling 17

Hit Threshold: 3 (large)

Alertness Modifier: +2

Weapon: +0 (bite), +5 (smash boat or boaters); a successful smash attack will splinter or capsize any craft with one or fewer masts, forcing passengers to make

off the prey's air supply, doing automatic bite damage each round, and rakes with its hind paws; rake attacks allow two claw attacks per round and the prey's Hit Threshold is at -1

Armor: -2 vs any (skin)

Stability Loss: +0

Mummy

A corpse preserved by desiccation, lacquer, or embalming, mummies are found in (among other places) Turkestan, Peru, Arizona, and the Canary Islands in addition to Egypt. Mummies are reanimated by various magics and need a spell or special condition (starlight, tana leaves, etc) to refresh their Health. Depending on the original enchantment or the mummy's purpose, it may regenerate 1 to 3 Scuffling each round.

Game Statistics

Abilities: Athletics 6, Health 9, Scuffling 11

Hit Threshold: 3

Alertness Modifier: +3 (its tomb only)

Weapon: +0 (fist)

Armor: -2 vs any (leathery skin); impaling weapons are useless; fire does +1 normal damage

Stability Loss: +1

Rat Swarm

For a swarm of rats, first determine the number of rats in the swarm. Increase Health and Scuffling by 2 for every 10 rats, and damage by +1 for every 30

Difficulty 4 Athletics tests to avoid being dragged down with the wreckage

Armor: -6 vs any (tough hide)

Stability Loss: +0

Lion

These statistics work fairly well for tigers; mountain lions, panthers, and cougars are smaller.

A lion can make one claw and one bite attack against a single target in a round.

Game Statistics

Abilities: Athletics 12, Health 11, Scuffling 20

Hit Threshold: 4

Alertness Modifier: +1

Stealth Modifier: +2

Weapon: +0 (bite), +1 (claw); if both claw and bite hit, the lion hangs on with its jaws to close rats. Every hit against a swarm kills 1 rat and disperses 9 others.

Use this same algorithm for swarms of rat-things (see p. 145), vampire bats, giant ants, scorpions, piranha, etc A swarm of normal-sized insects cannot be hit, and merely does a constant amount of damage each time increment spent inside the swarm.

Game Statistics

Abilities: Athletics 5, Health 3, Scuffling 3

Hit Threshold: 3 (small and nimble, but target-rich)

Weapon: -2 (bite); may be infected

Armor: none

Stability Loss: +0 unless phobic

Shark

What else could this be but the great white? Hammerheads, mako, and tiger sharks are faster and smaller (Athletics 13, Health 12) and their bite carries only a +2 damage modifier.

Game Statistics

Abilities (all in water only): Athletics 11, Health 21, Scuffling 25

Hit Threshold: 4

Alertness Modifier: +3 (only if blood is in the water)

Weapon: +4 (his teeth, dear)

Armor: -1 vs guns or spears (skin), -2 vs everything else

Stability Loss: +1 if the witness is in the water with it

Snake

This is pretty much any poisonous snake – a cobra in India or Egypt, a rattler or sidewinder in the American West, a copperhead around the Gulf of Mexico, a fer-de-lance in the Caribbean, a death adder or taipan or tiger snake in Australia, a black mamba or gaboon viper in tropical Africa, a bushmaster in Latin America, a banded sea snake in the Pacific Islands.

Treat snake venom as serpent-folk venom (see p. 146). Children of Yig have Athletics 11, Health 8, Scuffling 20.

Abilities: Athletics 7, Health 4 to 6, Scuffling 15

Hit Threshold: 3

Stealth Modifier: +2 (except rattlers)

Weapon: -2 (bite or spit); venom

Armor: none

Stability Loss: +0 unless phobic

Vampire

There are a lot of different types of vampires, many of which have magical spells in addition to their vampiric powers. This is a fairly standard Pulp vampire, influenced by Stoker and Lugosi. This does not model the vampire in *The Shunned House* or Curwen's vampiric phase in *Charles Dexter Ward.*

Prodigious Strength: By spending 2 Athletics points per feat, a vampire can lift up to 500 lbs., tear doors off hinges, move up to 2 range increments (long to close, or near to point-blank)

in a round, or leap up to 30 feet vertically.

Bite: The vampire can transfer Health lost by a bitten victim to his own Health or Athletics pool. If the victim fails a Difficulty 4 Stability test, she may not resist further bites from this vampire, and he can drink as much of her blood as he likes to a maximum of 6 Health per round. Three successful bite attacks over three nights transforms a victim into a vampire after her death.

Mesmerism: If the vampire wins a contest of the vampire's Health vs a target's Stability, he can perform any task listed under Hypnosis (see p. 43), and implant orders in her.

Transform: By spending 3 Health, the vampire can transform into a wolf or a bat. If reduced to 1 Health or below by normal (non-beheading, non-stake, etc) attacks, the vampire automatically transforms into mist.

Weaknesses: A vampire must spend all day in his native earth to refresh any points; all points refresh at sundown. A vampire casts no reflection (Sense Trouble test at Difficulty 4 to notice). A vampire cannot cross running water except at midnight, cannot bear the smell of garlic (3-point Health test to remain in the room with it), and is repelled by crosses or crucifixes (6-point Health test to confront one). A fatal beheading attack on the vampire does normal damage, but making such an attack requires an additional spend of 1 Weapons point by the attacker. A vampire suffers 3 points of Health damage automatically for each minute spent in full sunlight. A vampire can be harmed by holy water (treat as strong acid) or by ingesting garlic (treat as weak acid) or by fire (as normal). Vampires suffer additional damage modifiers as follows: +2 (touch of a cross or crucifix), +4 (wooden stake, see below).

Wooden Stakes: Staking a vampire in combat requires a spend of 2 Scuffling or Weapons points (for no die roll bonus) to hit the heart; staking a vampire while he sleeps requires only a 3-point, Difficulty 3 Stability test (6-point, Difficulty 5 if the attacker knew and liked the vampire in life). On a failure, the vampire awakens. A staked vampire can attempt combat, but can use no vampiric powers except his bite. He may spend two combat rounds removing the stake, if he wishes, and restore his vampire powers.

Return: A dead vampire must be beheaded, with his mouth filled with garlic, and buried at the crossroads or he will return to unlife. Alternately, he can be put to final rest if he is burnt and his ashes scattered into running fresh water.

Game Statistics

Abilities: Athletics 10, Health 7, Scuffling 16, Weapons 2

Hit Threshold: 4 or 5 (for fast vampires)

Weapon: +1 (claw), -2 (bite)

Armor: damage from physical weapons, except fatal beheading damage, refreshes the next round (but see above)

Stability Loss: +0 unless the vampire was known to the witness when alive

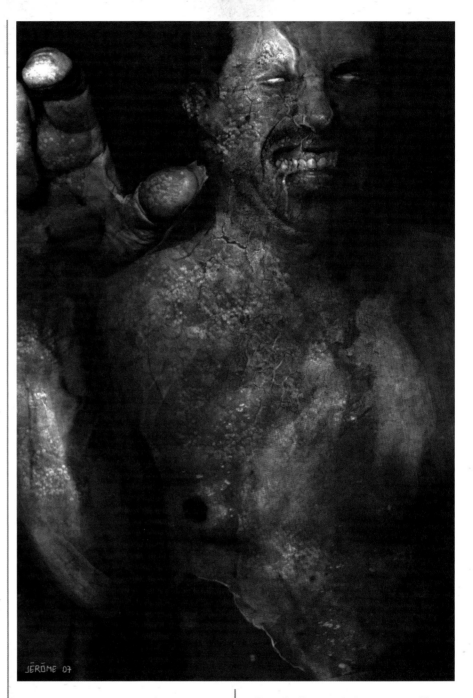

Wolf

The medieval werewolf uses a magical incantation or enchanted wolfskin to transform into one of these, a robust and ravening *canis lupus*, until sunrise. Transforming from human to wolf refreshes all pool points and heals all wounds, but not the other way. The full moon, the silver bullet, and the werewolf on hind legs are all inventions of Hollywood.

Use a slightly less robust version of these statistics to build a German shepherd or other guard dog, or a pack of wild dogs.

Abilities: Athletics 12, Health 6, Scuffling 10

Hit Threshold: 4

Alertness Modifier: +3

Weapon: +0 (bite)

Armor: -1 vs any (fur)

Stability Loss: +0

Yeti

The Abominable Snowman of the Himalaya, unless it's all mi-go prints. These statistics can build any of the hairy anthropoids of the wild places: Sasquatch, yowie, etc.

Game Statistics

Abilities: Athletics 8, Health 9, Scuffling 16

Hit Threshold: 4

Alertness Modifier: +2

Stealth Modifier: +1 (+2 downwind)

Weapon: +0 (fist), +0 (thrown rock)

Armor: -3 vs any (thick fur)

Stability Loss: +0

Zombie

The infectious bite is not true to Pulp zombies or to the *zombi* of Haitian lore, but it seemed kind of mandatory. The rest makes a pretty good Pulp zombie. The rock salt is derived from the Haitian legend that if you feed a zombi salt, he will die, or possibly return to his grave.

For a Herbert West-style reanimated corpse, remove the infectious bite and the vulnerability to rock salt, and increase Scuffling to 10.

Game Statistics

Abilities: Athletics 5, Health 7, Scuffling 7, Weapons 2

Hit Threshold: 3 (slow)

Alertness Modifier: -1

Weapon: improvised weapons, or -1 (Bite); every round after a successful zombie bite does damage, the victim must make a Health test against a Difficulty equal to the damage amount. If failed, the bite does double damage. Once the victim dies, he rises the next round as a zombie. Burning the wound with open flame sterilizes the infection, but does fire damage as normal.

Armor: none, but all weapons do half damage; firearms do only 1 point of damage even if point-blank; shotguns do 2 points of damage; shotguns firing rock salt do full damage

Stability Loss: +0 unless the zombie was known to the witness when alive

CULTS AND CULTISTS

"THEN, TOO, IT IS UNDENIABLE THAT A FRESH AND EVIL WAVE OF UNDERGROUND CULT ACTIVITY SET IN ABOUT THE TIME OF MY ODD MUTATION."

— "THE SHADOW OUT OF TIME"

The thready streams of tradition descending from prehuman gods and sunken continents have swollen with the ranks of the desperate and the greedy called forth by the times … or by the stars. How much of the renewed cult activity in the 1930s springs from the near-immanence of Yog-Sothoth and Cthulhu in the previous decade, and how much springs from the yawning shadows of poverty, war, and destruction – or if there is any difference — only Nyarlathotep knows for sure.

In game terms, a cult is the usual interface between the Mythos force at the center of the horror and the events that draw in the Investigators. Each cult has the following: Its general beliefs and antecedents, its distribution and strength, the sorts of things it does that might pique Investigators into meddling, and the sorts of things it might do in response to such.

Ahnenerbe

The *Studiengesellschaft für Geistesurgeschichte Deutsches Ahnenerbe,* or Society for Research into the Spiritual Roots of German Ancestral Heritage, began as an informal "Ahnenerbe Society" in 1928 dedicated to folk-occult (*volkisch*) research. In 1935, Reichsführer-SS Heinrich Himmler established it on a formal basis, setting Atlantis scholar Hermann Wirth and the pagan race-theorist Richard Darré as its directors. In 1937, SS Obersturmführer

Wolfram Sievers took over as Reichsmanager. In 1940, it became an official arm of the SS.

The mission Himmler gave the Ahnenerbe was to establish academic support for Nazi theories of race, prehistory, and folk belief. To Himmler, this research included topics like Atlantis, runic magic, song-sorcery, Druidism, the Holy Grail, and Freemasonry. Ahnenerbe agents or assets traveled to Finland, Sweden,

Iceland, Abyssinia, Brazil, Thibet, the Canary Islands, the Pyrenees, and Iran. Ahnenerbe specialists included past-life channelers, aura readers, psychometrists, and pendulum dowsers.

This is all historical truth. The exact nature of the Ahnenerbe activities on the fringes of Leng, Lomar, and Irem can only be guessed at. (But see the Totalitarianism box on p. 172 first.)

Distribution: Historically, Ahnenerbe operations comprised a few academic specialists (some cross-trained as SS men) bulked out by local guides. Anywhere the Nazis have influence, so might the Ahnenerbe.

Hooks: In a Pulp game, the Ahnenerbe is racing to uncover the Shining Trapezohedron, or the mummy of Abdul Alhazred, or the lost laboratory of the Elder Things (see p.131). In any adventure in Europe, Africa, or central Asia, the Ahnenerbe might be rival Investigators, trying to dig out the truth and twist it to support their paymasters' beliefs. Academic Investigators with ratings in Anthropology will be familiar with the Ahnenerbe, if only as an aggressively "Aryanist" research institute in Berlin.

Responses: Historically, the Ahnenerbe m.o. was to harvest as much information or as many artifacts as they could from a site and leave a political mess (either paid-off allies or ticked-off locals) for their competitors to deal with. In more Pulpy games, their responses widen to include trapping Investigators in the ruins before the flying polyps emerge…

Black Dragon Society

Historically, the *Kokuryû-kai,* or Black Dragon Society, was a small secret society of Japanese military and political officials dedicated to driving the Russians back behind the "Black Dragon" (or Amur) River. Founded in 1901 as an offshoot of a previous expansionist society, the *Genyòsha,* or Black Ocean, it was dedicated to ultranationalism, militarism, and expansionism. Its core ideology blended bushido, Imperial Shinto, and criminal callousness. Both the Black Ocean and Black Dragon had extensive criminal connections among the Triads and Yakuza alike. In American pulp fiction, and in a Pulp-idiom campaign, the Black Dragon is a sort of Japanese spy agency-slash-Mafia with a global reach.

The original "black dragon" of Japanese myth, the dragon king Ryujin, lived in a stone and coral palace underwater, which implies at least some connection between Cthulhu and the Black Ocean. The Black Dragon Society may thus be a local iteration of the Cthulhu cult, a secret society founded by a given Deep One or Serpent-Folk bloodline during Japan's tumultuous history, or some other Mythos movement altogether.

Distribution: The historical Black Dragon took special interest in restive religious movements such as Islamic groups in Russian Central Asia, or Buddhist groups in the European colonies of Indochina and Burma. The Black Dragon Society ran private spy and smuggling networks throughout Japan and East Asia, with contacts and assets extended as far as the Caribbean and Morocco, keeping an eye on the world's sea lanes for the Japanese navy. In a Pulp game, any Japanese naval officer might be a Black Dragon agent or asset.

Hooks: Incidents of sabotage, mysteries at sea, or "weird menace" Pulp criminality may carry Black Dragon spoor. In a campaign with a strong Black Dragon presence, Investigators with Streetwise in any Pacific port will know (or hear) of it, if only as a rumor.

Responses: Psychological warfare and propaganda to libel or blacken their ideological (and immediate) foes wherever they can. They historically used blackmail, hostage taking (kidnapping of relatives, for example), underworld contract killings, and even full-blown assassination against key targets.

Brotherhood of the Yellow Sign

According to occult rumor, the Brotherhood of the Yellow Sign is a cult of Hastur-worshippers (see p. 94) dedicated to driving the mi-go (see p. 142) off the planet Earth. Its leadership is likely based in K'n-Yan, and its secret chiefs may be able to materialize and dematerialize at will. The Brotherhood uses telepathy to contact its members (possibly piggybacking on the dreams of Hastur) and to scan for traces of mi-go mental alteration in the human population. They track mi-go colonies and mines, destroying them where they can and offering human servants of the fungi (or convenient innocents) as human sacrifices to Hastur.

The Brotherhood's secondary goal is to thwart any human

investigation into the works of Hastur, especially archaeological or other expeditions to sacred sites of Hastur.

The Keeper should note that the only evidence for such a society in the works of Lovecraft is given by the mi-go impersonating Henry Akeley. Hence, there may be no such cult, or its goals may be entirely other than noted here.

Distribution: The Brothers of the Yellow Sign mostly operate in large cities convenient to potential mi-go colonies: Boston, Lucknow, Lima, Denver, Mexico City, Geneva. However, they (or their K'n-Yani chiefs) may be in any large city or railhead in a mountain region. Senior Brothers often have jobs requiring (or covering for) travel: performing artists, import-export brokers, etc

Hooks: The Brotherhood will likely feed intelligence of mi-go activities to the Investigators, if the latter have raised their monster-killing profile at all. Failing that, the Investigators may hear about a party of city folk going up into the mountains out of season, or stumble on the evidence of the Hastur cult's other operations.

Responses: The Brotherhood uses poison gas of various sorts by preference, including gases that affect the mi-go. Its most common response to human enemies is to set them in the path of the mi-go, or vice versa.

Cult of Cthulhu

"Ph'nglui mglw'nafh Cthulhu R'lyeh wgah'nagl fhtagn." In his house in R'lyeh, dead Cthulhu waits dreaming. At some point in history, those dreams found echoes in willing, or weak, human minds. They found the idols of Cthulhu that He had brought down from Xoth. They became the creators of the cult of Cthulhu.

Or, perhaps, *cults.* The center of the cult is variously pinpointed as Irem of the Pillars in Arabia, though its leaders are supposed to be "deathless men" in the mountains of China. But cults of Cthulhu appear in many isolated and remote places across the globe, from Greenland to New Zealand. Cthulhu is worshiped by inbred tribespeople in the Philippines and by sophisticated merchants in Istanbul. Cthulhu's dreams find echoes in sensitive California Theosophists and brutal killers in the highlands of India. Unless the cult leaders – or the Xothian star-spawn of Cthulhu – are coordinating the whole thing through dreams and telepathy, the various cults of Cthulhu must perforce have a degree of independence of action.

Some cults merely exist to pass along the worship of the Great Old Ones and Cthulhu, keeping the rites alive against the great day when the stars come right and Cthulhu emerges to rule the world again. Others work to bring that day about by magical ceremonies. Some mistakenly conflate Cthulhu's dreams with their own beliefs about the coming new age. Others use the revelation of Cthulhu's power as a reason to kill and rape. But when the cult perceives a need for a professor to be silenced, or discovers that a seaquake has made some portion of R'lyeh briefly accessible, then it can assemble pilgrims to act on its behalf. Whether Great Cthulhu knows or cares about their actions is unknowable.

Distribution: Isolated cults of Cthulhu appear in all the locations mentioned above, as well as the interior of Africa, Haiti, South America, Alaska, and various pockets of inner Asia. The largest single networked cult of Cthulhu operates in virtually all of the world's seaports, among Lascars and other low types.

Some of these cult operatives have Deep One blood, and the Deep Ones may use the cult of Cthulhu for their own unguessable purposes.

Hooks: Any sort of "mystery at sea" can have a Cthulhu-cult explanation, from ghost ships to missing cargoes to uncanny storms. Individual Cthulhu cults such as the New Orleans cult of 1907 can also goad themselves into a frenzy of murderous mania (possibly connected with the waxing of Cthulhu's dream strength) and attract attention thusly. Cthulhu cultists might also break into museums to liberate alien artifacts, or Cthulhu's dreams might inspire an artist of the Investigators' acquaintance.

Responses: The seafarers' cult assassinates those who offend it, usually by poison injection. The hit is made to look like an accidental brush, and the victim's symptoms closely resemble a normal heart attack. In some cases, the cult might kidnap its victims and take them out to sea for questioning, before dropping them overboard to feed their allies.

Cult of the Skull

This is an example of a local cult, albeit a dangerous one. Around 1690 a group of wizards left the New England witch-cult to its fate, and founded the Cult of the Skull. These founding wizards guaranteed their cult's continuation by transmigrating their minds down their own bloodlines, possessing sons, daughters, wives, or whoever they need to increase their power both sorcerous and mundane. For ritual reasons, they traditionally jump only to

new bodies related by blood or marriage, and often intermarry with other powerful lineages. They worship Shub-Niggurath and Tulszcha, the Green Flame in the Earth, above other deities.

One question that those few who have encountered the Cult occasionally ask: are those guiding minds human now, after 300 years of unnatural life moving from skull to skull? Or were they ever? Could nonhuman entities have replaced – or inspired – the original cult leaders, now solely existing as parasites on the brains of their unknowing children and recruits? And even if they began as human, some of their chosen mates did not.

Distribution: The cult leadership includes members of the prestigious Waite, Eliot, Orne, Lyman, and Bishop families, who maintain homesteads throughout New England. The cult also maintains a presence in New York, for shipments requiring greater than average anonymity. The cult headquarters is an ancient megalithic site in the woods near Chesuncook, Maine. Beneath the standing stones, six thousand steps down, is the Pit of the Shoggoths.

Hooks: Any sort of deviltry or trouble in New England might have the Cult of the Skull at its back. The founders are overconfident (at least until the Upton fiasco of 1933) and the cults' scions openly mix with the fast set, occultists of all sorts, and dabble in every sort of debauchery. All it might take is a girlfriend who jilts the Investigator for an exciting new beau, and then seems "like an entirely different person..."

Responses: The Cult will not risk exposing the Maine sanctuary. It will use its own temporal power and influence to weaken or blacken their enemies' position in society, and then use magic to drive their foes mad. Once bankrupt and insane, foes can, if need be, brought to Maine for final disposal.

Starry Wisdom Sect

In 1844, Professor Enoch Bowen uncovered the Shining Trapezohedron, a mystical container for the aspect of Nyarlathotep (see p.96) known as the Haunter of the Dark, in the Egyptian tomb of the Pharaoh Nephren-Ka. The visions he received from the object led him to found the Starry Wisdom Church in his hometown of Providence, Rhode Island. Its rites were described as Egyptian occultism, and its icons resembled the statues of Easter Island more than Egyptian gods. By 1863, the Starry Wisdom had over 200 members; when Bowen died in 1866, Dr Raymond Flagg became the minister.

In 1871, following a series of publicized missing-child cases and at least one Irish riot, the town council of Providence moved against the Starry Wisdom Church. Its membership scattered, leaving its library of eldritch tomes and the Trapezohedron sealed in their old church on Federal Hill in Providence. Dr Bowen's daughter Asenath remained in Providence, and she may have nurtured a continued secret remnant. In 1935, a deranged artist named Robert Blake discovers the remains of the church and dies in a lightning storm. According to reports, a Dr Ambrose Dexter

recovers the library and the Trapezohedron that year and disappears.

Distribution: Offshoots of the Starry Wisdom have appeared in Townsend, Vermont (1863-?), Chicago (1863-1871; Celestial Providence Church, destroyed in the Fire), San Francisco (1871-1906; destroyed in Earthquake), Yorkshire (1881-1890; possibly led by Dr Flagg), Arkham, Massachusetts (1908-?; headed by someone calling himself "Enoch Bowen"), Los Angeles (1881-present; worship in Devil's Gate Canyon includes a number of Hollywood stars and power-brokers), and perhaps in your own campaign city.

Hooks: The sect has a specific penchant for child abductions, but any Nyarlathotep cult activity might lead back to (or through) the Starry Wisdom sect.

Responses: If the threat can be bought off, suborned, blackmailed, or recruited, the sect will try that first. The Los Angeles church, at least, has every imaginable inducement at its fingertips - money, sex, power, glamour, drugs, or whatever its enemies might desire most. Should the Investigators prove obdurate, the sect will try a demonstration of its magical power, most likely summoning a hunting horror to remove the thorniest persecutor. If the threat is both persistent and seems likely to bring the authorities down on them, the sect will pull up stakes and move to a new location, leaving sufficient low-ranking (but disgusting) patsies to take the fall.

Witch-Cult

As demonstrated by the Egyptologist Margaret Murray (an associate professor at University College until retiring in 1935), the various witch-cults of Western Europe were all part of a common underground religious resistance to Catholicism. They met in covens of 13 and venerated the Horned God (Pan, Cernunnos, or the Devil) and the Great Goddess (Diana, Berchta, or Aradia), practicing human sacrifice (usually of voluntary "sacred kings") in an unbroken religious line dating from the Neolithic Era. Among the witch-cult's members were Thomas a Becket, King Edward III (who founded the Order of the Garter as a covert coven), Joan of Arc, and other notables. Beginning in the 1450s, the Church (and its Protestant rivals) discovered the Old Religion's existence and responded in a frenzy of persecution, executing witches

and warlocks by the tens of thousands. The Salem witch trials in 1692 were one such action against the Old Religion. The witch-cult was splintered and driven into extinction by 1735, when Parliament's Witchcraft Act defined the offense of witchcraft as pretending to have magical powers.

So much for conventional anthropological wisdom. The truth is that the "Old Religion" worshiped Nyarlathotep (as the Black Man) and Shub-Niggurath. (Some cults worshiped other Great Old Ones as well.) The inquisitors did, indeed, burn it out where they could, but the roots of the Religion go back into the original matter of mankind and the Earth. You can no more exterminate the witch-cult than you can exterminate nature Herself.

Distribution: Any community where the Old Religion was once practiced might still host an isolated, secretive witch-cult. Likewise, refugees from the Inquisition or its Protestant equivalents may have brought the witch-cult to the New World. Witch-cults, at least in America, are isolated phenomena with no regular inter-coven links; in Britain, the cult may well have knit itself back together again. Known cult sites include Arkham, Massachusetts (where the witch Keziah Mason, just escaped from Salem, founded it in 1692 and directed it until her death in 1928), Maine, the New Forest in England, and Tuscany.

Hooks: Poisonings, crop blights, mysterious deaths in the forest, or any of the traditional witchly stigmata may spark an investigation. Houses once

used by witches may still hold their grimoires, their undying familiars, or their hyperspatial Gates, in addition to conventional hauntings.

Responses: A witch-cult prefers to arrange matters so that the victim goes willingly to his death, making a suitable sacrifice. Failing that, poisons, curses, the evil eye, raising storms, and communal Mythos magic are excellent ways to foil potential inquisitors.

Yithian Agents

A network of agents assists those members of the Great Race of Yith who travel to our time to record and study its lore. They offer support, provide materials to construct the return projector, and cover up the tracks of Yithians who stumble in our unfamiliar era. They also work to keep knowledge of the Great Race restricted to themselves.

In return, the Great Race provides their agents with advanced technological items and machinery, usually jury-rigged from contemporary items, and with the occasional snippet of unearthly lore. It is also in the Great Race's interest for its agents to be comfortable and wealthy, so they will arrange such matters to the best of their ability, but nothing must endanger the secret of Yith.

Distribution: An agent of the Great Race can be found anywhere that the Race might wish to sojourn in this century, both in leading academic centers (Berlin, Oxford, Yale) and places of more mysterious interest (Arabia, India and China, Norway, rural West Virginia). However,

Creating a Cult

With cults, it's the more the merrier. There should be only one or two truly global cults in any given campaign, unless it's a completely over-the-top Pulp brouhaha, but local cults can arise anywhere and everywhere. A small town might have (or be) one cult, or two feuding ones. In places of special Mythos significance like witch-haunted Arkham, the local sorcerous ecosystem can support six or a dozen cults without seeming ludicrous. And huge cities like London, New York, or Chicago can sport literally hundreds of sects, voodoo societies, theosophical study groups, revival tent churches, ethnic brotherhoods, quasi-Masonic guilds, occult fraternities, or murderous inbred families, any or all of which might be Mythos-influenced or Mythos-corrupted.

The first thing to decide about your new cult is its name. If you can't come up with a truly awesome name, don't bother coming up with a new cult, because repeatedly hearing "The Church of Blackest Claw" or whatever is just going to make your players giggle or quote metal lyrics. The name will give you insight and guidance into your cult's nature and perhaps even its rituals.

If you absolutely need a cult, but can't think of a name, take a page from von Junzt and leave it nameless. But then you have to build its ingredients separately: Which Mythos entity does it serve? Wittingly or unwittingly? What do its members believe? Is there a secret lore that key members know? Do they practice vile rituals, or simply aid each other with call-signs and passwords against the Day? What will they do to protect themselves? What's their signature means of murder, their warning sign, their venerated symbol? From that, you can probably figure out who founded the cult, its local (or global) history, and whether it has always been like it is now.

But if you start out with something like, say, the Spine of Apep, you've got a framework. It serves Yig or Nyarlathotep (Apep was a snake god and the enemy of Ra in Egyptian myth), probably wittingly with a name like that. Its members believe that they are the literal spine of Apep, the line of transmission of anti-Ra wisdom. There might be a secret lore, if say the head priests know they actually serve Nyarlathotep but the rank and file worship Yig. They might practice Tantric rituals awakening that Kundalini serpent in the spine. They will slink into the darkness by preference, but may set the sacred skeletal snakes on you if they must. Their warning sign is a hatched spiral, representing a snake's spine. Their venerated symbol is a snake spine wrapped around an ankh. It was founded either by ancient Egyptians or by crazed Egyptologists, it's been in Alexandria forever but just recently came to Manchester, and yep, it's pretty much always been like this.

the number of agents is small enough that obvious outsiders must sometimes be called in for assistance. In general, there will be more agents in a city where a Yithian is currently incarnated, but this is not always the case. Coordination of their activities across the gulfs of time is necessarily imprecise.

Hooks: A Yithian agent might be a mysterious stranger or a local fixer known to everybody. A mysterious artifact might get out onto the market, or a gung-ho agent might attempt to steal a dangerously complete compilation of the Pnakotic Manuscripts. It is more likely, however, that the Yithian's own actions will lead any Investigators onto the agents'

path than the other way around.

Responses: The first directive is secrecy. If that means a secret murder, with the body dropped in a quarry miles away, that's fine. If it just means a complete "cleaning" of a suspicious location – all books, items, and furniture removed overnight – that's good, too.

The Thirties

"I DO NOT RECALL DISTINCTLY WHEN IT BEGAN, BUT IT WAS MONTHS AGO. THE GENERAL TENSION WAS HORRIBLE. TO A SEASON OF POLITICAL AND SOCIAL UPHEAVAL WAS ADDED A STRANGE AND BROODING APPREHENSION OF HIDEOUS PHYSICAL DANGER; A DANGER WIDESPREAD AND ALL-EMBRACING, SUCH A DANGER AS MAY BE IMAGINED ONLY IN THE MOST TERRIBLE PHANTASMS OF THE NIGHT. I RECALL THAT THE PEOPLE WENT ABOUT WITH PALE AND WORRIED FACES, AND WHISPERED WARNINGS AND PROPHECIES WHICH NO ONE DARED CONSCIOUSLY REPEAT OR ACKNOWLEDGE TO HIMSELF THAT HE HAD HEARD. A SENSE OF MONSTROUS GUILT WAS UPON THE LAND ..."

— "NYARLATHOTEP"

Mormo was invoked in 1924. Cthulhu briefly awoke in 1925. Yog-Sothoth nearly broke through the barriers in 1928. This chapter is about the decade after that, when things got worse.

The "Dirty Thirties," as the farmers who fled the Dust Bowl called the decade, are still fairly familiar to us. If, as they say, the past is a foreign country, the 1930s are a near neighbor that mostly speaks the same language. Yes, moral codes (at least in public) were vastly different than our looser (or freer) era, and opinion polls record that people on the whole were more optimistic about the future then than they are now. They created Mickey Mouse; we created Eric Cartman. They created

Superman; we can't stop trying to kill him.

They listened to the radio, but not in their cars, and went to way more movies than we do. They smoked like chimneys, drank like longshoremen, and never cursed in front of the ladies. Many more of them danced — as social lubricant and leisure activity — and their dance music (and their dancing) was unmistakably different from ours. Singers sang "standards," not their own songs, while even middle-class folks bought tailored clothes, not "off the rack." Food in America and Britain was plain at best; the immigration waves of the post-WWII era had not yet liberated Anglo-Saxon diners from nonstop roast and potatoes, with a side of vegetable soup if you were adventurous. Baseball was the overwhelming American national pastime, and fans attended games in coat and tie. And the Chicago Cubs made it to the World Series three times in the decade.

But such strangeness aside, that era is still accessible in a way that medieval times, for instance, aren't. By and large, Westerners in the 1930s shared our assumptions (or recognizable versions of them) about democracy, science, law, religion, war, and romance. We can read a Lovecraft story, or a Raymond Chandler novel, without the footnotes we need for Shakespeare or even Jane Austen. And most immediately, we

can see and hear and immerse ourselves in the Thirties any time we want, by clicking on the Turner Movie Classics network or sorting our Netflix queue by year. We can see Humphrey Bogart, Clark Gable, the Marx Brothers, Marlene Dietrich, Myrna Loy, Jean Harlow, Greta Garbo, William Powell, Errol Flynn, Cary Grant, Carole Lombard, Charles Boyer, and Katharine Hepburn in all their black-and-white glory. The Thirties are right around the corner.

So, that decade full of wars, social turmoil, environmental crisis, poverty, murderous radicals, political deadlock, and cowardice – it turns out that it's not so far away as it might be. But at least they could dance during it.

A DESPERATE DECADE
"THE TIME WOULD BE EASY TO KNOW, FOR THEN MANKIND WOULD HAVE BECOME AS THE GREAT OLD ONES; FREE AND WILD AND BEYOND GOOD AND EVIL, WITH LAWS AND MORALS THROWN ASIDE AND ALL MEN SHOUTING AND KILLING AND REVELLING IN JOY. THEN THE LIBERATED OLD ONES WOULD TEACH THEM NEW WAYS TO SHOUT AND KILL AND REVEL AND ENJOY THEMSELVES, AND ALL THE EARTH WOULD FLAME WITH A HOLOCAUST OF ECSTASY AND FREEDOM."

— THE CALL OF CTHULHU

This is not one of those historical

Race

The world of the 1930s was a world of omnipresent, absolutely accepted racism. Racial barriers were supported by champions of law and science; only a very few radicals held otherwise. (A very few white radicals, that is. A rather larger share of black, brown, and yellow people also held otherwise.) From America's Jim Crow to Britain and France's colonial pass laws to Indian castes to Japanese xenophobia, legal codes enforced what everybody already believed. Many well-meaning folk (of all colors) supported domestic segregation and restricted immigration (if not lynching or race-baiting) as the only practical way to handle matters, regardless of their putative moral qualms about such policies. Even where the law was race-neutral (usually due to a providential absence of other races when the laws had been drafted), social codes were not. In genteel parlors and factory shop floors and military barracks the lines were clearly drawn, and drawn in color.

So how does this affect your game? The simplest way to handle the question is to ignore it: Investigators, allies, NPCs, and enemies might be of any race, just as they are in our utopian new millennium. The role of ethnic sidekick "just as good as a white man" (if not *quite* as good as the hero) is well established in 1930s pulp literature. Visits to Chinatown or Bronzeville or the Amazon jungles can be handled as, well, local color. This is perhaps the best option for Pulp-idiom games.

The next-simplest way is to construct all-white parties of Investigators who seek information or assistance only from fellow whites to battle creatures so alien as to moot the question. This is, somewhat unsettlingly, the Purist option. Lovecraft's (and Howard's) characters were almost universally WASPs, with one or two Irishmen as daring garnish.

Probably the most difficult, but perhaps the most satisfying, way to handle things is for the Keeper to pay attention to the question, and foreground it to the extent that it supports an interesting, or terrifying, story. A party of black Investigators in 1930s Mississippi battling decayed – but *white* – fisher-folk, vengeful conjure doctors worshipping the Black Man Nyarlathotep, and the Iloigor-infected (but socially connected) Klan would face challenges quite different from those confronting a tweedy bunch of New England professors.

But there's a catch, over and above the imperative to avoid preaching, and the need to be more aware of player sensibilities than usual. The story still has to work, both as horror and as a mystery. And the way you use the rules has to support this new condition. The use of Credit Rating would be historically almost entirely restricted to the Investigator's own race. Flattery, Reassurance, and Intimidation each have more potential pitfalls when the Investigator is one color and the NPC another. A Cop Talk core clue that a white Investigator could easily pick up from the Alabama sheriff just wouldn't logically work for a black Investigator, even if both Investigators are NYPD. Even in New York City, a Harlem cop and a Tribeca cop will encounter different reactions. And on a strict interpretation of the ability, the *only place* in *the world* of the 1930s where black Investigators can use Interrogation on a white person would be Haiti. Keepers in race-foregrounded games have to pay extra attention to their adventures, keeping clue opportunities realistic and appropriate, and double-checking to see if their laudable color-blindness points the Investigators into a blind alley.

The Keeper looking for specific rules guidelines might apply this option, which needless to say should only apply in race-foregrounded adventures. Interpersonal abilities used between strangers of different races *always require* a spend. This is abstract, not to mention still somewhat ahistorical, but it's an approach that represents the increased "social cost" of race barriers.

roleplaying books that feels the need to compete with Wikipedia. If you feel the need to know the name of the Belgian prime minister in 1931, or who won the Test Match in 1937, go look it up. Seriously, there's way more stuff – interesting stuff – on any given year in the Thirties somewhere

online than we could cover in a hundred books this size. All this section can be, or aims to be, is a filter put over the decade to bring up a backdrop for tales of horror and despair.

Poverty

The decade began with the Great Depression, which lasted in all industrialized nations until the coming of full employment with the Second World War. Millions went without work, and their families without incomes, for a decade. In the initial 1929 stock collapse, major American industrial firms lost 90% of their value within months. Banks failed, prices plunged, and farmers plowed crops under rather than sell them for less than they cost. US unemployment overtopped 30% by 1930, and remained above 15% for the remainder of the decade, spiking again in 1938 at nearly 20%. Family incomes – those that kept any income at all – plummeted by 40%. In Britain, unemployment averaged 20%, but was far worse (70%+) in the industrial north. In Germany, the tottering economy did not utterly crash, but the shocks wiped out the last vestige of trust in the Weimar Republic's competence and empowered Germany's political jackals. Everywhere, breadwinners lost their homes, entrepreneurs lost their businesses, and workers lost their dignity to piecework, make-work, and handouts. Resurgent unions saved some jobs, but slammed the factory gates hard against the jobless. The desperate turned to crime, to suicide, to radical politics … to anything that promised a way out.

The crash devastated the wealthy countries of the world, which weren't all that wealthy by our standards even before the blow hit. In 1929, nearly three-quarters of American families didn't make "a decent standard of living," meaning $2,500 a year (around $31,000 a year in 2007 dollars). Only about a quarter of Americans owned telephones. At most a fifth of them owned cars. But overall, Americans (and Londoners) had the highest standard of living in the world of the Thirties; Germany, France, and the rest of Britain were about 75% as rich. Italians made

only half of what Americans did, and Japanese and Russians about a third the American income level. In the colonies, of course, poverty was as endemic as it ever was in the Dark Ages; India's per capita wealth was barely a tenth that of America's.

Famine

And it was out there that people starved. In the great cities of the West, although there was hunger aplenty, there was no mass starvation. (About 300 people starved to death in New York City in 1931.) Even the horrific "Dust Bowl," that saw black soot fall like apocalypse snow in New York and Chicago, that uprooted nearly 3 million people from the Great Plains, didn't result in bodies bulldozed into pits or skeletal figures dying fly-bite by fly-bite.

But in African and Asian colonies, their economies twisted by commodity farming and then smashed by shrunken trade, there were spot famines and miseries aplenty. In Japan, drought struck rice farmers as silk-weavers lost their overseas markets. Africa and India were spared drought, but the wet weather worked its own evil in China, which had lost 2 million to drought in 1928-1930. The Yellow River floods of 1931 killed between 1 and 4 million people, and affected a quarter of the country. The Yangtze River flooded in 1935, killing twice as many as the Gansu earthquake, the decade's deadliest – 70,000 dead on Dec. 25. Drought then returned to China, sparking the "New Famine" of 1936, with 5 million dead.

Worst of all, in 1932-1933, Stalin's terror-famine intentionally starved 7 million of his own

people to death in the name of socialism and collective farming. Cannibalism ran rampant as farm families (in a blackly ironic final acceptance of collectivism) ate each others' children. The OGPU blocked the roads, turned back relief trucks, sent troops to loot food from peasant granaries, and piled 5 million corpses into mass graves in the Ukraine.

War

The world spent the 1920s hoping that the 20 million soldiers and civilians killed in the Great War of 1914-1918 would be the high-water mark of the century's deaths. It spent the Thirties preparing to drown that mark in blood. As with Famine, War rode hardest across China this decade. The Japanese invasion and conquest of Manchuria (renamed Manchukuo) killed a mere 60,000 people. The Chinese Civil War during that period, by contrast, killed 20 times that number of soldiers alone. Nationalists, Communists, and warlords together extinguished another 2 million lives in reprisals and civilian slaughter carrying out a squalid, primitive struggle amidst the alternately flooded and parched fields of what was once the richest country on Earth. When the Japanese resumed their conquest of China in 1937, they opened with the wholesale massacre of everyone they could find in Nanking, the Nationalist capital. The 300,000 dead in the "Rape of Nanking" were a down payment on the eventual Japanese slaughter of 1.2 million Chinese civilians through 1939, and touched off a further 1.3 million "incidental" deaths from typhus, cholera, and war-related starvation. The Nationalist resistance was no better,

Headline News

This is not intended to be a full-on chronology, but to at least put a few key dates into line. For fine detail work, look in the resources section of the Pelgrane Press website (pelgranepress.com).

1929

US stock-market crash (Oct. 29) precipitates global Depression.

1930

Stalin begins forced collectivization of Soviet farms (Jan 5). Clyde Tombaugh discovers Yuggoth, which he names Pluto (Feb 18). Mohandas Gandhi begins "salt march" civil disobedience campaign in India (Mar 12). Judge Crater vanishes (Aug 6). Ras Tafari crowned Emperor Haile Selassie of Abyssinia (Nov 2); Rastafarian movement burgeons in Jamaica in response.

1931

Jewish terror group Irgun founded in Palestine (Apr 10). Empire State Building opens (May 1). Yellow River floods, killing 1-2 million in China. Japan invades (Sep 19) and occupies Manchuria. Lucky Luciano begins building national organized crime syndicate; Al Capone imprisoned for tax evasion (Oct 24).

1932

In "the Crime of the Century," Charles Lindbergh's baby is kidnapped (Mar 2). Death of Charles Fort (May 3). President Doumer of France assassinated (May 7). Troops disperse the "Bonus Army" of 17,000 veterans in Washington, D.C. (Jul 28). Japan begins germ warfare experiments in Manchuria. Stalin begins terror-famine in Ukraine. Babe Ruth hits his "called shot" in Wrigley Field (Oct 1). Franklin D. Roosevelt elected President of the US in a landslide (Nov 8).

1933

US Marines withdraw from Nicaragua (Jan 2). Adolf Hitler becomes Chancellor of Germany (Jan 30). Anarchist attempts to assassinate FDR in Miami (Feb 15). Scottsboro Boys convicted (Apr 9). Chicago World's Fair. Autobahn construction begins. Albert Einstein emigrates to America, begins work at Princeton (Oct 17). Prohibition repealed in US (Dec 5).

1934

Gold Reserve Act makes private possession of gold illegal in US (Jan 31). Loch Ness Monster photographed (Apr. 19). "Night of the Long Knives" (Jun 30) purge of the SA in Germany. FBI guns down John Dillinger (Jul 22). Nazis assassinate Austrian chancellor Engelbert Dolfuss (Jul 25). US Marines withdraw from Haiti (Aug 15). Switzerland enacts bank secrecy laws. King Alexander I of Yugoslavia assassinated (Oct 9). Mao begins his "Long March" in China (Oct 16). Stalin rival Sergei Kirov assassinated in Leningrad (Dec 1).

1935

Twenty simultaneous "Black Blizzards" mark the height of the Dust Bowl (Apr. 14). Miskatonic University archaeological expedition to Australian Outback. Social Security enacted in US (Aug 14). Will Rogers and Wiley Post die in Alaska plane crash (Aug 16). Louisiana Senator Huey Long assassinated (Sep 8). Italy invades Abyssinia (Oct 2).

1936

Germany remilitarizes the Rhineland (Mar 7). The Pittsburgh Flood kills 70 and destroys 100,000 buildings (Mar 17). Franco's mutiny begins Spanish Civil War (Jul 17). Stalin begins purges and show trials of Politburo and Red Army. Boulder Dam (Hoover Dam now) is completed (Oct 9). Paul Robeson's version of "Gloomy Sunday" released. FDR re-elected (Nov 3). King Edward VIII abdicates to marry a divorced commoner; George VI becomes King (Dec 11).

1937

German planes flying for Franco bomb Guernica in Spain (Apr 26). Germany establishes rocket program at Peenemünde. Crash of the *Hindenburg* (May 6). Amelia Earhart vanishes over the Pacific (Jul 2). Japan begins new war on China (Jul 7); Rape of Nanking (Dec 13). Marijuana becomes illegal in US (Aug 2).

1938

Mexico nationalizes oil fields (Mar 18). Ruined Maya city of Caracol discovered. Italian physicist Ettore Majorana disappears from a ferry in the Bay of Naples (Mar 26). Route 66 completely paved. German government confiscates "degenerate art" (Jun 3). Bluesman Robert Johnson poisoned (Aug 16). Great New England Hurricane (Sep 21) hits Providence, RI Germany annexes Austria (Mar 12); Munich Conference sells out Czechoslovakia to Hitler (Sep 30). Orson Welles broadcasts modernized *War of the Worlds* on the radio (Oct 30). "Kristallnacht" pogrom in Germany (Nov 9). Living coelecanth discovered off Madagascar (Dec 22).

1939

Franco's victory ends the Spanish Civil War (Mar 28). New York World's Fair. First nylon stockings hit the market. Semyon Kirlian develops Kirlian "aura photography." Nazca Lines discovered in Peru. Nazi-Soviet Pact divides Eastern Europe between two empires (Aug 23). Germany invades Poland (Sep 1); WWII begins in Europe (Sep 3).

The Crawling Order: Totalitarianism

"No trials, or even definite charges were reported; nor were any of the captives seen thereafter in the regular gaols of the nation. There were vague statements about disease and concentration camps, and later about dispersal in various naval and military prisons, but nothing positive ever developed... Complaints from many liberal organizations were met with long confidential discussions, and representatives were taken on trips to certain camps and prisons. As a result, these societies became surprisingly passive and reticent."

— The Shadow Over Innsmouth

Perhaps the most terrifying thing about the 1930s is this: virtually every intellectual and political observer of the time believed at one point or another that the future was going to be written by Hitler or by Stalin, and they chose up sides accordingly. Lovecraft began as a fan of Hitler, and converted late in life to supporting a sort of dirigiste collectivist technocracy. (His description of the Yithians' civilization as "a kind of fascistic socialism" is not intended horrifically.) The rise of Cthulhu in the secret places of the world mirrors the rise of totalitarianism, not merely in overseas labor camps from Dachau to Vorkuta, but in the salons and soirees of New York and London. This provides *Trail of Cthulhu* games not merely an endless supply of potential bad guys, but a potentially powerful thematic element as well. But using totalitarianism for either purpose runs a few risks, and implies a few choices.

The first possible direction is the one taken by F Paul Wilson's novel *The Keep*, in which a rabbi and an SS commandant must ally to battle an inhuman monster. In this approach, the horror of the Mythos is such that it overwhelms all human politics, and one can assume that "right-thinking" agents of the NKVD and the Gestapo would agree. This raises the unsettling possibility that the actual best, most workable solution to the interpenetration of humanity by Cthulhoid horror is the one followed in *The Shadow Over Innsmouth*, and one that anti-Mythos Investigators in Berlin, Moscow, Rome, Tokyo, or Madrid would reflexively follow: concentration camps, secret prisons, and (one presumes) mass graves somewhere desolate. Forcing players to make – or even accede knowingly to — such choices should be done deliberately, if at all.

Of course, this knowledge alone – that their governments have decided to use such tactics — may be enough to keep some player groups conveniently reluctant to call in the FBI or MI5. Another method of seeding this dramatically useful distrust is to imply that at least some elements in some human governments are attempting to harness the Mythos for themselves. This can be a sort of "Arkham Project" scenario, in which the bureaucrats don't actually know or care what they unleash, or an implication of spreading, viral cultism as interrogators discover just what kind of powers (and what kind of Powers) their prisoners had access to.

This approach is reinforced if the Keeper chooses to go the "Indiana Jones" direction, in which evil Nazis (or Commies) are hunting the living idol Chaugnar Faugn or searching for the ruins of Commoriom in the Greenland ice sheet, and the bold Investigators must beat them to it and stop them. After all, why would Hitler's goons be looking for the *Necronomicon*, if not to use its powers to fuel the blitzkrieg? This makes both narrative sense – if the powers of the Mythos exist, surely people as bent as the Nazis would be looking into it – and dramatic sense – Stalin is evil and dangerous, Yog-Sothoth is evil and dangerous, bingo. But it runs the risk of sliding into "Nyarlathotep invented the Nazis," or worse yet "Nyarlathotep magicked the Nazis into being so evil." This trivializes the decade's human history of genocide and oppression, turns real living atrocities into pulp supervillainy, and lets us all off the hook.

Even less forgivably, it also makes the story boring and predictable – all the anti-fascists must be anti-Cthulhu, too! Keep in mind that in real history, most of the anti-fascists were devoted servants of an ideology every bit as inhuman and murderous, and even the "good guys" got into bed with Hitler and Stalin when it suited them. If you're going to mix the Mythos and politics, try to at least occasionally look at the story from the perspective of cults and gods to whom the entire human race are insects, and to whom Gandhi and Tojo are both indistinguishable mayflies – or potential tools.

Brigades. Both Franco and the Republicans committed tens of thousands of political executions – the "necessary murder" in Auden's poem – and another 50,000 Spaniards died of apolitical hunger and germs. In a further preview of coming attractions, German bombs killed 10,000 Spanish civilians from the air. Air superiority, Soviet selfishness, and Franco's considerable strategic skill ended the war with fascism victorious.

Fascism also won in Libya, as Italy defeated Senusi rebels in 1930–1932, and Abyssinia, where 400,000 died to make Mussolini master of the upper Nile. War spread across South America, too. Beginning in 1932, Western mercenaries honed their craft fighting the Chaco War across the endless sawgrass plains between Bolivia and Paraguay for a fortune in oil. When a 1935 military coup in Bolivia left Paraguay the final winner by default, 100,000 South Americans were dead. There didn't turn out to be any oil in the Chaco after all.

killing 1.6 million Chinese for collaboration or political crimes, or simply to deny their labor to the invader. Following the Long March away from the battle front, Mao's Communists sat this phase of the war out, killing under 100,000 civilians.

By contrast, the "rehearsal war" in Spain was practically civilized, with its ideologically driven rapine and firing squads.

It served as a practice ground for the expansionist totalitarians: Soviet tanks defended – and looted – the Republican government, and faced off against the Italian artillery and German bombers that put iron in the gloves of Franco's Nationalist troops. Approximately 100,000 soldiers died on each side, including 25,000 foreign fighters from the fascist Condor Legion to the communist International

THE NIGHTMARE COUNTRIES

"SEEKERS AFTER HORROR HAUNT STRANGE, FAR PLACES. FOR THEM ARE THE CATACOMBS OF PTOLEMAÏS, AND THE CARVEN MAUSOLEA OF THE NIGHTMARE COUNTRIES."

— THE PICTURE IN THE HOUSE

This section gives brief views of various locations around the world of the Thirties, roughly organized by continent. More mundane details both historical and geographical are available online or in other references. We especially recommend period travel guides, such as Baedeker's or Cook's, as well as the Federal Writers' Project guides for the US, although even modern-day tourist guidebooks like the *Lonely Planet* series have astonishing amounts of useful game information.

With that said, we focus primarily on the needs of the Mythos tourist. The Cthulhu Mythos section in the entries indicates both ongoing Cthulhoid activity, and rumors that Investigators with ratings in Cthulhu Mythos might well have come across in one or another moldering tome or nightmarish vision.

Abyssinia

Despite the Italian conquest in 1935-1936, unrest continues in the mountains of the south and the deserts to the east. Entering Abyssinia after that date requires Italian permission, or a lengthy and dangerous covert overland journey from British East Africa. Edmund Kiss, a novelist and mystic attached to the Ahnenerbe, mounts an expedition to the highlands in search of fragments of the "second moon" and Lemurian ruins in 1936.

The Abyssinian royal family traces its descent from the Queen of Sheba and King Solomon. A church in Axum supposedly holds the Ark of the Covenant, brought here by Solomon's son Menelik.

Cthulhu Mythos: Coptic monasteries here hold records of certain lineages supposedly descended from Irem via the Queen of Sheba and King Solomon. *The Book of Enoch* is only the best-known work of occult lore to be discovered here.

Antarctica

US Admiral Richard E. Byrd mounted an aerial survey of Antarctica in 1928-1930 from a base on the Ross Ice Shelf. In 1929, he overflew the South Pole. In 1933-1935, he mounts a second expedition, and nearly goes mad after spending five months completely alone at "Advance Base" in 1934. Two British expeditions (1929-1931 and 1934-1937) explore and claim portions of the continent. Alfred Ritscher heads a German expedition to Queen Maud Land in 1939, renames it "Neuschwabenland" and claims it for Germany with air-dropped swastika markers.

Cthulhu Mythos: The Miskatonic University Dyer-Lake Expedition of 1930-1931 discovers a primordial city of the Elder Things and a previously (and since) unknown mountain range they surveyed at 35,000 feet. The mountains' failure to appear on later surveys implies that Dyer may have unwittingly entered a parallel plane, possibly Dho-Hna, Leng, or Kadath in the Cold Waste.

Belgian Congo

Less of a hellhole now than during the genocidal "Congo Free State" period of direct Belgian royal control, borderline slavery and the occasional massacre still keep the Congo's rubber and copper coming. The 25,000 square miles of jungle in the colony are essentially impassable to whites outside the river valleys.

Cthulhu Mythos: The nightmare of Belgian rule sparked the millenarian cult of Ahtu (Nyarlathotep) here in the 1880s; though stanched by Dame Alice Kilrea in 1902, it may yet flourish back beyond the Baenga country.

The last of the Anziques, a mysterious tribe of cannibal magicians with a peculiarly Caucasian appearance, fled into the Belgian Congo from the French Congo in the early 1870s. They may have been one offshoot of a mysterious white kingdom supposedly discovered in that region by Sir Wade Jermyn in the mid-18th century.

Brazil

The populist President Getúlio Vargas, elected in 1930, increasingly models his government on dictatorial lines. Brazil's openly fascist Integralist "Green Shirt" movement (popular with the 1 million Brazilians of German extraction) battles Communist agitators in the streets until 1938, when Vargas bans all paramilitary bodies, having seized openly fascist control himself by means of a new constitution in 1937.

The psychic channeler and healer Zelio de Moraes founded Umbanda, a blend of Spiritualism and Macumba (the traditional Afro-Brazilian religion similar to Voodoo) in 1920; by 1938 it has centered itself in the white and mestizo Rio de Janeiro middle- and upper-class. It involves spirit communication with the *caboclos*, or "Those Who Come From The Forest," and the *pretos velhos*, the "Old Slaves."

Brazil is the site of two Tunguska-style events this decade: the upper Rio Curacá valley in 1930, and the Rupununi region on the border of British Guiana in 1935.

Future Ahnenerbe asset Edmund Kiss explored the Amazon delta in 1928.

Cthulhu Mythos: The explorer Percy Fawcett disappeared into the Brazilian interior in 1925 searching for the lost city of Muribeca with a mysterious basalt idol he identified as Atlantean.

Burma

Burma is part of the British-controlled Empire of India. The Galon rebellion, named after the giant serpent-killing Burmese magical bird (similar to the Garuda of India) breaks out after earthquakes rock Pegu and Pyu in October 1930. A tattooed blond fortune-teller named Saya San proclaims himself Bird King of Burma, and channels spirits to possess his soldiers. He uses astrology, sorcery, and alchemy as weapons of war; the British hang him and his followers in 1932.

Cthulhu Mythos: The Hawks Expedition of 1905 discovered the lost city of Alaozar on the Plateau of Sung, but was attacked by Tcho-Tcho tribespeople and wiped out. The last survivor, Eric Marsh, dies in 1934 and publishes his narrative. The Tcho-Tcho of Alaozar worship the Twin Obscenity, Zhar and Lloigor. The Plateau of Sung is the source of the potent black lotus, which has power over dreams, death, and madness.

This may be connected to the cult of Ghatanothoa in Burma.

Easter Island

An island territory governed by the Chilean Navy, Easter Island is most famous for its enigmatic *moai* statues. They face inland; 887 are known. Between 1770 and 1838, the islanders toppled all the moai from their plinths, usually onto their face.

In 1932, Hungarian engineer Guillaume de Hevesy proposes a kinship between the undeciphered *rongo-rongo* script of Easter Island and the undeciphered alphabet of pre-Aryan Mohenjo-Daro in India.

Cthulhu Mythos: Easter Island is the closest land to the location indicated in the "Johansen Narrative" (47°9' S by 126°43' W) as the site of Cthulhu's sunken city R'lyeh.

Egypt

Technically independent of British control under its King Fuad I (succeeded by his son Farouk after 1936), Egypt resents continued British control over its military and operation of the Suez Canal. German, Italian,

and Soviet agents have their own networks of dissatisfied religious leaders, ambitious junior officers, and smugglers in Cairo, Alexandria, and Port Said. The trade in illicit artifacts, mummies, and papyri thrives despite official condemnation and suppression; Streetwise will allow Investigators to connect with willing sellers.

Major Egyptologists with excavations and digs in the 1930s include: Pierre Montet at Tanis, John Pendlebury at Akhetaten, Jean-Philippe Lauer at Saqqara, Gunther Roeder at Hermopolis, and George Reisner at Giza. (Weird freelance scholars such as the fascist French mystic René Guénon at Cairo and the Theosophist E.A. Schwaller de Lubicz at Luxor also study various monuments and sites.) Harvard, Miskatonic, the British Museum, and the German Archaeological Institute (DAI) maintain active presences throughout the country. Obtaining dig permission requires academic tenure, affiliation with an approved organization, and at least one Bureaucracy spend.

Cthulhu Mythos: There are at least two cults of Nyarlathotep worshippers active in Egypt claiming descent from Nephren-Ka: the politically active Brotherhood of the Black Pharaoh and the dilettantish Children of the Sphinx.

A Bedouin cult worships a monstrous Thing dwelling under the Pyramids, and one of Ghatanothoa's surviving cults lurks in Upper Egypt.

Egypt also boasts a vampire who calls himself Seth, a remnant tribe of serpent-folk in the Nile

marshes, and an immense ghoul colony in Cairo's City of the Dead.

Necromancers and other would-be wizards haunt the library of Al-Azhar and the Egyptian Museum.

Germany

Once he becomes Chancellor in January 1933, Hitler rapidly consolidates dictatorial power. Jewish Investigators, even those from America or Britain, will find conditions here increasingly hostile as the decade progresses. Refugees fleeing Germany are often forced to sell their belongings – including libraries and ancestral artifacts – for a fraction of their value.

The Nazis hold their first great book-burning (at which many "decadent" works might be dangerously salvaged) on May 10, 1933. The Nazis ban Freemasonry for Wehrmacht personnel in May 1934, and begin their crackdown on rival secret societies thereafter. By 1935, Crowley's OTO, the Theosophical Society, the Golden Dawn, and the Brotherhood of Saturn (among other magical societies) have all been banned, and their libraries and ritual paraphernalia seized by the RSHA Amt VII B, a division of the SS.

Cthulhu Mythos: The Great Old One Cyäegha, the Sleeping Eye, lies imprisoned in a cavern beneath the Dunkelhügel hill near Freihausgarten, guarded by the five Vaeyen: "The Green Moon," "The White Fire Which Is Darker Than The Night," "The Winged Woman," "The White Dark Which Is More Red Than The Fire," and "The Black Light."

German scholars in the 19th century such as von Junzt, Dostmann, and Mülder uncovered vast amounts of Mythos material, which likely rests in University libraries at Cologne, Frankfurt, Vienna, or Berlin.

Greenland

Norway and Denmark dispute jurisdiction over this ice-covered island until a 1933 ruling by the Permanent Court of International Justice.

Although the Ahnenerbe has plans to visit the island, which it identifies with the mystical Aryan homeland of Thule, it succeeds only in mounting the Otto Rahn and Bruno Schweizer expeditions to Iceland in 1936 and 1938.

Cthulhu Mythos: Professor William Channing Webb, while searching (unsuccessfully) for runic inscriptions, stumbled upon a tribe of degenerate Cthulhu-worshipping Esquimaux in high West Greenland in 1860.

The ice of Greenland conceals the lost civilizations of Hyperborea and its successor kingdom, Lomar. Fanes of Tsathoggua, remains of the prehuman Voormis, and the fearsome gnoph-keh dot the tundra.

Haiti

The United States winds down its two-decade occupation of Haiti, withdrawing completely in 1934. The Americans have eliminated banditry and aroused much resentment with their attempts to suppress Voodoo, a religion resurging in popularity as times remain hard.

Journalist William Seabrook's 1929 book on Haiti, *The Magic Island*, spread knowledge of zombies and Voodoo in general (which he differentiates from *ouanga*, or malevolent magic) to the outside world.

Cthulhu Mythos: The Voodoo serpent loa Damballah Wedo is known to cultists of Yig as the Crawler of Midnight.

As "Don Pedro," a Spanish magician involved in the great slave revolts of the 1790s, Nyarlathotep inspired the violent "Petro" rites of Voodoo.

Some Voodoo cultists worship Cthulhu as Agwe, the underwater loa, and cult activity in Haiti generally increases at times

of increased Cthulhoid dream-sendings or similar activity.

Louisiana

The populist crusader Huey Long, "the Kingfish," was elected governor of Louisiana in 1928, and served simultaneously as governor and US senator during 1931-1932. His hand-picked successor, Oscar Kelley Allen, succeeded him as governor, freeing Long to spend full time in the Senate building a national constituency for radical reform. His opponents, including FDR, called him a fascist; his 1935 assassination curtails his plan to run against Roosevelt in 1936. His brother Earl Long inherits the Kingfish's machine, and serves as governor from 1937 to 1939.

Among the major Voodoo doctors and queens in New Orleans during this decade are Mother Catherine Seal (of the Manger of True Light), Father James Joseph (of Jerusalem Temple Baptist Church), Luke Turner (nephew of the great Voodoo queen Marie Laveau), and Laure Hopkins, a.k.a. Madame LaLa.

Beginning in 1935, the archaeologist Clarence H. Webb excavates Indian mounds at Poverty Point in the northern part of the state.

Cthulhu Mythos: In 1907, New Orleans police inspector John Raymond LeGrasse led a major raid into the bayou country to break up a cult of Cthulhu worshippers. Among the discoveries left unplumbed were a white polypous avatar of Cthulhu in a bayou lake.

The occultists Étienne-Laurent de Marigny (the executor of

Randolph Carter's estate) and Henricus Vanning lead a group of magical adepts known as the Coffin Club in New Orleans until Vanning's mysterious death by crocodile bite during the 1937 Mardi Gras.

Mongolia

Once the center of a vast empire stretching from Burma to Hungary, this Communist country and its neighbor Tannu-Tuva have been Soviet client states since 1921. In that year, the Red Army captured and executed the "Mad Baron" von Ungern-Sternberg, who believed himself to be the "King of the World" prophesied to emerge from Inner Asia in certain arcane Buddhist texts.

Between 1920 and 1930, the paleontologist Roy Chapman Andrews mounted several expeditions into the Gobi Desert searching for dinosaur eggs and skeletons. He may also have been working as an agent for US Naval Intelligence during that time.

The occultist, mystic, and painter Nicholas Roerich explored Mongolia during his 1925-1928 Asian trek, and again in 1934-1935 on a mission (ostensibly to gather drought-resistant plant specimens) from US Secretary of Agriculture (and future Vice-President) Henry Wallace.

Cthulhu Mythos: During warmer, wetter ages, Mongolia was the center of a vast primordial empire (known to Theosophists as the "Uighur" or "Naga" Empire) that rivaled Mu. That empire may have vanished from space-time entirely, existing solely on some other vibratory plane.

Other texts hold that Mongolia once held the Lake of Hali and that Carcosa manifested there when Hastur ruled on Earth.

The connection between these two legends, and between either vanished city and the Russian legend of Belovodye ("The White Lake") remains unknown.

After the Copeland-Ellington Expedition vanished in 1913, Miskatonic University anthropologist Harold Hadley Copeland appeared three months later in Mongolia, raving mad and carrying the Zanthu Tablets. Upon his suicide in 1926, Copeland's will bequeathed the Tablets to the Sanbourne Institute of Pacific Antiquities in Santiago, California, from which they are stolen in 1933.

Peru

Following a military coup in 1930, Col Luis Sánchez Cerro serves as President (barring a period in 1931 when leftist revolts by a pan-Indian group, APRA, forced him from office) until his assassination on April 30, 1933. His successor, Oscar Benavides, bans APRA and the Communists. Benavides battles strikes and leftist mobs, remaining in power (despite losing the 1936 election) until 1939. Undeclared border wars break out with Colombia in 1932 and Ecuador in 1938.

Hiram Bingham's "discovery" of Machu Picchu in 1911 rekindled interest in Peruvian archaeology and Andean archaeology generally. Among those interested is the mystic Edmund Kiss, who explores Lake Titicaca and Tihuanaco in neighboring Bolivia in 1928-1929. Kiss plans to return to Peru for the Ahnenerbe in 1940.

Cthulhu Mythos: A major Cthulhu cult flourishes in the mountain gorges northwest of Cuzco, in the Salapunco region near Machu Picchu. The Indian cultists identify Cthulhu with the Inca (and pre-Inca) god Viracocha, the "power of the water," who destroyed and re-created the world only to withdraw to the Pacific, promising to come again.

A cult of Ghatanothoa exists in Peru, according to von Junzt.

San Marco University in Lima has a Greek copy of the *Necronomicon*.

Rumania

Under the increasingly dictatorial rule of King Carol II, Rumania has an active fascist underground, known as the Iron Guard. Bucharest is a lovely city known as the "Paris of the Balkans." After the Great War, Rumania annexed Transylvania, formerly a province of Hungary. Hungarian nationalism remains a vexing problem in that region.

Dr Franz Altheim of the Ahnenerbe spends some time searching for ancient Dacian ruins in Rumania in August 1938.

Cthulhu Mythos: In October 1928, a titanic explosion destroyed Castle Ferenczy in Transylvania, long a rumored plague spot of Yog-Sothoth worship and cult activity. Did any artifacts – or Ferenczys – survive?

According to occult legend, the "Scholomance," the Devil's School, exists beneath the waters of a lake south of Hermannstadt (Sibiu) in Transylvania. Its rumored pupils include Johann Faust and Count Dracula. It may contain a spawn or avatar of Hastur or Cthulhu.

A cavern beneath the Carpathians leads to the underground tomb of Nyogtha, That Which Should Not Be. (Other caverns of Nyogtha are in Syria, Chinese Turkestan, New Zealand, and Salem, Massachusetts.)

Saudi Arabia

Under its founding king, Abdul-Aziz Ibn Saud, Saudi Arabia consolidated its control over the Arabian peninsula in a series of wars between 1924 and 1932. A war with Yemen in 1934 reduces that country to vassal status, leaving only the British colony at Aden (and to a lesser extent, the British protectorates along the Gulf coast) outside Ibn Saud's will. Non-Muslims are forbidden to enter Mecca, and need special permission from the King to travel to the Arabian interior.

Unproductive searches for oil continue until a strike at Dharan in 1938. Thanks to Ibn Saud's traitorous British advisor St John Philby (whose son Kim is recruited by the OGPU in 1934), that oil concession goes to the American Standard-Texaco combine of Aramco. Philby also explores the Rub al-Khali or "Empty Quarter" in 1932 searching for the lost city of Irem, and spends much of the decade negotiating with Germany and Spain to supply Gulf oil to the German Wehrmacht.

Cthulhu Mythos: The site of Irem of the Pillars, in the Crimson Desert, is a pilgrimage location for wizards, necromancers, and members of the Great Race of Yith. In some fashion, it sits on the Border of space and time

themselves, with the Hand carved above its gates grasping for the Silver Key. Beneath Irem are the twin shrines to Nug and Yeb.

Irem is also near the "Nameless City," the home of the masqut. According to various sources, the Nameless City is a fane of Hastur while Irem is the center of the Cthulhu cult.

Soviet Union

Stalin rules the Soviet Union with purges, terror, and famine. The Gulag system of slave-labor camps and colonies, run by the OGPU (which becomes the NKVD in 1934), grows by leaps and bounds during this decade, from 200,000 prisoners in 1931 to 1.1 million in 1935 to 1.65 million in 1939.

The official ideology of the Soviet Union rejects supernatural belief, including belief in the Mythos,

which means that any number of shamans, priests, or cultists might be slowly starving to death while digging a canal through the permafrost or mining gold in Siberia. However, the influential "socialist realist" writer Maxim Gorky nurtures a small circle of Gnostic philosophers and artists, and remains a firm believer in telepathy, until his mysterious death in 1936.

"White" Russian exiles in Europe and America, like refugees from Germany, may be compelled to sell their heirlooms to the curious.

The Comintern supports artists, musicians, and writers who toe the Stalinist line, which can be an excellent source of income or contacts for Investigators who do likewise.

Cthulhu Mythos: The Tunguska explosion of 1908 is rumored

to have been a summoning of Azathoth, perhaps by a cult of nihilists in a Czarist Siberian labor camp.

There is a frozen city above the Arctic Circle inhabited by those who Ithaqua has carried off over the centuries.

South Pacific Mandate

Comprising the Marshall, Caroline, and Mariana Islands (except the American territory of Guam), the League of Nations turned the "South Pacific Mandate" over to Japan after the Great War. Beginning in 1934, Japan fortifies Truk, the "Gibraltar of the Pacific," as well as Saipan, Tinian, Palau, and Yap. The Japanese government consequently closes the Mandate area to foreigners.

During this period, the Japanese Navy's "Strike South Group" sponsors archaeological expeditions from Taihoku Imperial University that discover giant human bones and hieroglyphically inscribed wooden fragments on Ponape and Kusaie.

Cthulhu Mythos: According to Miskatonic University anthropologist Harold Hadley Copeland, the island of Ponape is the home of the Great Old One Zoth-Ommog, and its megalithic Nan-Matal ruins are remnants of Mu.

From the *Ponape Scripture* transcribed by Captain Abner Ezekiel Hoag in 1734, Ponape is known to have supported a Deep One cult similar to that in Innsmouth, implying that a major Deep One city rests beneath the Pacific amid the Caroline Islands. Ponape remains an epicenter of Cthulhoid art and ritual activity.

Spain

Spanish museums or private collections may hold reed codices, idols, gold artifacts, or other items taken from the Maya, Aztec, or Inca civilizations (as well as books, art, or objects looted by Spanish armies from Italy in the 16th century or Germany in the 17th). Under wartime pressures and privations, those items could be available for the right price, or bold thieves could grab them under cover of a bombing or attack.

Entering the country during the Spanish Civil War (1936-1939) will require contacts among German or Italian arms-dealers (to enter Nationalist-held territory, via Seville) or the Comintern (to enter Republican territory, via Barcelona or Cartagena). Either sort of contact exposes

Investigators to imprisonment or execution by the other side (or to purges by Soviet agents in either case).

Cthulhu Mythos: The former temple of Chaugnar Faugn, in the Pyrenees, may yet hold unsavory lore.

Adolf Schulten's theory that the Spanish city of Tartessos (now submerged off the shore of Cadiz) was the original Atlantis may actually derive from the Deep One colonies in those waters.

Thibet

The 13th incarnation of the Dalai Lama dies in 1933, and the new avatar is not born until 1935 and not enthroned until 1940. During the interim, the Reting Rinpoche, a powerful lama, heads the country. James Hilton's 1933 novel *Lost Horizon* popularizes the myth of Shambhala, or Shangri-La, and associates it with Thibet (or Tibet).

Thibet has no motor vehicles and no airstrips; travel is by foot or on animal back. Entering Thibet through India requires British permission or subterfuge. Entering the country across China requires a great deal of luck or fortitude.

The American naturalist Brooke Dolan heads two expeditions to Thibet in 1931 and 1934-1935. Among his party both times is the ornithologist Ernst Schäfer. In 1939, now-SS Hauptsturmführer Schäfer heads an Ahnenerbe expedition to Thibet with the goal of seeking the primordial Aryans among the lama caste, securing copies of Thibetan holy and magical texts, and biological research.

Cthulhu Mythos: Elements of the pre-Buddhist religion of Bön in Thibet bear strong similarities to Mythos teachings and practices. This may be due to its antiquity, or to its geographic (or spiritual) proximity to the blasphemous corpse-eating cult of inaccessible Leng. For example, the Thibetan national epic of King Gesar takes place in the "kingdom of Ling."

The plateau of Tsang houses Chaugnar Faugn. It also holds a non-human race that worships the sacred powers of plague and pestilence. Tsang-ka cultists infiltrated the San Francisco medical establishment in 1899, and may have caused the San Francisco black plague outbreak in the following year, along with a number of cases of "black fever" in the prison system.

The Copeland-Ellington expedition of 1913 sought proof of Muvian survival on the plateau of Tsang, but ended in disaster (see Mongolia, p. 178).

The lamasery of Nen-mka in northern U-Tsang was dedicated to the worship of Hastur and Azathoth before being broken up by Thibetan soldiers in 1911.

The mi-go are active in the Thibetan Himalayas, and their traces have been mistaken for Yeti tracks.

Money

In the 1930s, much like the modern era, the plethora of local currencies are mostly irrelevant. Virtually all serious business, and even more criminal business, is done in one of three currencies: the US dollar, the British pound sterling, and the French franc. Almost anywhere in the world, a fat wad of one of these three currencies and the Streetwise ability will get you what you need without bothering about exchange rates. Except, of course, between those three: in 1935, to pick a year at random, the pound was worth about $5, and the franc about 7 cents. (Once things get dicey in Europe, the Swiss franc – about 33 cents in 1935 – comes into its own.) Totalitarian states prefer to sell only in outside currencies, and buy only with their own, but cannot always get such sweetheart deals. Internally, they can enforce whatever farcical exchange rate they like, although trading nations need to maintain some realism: the Reichsmark is rather closer to the official 40 cent exchange rate in 1935 than the Japanese yen is to 84 cents or the Soviet ruble is to $8.71.

TECHNOLOGY, WEAPONS, AND EQUIPMENT

"I SET OUT FOR HOME, WHERE I BATHED, ATE, AND GAVE BY TELEPHONE AN ORDER FOR A PICKAXE, A SPADE, A MILITARY GAS-MASK, AND SIX CARBOYS OF SULPHURIC ACID, ALL TO BE DELIVERED THE NEXT MORNING..."

— THE SHUNNED HOUSE

The technology of the Thirties should be familiar fare to any player who has watched her share of World War II movies. It's a heavy, industrial, mechanical tech, full of diesel, propellers, and whirring cogwheels. The workhorses of the world are the railroad engine, the steel mill, and the hydroelectric dam. Television is cutting-edge mad science, computers are still just mathematicians' daydreams, and oil has been "the new coal" for over a decade now.

Vehicles

In general, if an Investigator has a Driving ability rating, he has a motor vehicle suitable to his Credit Rating. As a general rule, cars between $500 and $1,000 are about right for Credit Rating 4 owners. Cars over $3,000 are driven primarily by Credit Rating 6+ owners, or by their chauffeurs. That said, the Keeper may allow Investigators to own used or rebuilt cars (which may require more frequent Mechanical Repair tests), inherited cars (which down-on-their-luck Dilettantes can't replace if wrecked by a monster), or stolen cars (with a Cop Talk, the cop just impounds the vehicle without charging the driver).

An Investigator must have at least a Driving rating of 2 to own (and be able to drive) a motorcycle, but they are extremely affordable and widely available used or rebuilt at any Credit Rating over 0.

The motor vehicle table gives statistics for a sampling of representative and evocative period cars and trucks. Speeds represent top road speeds; cruising speed is normally two-thirds, or even half, that amount. The Keeper is welcome to move prices and speeds up and down to indicate closeout sales, lemons, or precision-tuned racing vehicles. Most cars have two running boards each capable of carrying a clinging Investigator at a pinch. The Keeper may require tests of Athletics to stay on if the driver spends any Driving points during the ensuing chase sequence.

Under off-road conditions, a

Monsters vs Machines

Most monster chases will likely occur on foot, or pseudopod, or tentacle, or what-have-you. But in Pulp games especially, a monster may pursue the Investigators' vehicle as it flees the scene, in a test of the Investigators' Driving (or Piloting) vs the monster's Athletics. A ghoul, Deep One, or similar beast might make an Athletics test (Difficulty 6) to leap onto the running board of an escaping car and continue the fight that way.

Failing that, most monsters cannot outrun a speeding car, or outfly a speeding plane. If the Investigators make their initial test, the vehicle evades such slowpokes and the scene is over. Although the Keeper is welcome to change monster speeds in her game, we suggest instead ambushes, or presenting some obstacle (muddy roads, dense fog, cultists with spiked chains in the path) that the monster can avoid but the vehicle cannot. Monsters also have any number of interesting attacks that they can make on a fragile car or even-more fragile airplane. A Hound of Tindalos or dimensional shambler can even appear inside a moving vehicle, for extra fun.

With all this in mind, the following monsters can probably hold their own in a car chase and make it a full-fledged contest: byakhee, hunting horrors, mi-go (chasing cars from the air by cutting across "as the crow flies"), nightgaunts, shantaks, and shoggoths (off-road). Shan can maintain a chase until the Investigators can escape the environs of Goatswood (up to the Keeper – who may rule that the shan are trying to herd their prey deeper into the forest). In their own terrain, gnoph-keh and sand-dwellers can probably sustain a chase against cars for two or even three rounds.

In the air, only byakhee and shantaks can sustain a long chase against an aircraft, although the Keeper may rule that hunting horrors or nightgaunts require 2 successful tests to evade rather than the standard 1.

Xothians, of course, can easily pace any ship or boat that humans can construct.

vehicle's speed is halved, except for those vehicles indicated with an 'OR' in the table. Their speed is only reduced by one-fourth. Poor driving conditions, hills, and so forth cancel out; each party to a chase is usually affected equally, although the Keeper may always rule otherwise for extremely specialized circumstances.

Motorcycles may mount sidecars; if so, their top speed is halved.

A truck can carry the amount of cargo indicated in its description;

a "1-ton" truck, for instance, can carry 1 ton of cargo. (It weighs considerably more than 1 ton, even empty.)

Car chases work like normal chases, with Driving instead of Fleeing as the contested ability. In straight car chases, if a car's top speed is lower than its competitor's by 10 mph or more, the driver of the car with the lower top speed has a +1 to all Difficulty Numbers in the driving contest; if it's lower by 30 mph or more, the add is +2. The

Vehicle Table

Vehicle	Cost	Speed (mph)	Notes
1928 Indian 101 Scout motorcycle	$200	75	Provides automatic +1 to roll in all off-road Driving tests; OR
1936 Harley-Davidson 61E "Knucklehead" motorcycle	$300	120	OR
1927 Ford Model A	$400	75	Two-seater with open rumble seat in back
1935 Willys 77 sedan	$500	75	
1933 Chevrolet ½-ton pickup truck	$550	60	OR
1935 BMW R-12 motorcycle	$600	70	OR
1933 Reo Speed-Wagon 1-ton light delivery truck	$650	80	Refreshes 1 Driving pool point per scene
1935 DeSoto Airstream coupe	$700	85	
1937 Ford ½-ton panel van	$700	60	
1932 Dodge 1-ton truck	$750	75	
1935 Packard One-Twenty touring car	$1,100	85	
1936 Lincoln-Zephyr V12 sedan	$1,250	90	
1934 Chrysler 8 Airflow sedan	$1,350	85	
1930 Ford 2½-ton truck	$1,600	55	OR
1935 Auburn 851 Speedster	$2,000	100	
1937 Studebaker President 8 sedan	$2,500	75	
1931 Stutz Bearcat roadster	$3,500	70	Two-seater; Provides automatic +1 to roll in all road Driving tests
1930 Cadillac V16 sedan	$5,400	90	
1937 Jaguar SS 100 Sport	$9,500	100	
1932 Maybach DS8 "Zeppelin"	$16,000	105	
1938 Mercedes-Benz "Grosser" 770 touring sedan	$20,000	80	Often encountered as an armored (+4 against bullets; top speed 60) limousine
1932 Duesenberg SJ coupe	$25,000	130	Two-seater
1935 Rolls-Royce Phantom III limousine	$50,000	90	Seats eight

Keeper may rule that local traffic conditions, twisty narrow streets, or other considerations obviate this advantage. She may also rule that the much faster car speeds away and ends the scene, if it makes better dramatic sense than gaming out a car chase.

The aircraft table is similar, although access to aircraft is usually restricted to Investigators with the Occupation of Pilot or with Credit Ratings of 7+. Aircraft with 'SE' noted are single-engine light aircraft. (High-performance single-engine fighter planes such as the Spitfire require a dedicated Piloting slot, although a kindly Keeper may allow a "bush pilot" to fly one at a +2 Difficulty penalty.) Speeds are top burst speeds; cruising speeds, like those for ground vehicles, are normally half to two-thirds as fast. Climb angles, ceilings, turn radii, and so forth are outside the purview of the GUMSHOE rules.

Weapons

Because you demanded it: more complete weapons statistics for common or evocative firearms of the 1930s. See the table overleaf.

Aircraft Table

Aircraft	Cost	Range (miles)	Speed (mph)	Notes
1917 Curtiss JN-4 "Jenny"	$2K	250	75	Typical barnstormer biplane; two-seater; SE
1924 Dornier Do J "Wal" seaplane	$14K	2,250	110	2-4 crew + 10 passengers
1933 DeHavilland DH.89 "Dragon Rapide"	$20K	550	150	1 crew + 8 passengers
1934 Cierva C.30A autogiro	$20K	285	110	Single-seat; can land near-vertically; requires only short takeoff
1929 Lockheed Vega 5	$30K	675	185	Six seats; provides automatic +1 to roll in all mid-air Piloting tests; SE
1933 Boeing 247	$44K	745	200	3 crew + 10 passengers
1935 Douglas DC-3 cargo plane	$47K	1,500	150	3 seats + cargo space can hold 20 people; refreshes 1 Piloting point per scene
1934 Sikorsky S-42 flying boat	$50K	1,950	180	4 crew + 37 passengers
1938 Supermarine Spitfire	$160K	1,150	380	Not for sale; one-seat fighter plane; 2 cannons, 4 machine-guns
1928 *Graf Zeppelin* airship	$3 million+	10,000	75	Not for sale; 36 crew + 24 passengers

Firearms Table

Damage	Weapon	Shots	Cost	Notes
Light firearms; +0 damage	Webley & Scott Police Model .32 ACP automatic pistol (1906)	8	$10	
	TT-33 Tokarev 7.62 mm automatic pistol (1933)	8	$45	Soviet military/police sidearm
	Nambu Type 14 8mm automatic pistol	8	$40	Japanese military sidearm
	Mauser "Broomhandle" 7.62 mm automatic pistol (1896)	10	$50	
	Remington .41 Short double Derringer (1866)	2	$20	+1 to Difficulty of any test to find on carrier; only point-blank range
	Colt Police Positive .32 revolver (1907)	6	$15	US police sidearm
	Walther PPK .32 automatic pistol (1931)	7	$70	
	Remington M34 .22LR sporting rifle (1932)	20	$45	
	Mannlicher-Carcano M1891 6.5 mm bolt-action carbine (1892)	6	$20	Italian combat rifle; statistics also apply to Japanese Arisaka Type 44 combat rifle
	Winchester M1912 20-gauge pump shotgun (1912)	5	$50	
	Remington M32 20-gauge shotgun (1932)	2	$35	Double-barreled
Heavy firearms; +1 damage	Very 12-gauge flare pistol (1882)	1	$30	Only does damage at point-blank (no bonus) or close range; starts fires if it hits flammable material at up to long range
	Colt M1911A1 .45 ACP automatic pistol (1926)	7	$50	US military sidearm; all tests to repair or un-jam are at -1 Difficulty
	Luger P08 9mm automatic pistol (1908)	8	$50	German military sidearm
	Walther P38 9mm automatic pistol (1938)	8	$75	German military sidearm
	FN Browning High-Power 9 mm semi-automatic pistol (1935)	13	$75	
	Webley No. 1 Mk IV .455 SAA revolver (1915)	6	$25	U.K. military sidearm
	Smith & Wesson .38 Special revolver (1902)	6	$30	US police sidearm
	Smith & Wesson Model 27 .357 Magnum revolver (1927)	6	$80	
	Thompson M1921 submachine gun (1921)	20, 30, 50, or 100	$200	See p. 65
	"Schmeisser" MP28 submachine gun (1928)	32	$200	See p. 65
	Mauser 98K 7.92 mm rifle (1935)	5	$125	German combat rifle; statistics also apply to Soviet Moisin-Nagant M10 7.62 mm combat carbine (cost $100)
	M1 Garand .30-06 rifle (1936)	8	$120	US combat rifle
	Lee-Enfield MkIII .303 rifle (1907)	10	$100	U.K. combat rifle
	Winchester M1912 12-gauge pump shotgun (1912)	5	$50	
	Remington M32 12-gauge shotgun (1932)	2	$35	Double-barreled
Very heavy firearms	Holland & Holland Double Express .600 elephant rifle (1903)	2	$500	Does +2 damage; next round action must be an Athletics test (Difficulty 3) to remain upright
	Browning Automatic Rifle (BAR) .303 machine gun (1918)	20	$500	Does +2 damage; requires bipod or prone firer

Remember, all shotguns are considered heavy firearms at point-blank range, and light firearms at near range. At point-blank or close range, add an additional +1 to damage if you fire both barrels of a double-barreled shotgun simultaneously.

Hardware and Sundries

And what would a historical setting section be without a price guide? A page or two shorter, that's what. The table overleaf is intended to paint a broad picture; prices for clothing, food, and other goods varied as much in the 1930s as they do today. If you don't see an item, as a rule of thumb, divide its 21st-century price by 12.

Exotic Equipment

"WE HAD DEVISED TWO WEAPONS TO FIGHT IT; A LARGE AND SPECIALLY FITTED CROOKES TUBE OPERATED BY POWERFUL STORAGE BATTERIES AND PROVIDED WITH PECULIAR SCREENS AND REFLECTORS, IN CASE IT PROVED INTANGIBLE AND OPPOSABLE ONLY BY VIGOROUSLY DESTRUCTIVE ETHER RADIATIONS, AND A PAIR OF MILITARY FLAME-THROWERS OF THE SORT USED IN THE WORLD WAR, IN CASE IT PROVED PARTLY MATERIAL AND SUSCEPTIBLE OF MECHANICAL DESTRUCTION..."

— THE SHUNNED HOUSE

In "The Shunned House," Elihu Whipple obtains the Crookes tube and flame-throwers by his "natural leadership," not by slapping cash down on the barrel. If the Investigators decide they need arcane machinery, illegal goods, or military weapons for their monster stakeout then they should earn them the old-fashioned way – with interpersonal abilities.

Scientist Investigators can use Reassurance to borrow the Tesla coil from the lab, military officer Investigators can employ Intimidation to get land-mines from an armory clerk, and so forth. With a white coat or hard hat, Disguise can get the Investigator access to labs or construction equiment; Flattery might get the reclusive NPC inventor to bring his microwave beam along. Players can use their Investigators' pre-existing contacts to rustle up weird gear, or in extremis default to Credit Rating ("surely I went to Yale with someone who owns an autogiro") or Streetwise ("we're in luck; there's a chemical plant in Gary with a bent guard where we can get all the pesticide we need"). The overarching goal should be to knit strange equipment into the story, rather than just letting the Investigators stop off at Crookes Tubes R Us.

Technologiy, Weapons and Equipement

Clothing and Accessories	Price	Notes
Boots, leather	$3-$10	
Clothing, ladies', one outfit	$3-$12+	Dress, stockings, hat
Clothing, men's, one outfit	$13-$27+	Suit, shirt, tie, socks, hat
Coat, leopard/mink	$90/$585	
Coat, trench	$11	
Gear, arctic	$60	Parka, boots, gloves
Gear, safari	$25	Leather jacket, khaki shirt and trousers, pith helmet
Gear, seafaring	$15	Peacoat or raincoat, cap, work shirt, sweater, canvas trousers
Shoes, ladies'/mens'	$1+/$4+	
Spectacles	$9	
Tuxedo	$25	Still called a "dinner jacket"
Watch, pocket or wrist	$2-$20+	

Food and shelter	Price	Notes
Apartment, per month	$12-$50+	
Bread, loaf	$0.05	
Coca-Cola, 12 oz. glass bottle	$0.05	
College tuition, year	$200-$2,000	Harvard College: $4,500
Hotel room, per night	$0.25-$3	Waldorf-Astoria, NYC: $5-$10
House, three-bedroom	$2,800	
Meal, automat	$0.10-$0.25	Coffee is always a nickel
Meal, home-cooked	$0.65	3-lb. roast, potatoes, onions
Meal, restaurant	$0.25-$1+	Steak dinner at the Rainbow Room, NYC: $3, plus $1 for wine
Milk, quart	$0.10	
Movie ticket and popcorn	$0.20-$0.50	Newsreel and cartoons included
Whiskey, shot/bottle	$0.35+/$4+	Less for rotgut

Adventuring Gear	Price	Notes
Alarm clock, wind-up	$1-$5	Makes an ideal bomb timer!
Ammunition, 50 rounds	$0.30	Shotgun shells $0.70 for 25
Bicycle	$24-$45	Top speed 20 mph; OR
Binoculars, 8-power	$25	$12 for 5-power
Camera	$5-$40	$0.20 for one roll of b&w film (8 shots)
Camera, 8mm motion-picture	$30-$50	$4 for one reel of b&w film (8 mins)
Chain, per foot	$0.50	$1 for a padlock
Cigarettes, per pack	$0.15	$2 for a box of cigars
Flashlight, 2-cell	$1	$0.05 per battery
Gas mask	$5	
Geiger counter	$10	
Generator, portable	$120-$300	
Gold, per troy ounce	$35	Jewelry and rare coins will be more
Guitar	$9	
Lantern, kerosene	$4	
Medical bag and kit	$20	
Tools, carpenters' or locksmiths'	$10	
Trap, break-leg	$6	Sense Trouble to avoid or Conceal to plant; does +1 damage and immobilizes limb
Typewriter	$20-$45	$50-$70 for portable
Welding/cutting torch and tanks	$95	$8 acetylene refill
Zippo lighter (1932)	$1	

Transportation and Communication	Price	Notes
Airfare, per mile	$0.12	Travel time 90-150 mph
Bribe, for speeding/illegal firearms/ illicit entry/smuggling (plus Cop Talk, Reassurance, etc)	$5/$20/$10 /$10-$100	A policeman's pay is about $3 per day
Gasoline, per gallon	$0.19	
Native bearer, per day	$0.05-$0.25	Native guide $1 per day
Ocean liner fare	$10-$100+	600 miles per day, weather permitting
Pullman sleeping-car ticket, per mile	$0.02-$0.07	Average 40 mph or 900 miles per day, depending on stops
Telegram, per word	$0.05	$0.25 international
Tires, set of 4	$4-$10	
Train ticket, day trip, per mile	$0.04	Average 35 mph, depending on stops

Putting it all together

"It occurred to us, too, that our venture was far from safe, for in what strength the thing might appear no one could tell. But we deemed the game worth the hazard, and embarked on it alone and unhesitatingly..."

— "The Shunned House"

The purpose of playing *Trail of Cthulhu* is to collaborate in telling a horror mystery story. In this collaboration, it's the players' job to feel the horror, to figure out the mystery, and to willingly involve themselves in the story. It's the Keeper's job to make the players' jobs possible in the first place.

Tips For Players

"A new and burning curiosity grew within me, compared to which my boyish curiosity was feeble and inchoate. The first revelation led to an exhaustive research, and finally to that shuddering quest which proved so disastrous to me and mine."

— The Shunned House

A monster investigation is full of dead ends, red herrings, and utter confusion. *Roleplaying* a monster investigation shouldn't be. Herewith, then, we provide a few techniques or concepts to take on board that can help maximize your own fun.

Believe You Might Succeed

Yes, this is a game of horror, in which your Investigator might well be slaughtered, carried off to Yuggoth, or driven irrevocably insane. That said, the best way to fail is to become defensive and do nothing. Don't let the fear bring your planning ability to a halt. Instead, talk through the most obvious options, quickly pick the one that seems the most appealing, and then execute that plan. Will something horrible happen? Of course it will — it's a horror game! Something horrible will happen no matter what your plan is. At best, you'll find one that requires desperation and daring, and might still cost you your lives. But no fun whatsoever will happen unless you choose something to do and do it.

So be bold and seize the initiative. Pick the type of terrifying risk you're most able to confront and go after it with both hands. Who knows? Maybe you'll surprise the Keeper, if not the monsters. As in any game, the Keeper will allow any halfway credible approach you come up with a good chance of success, and will place nasty obstacles in your way to make it more exciting. Pick something quickly, grit your teeth, and send your Investigator into that warehouse.

In the world of the Cthulhu Mythos, safety is an illusion, so you might as well do *something*.

Justify Your Casting

When you created an Investigator, you cast a character – a hero — in a story. True, it's often a story about an ordinary cop or college professor who stumbles into cosmic horrors that transcend the universe. Realistically, many people would likely respond to extreme violence and eruptions of supernatural awfulness by curling up into a ball and doing nothing. Those people are called "non-player characters."

The Cthulhu Mythos is hard enough on your Investigators without you making them freak out, too. Plus, paralysis is boring, at least after the obligatory denial or disbelief in the "this ... defies every known law of science" sequence. When you create your Investigator, or develop her personality during play, think about realistic ways to portray her as proactive and resourceful, even in the face of mind-shattering horror.

Players in horror games often make the mistake of thinking solely about how realistic their responses are. Instead, make interesting choices and then find a way to make them realistic. An interesting choice is one that keeps your Investigator moving and doing things.

Drives Drive You Forward

If you still find yourself unable to justify some near-suicidal plan, think of your Drive. Come up with some reason to Drive yourself into danger, and pick up some needed Stability for doing it along the way. Look to your Drive as a source of action and inspiration, and use it to decide which near-suicidal plan is right for your Investigator.

When Stuck, Look For More Information

If you are legitimately stuck, and not just rejecting perfectly viable courses of action, don't just stick close to home hashing over your options. Investigative scenarios often bog down into speculative debate between players about what *could be* happening. Many things *can* be happening, but only one thing *is*. If more than one possible explanation ties together the clues you have so far, you need more clues.

Whenever you get stuck, **get out and gather more information**. Ask yourself what you need to know in order to formulate a plan. Then figure out how to get that information, and go out and get it. Keep a written record of all the clues, particularly the core ones that the Keeper has thrown at you, pick one that hasn't been followed up, and pursue it hard.

Talk To People

Many groups are reluctant to use their Interpersonal abilities, figuring that they can get into less trouble by sticking purely to physical clues, or thumbing through well-lit libraries in the next county. This is a disastrous mistake. Talking to witnesses, experts, and informants is by far the best way of gaining information about your situation. With information, you can find

that coveted least-worst plan that will lead you to the grim final confrontation.

Keep Moving Forward

Expect to find only one major clue per scene. Although you shouldn't be too quick to abandon a scene for the next one, most groups make the opposite mistake, returning endlessly to the same few places or witnesses, hoping to scrape more info out of them. If you find a clue that leads you somewhere else —go there! Chances are, once you're there, you'll find another clue, that will in turn lead you to a new scene, with a further clue that takes you to a third scene, and so on. Unsuccessful groups endlessly re-plough the same ground. Successful ones follow a trail, just like in a kid's game of treasure hunt.

Deputize Yourself

An ordinary person might be reluctant to go out and involve themselves personally in investigations best handled by the professionals. But you've stumbled into a world of unearthly menace where, as far as you know, there are no professionals. You may feel cosmically ill-prepared to face the threat in front of you, but you know that no one else is up to it, either. As improbable as it may seem, you must take on the mantle of unofficial investigators.

Rely on your Interpersonal abilities to gain entrance to situations that would normally be closed to regular folks. Come up with suitable cover stories if need be.

Passively playing the good citizen won't save you. You must carry

the ball into the enemy's court, and part the dark veil of the unknown. A few moments of reluctance is understandable and realistic. More than that is boring. Accept your weird new role in life, and make the most of it.

TIPS FOR KEEPERS

"MAN MUST BE PREPARED TO ACCEPT NOTIONS OF THE COSMOS, AND OF HIS OWN PLACE IN THE SEETHING VORTEX OF TIME, WHOSE MEREST MENTION IS PARALYSING. HE MUST, TOO, BE PLACED ON GUARD AGAINST A SPECIFIC, LURKING PERIL WHICH, THOUGH IT WILL NEVER ENGULF THE WHOLE RACE, MAY IMPOSE MONSTROUS AND UNGUESSABLE HORRORS UPON CERTAIN VENTURESOME MEMBERS OF IT."

— THE SHADOW OUT OF TIME

Running a *Trail of Cthulhu* adventure begins with building a *Trail of Cthulhu* adventure. We call this game "investigative horror," and it's important to keep a handle on both the investigation and the horror, which is to say that an adventure should have a structure and it should have a feel. The structure, or skeleton, lets the story move and stand up. The feel, or atmosphere, lets the story live and breathe. Both are necessary, and each should inform the other.

Designing Scenarios

In *Trail of Cthulhu,* the Investigators stumble onto or track down an occult mystery, they discover or deduce the horrifying Mythos truth behind it or the vile Mythos monster or conspiracy responsible, and they take desperate action to end, postpone, or avert the horror. They may kill the sorcerer responsible, or dynamite the old cavern so the Thing can come out no more. They may destroy all monsters, or practice some ritual to banish or blockade them. They may steal the key tome or artifact, or just sink it in Narragansett Bay. In some campaigns, they may even call in the FBI and the Navy to demolish the whole town. Or, of course, they might go insane and leave the horror out there to attract the next batch of Investigators.

Mystery Structure

As Keeper, you design each adventure with three key elements: the hook, the horrible truth, and the trail of clues.

The hook. This is the event, whether a conventional haunting, a gruesome crime, or a mysterious letter, that attracts the attention of one or more Investigators. Examples:

- *A murder seems to have been committed in an inhuman fashion, or in a way described in some hoary Mythos tome.*

- *Strange lights or figures appear in some distant or remote place, or in a haunted location such as a witch's house or a graveyard.*

- *An occultist, artist, or scientist, or perhaps a friend or relative, dies or disappears mysteriously.*

- *A psychic, a spell, a nightmare, or an ancient grimoire predicts disaster soon.*

- *A strange figure tries to get*

access to a library, graveyard, or the Investigators' home.

The horrible truth. This sets out what is going on. If it's an anomalous incursion by the Mythos as in "The Colour Out of Space," or an ongoing infestation as in "The Whisperer in Darkness," the Keeper determines what the Big Bad is, how it got there, what it wants, and where it's going. If it's a crime or plot by cultists or a solitary madman, the Keeper does the same for them, and decides how they fit into the larger Mythos picture, if at all. In both cases, the Keeper must figure out how the hook fit into the overall story – if it was triggered accidentally, coincidentally, deliberately, or carelessly, and why. The Keeper then determines what will happen if the horror goes unchecked – do the mi-go just keep mining Vermont, does Simon Orne raise an army of revenants to set up another adventure, or does the world end with Yog-Sothoth blasting through the skin of North America?

The Keeper also determines what has to happen to solve the problem, if only in this local area or at this specific time. This, unknown to the players, is their **victory condition** for this scenario – what they have to do to thwart the Mythos and bring the story to a positive conclusion.

Once the Keeper has worked out the logic of the story from the Mythos point of view, she then thinks in reverse, designing a **trail of clues** leading from the hook to an understanding of the horrible truth and its Mythos enablers, sufficient to get to work defeating it. Following this trail of clues should ideally allow the players to deduce, or at least trigger, the

victory condition.

Optionally, the Keeper may also plan a series of **antagonist reactions**. These lay out what the monsters, aliens, or cultists do when they find out that they're being investigated. The Keeper determines what conditions trigger them, and what the antagonists attempt to do. These may include further crimes, giving the team more to investigate. Cultists or aliens may try to destroy evidence, hinder the investigation by planting false leads, or to intimidate or dispose of potential witnesses, including accomplices they no longer trust They may attack the investigators. Foolish, overconfident, or risk-taking villains may take them on directly, as might alien, uncaring, ravening, or oblivious monsters. Clever villains will strike from a distance, perhaps using magic or summoned beasts, taking great pains to cover their tracks. See Responses in the Cult section p. 167 for inspiration.

Spine and Skeleton

A straightforward investigation can be seen as a series of scenes arranged in a straight line, with multiple ways to move from each scene to the one following it. Improvisation consists of reacting to the players by switching the order of scenes around, or interpolating new scenes in this order. This is simple to write and run, but difficult to hide.

A looser structure will still consist of an investigative line, in which the Investigators pursue a series of core clues until they achieve a resolution of some sort. This is called the **spine.** In your notes, it can consist of large sections of fleshed-out narrative, or a

✦ Victory is Impossible

Some Lovecraft stories have no victory condition: *The Colour Out of Space*, for example, implies that nothing has to happen, and the monster will leave of its own accord, or not. Others, such as *The Whisperer in Darkness*, imply that nothing can be done at all, and the Mythos will win in its own time regardless of player action. This will not satisfy most gamers, but it's a great conclusion for a hard-core Purist campaign, complete with anagnorisis (see p. 76).

barebones list of the elements that need to occur to comprise a minimally satisfying narrative. See the introduction to the adventure included in this book, *The Kingsbury Horror*, for a sample spine.

Surrounding this rudimentary spine are confrontational scenes, in which any of the following can happen:

- The creatures (or other antagonists) make an aggressive assault on the lives or sanity of their targets, whether these are the Investigators, recurring members of the series' supporting cast, or supporting characters involved only in the current scenario.

- One or more Investigators pursue their personal goals, or advance another investigation occurring in parallel to this story.

- Something strange or uncanny happens, possibly providing yet more information about the nature of the threat, while usefully eroding the Investigators' Stability and building tension. This helps make the final confrontation more dangerous for the Investigators, and hence more dramatic for the players.

- A strong supporting cast member (ally, villain, or bystander) offers a tempting distraction, a red herring, or an alternate take on the mystery. These sorts of scenes should be kept to a minimum, but they can add real depth to a setting and to a story.

Confrontational scenes can be even looser than the spine. In your notes, they can consist of carefully detailed prose descriptions. However, unless you're preparing an adventure for someone else to run (as in the case of *The Kingsbury Horror*) you're probably better off with rudimentary point form notes. By keeping your notes sparse, you can give yourself a foundation of ideas to improvise from, without spending undue time writing up scenes that might not occur.

Floating Core Clues

It can be useful to structure a scenario with one or more free-floating core clues. These typically advance the story from one distinct section to another. Where an ordinary core clue is linked with a particular scene, a floating clue can be gleaned in any one of several scenes. The Keeper determines during play which scene gives up the clue.

Floating clues allow you to control

Not-So Weird Menace

There was a flourishing subgenre of pulp stories known as "Weird Menace" tales. In these stories (which descend directly from early Gothics such as *The Mysteries of Udolpho*), a sadistic villain uses the trappings of Gothic horror to advance a sinister scheme. *But* the seemingly supernatural events all have rational explanations, usually trickery and coincidence, or at most hypnotism. (This format was later revived as the "Scooby-Doo" plot, but "Weird Menace" sounds better.) These sorts of scenarios, in which the San Francisco Mob is faking a sea-monster to cover up its smuggling operation, or a vile baronet is attempting to drive his weak-willed sister insane to gain the inheritance, make an interesting change of pace. Such a story might focus on one of the Investigators' Sources of Stability, and provide a kind of breather story in between globe-threatening dangers. They take essentially the same structure, but require less thematic juice, since the whole point of the tale is that the theme is a lie … or is it? It can be fun to plant just one tiny clue to actual Mythos activity somewhere in the tale, just to tweak player paranoia.

Multiple Spines

An even more robust mystery plot may have several potential trails of clues leading from one or more hooks to the same horrible truth. Done correctly, such an adventure can feel extremely organic, as any player choice leads to a useful core clue. It can even ramp up the paranoia, if the Keeper has a sense of style and timing – the Cthulhu cult *is* everywhere! Done poorly, of course, it can seem over-obvious or forced, so we recommend mastering the basic structure before you start adding new spines to scenarios.

A multi-spine adventure or complex of adventures can be a fair bit of work to design to its full potential, but in many games, you can re-use unexplored trails as sequel adventures involving other branches of the cult or conspiracy, or as bolt-holes and backup plans for the bad guys.

the pacing of a scenario. They allow the characters to play out all of the fun or interesting experiences in one section of the scenario before the story takes a dramatic turn. For example, you might want them to separately meet all of the suspected Mordiggian cultists before they, and the Investigators, get locked up for the night in an old dark house. To achieve this, withhold the core clue that moves the Keepers to the dark house until after they've met all of the relevant supporting characters. That way, you prevent them from leaping ahead into

the narrative without getting all the information they need to fully enjoy what follows.

Likewise, a floating clue allows you to perform like a ruthless editor, skipping unnecessary scenes when you need to kick the narrative into a higher gear. Let's say you've chosen five possible scenes in which the Investigators might logically get a necessary core clue. You figure that this phase of the adventure should take about an hour. If the players breeze through the scenes in ten minutes apiece, you can save the core clue for the last scene. If they linger, taking twenty minutes per scene, you'll want to make the core clue available after the third scene.

Player frustration level usually serves as a better trigger for a floating core clue than a predetermined time limit. If they're having obvious fun interacting with the vivid supporting characters you've created, or being creeped out by uncanny phenomena, you can give them more of what they want by saving the core clue for the final scene. On the other hand, if you see they're getting bored and frustrated, you can slip in the floating clue earlier.

The scenario in this book uses a floating core clue structure.

Leveraged Clues

A staple element of police procedural shows is the crucial fact which, when presented to a previously resistant witness or suspect, causes him to break down and suddenly supply the information or confession the detectives seek. This is represented in GUMSHOE by the leveraged clue. This is a piece of information which is only available from the combined

use of an interpersonal ability, and the mention of another, previously gathered clue or object. The cited clue is called a prerequisite clue, and is by definition a sub-category of core clue.

Statistics for NPCs

Potentially violent NPCs should have relevant General abilities defined. Add more as they are required. NPCs who aren't likely to do more than talk to Investigators don't need General abilities defined, let alone investigative ones, so don't bother defining them – a simple description, with some roleplaying notes will suffice. They will often hold clues to be revealed based on the interpersonal abilities of the Investigators; these also provide roleplaying handles for the Keeper.

If you don't want to define the exact interpersonal abilitiy for a particular clue, in which NPCs provide, you can simply list the NPCs suspectibilities – the interpersonal abilities which are most likely to make them cooperate, and those which will make them clam up. These can be used in future scenes, too. NPCs who use their abilities to help the Investigators, for example, a mountain guide, should have at least the basics covered (Athletics, Health, Stability, any offensive skills, and any other General skills they are likely to use). Occasionally, the Investigators might employ a specialist to use investigative skills – this is usually just an indirect way of spending their own points, for example Credit Rating to get a medical opinion. In such a case, you don't really need to list their abilities explicitly. You simply decide whether or not they've succeeded based on the NPCs occupation, your description, and the needs of the adventure.

Calling On Abilities

The rules offer a number of ways to call on abilities, depending on the situation. Choosing the right way to call on an ability is crucial to the forward momentum of your investigative plot. Make this choice according to the consequences of failure.

If the consequence of failure is that a character fails to get a piece of crucial information, success should be automatic provided that the character has the ability in question, and the player thinks to ask for it. Even at that, you may need to improvise during play if no player steps up to claim the needed clue, bending the details of the scenario so that a different ability (one possessed by another player, perhaps) will garner the same information. In other words, core clues should ideally have more than one potential delivery route.

If you have a piece of information that offers a fun sidelight on the action but is not essential to move through the story, you can make this available with a 1- or 2-point spend. Choose the cost of the spend according to the entertainment value of the information, *not* the game-world difficulty of completing the task. Look at the Example Benefits sidebar on p. 53 for inspiration.

Drama should supersede realism, and the GUMSHOE rules and structure are fundamentally dramatic. You should build scenarios likewise. For example, the sorts of locks

that Investigators encounter will depend on their narrative function, not on the quality of the cultists' local hardware store. In dramatic terms, a locked door is like a clue the players can't find: frustrating and meaningless, or an intentional narrative re-routing mechanism, or usually both. Locks that hide clues should be pickable with the Locksmith ability – locks that seal the Investigators in with the formless spawn of Tsathoggua should require dramatic

Mechanical Repair tests.

If an action's consequence of failure might be madness, death or injury, by all means make it a test. If game world logic suggests that a supporting character will actively oppose the Investigator, make it a contest.

In a horror game, mayhem suffered by the protagonists is not an impediment to forward movement. Trail of Cthulhu

The Cthulhu Mythos Ability

Using the Cthulhu Mythos ability is the poisoned "Get Out of Jail Free" card in *Trail of Cthulhu*. A player whose Investigator uses this ability is likely signaling one or both of two things: he wants a big hint to the mystery and is willing to pay for it, or he wants to confirm his deductions and roleplay some juicy Lovecraftian madness.

The Keeper should oblige on both fronts. In the second place, the Keeper should feel free to quote horrific couplets, drop monstrous names, and generally emphasize the cosmic at the expense of the quotidian in this revelation. She should also tailor the revelation, as much as possible, to hit the Investigator's specific weak points and to corrode his Pillars of Sanity (see p. 46). But primarily, to the extent she can without completely wrecking the adventure, she should unveil the horrible truth, confirming at the very least the identity of the relevant Great Old One who lurks Behind It All, and the outlines of the monstrous scheme at hand. Some sample revelations:

- Cthulhu's island home recently rose above the Pacific Ocean; the cult seeks to open his tomb.
- This alien civilization was more advanced than humanity is physically or mentally capable of ever becoming, and its survivors are degenerate and homicidally insane.
- Hastur has poisoned the minds of the whole collective.
- Old Man Whateley bred Yog-Sothoth with his daughter, and one of the resulting twins is still alive.
- During the eclipse, cultists can use a sufficiently powerful ritual to open a door for Nyarlathotep.
- A 300-year-old wizard learned to resurrect the dead from Yog-Sothoth.
- Ghouls infest the London Underground, and the government already knows about it.

The revelation need not explicitly reveal the victory condition, much less provide specific spells, techniques, or monstrous vulnerabilities. Such information comes from research in Mythos tomes, interrogating cultists, discovering diaries or inscriptions, and so forth.

In a standard *Trail of Cthulhu* scenario, the entire trail of clues from hook to victory condition should be accessible – albeit harder to navigate — without any Investigator using her Cthulhu Mythos ability. Likewise, using the Cthulhu Mythos ability provides Investigators a glimpse of the destination, and perhaps a view of the countryside, but not a road map.

With that said, a hard-core Purist *Trail of Cthulhu* scenario may well require the use of Cthulhu Mythos to solve. Such scenarios may very well end in anagnorisis (see p. 76).

---

characters, especially in Purist games, are expected to die early and often. The player turns to his defunct Investigators' contacts or connections (see the Intimate Correspondent, p. 31), creates a new character, the Keeper inserts him as close to the scene as possible (or narrates something like "Three days later, after picking up Father Micah from the railway station…") and bingo, you've got more meat for the grinder and the story continues.

For this reason, we advise you to structure *Trail of Cthulhu* campaigns in an episodic manner, so that no ongoing plotline depends on the continued survival of any particular Investigator.

Ripped From the History Books

"THE WHOLE MATTER BEGAN, SO FAR AS I AM CONCERNED, WITH THE HISTORIC AND UNPRECEDENTED VERMONT FLOODS OF NOVEMBER 3, 1927."

— THE WHISPERER IN DARKNESS

Horror elements become more frightening when juxtaposed with recognizable elements of ordinary life. *Trail of Cthulhu* is set in a historical era with no shortage of horrors even in ordinary

life. Even if she isn't running a "Nazis for Nyarlathotep" game, the Keeper should try to blur the distinction between esoteric horror and exoteric history.

To create scenarios, scan through history books, biographies, collections of weird phenomena, cultural compendia, or even period novels for the most peculiar, anomalous, or outrageous events of the era, or of your campaign month and year. Add an additional layer of backstory, explaining that the Napier, New Zealand earthquake of 1931 was caused by a Tsathoggua-worshiping cult, or that a special Black Dragon team moved into Nanking's art museums during the massacre to loot Mythos statuary. How did the Mythos influence, exploit, or create the event? Use the event or its aftershocks as the hook for a scenario, and half your adventure is already done.

Should demand warrant, we'll produce more scenarios ripped from the history books and dipped in oily green Cthulhoid ichor. In the meantime, however, there's nothing stopping you from libelously speculating on J Edgar Hoover's real interest in the Innsmouth detainees and their amorphous sexuality.

The Skeptical Authorities

"OPINIONS WERE DIVIDED AS TO NOTIFYING THE MASSACHUSETTS STATE POLICE, AND THE NEGATIVE FINALLY WON. THERE WERE THINGS INVOLVED WHICH SIMPLY COULD NOT BE BELIEVED BY THOSE WHO HAD NOT SEEN A SAMPLE ..."

— THE DUNWICH HORROR

It is a standard trope of horror that the traditional guardians of order and normality, such as the police, civil authorities, and news agencies, are resolutely blind to what the protagonists are going through. The usual Lovecraftian scenario involves obsessed or nearsighted Investigators uncovering an awful truth that they cannot, *dare not* reveal to society at large.

There is a sound dramatic reason for this. Successful horror depends upon a sense of isolation, whether this is geographical (a ruin in Antarctica) or social (you're obviously a dangerous lunatic). The reassurance of a support network is poison to

Imprisonment As Plot Device

Obstacles where the punishment for failure is imprisonment or other loss of freedom to maneuver should be introduced with caution. If the characters can gain information while captured, and will be presented with a fairly easy avenue of escape afterwards, by all means, include them. You can allow tests or contests to avoid such consequences.

However, plot turns in which characters are arrested by the authorities and cannot escape invariably bring game sessions to a screeching, thudding halt. Either allow the characters to avoid them with automatic successes on Interpersonal abilities, or build an escape hatch into your story. Investigators with high Credit Ratings erve this purpose well. Assuming that the players are jailed in an industrialized democracy or Western ally, the dilettante's lawyers or political connections can always get the characters sprung, after a suitable interval of nail-biting and discomfort.

Be wary of plot construction that demands characters accept captivity to gain crucial information. Many players would sooner have their Investigators trepanned by the fungi from Yuggoth than accept even a brief sojourn in comparatively cushy confinement. Unfortunately, with this player type, you won't get very far by pointing out that getting captured is a Pulp staple. Their attitude is rooted in a deep-seated desire to maintain emotional control, and is not typically susceptible to argument.

the sense of creeping unease that horror seeks to cultivate. Eventually, once the protagonists have already been through hell, society may come to their aid, recognize that they were right all along, and dynamite the Innsmouth waterfront, but this only happens at the end of the investigation, if at all.

The Keeper should enforce this convention stringently, cutting off player access to outside support. This is easier in the 1930s. There are no cellphones and no CBs. Phones in small towns like Innsmouth (if they even have phones) are on party lines, and the villains are almost certainly listening in. Phone and telegraph lines can be cut. Shortwave radio is new and experimental, and the sets are too bulky to bring along. Roads are narrow and ill-paved,

even in much of the Northeast, and susceptible to a "convenient" mudslide, flood, or bridge collapse. If your car breaks down (or is sabotaged), there aren't rental agencies waiting to replace it. The police don't have civil rights lawyers and neighborhood advocates on their back, and can afford to be politely skeptical or downright rude. They can threaten to run you in for wasting their time or vagrancy, with no *Miranda* rights and no phone call, depending on how you approach them.

All of these limitations then act as motivators for the players to press ahead with the investigation. Unless they can *prove* that sinister events are afoot in this quiet seaside resort, the police will be worse than useless. Unless they can find out for certain exactly what web of occult association links the murder victims, they are liable to join them. If they don't find out what happened to Alonzo Typer, nobody will. There isn't a police station around for miles, the phones aren't working, and he could already be dead...

The Keeper may find it hard to give the players the impression that running to the authorities would be a bad idea. Drives and character background help with this, as some characters will naturally recoil from police involvement, but in case these are not enough for the story, the following three classic demotivators may help:

- *The police would never believe us.* Who in their right mind would go running down to the police station babbling about walking corpses made of grave worms?

- *The police would assume we were responsible.* Have the Investigators had to kill anyone? Have they been put into a position where it looks like they've killed someone?

- *The police are in on it.* Worst of all is the possibility that the authorities themselves are somehow complicit in the horror. Can you really trust them to watch over you?

Note that police detective Investigators may know these risks even better and more intimately than naïve dilettantes or stodgy professors.

Managing Scenarios

An investigative story in any medium is, by its very nature, highly structured. The investigators learn of a mystery, then move through a series of scenes, each of which concludes in the acquisition of a clue which segues into the next scene. The story reaches its climax when the investigator discovers and reveals the answer to the mystery. It may or may not conclude, for extra punch, in a physical confrontation with the story's now revealed-antagonist.

Structure can be difficult to achieve in the roleplaying medium. Guide the players too little and they lose the thread, resulting in a loose and sloppy narrative that provides none of the neat, order-making pleasure the genre is meant to provide. Guide them too much and they feel that their freedom of action has been taken away from them, and that they're merely observers moving through a predetermined sequence of events. (As you probably know, this latter syndrome is known in roleplaying jargon as *railroading*.)

The trick to successfully running investigative scenarios is to strike the right balance between the two extremes. The exact balance is a matter of collective taste. Groups prone to flailing about may welcome a strong structure with clear goals, a straight narrative path and definite resolutions. Players who resolve questions of procedure with swift efficiency, or who prefer to focus on characterization over storyline, require a looser hand on the structural tiller.

Streamlining the Twentieth Century Limited

Some groups are hyper-sensitive to issues of railroading. These concerns, which are absolutely legitimate, may be based on past bad experiences with controlling Keepers who forced them to enact essentially passive roles in unalterable, preset storylines. If members of the group are avid roleplaying theorists, they may respond out of a general ideological feeling that players ought to shape and drive the story, taking on responsibilities traditionally given to the Keeper.

The most important way to prevent players from feeling railroaded is to remain flexible and reactive to the choices the characters make. We'll discuss this a bit more in the next section.

However, nearly as crucial is avoiding the appearance of railroading.

Some players may feel that the GUMSHOE system's reliance on automatic successes inevitably leads to a railroaded result. In practice, this simply isn't so. The degree of narrative flexibility a *Trail of Cthulhu* Keeper exercises is entirely unrelated to the game's resolution mechanic, or relative lack of same. Flexibility remains up to you, the Keeper, and to your ability to improvise within the basic structure of the investigative story, as it does in nearly any set of roleplaying rules.

As proof of this, we cite a weird phenomenon that occurred during playtest of a GUMSHOE scenario. The groups that expressed the strongest misgivings about possible railroading were those

The Continuing Conspiracy: Campaign Design

A campaign is a continued sequence of scenarios uncovering the same vile conspiracy or horrible truth, the equivalent to the "story arc" or "season arc" of an ongoing television series. Campaign design is essentially scenario design writ large. Each adventure becomes a "scene" of the campaign, and the campaign structure breaks down as follows:

Opener: This adventure is the "hook," and must contain enough juice to get and keep the players' interest for the ongoing story arc. Its confrontations should emphasize the campaign's overall theme, and should ideally include a glimpse or foreshadowing of the ultimate Big Bad for this story, perhaps as a cut scene played out with doomed NPCs.

The Big Bad: This is the source of the multiple manifestations of the Mythos that the Investigators will encounter over the course of the campaign. It might be a single Great Old One, a nefarious cult, a sorcerous mastermind, an alien infestation, or some combination of the above. As with the "horrible truth" in an individual scenario, the Keeper should determine what the Big Bad's activities, aims, and resources are, and how the Big Bad can be thwarted, at least temporarily.

The Build: This is the macro-level of the "trail of clues." Each adventure should logically and dramatically build to the next one, rather like unpeeling an onion layer by layer. For example:

• The Investigators exorcise a haunted house of its Mythos taint.
• The Investigators discover and bust up a cult that held rituals at the house.
• The Investigators discover that the cult's founder, the house's architect, is still alive and working evil.
• The Investigators thwart the architect's plan to take over Stonehenge.
• The Investigators confront and kill the architect in his place of power.

In each adventure, the Keeper should reveal one or more portion of the Big Bad's plans, and provide one or more needed element to thwart it. Some adventures may be entirely "antagonist reaction" adventures, in which the Big Bad or its agents try to trap, ambush, or suborn the Investigators. These should likewise provide needed clues or elements. Like floating core clues, some adventures might float around the arc, triggered by Investigator action or plugged in when the Keeper senses the need for a change-up.

Not all scenarios during the campaign need to lead directly to the Big Bad; some may be foreshadowing (or after-echoes) of another arc, some may be "palate cleansers" or provide interesting character interactions, and some might be driven by the campaign calendar – if the Investigators are in Providence during the great thunderstorm of August 8, 1935, they may well be drawn into the events of *The Haunter of the Dark* even if the larger campaign is a contest against the mi-go.

Campaign Connections

In an organic campaign, knowledge obtained during one scenario will provide the necessary hooks into the next adventure, or into any number of potential adventures. Keepers should strive to see that at least one clue in a given adventure points somewhere else, as well as to the next scene in the current scenario. Sometimes, the connection to the next scenario is the "clue reward" for defeating the adventure's antagonist; sometimes it shows up during the initial investigation or only gains its importance in hindsight. It might even appear as a cut scene with no real connection to the adventure plot, as in *The X-Files*, when "Deep Throat" would appear and give cryptic advice to Mulder that only made sense several episodes later.

Some possible connections include:

• Letters from one strand of the Big Bad to another
• Business cards, matchboxes, or other leads to locations
• Photographs depicting known villains in interesting or identifiable places, or with identifiable or enigmatic other NPCs
• Brochures, pamphlets, letterheads, or other leads to organizations
• Cult symbols on bodies, walls, figurines, hand-bound books
• Case notes from previous (usually dead) investigators
• Testimony, expert opinion, hearsay, rumor, references, cryptic phrases, or confessions obtained from NPCs such as officials, scholars, reporters, gossips, bystanders, allies, or cultists
• Art or artifacts, in photographs, books, or collections; might lead to the artist, the museum, or the curio shop
• Shipping manifests, invoices, packing labels, or railway schedules
• Intriguing pins (or markings) on maps, especially maps of places with no seeming relevance to the current adventure
• Physical surveillance of cultists or targets ("Why is he going there? Doing that? Talking to her?")
• Physical links, from secret panels to hyperspace Gates
• Newspaper cuttings of similar events or phenomena across the country or around the world, found in a scrapbook, a newspaper morgue, or a locked case
• Leads in books (especially Mythos tomes), lectures, or unpublished doctoral theses; including hand-written notes by previous readers
• Insane rantings, scrawled, typeset, howled, or recorded
• Places, people, and events mentioned in diaries, reporters' notebooks, or Mythos tomes

Managing Resource Management

The mechanical tension in *Trail of Cthulhu* comes from GUMSHOE's "resource management" nature. Investigators (and their players) have a limited number of pool points to use while accomplishing the mission or solving the mystery.

Investigative pool points should not be a problem. **No core clue needed to solve the mystery should depend on spending pool points.** The mechanical role of investigative pool points is to manage spotlight time, and as a method for the players and Keeper to signal "oncoming coolness" to each other. A player who says "Can I spend a Bureaucracy point here?" is requesting something cool for his Investigator to do or discover during the scene. When the Keeper says, "Do you want to spend an Art History point here?" she's signaling that there's something awesome available during this scene that she thinks the player (or players) would enjoy. This repartee will eventually become nearly seamless and automatic.

General pool points, however, are the very devil. If the Investigators reach the standing stones at full Stability, Health, Athletics, and Firearms, they're not going to be too terrified unless Shub-Niggurath Her Own Bad Self is there backed up by the Red Army Choir. But if they drain away too much Stability casting spells, or exhaust all their Scuffling battling cultists, they won't survive the climax no matter how well they've reasoned out the solution. It's vitally important that the Keeper, er, keep an eye on the party's pool points, especially Stability and at least one "fight or flight" pool (Athletics, Fleeing, Firearms, Scuffling, or Weapons). Given the Investigatorial ability to drop Health and Stability to -11 without *fatal* result, in most cases, Investigators should reach the climax with their key pools hovering in the low single digits.

The Keeper can work to hit this mechanical sweet spot in three ways. First, tailor the ability caps at the beginning of the game to create the level of tension you seek. As suggested in the sidebar on p. 26, Health and Stability ratings of of 12 are good caps to consider. Increasing the Sanity ceiling to 12 or even 15 minus Cthulhu Mythos provides a potentially longer-lasting character without reducing the potential danger and tension from any single encounter. Decrease the caps if you want characters mental stability to be more fragile. This can encourage early mental instability in campaign, allow madness to appear in a short one-off game, or make lesser threats to cause madness. Second, whether you cap ratings or not, definitely tailor the threat levels to the party's resources. If they have four Investigators with 30 Stability points between them, don't write adventures that call for more than 15 or so Stability tests without intentionally planning one of two things: a "killer" adventure, or a refreshment interim. (Players will likely spend 1 or 2 Stability points on tests, even if they succeed.) Those 15 tests might include three major supernatural encounters (three encounters times four Investigators is 12 tests) and three "mandatory" spells. (Making sure that the Investigator who knows the essential spell avoids Stability tests is the players' job.) Every group is different, spending points or hoarding them at different rates. It may take you a couple of adventures to learn your group's "burn rate," but it's a key datum for you as Keeper.

The third, and equally important, management technique is adding encounters if the party seems to be "too healthy." **The object of the game is horror, and horror comes from a threat.** The threat should be both fictional ("If we don't get past this hedge maze, the lloigor will swallow Caerleon") and mechanical ("If we meet another batch of byakhee, we're not going to have any Stability points left when we meet the lloigor."). This "soak" encounter doesn't always have to be a monster attack, although that always helps. It can be a horrible nightmare, a magical phenomenon, or even a "mundane" horror like a grotesque murder. This technique has the added advantage of being dramatically effective, too; it's the faithful "tension-and-release" model that works on everything from slasher flicks to roller-coasters. Adding a "soak" encounter on an ad hoc basis usually works okay, but it's better yet if the Keeper pre-designs it to be a natural – or even obvious – part of the adventure. "We're have to get to Caerleon by daylight – but that old rummy swore that 'the corpse that flies' haunts this hedge maze!"

whose Keepers had done the most improvising during the scenario.

This result can be partly attributed to variances in group tastes, but also suggests the enormous importance of maintaining the *perception* of free choice. When you're on a roll as a Keeper, you can create the perception of free choice even when players respond predictably to the scenario. On an off night, you can convey the impression of constricted options even you're improvising furiously to keep up with their completely unexpected choices.

Here are five ways to maintain the perception of narrative freedom:

- When using a prewritten adventure, paraphrase as much as possible. **Avoid reading right from the scenario.** Even if it's well-written, your narration, no matter how halting and tentative, will seem more spontaneous than canned text. Some Keepers read too much of the scenario out loud because they have trouble extracting the necessary nuggets from a pre-written text. Judicious use of a highlighting pen can work wonders to zero in on the best details, which you can then weave into your own extemporaneous sentences.

- During scenes of character interaction, listen carefully to player dialogue and respond accordingly. **Riff with the players.** This is more important than spewing the supporting characters' clues or talking points, even if that means altering the characterization from what you see on the page.

- **Encourage players to flesh out details of the setting and situation.** If they ask you what the weather is like, ask them what they want it to be. If they ask if there's a desk in the hotel room, or a wet bar in the library, or a boat at the pier, tell them that it is and ask them to describe it. On rare occasions the mystery plot will turn on such details, and you'll have to pull back from this technique and stick to your clue trail. Otherwise, seek

out opportunities for player input. This also helps make the setting more detailed, more interesting, and thus more important to the players.

- **Tailor NPCs and situations to the Investigators.** If a player portrays a sloppy, rumpled reporter, confront her with a neat-freak, press-hating authority figure. An Investigator (or a player, ahem) known to fall for sexy librarian types should meet successions of sexy librarians, and so on.

- Introduce story elements giving players opportunities to **flesh out their Investigators' backstories.** Weave old friends, acquaintances, mentors, colleagues, and rivals into your supporting casts.

If you yourself are still worried that GUMSHOE encourages or requires railroading, take heart in this last result from GUMSHOE playtests. Each group submitted an account of the events of the sample adventure that differed radically from everyone else's.

Improvising with GUMSHOE

Although the advice here is designed to help you prep adventures in advance, there is nothing inherent in the GUMSHOE core clue and point-spend system that requires you to predetermine what happens in an adventure, any more than there is with a system where your players roll for information.

Even if you want to improvise most of the adventure, we recommend you have some fairly solid ideas on paper before you start (use The Basic Mystery Structure on p. 192). Then take note of the build choices the players have made in creating their Investigators. This signals to you the type of scenes they want to experience, and also reminds you to give out clues which give each player spotlight time for their characters. Refer often to the Investigator Matrix for your game. Make sure there is always at least one dangling core clue available, and take a careful note of any clues you give out.

It's most likely that you, and your players will want a predetermined mystery and solution, even if you are mostly improvising, but again, there's nothing inherent about GUMSHOE which prevents you from using a "twenty questions" approach, where you haven't decided any more than the initial set-up. As a "twenty questions" game progresses, each clue will disclose the mystery and narrow down possible solutions until there is only one which fits all the clues you have revealed. This is the solution. Watch out, though, some players hate it when you haven't decided whodunnit, particularly if you conceal the fact that you are using this technique and they find out. Others will embrace it, even knowing you are using it. You know your own group, and your own abilities.

In each case the wide variances of incident arose from disparate player choices. Just like it's supposed to.

Any Direction is Forward

Although it may be, oddly enough, more important to maintain apparent than actual narrative freedom, we should still endeavor to provide the real thing to the maximum extent possible.

Fortunately, it's easier to provide freedom than it is to seem like you're providing it. Simply ensure that any clue, especially any core clue, is available not only to Investigators using the ability specified in the scenario, but to *any player who provides a credible and entertaining alternate method of acquiring that clue*. The scenario is a foundation to work from, which ensures that there is at least one way to move through the story. It should never be regarded as the only way to get to the resolution. A group of players will often come up with better ideas than the

scenario writer ever could. Give yourself permission to go with them.

One slight exception pertains: this advice pertains only to clues available in the current scene. Allow players to leapfrog scenes by acquiring information they're meant to get later only when pacing permits. If you're early in a session when the threat of leapfrogging occurs, and you're not confident you can improvise enough new intervening scenes to make a full evening's entertainment, by all means block the players' efforts. If you're zooming toward evening's end, leapfrogging may prove a blessing — just be sure to squeeze in all of the necessary ancillary information the players might miss by skipping ahead.

Scenes in the middle of an investigation can often be juggled around with no ill effect to the storyline. When this is the case, it's always better to let the players dictate pacing than to force them back into the order of events

envisioned by the scenario.

If you've prewritten an adventure and the PCs veer off, that's fine. If it's interesting, see where it takes you. If they seem to know where they are going and what they want to do, keep offering more leads. Eventually, if you want to get back to the beaten track, offer more clue bait to take them back to a pre-planned scene.

The scenario is only the blueprint. The building happens during play.

Ending Scenes

In a novel or TV episode, writers can freely cut to the next scene when their characters have acquired all of the clues available in the current one. The characters might stick around for hours tying up loose ends and pursuing fruitless questions, but this doesn't happen on screen. We, the audience, are not forced to sit through such sequences.

This kind of concise editing isn't so easy in the roleplaying medium.

Putting it all together

Players don't know when they've got all the clues.

Here's a simple trick to gently steer them onwards, without unduly breaking the illusion of fictional reality:

Before play, take an index card and write on it, in big block letters, the word SCENE. As soon as the players have gleaned the core clue and most or all of the secondary clues in a scene, and the action begins to drag, hold up the card. When the players see this, they know to move on. (Of course, you have to explain the cue to them before play begins.) Easy, efficient, yet somehow not nearly as disruptive or jarring as a verbal instruction.

Cutaways

One of the huge mistakes characters make in horror movies is to split up in the face of danger. As the Keeper, you should always be encouraging players to make it.

You'll also want to run solo scenes, or sequences with only a few cast members present, during mundane scenes that develop character and further the Investigators' personal goals.

To do this, you'll need to rely on the cutaway technique. Here you spotlight the actions of a few players while the others look on. In some genres, gamers can get restless while out of the spotlight. In a properly bloodcurdling horror game, they'll likely be glad for a few moments of respite when it's somebody else's hard-to-reach places being chewed on by Brown Jenkin.

A few keys to successful cutaway use:

- Allow all players to observe cutaway scenes they're not involved in as spectators. Require them to separate their own knowledge from Investigator knowledge. Properly managed, it's always more ominous to know what horrible events might be in the offing than to be surprised. This mode of suspense is what makes Alfred Hitchcock's movies – and plenty of Lovecraft stories – so inexorably compelling. (Which is not to say that there's anything wrong with the occasional out-of-nowhere jolt.)

- Keep scenes short and snappy. Think about how quickly ensemble TV shows pop from one story thread to the next. Relentlessly intercut. Cut on cliffhanger moments, or when the spotlight player(s) need time to think of what to do next.

- See that something interesting is happening to everyone at the same time. This may be challenging, as it is often the wary player's goal to make sure that nothing interesting ever happens to his player.

Maintaining Menace

More so than in more adventure-oriented roleplaying games, your primary duty as Keeper is to sustain a mood of unease. Occasional moments of comic relief and relaxation can work in your favor, softening up the players for the tension to come. However, if your players are more bored or complacent than scared, take whatever immediate action you can to ramp up the creep factor. Whether you throw in a

Compensating For Spotty Attendance

Older gamers most likely to enjoy an investigative campaign are sadly prone to scheduling disruptions. If your group is typical, you may not be able to rely on any particular player showing up on a given night. To compensate for this, give each player a pool of free-floating investigative points, which they can spend to gain a clue in investigative abilities they don't have. When this occurs, explain it as the character remembering a fact or technique taught to them by their absent teammates. Adjust the quantity of points as needed for your group's requirements.

nightmarish telepathic image, a grotesque and flyblown corpse, or a horde of sand-dwellers burrowing up through the dunes beneath, remember that subtlety only goes so far in horror. Don't be afraid to grab the players by the metaphorical lapels. Horror is not meant to be fair. It's best if you don't have to abandon your storyline's internal logic to toss in a scare, but that's a secondary consideration to keeping the fright going. Emulate the shamelessness of horror movie directors. Throw in unrelated scares to make the players jump. Use dream sequences and hallucinations if need be. A sustained mood comes before everything else.

Campaign Frames

"But more decisive steps were in the air, and it is in the secret assemblages of sworn and tested sailors and faithful old privateersmen in the Brown warehouses by night that we must look... Slowly and surely a plan of campaign was under development..."

— The Case of Charles Dexter Ward

If a Trail of Cthulhu campaign is like a television series "story arc," a campaign frame is like the series itself. The campaign frame, or campaign premise, is the basic overarching narrative structure from which the Keeper suspends the various campaigns and stand-alone adventures that the game comprises.

To construct a campaign frame, the Keeper should define the following basic building blocks. She may choose to define them collaboratively with the other players, or to present a series of options for the players to pick from, or develop the frame secretly and tell the others only what they need to know to design their Investigators. Three sample campaign frames follow this section, with some sample answers filled in.

Setting: The time and place that the game will begin, and where most of the action will be set. While the default Trail of Cthulhu setting is the 1930s, somewhere in the Western world, the Cthulhu Mythos spans all times and places. The Keeper should provide setting focus with boundaries; will the game be restricted entirely to Arkham, to the Deep South, or to a single large city like London? Will it be primarily rural or primarily urban? Will it be set equally in Britan and on the Continent? Will it be a globe-trotting game? Are hyperspatial Gates or Mythos time-travel likely to play a key role? What languages will come in handy? Players shouldn't bother creating Investigators who will be useless, or who stick out like sore thumbs, in the majority of the setting. Setting and boundaries can shift with individual campaigns, but the Keeper needs to set a default, and a starting point.

Style: To start with, decide whether the game will be Purist or Pulp in intent, or a mélange of both. Will it emphasize cosmic dread, or bloody splattering gore? Will the Keeper's setting enforce the laws (against firearms possession, say) strictly, or let Investigators slide past their fourth arson investigation with a wink? Will it have a strong techno-thriller feel, or center on Gothic emotional conflicts? Will race or politics play a major role in stories? Should the players prepare to portray vivid, realistic psychological damage, or to just gibber and run amok when the dice dictate it?

Mythos: Strongly related to style, the Keeper should decide on the general scope of the Cthulhu Mythos in her world. Unlike style, she should keep this parameter as a secret to be uncovered in play. How omnipresent is the Mythos, and what is its nature? Does it underly all occultism and religion, or just occultism, or just "evil" occultism? How many *Necronomicons* are out there? Are Elder Signs common or rare? Can you find the word "Cthulhu" in any reference book? How much, if anything, do the authorities know about the Mythos, and what are they doing about it? Which gods or titans take center stage, and which don't even exist? The Keeper can also pick a particular Mythos flavor: pure Lovecraft, Derlethian dualism, weird Clark Ashton Smithery, or everything-in-the-basket Lin Carter.

Investigators: The most important question is: what brings the Investigators together? Even if the Keeper decides everything else in secret, she might well want to get the players' input on this question. Is it just a coincidence? Do the Investigators all have some connection that will turn up later in the game – a common ancestor, college professor, or patron, say? Do they all just meet at the auction house or hiring hall? Are they all members of the same secret society, MU fraternity, or police department? Both the setting and the style will influence Investigator design, so the Keeper should at least provide some hints: "The story

begins in Australia, and all your Investigators should be pretty robust and have some interest in astronomy."

Continuing NPCs: The Keeper should spend a little time coming up with "recurring guest stars," NPCs who will either drive the story or otherwise repeatedly interact with the Investigators. They might include a rival group, suspicious local authorities, the neighborhood priest, a borderline villain who feeds them clues when it suits him, or even "celebrity guest stars" like Howard Hughes, J Edgar Hoover, or Aleister Crowley. The Keeper should absolutely incorporate Investigator-driven or player-created recurring cast members such as Sources of Stability, proteges and intimate correspondents, and the Investigators' contacts and connections (see p. 31) from Cop Talk, Credit Rating, and various Occupations.

Rules Variations: If the setting or feel deserve it, the Keeper should develop any rules variations. This might include new Occupations, subdividing abilities, or additional types of magic. This is also where to note any specific ability caps or uses of Pulp or Purist rules options.

Pitch: Finally, see if you can boil the campaign frame into a pitch line suitable for selling your game to the players, like writers sell TV pilots to the network: "It's like *The X-Files* in Stalinist Russia!" "It's Grant Morrison vs August Derleth, and anything goes!" "It's like House, only set at Arkham General!" "It's Lovecraft meets Orwell: Deep Ones in the

Spanish Civil War!" These pitch lines are hardly mandatory, but they can help players grasp the elements of your style that you haven't put into words: "It's like *Buffy*" is different from "It's like *Supernatural*," even though both shows are about monster-hunting.

The Armitage Inquiry

"MY GOOD FORTUNE IN SECURING THE BACKING OF MISKATONIC UNIVERSITY WAS GREAT ... WE WERE NOT TOO SPECIFIC WITH THE PUBLIC ABOUT OUR OBJECTS, SINCE THE WHOLE MATTER WOULD HAVE LENT ITSELF UNPLEASANTLY TO SENSATIONAL AND JOCOSE TREATMENT BY THE CHEAPER NEWSPAPERS."

— THE SHADOW OUT OF TIME

Enough professors at Miskatonic University have stumbled onto the Mythos in the last several years to create a critical mass of dangerous knowledge. Under the direction of Dr Henry Armitage, they have decided to do something about it. He has formed an informal "Inquiry Group," similar to the interdisciplinary collection of scholars who advised President Wilson at the Versailles talks in 1919.

Setting

This campaign frame takes a "base and mission" structure, centered on Miskatonic University in Arkham, Massachusetts. It begins in the Fall 1935 semester, after the return of the Dyer-Peaslee Expedition from Western Australia. Campaigns and individual adventures might take place anywhere that Miskatonic University scholars could go, from academic conferences in Berlin to archaeological digs in Egypt, to "day trips" to the Dunwich backcountry. Using Lovecraft's writings as a guide, about half or two-thirds of the adventures will take place at least partially in New England, but anywhere is fair game. A campaign might be a series of mysteries, or a single major expedition.

Style

The style is up to the Keeper, as the Miskatonic setting rewards Purist play as much as the globetrotting possibilities suggest Pulp. A tweedy, academic tone, with occasional dips into mad science, seems to fit the material better than emotional and psychological torment, although plenty of college novels would disagree.

Mythos

The Mythos is barely known. As recently as 1908, only two anthropologists in America had ever read or heard the word "Cthulhu." Teasing the true Mythos out of the rambling, arcane, elliptical tomes and records available even at the Orne Library is a full-time job, and must be amplified with constant and diligent field research. The authorities know essentially nothing, and the Inquiry is determined that things should stay that way.

Investigators

Investigators are all professors, graduate or undergraduate students, or librarians at Miskatonic University. (The Keeper can stretch a point to include former cops on the University security payroll, veterans returned to college, doctors at the medical school, and similar.) They all participated in an initial expedition or local adventure that uncovered some aspect of the Mythos. (The Keeper can run this initial expedition as the first scenario, or merely recount it in flashback.) They have all agreed to work with Dr Armitage to secretly plumb the depths of the Mythos.

Continuing NPCs

The continuing characters in this frame are the Investigators' fellow professors and members of the Inquiry. They can be contacts, rivals, or even (secretly) villains. The "Dunwich Three" (Armitage, Morgan, and Rice) form a kind of "inner circle" within the Inquiry, keeping secrets and rationing access to the *Necronomicon*. Members of the Inquiry as of 1935 include:

Dr Henry Armitage (b 1855): Head librarian and specialist in medieval epigraphy, occultism, and linguistics. Took his D. Litt. at Cambridge, and may have Mythos contacts at that University. Retires (becoming Director Emeritus) in 1936 to head the Inquiry full time.

Dr Ferdinand Ashley (b 1891): Associate professor of archaeology, specializing in Egyptology. Participated in the Western Australia Expedition. Like Morgan, young enough for field missions.

Dr William Dyer (b 1880): Professor of geology, survivor of the first Miskatonic Antarctic Expedition. Believes strongly in secrecy and preventing further expeditions.

Dr Tyler M Freeborn (b 1906): Assistant professor of anthropology, and a participant in the Western Australia Expedition. A self-proclaimed Communist and radical, he clings to his tenure track by his fingernails against a storm of inter-departmental opposition. Devoted to field work, but his professional research sometimes takes precedence over Inquiry work.

Dr Cyrus Llanfer (b 1871): Assistant director of the Orne Library, becomes head librarian in 1936. Has no real understanding of the Mythos, but is entirely loyal to Dr Armitage.

Dr William Moore (b 1886): Professor of geology, specializing in paleontology. Co-head of the Starkweather-Moore Antarctic Expedition in 1932-1933. Its findings are officially minimized.

Dr Francis Morgan (b 1891): Associate professor of archaeology, specializing in the American Southwest, but with experience in Egypt and Mesopotamia. Logical and scientific in orientation. Still young enough for field missions.

Dr Nathaniel Peaslee (b 1900): Professor of psychology, specializing in abnormal psychology. A devotee of Jung, he is driven by revenge for the suffering of his father, Professor Emeritus Nathaniel Wingate Peaslee, who has been in a sanitarium since his return from Australia.

Mrs. Agatha Warren Pickman (b 1849): The eccentric and domineering head of the Nathaniel Derby Pickman Foundation, which provides financial support for some Inquiry operations. Mrs. Pickman insists on propriety, decency, and to-the-penny accounting. She often calls Dr Armitage "young man."

Dr Warren Rice (b 1866): Professor of classical languages, specializing in Semitic and Near Eastern tongues. Pessimistic and pragmatic.

Dr Ephraim Sprague (b 1886): Essex County medical examiner and private physician. Not associated with Miskatonic University, but obviously a key and useful ally.

Dr Albert Wilmarth (b 1861): Professor of English, specialist in New England folklore. He becomes Chairman of the English Department in 1930. Between his departmental responsibilities and his delicate temperament (following the Vermont nightmare) he now sends graduate students and junior faculty to gather folklore first-hand.

Depending on the specific nature of the campaign, other continuing NPCs might include rival scholars from other universities, Ahnenerbe agents, and unhelpful department heads or University bureaucrats.

Rules Variations
Members of the Inquiry can use academic abilities they don't actually possess, albeit at one remove. Each Investigator should pick a patron from the list above (or make one up); this is the scholar who introduced them into the Inquiry. During an investigation, they can write, telegraph, call, or otherwise seek the advice of their patron; if a response is possible, their patron will provide one. Investigators may wind up dragged into inter-academic rivalries on their patron's behalf, or otherwise find their lives complicated by their connection. You could

also consider reducing the number of academic abilities the Investigators take to ensure they need to use their patron's services.

At the Keeper's discretion, any member of the Inquiry might be able to go to Dr Armitage, who will research the question in the Orne Library. He may, however, keep the answer to himself, or he may get the Investigators into hot water "returning the favor."

Pitch
Might range from "It's Indiana Jones meets the Watchers' Council from *Buffy*!" to "It's Donna Tartt's *The Secret History*, Lovecraft style."

Project Covenant
"DURING THE WINTER OF 1927-28 OFFICIALS OF THE FEDERAL GOVERNMENT MADE A STRANGE AND SECRET INVESTIGATION OF CERTAIN CONDITIONS IN THE ANCIENT MASSACHUSETTS SEAPORT OF INNSMOUTH."

— THE SHADOW OVER INNSMOUTH

On February 13, 1928, in cooperation with Treasury agents and the FBI, US sailors and marines raided Innsmouth, Massachusetts, after President Coolidge secretly placed the town under Federal martial law. The Coast Guard cutter *Urania* and the Navy submarine *S-19* deployed off Devil Reef, dropping depth charges, firing torpedoes, and taking soundings, as well as landing sailors on the Reef itself. Much of the town was burned and dynamited, and hundreds of Innsmouth residents were arrested and shipped to secret camps and military prisons. This was Project Covenant, and what it discovered has been hushed up or denied at every level of government. J. Edgar Hoover, director of the FBI, refuses to discuss the affair even with his closest advisers, although he occasionally travels to certain isolated sites in the California desert. President Roosevelt may not even know the operation happened. Nobody will discuss it, or what it meant.

With former President Coolidge's death on January 5, 1933, the survivors of Project Covenant have nowhere left to turn when they start seeing the same sorts of things they saw that cold night in Innsmouth. Except to each other. They form a secret cabal within the US military and intelligence services, and provide cover and leads for each other where they can. They call themselves "Covenanters," or "Friends of Ezra" (after Ezra Weeden, an 18th-century patriot who defeated a wizard), and use variations on "Ezra," "Samson," and the Ark of the Covenant as code words, contact signals, and warning signs.

Setting
Anywhere the US government or military might reach, Project Covenant might act. That primarily means the continental U.S., but Alaska, Hawaii, Panama, the Philippines, Guam, the Virgin Islands, and Puerto Rico are all equally fair game, as is the Yangtze River (home to the US Navy's Yangtze Patrol until 1941). The FBI ran spy rings in Latin America during the 1930s, and the Navy patrols the Caribbean, so undercover adventures might be set anywhere from Cuba to Argentina.

In a globetrotting Pulp game,

Covenanters might mount covert operations anywhere in the world that they have assets or "friendlies," such as US Embassies, or even Royal Navy bases.

Style
Up to the Keeper, but the likely emphasis on gunplay and espionage implies a Pulp feel to the game. The mood is likewise implicitly grim and gritty. Politics are likely to play a fairly significant role, as is the psychological strain on Covenant operatives.

For a different sort of style, the ongoing Project Covenant can be an official (though still secret) operation within the FBI and Navy bureaucracies, probably alternately claimed as turf and completely denied by each.

Mythos
Project Covenant begins by confronting Dagon and Cthulhu, and they are likely to remain at the forefront of any ongoing investigation involving naval personnel. Tossing the entire Mythos in at once vitiates the theme of slow discovery; an entire campaign might center on the horrible revelation of the mi-go or a cult of Hastur. Whether any other unit of the US government – or other governments – is confronting, or attempting to exploit, the Mythos should be another major mystery in the game.

Investigators
Investigators are preferentially agents of the US government or members of the US military (most likely the Coast Guard, Navy, or Marine Corps), but might be senior civilian or semi-governmental assets such as oil

company engineers, Miskatonic University professors, New Orleans police officers, or the like. They may be veterans of the original Covenant raid, or of later operations by the Friends of Ezra. The Keeper may choose to run their "cherry" operation as the introductory adventure, recruiting the survivors into Covenant afterward.

Continuing NPCs
These are the core members of the Covenant conspiracy within the US government. All were directly involved in the Innsmouth Raid, and could only speak about their experiences with each other. They use their connections and influence to plan, cover up, and exploit ongoing counter-Mythos operations, and to recruit new members to the Covenant.

Assistant Director **Cleveland Drew,** US Secret Service (b 1888): The mastermind of the Raid, he maintains contacts throughout the bureaucracy. His pull in the Treasury and Labor Departments keeps Covenant pay records hopelessly snarled.

Dr **David Frushour,** Smithsonian Institution (b 1898): An Treasury agent during the Raid, he was injured and retired on disability. Following a doctoral program in anthropology at Miskatonic University, he got the Smithsonian post. He tracks Covenant findings, and serves as the cabal "historian," storing its trophies and artifacts in the warren of basements beneath the Museum of Natural History.

Master Sergeant **Emile Grabatowski,** USMC (b 1880): Raid veteran, based at Naval Air Station Pensacola. He trains

Covenant personnel, as best he can, to fight Deep Ones and other inhumans.

Captain **Robert Harrow**, USN (b 1894): Commander of the S-19 during the Innsmouth Raid; now works at the Office of Naval Intelligence (ONI) in Washington.

Captain **Curtis Henley**, USCG (b 1893): Commanded a patrol boat during the Raid, now the captain of the cutter *Hancock*, based out of Boston.

Colonel **Joseph "Fighting Mad" Maines,** USMC (b 1885): The Covenant's chief patron in the regular military. He has taken a much-despised "desk job" in Washington to help run the cabal.

Special Agent in Charge **Albert Ryan**, FBI (b 1890): Drew's main FBI liaison during the Raid, he knows where enough bodies are buried that Hoover – probably – won't interfere in his Covenant operations, as long as he keeps the profile subterranean.

The Investigators may have been recruited by any of these men, or by another "control." They may also have commanding officers, subordinates, or other "innocents" who recur in their adventures – some of them might make good replacement Investigators after a messy death on assignment.

Rules Variations
In addition to any special Pulp rules the Keeper uses, she may want to introduce the following new Occupation, and expand the Military Occupation as indicated below:

Federal Agent
You are a sworn agent of the US Government, with all the power and responsibility that implies. (This template may also be used for agents of His Majesty's Government.)

Occupational Abilities: Driving, Evidence Collection, Reassurance or Intimidation, Law, Assess Honesty.

Alcohol Tax Unit: add Accounting, Conceal, Shadowing, Streetwise.

FBI: add Firearms, Interrogation, Sense Trouble, Shadowing.

Secret Service: add Athletics, Firearms, Scuffling, Sense Trouble.

US Marshals: add Cop Talk, Firearms, Scuffling, Shadowing.

Credit Rating: 3-5

Special: Credit Rating is capped at 5. Not until 1942, when William Donovan creates the OSS from his Yale banker contacts, does the wealthy aristocrat enter the US intelligence world.

A Federal agent can use Bureaucracy to pull strings within his own agency or department, Credit Rating to activate contacts within other government agencies, and either Law or Intimidation to enter almost any premises in US territory.

Military
Here are two more specialties within the Military Occupation (see p. 15) that might turn up in Project Covenant teams.

Coast Guard: add First Aid, Mechanical Repair, Piloting.

Intelligence Officer: add Bureaucracy, Cryptography, Library Use.

Pitch
Might range from "It's *The Untouchables* meets *Delta Green!*" to "It's The *X-Files* vs Fu Manchu!"

Book-Hounds of London
"THESE CYCLES OF EXPERIENCE, OF COURSE, ALL STEM FROM THAT WORM-RIDDLED BOOK. I REMEMBER WHEN I FOUND IT – IN A DIMLY LIGHTED PLACE NEAR THE BLACK, OILY RIVER WHERE THE MISTS ALWAYS SWIRL. THAT PLACE WAS VERY OLD, AND THE CEILING-HIGH SHELVES FULL OF ROTTING VOLUMES REACHED BACK ENDLESSLY THROUGH WINDOWLESS INNER ROOMS AND ALCOVES. THERE WERE, BESIDES, GREAT FORMLESS HEAPS OF BOOKS ON THE FLOOR AND IN CRUDE BINS; AND IT WAS IN ONE OF THESE HEAPS THAT I FOUND THE THING."

– THE BOOK

The global Depression has driven an unprecedented number of collectors – both individual and institutional – to sell off their holdings for whatever they can get. The global crisis has also driven an unprecedented number of over-educated, morally bankrupt aristocrats and resentful would-be Great Beasts to experiment with black magic … including the Cthulhu Mythos. Between the two groups, sellers and buyers, a specialty market has sprung up in blasphemous tomes, no questions asked.

You cater to that market, finding books at estate sales or abandoned churches across the Home Counties, tracking

It's a hard old world out there, and mayhap the hardest thing about it is that you have to save it from your own customers now and again.

Setting

This campaign frame works best if restricted to London and its immediate surroundings, with only occasional trips out to stately homes and poorly guarded regional libraries. Brichester might make a good second lobe for a campaign, if the Keeper wants to expand it, or is justifiably fond of Ramsey Campbell's setting.

Style

The style of this game should be skeevy, crawly, and underhanded. The Investigators aren't nice people, and the people they meet are worse yet. This is a game of urban survival, creepy low-light magic, and the kinds of things you see in old, horrid books. Combat should be downgraded, and obsessions and psychological damage of one sort or another should be nigh omnipresent. Consider it "Ramsey Campbell Purist."

Mythos

Within this specialized underground, the Mythos is known, but hedged round with superstition and misunderstanding. The book-hounds may initially underestimate the larger significance of the lore they traffic in, or go in with their eyes wide open, like smugglers of nuclear material in the 21st century. With a campaign frame like this one, variety will be the spice of life; everything that might logically plague the Investigators, their customers, and their competitors should. The

down rumors and doing your competitors dirt. You've had to learn the difference between the 1452 and the 1472 editions of Wormius, and why neither should be opened at Ludgate, or anywhere during a full moon. Sometimes you touch up an imperfect von Junzt, and sometimes you might liberate a Prinn first edition from an insufficiently caring owner.

1930s Rare Book Prices

Rare book prices hit an all-time high in the 1920s, exemplified by the Jerome Kern library auction of 1929, which realized $1.7 million ($21 million in 2007). With the Depression, the bottom fell out of rare books as it did everything else: a Shakespeare First Folio that sold for $66,000 in 1927 sold for $22,000 in 1941, while a copy of Shelley's *Queen Mab*, with the poet's handwritten annotations, sold for $68,000 in 1929 and only brought $8,000 as late as 1951! There are exceptions; in 1933 the *Codex Sinaiticus*, a 4th Century Bible was sold by the Soviet government to the British Museum for over $500,000.

A few further examples:

Blickling Homilies: 10th-century parchment (150 pages), $55,000

The Tickhill Psalter: near-perfect early 14th-century illuminated vellum manuscript, $61,000

Roman de la Rose: mid-14th century mystical illuminated vellum manuscript, $6,800

Boccaccio's *De la Ruine*: 1476 printing with copperplate illustrations, $45,000

Hypnerotomachia Poliphili: 1499 Aldine printing of a mystical work with woodcuts (450 pages), $700

Cervantes' *Don Quixote*: 1605 Madrid printing (2nd edition), $2,200

Cotton Mather's *Wonders of the Invisible World*: 1693 London printing (2nd edition), $70

Francis Barrett's *The Magus*: 1801 London first edition grimoire, $12

Shelley's *Hellas*: 1822 suppressed first edition, $2,100

Frazer's *Golden Bough*: 1911 London third edition, 11 vols., $18

These are auction prices, mostly taken from the 1935 and 1936 issues of *American Book Prices Current*, which is recommended for Keepers who want to get a sense of the used book market. Mythos tomes might bring far more from a knowledgeable buyer (what price godhead?), or they might turn up for a few shillings in the stacks of a seller who knows not what he has. Copies with wizardly annotations might bring considerably more; copies with the all-important magical diagrams cut out might be essentially worthless to a Mythos sorcerer but still quite valuable to a mundane (or foolish) collector.

whole world should be creepy, uncanny, and dangerous. That said, this background cries out for Y'golonac, the King in Yellow, Quachil Uttaus, and plenty of rat-things.

This sort of game will benefit from lots of non-Mythos monsters and occultism to act as "protective coloration," and to otherwise add variety. The Mythos tomes may be McGuffins, or their use (or destruction) may be the key to solving the mystery, depending on the scenario.

Investigators

Investigators are people active in London's underground trade in occult books (and possibly in other dubious literatures such as pornography). They will likely come from one of the following Occupations: Antiquarian, Criminal, Dilettante, Hobo, or Private Investigator. (That said, Artists, Authors, Clergymen, and Professors might easily find themselves involved.) They likely form a loose ring of book-hounds, operating out of a given store or library.

For properly dodgy desperation, all Investigator Credit Ratings should be capped at 4, and all Investigators should begin with no free rating points in Credit Rating. Players may still build aristocratic Investigators, but they will be from families long gone to seed, or horrible black sheep no longer invited to decent parties.

Continuing NPCs

Should initially include at least two rival book-hounds and their hangers-on, three or more major collectors (likely Mythos victims, sorcerers, or cultists) of various social strata, and key locals such as pub-keepers, grave-robbers, gang bosses, and bent coppers. Enough, in other words, to give the setting lots of potential for betrayal and double-crossing, and enough to give it life off the page.

Rules Variations

This campaign frame invites a finer grain of abilities in the realm of books, and presents the thematic possibility of idiosyncratic "street magic."

New Abilities

Much as *The Esoterrorists* expands the basic GUMSHOE abilities list to detail the various technical wizardries of the postmodern policier, this campaign frame benefits from the addition of focused book-specific abilities.

Bibliography (Academic)
You're an expert on books from an aesthetic, historical, and technical point of view. You can:

- distinguish real tomes from forgeries

- tell when a book has been retouched or altered, or pages have been tipped in or otherwise placed where they were not originally

identify the age of a book by style and materials

- call to mind historical details on famous books, printers, bookbinders, and publishers, and those around them

- recall details of book sales and auctions, and accurately price a given book

- know or estimate what libraries (institutional or private) might hold a specific volume

If this Ability is not available in the game, these talents and skills are otherwise subsumed under Art History. If it is available, it is an Occupational ability for Antiquarians.

Document Analysis (Technical)
You're an expert in the study of physical documents (as opposed to the contents of a text). You can:

- determine a document's approximate age

- identify the manufacturer of paper used in a document

- tell forged documents from the real thing

- identify distinctive handwriting

- match typed documents to the typewriters that produced them

- find fingerprints on paper

If this Ability is not available in the game, these talents and skills are otherwise subsumed under Chemistry, Evidence Collection, and History. If it is available, it is an Occupational ability for Antiquarians and Police Detectives.

Forgery (Technical)
You can create a false document, forge handwriting with a sample to work from, or (given time) fake an entire book. This ability does not convey any special skill at creating "aged" paper or ink, or at bookbinding, or any ability to write or otherwise create a given volume.

If this Ability is not available in the game, these talents and skills are otherwise subsumed under Art (Calligraphy or Printing).

Textual Analysis (Academic)
By studying the content of texts (as opposed to their physical characteristics as documents) you can draw reliable inferences about their authorship. You can:

- determine if an anonymous text is the work of a known author, based on samples of his work

- determine the era in which a text was written

- identify the writer's region, and level of education

- tell a real work by an author from a false one

If this Ability is not available in the game, these talents and skills are otherwise subsumed under History.

Ability Emphases
Investigators in a Book-Hounds game may wish to ensure their team covers a few less usual areas that are not new abilities per se: Art specialties such as Engraving and Printing; Chemistry for ink and paper treatment; and Craft specialties including Bookbinding, Leatherworking, and Papermaking.

Idiosyncratic Magic
Book-hounds, their customers, their contacts, and all those who haunt the Mythos black market are superstitious, obsessed, and widely read in the occult. This is the kind of combination that leads people to try magic, and in keeping with the weird, uncanny setting, some of it might work.

As an entirely optional rule, the Keeper can allow an Investigator (or NPC) to make a 3-point Stability test to exchange 2 Stability pool points for 1 pool point from another Ability. The exchange can happen after the die roll. The player must say what weird ritual action her Investigator is (possibly retroactively) performing, give some notion of the oddball theory by which it works, and tell where she learned it if this is the first time she has made this particular exchange. The primary restrictions are: no player (including the Keeper) should consider it grotesquely abusive, it must be strange and eerie, and it should have a necessary condition. Keeper is allowed to enforce these conditions for similar trades from here on. For example:

"Rose really needed to make that Sense Trouble test – I'm trading 4 Stability for 2 Sense Trouble, so she gets a '5' on the die roll instead. Rose is smoking cigarettes soaked in rats' blood and saffron oil, since we think the plague demon we're hunting is from Russia where saffron grows, and she's watching the smoke pool around its invisible hidey-hole. She learned this trick from that crazy White Russian who used to trade books for vodka money down in Spitalfields last winter."

Creative Keepers and players will be able to justify all sorts of weird, eccentric magics to boost Athletics ("I twist the strand of human hair around my neck and pull myself over the fence"), Disguise ("I've got his mummified thumb in my ruddy mouth, of course I look like him"), Fleeing ("I cut my finger, let it soak my glove in blood, toss it onto the boot of that speeding car, and run the other way"), Shadowing ("I'm only looking in shop windows with her first initial in them"), and so forth.

Keepers may rule that any idiosyncratic magic must have a Mythos source (forcing Investigators to read their wares), that it must involve the caster's blood (either a token amount, or 1 Health point), or any other restriction she feels suitable. At the Keeper's discretion, some parts of London may be more conducive to certain magics (the Isle of Dogs for hunting magic, say), lowering the Difficulty of the Stability test from 4 to 3.

Pitch

Might range from "It's James Ellroy's *Ninth Gate*!" to "It's *Unknown Armies* meets Iain Sinclair!"

The Kingsbury Horror

Hacked From the History Books

The Cleveland Torso Murders occurred exactly as described here. With the exception of the fig leaves, I have added nothing to the facts of the case. One-Armed Willie, the "crazy Greek," and the Aztec blood cult are all actual leads pursued during the investigation, although I confess that I've provided more creative explanations than the impoverished historical record sees fit. Other strange but true leads included a vampire Voodoo killer, Flo Polillo's bizarre search for puzzles before her death, and the elderly scientist who built a death ray. For space's sake, I've omitted them all and much more with great reluctance – that last one sounds beautifully like Yithian technology fallen into the Run through Charybdis' wake.

Sheriff O'Donnell did mount his own "spoiler" investigation, albeit a year later than our timeline has it. (He arrested Dolezal, who died in police custody.) The solution given here to the mystery is impossible, however, and I have changed more than just the name of the Cleveland visionaries who built Shaker Heights and the Cleveland Interurban Railway.

Historical details came from *Torso*, by Steven Nickel, which I recommend to any fan of true crime and Depression.

The Horrible Truth

Orem van Schaen, a deranged classicist and scion of twin Cleveland rail and real-estate barons Castor and Pollux van Schaen, is the Cleveland Torso Killer. Never particularly stable, he came unhinged when he discovered an engraved Red Stone during a European trip in 1928, and brought it back to Cleveland with him. He is attempting to summon Charybdis, the legendary whirlpool demon from Homer's *Odyssey*. He has been assembling suitable heads, and energizing them with enough murderous magic, to construct Scylla, Charybdis' twin monstrosity, in the (as it happens) accurate belief that the creation of Scylla necessarily calls forth Charybdis. With the killing of victim #10, he has six suitable heads, and Scylla can emerge. As Charybdis begins to manifest, the city's hold on time itself begins to come unstuck around the edges.

"MY GRANDFATHER AND HIS WIDOWED SON WALTER NOW COMPRISED THE CLEVELAND HOUSEHOLD, BUT THE MEMORY OF OLDER TIMES HUNG THICKLY OVER IT. I STILL DISLIKED THE PLACE..."

-- THE SHADOW OVER INNSMOUTH

In this scenario, a team of Investigators delves into the mystery of the grotesque Cleveland Torso Murders, and discovers that the truth is perhaps more appalling yet. It is more impressionistic than direct, but a line of reasoning – no matter how illogical – does run through it. It can serve as an introduction for an ongoing *Trail of Cthulhu* campaign, as pieces from the pattern of menace can point survivors in a number of different directions.

This scenario will likely take two sessions to run, and can be played in either Pulp or Purist mode. It begins on August 12, 1938, in Cleveland, Ohio.

If you are not the Keeper, reading this chapter will fatally spoil your fun. If you are the Keeper, not reading this chapter carefully before running the scenario will fatally spoil everyone's fun.

The Spine

The Spine of this scenario is as follows:

Briefing by Sheriff O'Donnell:
The Sheriff assembles the

Welcome to Cleveland

Cleveland, Ohio in the Thirties is America's seventh largest city, with a population just under 1 million. Besides "native whites," there are Germans, Poles, Irish, Italians, Slovenes, Serbo-Croats, Czechs, Mexicans, and a smattering of Rumanians, Syrians, Greeks, and Carpathian-Russians. (Cleveland's 72,000 black residents stay in the Cedar Central ghetto along Central Street.) A quarter of the city is out of work, despite the blazing steel mills and oil refineries, chemical works, and factories lining the basin of the Cuyahoga River. This industrial hell is the Flats, 60 feet below street level. Running southeast from the Flats, paralleling the river between Woodland Avenue and Broadway, is a prehistoric river bed called Kingsbury Run. It holds the waste and effluent from the Flats, the trash of the city, weeds and poison sumac. The Run and Flats together hold perhaps 100,000 hoboes, bums, and homeless, the human waste and effluent from the Depression. Their shanties and tent cities flow past the commuters who ride the Cleveland Interurban Railroad (CIRR) line from downtown's Union Station (surmounted by the 708-foot tall Terminal Tower, the eighth tallest building in America) to the exclusive Shaker Heights neighborhood. The CIRR is built on the old Nickel Line railroad tracks right down the middle of the Run.

Just east of the Flats is the "Roaring Third," the most corrupt police precinct in the city, which is saying something. Prostitution, the drug trade, dive bars, and gambling flourish. It's a warren of slums and tenements, single-room apartments that ask no questions as long as travelers pay in cash. (It is also, as such neighborhoods tended to be, the only racially and ethnically integrated part of the city, home to 39 different languages.) During Prohibition, Cleveland, like St. Paul and Hot Springs, gained a deserved national reputation as an "open city" for gangsters – the city government and police department gladly accepted bribes to keep the heat off of any fugitive from justice who could afford it. The racketeer Moe Dalitz and the "Mayfield Road Mob" (the Milano and Pollizi brothers) run the city to suit themselves.

The independent Republican Mayor Harold H. Burton wants desperately to clean up his city, against the opposition of the Democratic machine, the Dalitz mob, and his own police department. In 1935, he appointed Eliot Ness, the "Untouchable" G-man who broke Capone in Chicago, as Cleveland's safety director. That same year, the killings began.

Investigators, briefs them, gives them a copy of the county case file on the "Butcher of Kingsbury Run," and turns them loose on the mystery. This, along with the Torso Murders themselves, is **the hook.**

Seeing the Red Stone: At least one Investigator sees the Red Stone in the photographs in Frank Dolezal's apartment.

Fingering the Butcher: As they explore the seamy side of Cleveland during the hot Depression summer, the Investigators piece together enough clues to suspect a scion of Cleveland aristocracy.

Time Slips: At the same time, the Investigators also experience enough strangeness to suspect

a major Mythos manifestation is approaching. Both **trails of clues** lead to the same **horrible truth** (see sidebar).

Two More Bodies: As if history itself prods the Investigators along, two more bodies show up in Cleveland.

Stopping Charybdis: Having linked their parallel murder and Mythos investigations, our heroes must beard the Butcher in his den and stop Charybdis from drowning the world.

Premise

The Investigators (or at least one of them) need to be the sorts of people who Sheriff Martin L. O'Donnell would hire to solve a series of brutal killings. The

players should also decide among themselves whether and how their Investigators knew each other before this case.

Sheriff O'Donnell doesn't have many deputies he can rely on, and as a loyal Democrat, he can't work with Mayor Burton's police investigation. The whole point is to make Eliot Ness look bad by solving the murders before he does, and to avoid kicking over any other anthills in Cleveland. The few deputies he has available have raised their profile in the Third too much, and might attract unwelcome police attention if he uses them any more. O'Donnell needs fresh faces on the street and fresh eyes on the case.

Investigators can be from Cleveland, and thus well known to

O'Donnell as interested in "queer stuff" like these killings, or they can be from out of town, and the sheriff can trust them not to have any local loyalties that trump his. Is a professor a "noted expert in abnormal criminal behavior"? Is a dilettante "Martin's brother's boy, just down from Yale, but a good Democrat"? Maybe a journalist works for the Cleveland *Press*, resentful of Ness' sweetheart deal feeding scoops to the *Plain Dealer*. (In the "Project Covenant" campaign frame, the Investigators can be tasked to look into the killings by the cabal.) Ideally at least one Investigator will be a P.I. or a former police detective who can bring the other Investigators on as "my associates," but any halfway plausible explanation the players come up with will work – O'Donnell needs results, and he's paying them ($25 a day, plus expenses) off the books anyway.

With a 1-point **Cop Talk** spend, O'Donnell can also give the Investigator who spent the point a Cuyahoga County deputy sheriff's badge. He makes clear that he doesn't want a lot of noise about the investigation to get back to Cleveland P.D., which means no search warrants needed -- but no arrests without solid evidence. "This badge might close as many mouths as it opens," he says, before laying out the facts of the Torso Murders.

Sheriff O'Donnell Spells It Out For You

Give the players as much background as you think they can stand. If they get restless or bored, you can cut to the chase; O'Donnell will throw them a thick case file and send them packing. The case file is not the

Cleveland Police Department file on the Butcher; that would be many boxes of documents, and it is privileged Ness information that the rival Sheriff has no access to. This file contains the public filings on the case (warrants and such), copies of news stories, and the results of the sheriff's department's previous (and sketchy) legwork. It provides 1 dedicated pool point concerning details of the murders to any investigative ability for the Investigator holding it. (This is called a **File Spend** in these scenario notes.) The point refreshes between scenes.

The basic facts are these: Between September 1935 and the present date, an unknown assailant has kidnapped, beheaded, and dismembered at least 10 people. The "Butcher," as the press calls him, kills his victims at some unknown site, moves the remains, and leaves the bodies in pieces to be discovered later. Some bodies show reddening, or seem dried and leathery; possible signs of chemical treatment intended to remove trace evidence. Some of the victims' heads are left nearby; others are still missing.

The Keeper should photocopy the Case Summary nearby (permission granted) for the players' use.

At First Glance

The best lead that O'Donnell has is Lester's, a dive bar in the Roaring Third on E. 20th and Central. His deputies, working nights around other cases, have discovered that all three identified victims – Edward Andrassy, Flo Polillo, and Rose Wallace – were regulars there. They kept company with a volatile, burly man called "Frank,"

who further investigation has tentatively identified as Frank Dolezal, an unemployed bricklayer and sometime pimp. In 1936, he lived at 1908 Central Ave., a block from where Flo Polillo was dumped. O'Donnell can also give them a "last known address" for Dolezal.

Frank Dolezal's Apartment (2941 E. 22nd)

The Investigators can break into this cold-water second-story apartment (with **Locksmith**, or with a swift kick, but the former won't leave obvious signs of forced entry) and search it, or brace Dolezal, or both, perhaps waiting in his flat for him to return from another day of drinking and doing nothing. They may also talk to Frank's neighbors.

Searching the Apartment

Dolezal's apartment is a cheap flop, with very little in the way of furniture or personal effects. A notebook on the side table has a list of 25 names and addresses, the farthest away in Ontario, California, none of them matching known figures in the case.

Evidence Collection (Core clue): A hollow brick under the windowsill holds white powder in a twist of paper (**Streetwise** or **Pharmacy** to identify as cocaine), and a packet of three black and white photographs.

The photographs show: *An unknown man having sex with Rose Walker.* His face is not visible. He has a peculiar tattoo high on his shoulder, resembling an arrowhead pointing into a curve. **Anthropology** suggests that it looks like a primitive glyph. (Either a 2-point Anthropology

CASE SUMMARY -- "TORSO MURDERS"
Office of the Cuyahoga County Sheriff -- DO NOT CIRCULATE

Victim #1: John Doe I
Found 9/23/35 in Kingsbury Run near E. 49th & Praha; emasculated and beheaded; est. dead
between 1 and 4 weeks when found.
Victim #2: Edward Andrassy, small-time crook and hustler
Found 9/23/35 approximately 30 feet from Victim #1; likewise emasculated and beheaded; est.
dead 2-3 days.
Victim #3: Florence Polillo, AKA Flo Martin, AKA Clara Dunn, prostitute
Found 1/26/36 behind Hart Mfg. at 2315 E. 20th (just north of the Run); arms and legs severed,
legs bisected at knee, torso bisected at waist; head missing; identified by her fingerprints;
wrapped in newspapers from 1/25/36 and 8/11/35; est. dead 2-4 days. (Victim's clothes
discovered 1/17/38 in Kingsbury Run.)
Victim #4: John Doe II, sailor?
Found 6/5/36 in Kingsbury Run near E. 55th; beheaded; six tattoos on body; laundry mark "J.D.";
est. dead 2 days.
Victim #5: John Doe III
Found 7/22/36 in Big Creek near Clinton Rd.; beheaded, no mutilations; may have been killed on
scene; est. dead 2 months.
Victim #6: John Doe IV
Found 9/10/36 in sewer tunnel in Kingsbury Run near 37th St. Bridge; beheaded, emasculated,
torso bisected, dismembered; head and arms missing; est. dead 2 days.
Victim #7: Jane Doe I
Found 2/23/37 near Euclid Beach at E. 156th; dismembered, torso bisected, beheaded; head and
limbs missing; cause of death heart failure; est. dead 3-4 days. (Lower half of torso found
5/5/37 in Cuyahoga River at E. 30th.)
Victim #8: Rose Wallace (?), prostitute
Found 6/6/37 on bank of Cuyahoga under Lorain-Carnegie Bridge; beheaded and dismembered;
limbs and one rib missing; wrapped in newspaper dated 6/5/36; est. dead 1 year. ID made by
son and dental records, but Rose Wallace reported missing only 10 months previous.
Victim #9: John Doe V
Found 7/6/37 in Cuyahoga River beneath W. 3rd and Erie RR Bridge; dismembered, beheaded,
torso bisected, limbs bisected at joints, disemboweled; heart and head missing; cuts
unusually erratic; blue cross tattoo on leg; wrapped in newspapers from 6/37; est. dead 2-3
days.
Victim #10: Jane Doe II
Found 4/8/38 in Cuyahoga River at Superior Ave.; dismembered, beheaded, torso bisected,
limbs bisected; arms, head, and lower right leg missing; cuts unusually erratic; drugs
found in victim's blood; est. dead 3-5 days.

Potential Additional Victims:

Mahoning Swamp Bodies
Six men found (4 bodies, 2 heads) in Mahoning River swamps near New Castle, Penn., 1923-1924.
John Doe 0, Black
Found 7/24/29 in Kingsbury Run 6 blocks N of site of Victims #1 and #2; beheaded, left arm
severed; head and arm missing; time of death unknown.
Jane Doe 0, "The Lady in the Lake"
Found 9/5/34 on the same site as Victim #7; bisected, dismembered, and beheaded, head,
uterus, and limbs missing; body chemically preserved and treated.
John Doe 00
Found 7/1/36 in a boxcar in the Erie RR yards in New Castle, Penn.; beheaded and mutilated;
head missing; wrapped in newspapers dated 7/33; est. dead 10-14 days.

spend or a later **Library Use** at Western Reserve University will identify it as a canine totem from the Balkans approximately 5,000 years old.) The room looks like an anonymous Cleveland flop.

The same man having sex with Edward Andrassy. His face is not visible. This picture appears to have been taken through a window; the corner of a painting is visible behind the two. With **Art History,** it can be identified as an Italian futurist work from before the War. (A 1-point spend garners the title, *Whirlpool,* and the artist, Glaucco Aioli.)

The same man having sex with Flo Polillo. The room looks sumptuously furnished, although **Architecture** can tell that it is built of pre-stressed concrete rather than normal residential construction. Behind them, leaning against the wall, is an engraved bas-relief in what looks like marble or soapstone. Under magnification, it depicts a ship being attacked by a horrible monster with six snarling, canine heads. A man in a crested helmet stands at the bow, looking on in horror. The stern is obscured by Flo Polillo's head. **Archaeology** or **Art History** identify the scene as the attack of Scylla on Odysseus' ship, from the *Odyssey*. Examining the picture closely enough to identify the relief creates a strong sensation of being watched, along with vertigo and a powerful onrush of déjà vu, for a 2-point Stability test.

Meeting Frank Dolezal

If the Investigators are planning to ambush Dolezal either in the street outside or in his apartment, they need to make a Stealth test. (Since Frank is more than a bit drunk, the Difficulty is 3.) If they succeed, he will spill what he knows after a few minutes of **Intimidation**, or even faster if confronted with the photographs. If the Stealth test fails, Frank is alerted to their presence and comes at them swinging a butcher knife he has concealed.

Frank Dolezal
Athletics 5, Health 5, Scuffling 6, Weapons 2

Weapon: -1 (butcher knife)

All the Investigators should know that gunshots will draw police, which will make Sheriff O'Donnell upset. Once Frank is defeated, he will talk.

Dolezal was just a pimp who catered to clients with a taste for slumming it. He admits to having beaten Flo, claiming that she deserved it. Every so often, he goes into a fugue state in which he describes cutting Flo up after "a fight on Saturday fit to make the dogs howl." Any Investigator (especially an alienist) with **Psychoanalysis** can tell Dolezal is not entirely sane; **Psychology, Oral History**, or **Interrogation** can tell that his story contradicts itself, and is probably not true. He does, however, tell a very convincing tale of hiding Flo's body in the cans behind Hart Manufacturing. Using the **File Spend** reminds the Investigator that Flo was killed, according to the examiner's estimate, on a Friday. He claims he doesn't know who the man in the pictures is (**Psychology** says he's not lying), and that he got them from another pimp, One-Armed Willie. He hasn't seen Willie around since.

Cleveland by Night
As the Investigators wander through Cleveland, the following scenes can happen whenever the Keeper decides it's time for another scene. They are most likely to start with either Lester's Tavern or Nadie's Tattoos, but again, it's all up to your sense of pacing as Keeper. Scenes with floating core clues are indicated.

Lester's Tavern
The clientele are desperate loners; amputees, hoboes, blind pencil salesmen, and aging prostitutes. With suitable Interpersonal ability use by the Investigators, they will describe Frank Dolezal as "barking mad" and "surly" and "hair-trigger" and similar epithets. The speaker will often aver that "He might be the Butcher hisself, see if he ain't," and after one such pronouncement, a wretched-looking hobo soak will contradict the speaker.

Reassurance (Core clue): If bought a Reassuring drink, the 'bo will tell how he met "The Hobo Doctor" at "this very bar." He was always good for a drink, and he knew Flo Polillo. He was well-dressed, about thirty, called himself a doctor, used hair pomade, and "talked a storm." He was very interested in tattoos that people had. He offered people lifts at closing time "in a big black car," and he left with Flo "a couple days before" her death. Nobody saw either of them since. The unknown man in the photos uses hair pomade. (Hobo Investigators can use their **Streetwise** here, as well.)

Lester's can be the spot for Investigators to pick up any other helpful rumors or gossip the Keeper decides to plant. On their second visit, for example, following a **Reassuring** drink for the house, they might hear about the "Mexican headhunters" or the "crazy Greek," to prep them when those figures appear. However, if the Investigators prefer to prowl the mean streets of Cleveland shaking down suspicious characters, they can get the same sort of leads that way.

Nadie's Tattoos

The Investigators will most likely notice this Mexican tattoo parlor while walking through the Third, probably as an Inconspicuous Clue (see p. 55).

Evidence Collection or Streetwise (Core clue): In the window, displayed on fading paper, is the design from the unknown man's tattoo, only in this case filled in with emerald green snake scales and sporting white bone skulls at the four ends.

A **Streetwise** Investigator will know that the tattooed, eye-patch wearing operator, **Mondo,** is a gang member, and will not mention anything about the sheriff or the Butcher, but work elliptically around to the subject of the tattoo design. Failing that, **Flattery** will also work – Mondo is proud of his designs.

Should the Keeper wish it, and things go wrong, a fight can break out with Mondo and his pals. (The precise number of his pals is up to the Keeper.) At the conclusion of the affray, if the Investigators are victorious, **Intimidation** can also get the answers they crave.

Los Cazadores de Cabezas, The Headhunters

This Mexican gang began as commercial fishermen until they accidentally crossed paths with the incipient Charybdis-energy surrounding the Butcher as he examined a future ritual site. They suffered a religious epiphany, and discovered their new goddess.

They worshipped Scylla, the demon the Butcher was building, calling her Coatlicue, after the Aztec goddess of fire and death. As the **Anthropology** ability reveals, she wears a skirt of living serpents and skulls, and her hands and feet are clawed like dogs' paws.

The Headhunters' actual career is up to the Keeper; did they harvest any skulls, or did Eliot Ness break them up first? Does their remnant still have a cult center somewhere in the Third? They can be a red herring, or they can have made contact with their unwitting founder and be part of the trail of clues. (If so, **Evidence Collection** will find a fair number of CIRR tickets in their compound, very unlikely for Mexican poor folk in 1938.) If the cult is still functioning, their hideout will feature three things:

A copy of the Red Stone, painted in garish Aztec colors and designs, showing a boat being smashed between two giants: the god Huracan and the goddess Coatlicue, while a Jaguar Knight looks on helplessly. (A 1-point **Anthropology** spend will recall that the Aztecs had a myth similar to the Greek tale of the Clashing Rocks, which Odysseus avoided in the *Odyssey*.) At the Keeper's discretion, it may also impose a Stability test.

A pyramid of skulls, as many as they have collected. (Some might be looted from graveyards, if the Keeper doesn't want to needlessly multiply decapitations.)

The Brood of Coatlicue, a nest of living skulls attached to vines growing in pots all around the humid room. It will attack unbelievers.

Brood of Coatlicue

Abilities: Athletics 11, Health 7, Scuffling 16

Hit Threshold: 3 (rooted)

Weapon: +0 (bite); each skull can bite one opponent at close or point-blank range at no Hit Threshold penalty.

Armor: Physical weapons, except those that crush skulls or cut vines, do only 1 point of damage. Fire does normal damage.

Stability Loss: +0

The Keeper can also plant evidence of the cult's ties to other Mythos threats to jump-start an ongoing campaign; cults to Yig in Mexico, for example, or via other fishermen to the Deep One threat in Cleveland personified by the Williamson family in "The Shadow Over Innsmouth."

"Los Psychos" Gang Members
Athletics 6, Health 6, Scuffling 7, Weapons 4

Weapon: +0 (chains, baseball bats), -1 (knives, blackjacks)

Mondo says the symbol represents "a goddess from the old times, with snake skulls in her dress," and that a gringo gave him the basic design, but he added the flashy parts. (If asked to describe the gringo, he says "Young, pushy, big mouth. Shiny hair. They all look the same. Showed me what he wanted, and I gave it him, the dog on the shoulder." If pressed, he will seem confused about calling it a dog.) He designed that tattoo for a gang called the Headhunters, "until Ness busted them."

The Picture in the Tavern

Either Mondo, or someone at Lester's, can point Investigators looking for the Headhunters' trail toward La Sirena, a Mexican bar and gambling establishment near the riverfront. The name comes from a traditional Mexican Loteria card prominently displayed in the window, depicting a mermaid.

Gringos are distinctly unwelcome, unless they're gambling and losing. Nobody will talk about anything, although a 2-point **Credit Rating** spend washes away any such resentment. If the ice is broken thusly, the bartender or dealer will allow that yes, the *Cazadores de Cabezas* used to come here. They came here when they were just fishermen, and when they were big gangsters, too. Now, they are in jail or in hiding, and they come here no more.

Evidence Collection (Core clue): Many of the photographs hanging on the wall of the bar show various fishing boats with their Mexican crews. In one, however, a white man is standing on the dock above the crew, obviously caught in the frame by accident. With **Architecture,** the dock is recognizable as the Erie Railroad Dock on W. 3rd, where victim #9 was found. The date in the corner of the picture is 8/11/35, the date on the newspapers that wrapped Flo Polillo's body. Odder yet, the white man's jaw resembles that of the john in the "insurance" photos. Upon that discovery, the Investigator who saw the bas-relief recognizes the resulting composition as the same – a row of men with one man in profile raised above them, extending an arm in protestation. Once the Investigator sees the resemblance, the sky in the photo seems to roil, as if a cyclone were forming above the fishing boat, triggering a 2-point Stability test.

Meet One-Armed Willie

Either a lead at Lester's or a sudden impromptu Sense Trouble ("That black guy's sleeve is flapping in the wind.") at Difficulty 5 lets the Investigators know that One-Armed Willie has swum into their ken. He must be chased down, beginning with a Shadowing test against Difficulty 4. (He's suspicious, but he's got one arm and stands out in any crowd not in the ghetto.) If successful, the Investigators can trap him in a dead end alley; if not, it's time to test Athletics, since he doesn't stick around to find out what the scary white folk want.

One-Armed Willie
Athletics 9, Health 3, Scuffling 4

If he escapes, great! The Investigators can have run themselves into some creepy part of Cleveland suitable for a time-slip (see below). Eventually, he'll show up again. He has to.

Once finally run to ground, Willie just breaks down and sobs. He's incoherent, moaning about how "the doctor already showed me papers says I'm gonna die in the past." "I been spit up by the whirlpool, just like in the story, and I'm gonna get sucked back in. The doctor gonna cut my arm off and kill me in 1929, and the one that gets away just runs until he sucked back in." **Reassurance (Core clue)** can calm him down and change his ranting to muttering, but can do nothing for what is obviously a far-gone case of delusional paranoia.

Investigators can ask a calmer Willie anything they like, but his useful responses are as follows: "Where does he cut your arm off?" "Under the train." "What whirlpool? What story?" "Cribdis. Greek story. Next to the dogs." "Who is the doctor?" "Rich white man with greasy hair. Live under the train." "Did he kill Flo? (Or Ed, or Rose.)" "Didn't know he was the doctor the first time before he killed me, so I shopped him Flo an' Ed an' Rose. Builds dogs out of 'em." "Saw the boat in the pitcher. Caught in the whirlpool."

During this colloquy, **Medicine** indicates that Willie is malnourished and suffering from exhaustion and exposure. His arm seems to have been neatly severed, and then scarred over, possibly as many as, oh, nine years ago.

Once the Keeper judges that Willie has been as informative, or as interesting, as he is going to get, Willie begins to bleed all over them, from a sudden wound in his neck. They hear the sound of a great, rushing wind, and Willie's head simply tears loose and disappears in a mist of blood and snarling noises. Any Investigator specifically watching Willie has her vision grey out and grow patchy; any visible light seems to be sucked away toward the Kingsbury Run. Willie's body falls backward, its good arm flailing, and Willie, too vanishes with a sucking splash. The manifestation is over, and witnesses to Willie's piecemeal disappearance make a 5-point Stability test.

The Crazy Greek
Eventually, habitues of Lester's will mention the "crazy Greek" seen running along the Run with "big knives" in his overcoat. If the Investigators don't bother with Lester's, they will eventually run into the crazy Greek during their wanderings.

He is short, wiry, barefoot, and clad in leather trousers and a hobo coat too big for him. He has a reddish beard, a beaky nose, and rotten teeth. He babbles at those he encounters, and if they seem dangerous, he waves his big knives at them.

Languages: An Investigator with Greek recognizes the crazy Greek's babbling as Homeric Greek, not modern Greek. An Investigator with Homeric Greek can talk to him, beginning with Reassurance.

Archaeology: His "big knives" are a Mycenaean broadsword and dagger, banged up by heavy use, but otherwise in museum condition.

Psychoanalysis: He suffers from severe panic attacks, and is probably insane.

Teiresh, the Crazy Greek
Athletics 8, Health 7, Scuffling 5, Weapons 6

Weapon: +1 (sword), -1 (dagger); he can attack with one or the other

In his brief interval of lucidity, he explains that his name is Teiresh, he lost his ship when the Render (*Skyllo*) attacked, and that the river doesn't look the same as it did, the figs are bad here and you can hardly find any, he didn't know where that wall of grey came from, and where is the Troublemaker? (*Odishowax?*)

He then panics again, and runs off waving his sword. If restrained, he will escape when no longer watched.

Meet Detective Merylo
If the Investigators have been sloppy, firing a lot of guns, flashing their badge unwisely, or otherwise setting too high a profile, they will get a visit from Detective Peter Merylo of the Cleveland Police Department. He warns them to stay out of his case and to tell the Sheriff to stick to finding lost dogs. With a **Cop Talk**, he doesn't have a few of the boys in blue beat the Investigators up. He will not listen to fool theories about cults, or time vortexes, or accusations against leading citizens from obvious political hacks like the Investigators.

Cleveland's Finest
Athletics 7, Firearms 4, Health 8, Scuffling 6, Weapons 4

Weapon: -1 (nightstick or sap); cops won't shoot (+0 .32 Police Specials) unless the Investigators are stupid enough to draw down on them.

This encounter can be used as a "soak encounter" if the Keeper wishes, or left out if the Investigators are doing a reasonable job of keeping things on the down low.

Eddies of Charybdis
These time slip encounters should start happening after the first Investigator has seen the Stone in the photograph, and with greater frequency as dramatically appropriate. It's best if they happen to lone Investigators first, and then to increasingly large teams. They can happen at any time of the day or night; Charybdis deforms time to suit drama. The Keeper should absolutely feel free to make up her own time-slip phenomena. Once enough of them have occurred, if the Keeper wants to skip ahead to the discovery of the next two bodies, or even to Ness' final raid on the Flats, she can justify it by dropping the Investigators through a time-slip themselves.

Newspaper Ghosts. A newspaper blows past you in a spiraling wind. When you grab it out of the air, it is dated years ago. (If the Keeper wants, it can match one of the dates the Butcher uses to wrap his kills.) No test.

Back on the Bridge. While crossing a bridge over the Run or over the Cuyahoga River, you suffer a huge burst of déjà vu and cross it a second time. 2-point Stability test.

Dried Birds. If the Investigators

are in a car, they are pummeled by falling dead birds, dried and leathery. On the street, the things simply drop silently from the sky. **Biology** identifies the birds as passenger pigeons, extinct for a generation or more. 3-point Stability test.

Future Sky. An incredibly loud noise comes from overhead, and you look up to see an enormous airplane with no propellers slowly cross the sky, leaving a white trail that spirals toward the Run. 3-point Stability test.

Car Dumping a Body. It's night on the Jefferson Street Bridge above the Cuyahoga, near the Kingsbury Run. You see a black Cord stop and the driver get out, remove a body from the back seat wrapped in paper, and hurl it over the railing. From the sound when it bounces off a roof, and the multiple splashes, you know it was in pieces. You cannot identify the driver, except to note he has pomaded hair. The Keeper should emphasize the dreamlike or ghost-like nature of this time-slip; the Investigators cannot affect these events. 3-point Stability test.

Flashback. This can be an opportunity for roleplaying and deepening your character; while walking in sight of the Run, you have a vivid waking dream and replay the worst thing that ever happened to you involving dogs or drowning. (The player should make this up if need be.) 3-point Stability test, or worse if the Investigator already has a pre-existing paranoia, or the "worst thing" was a Mythos shock.

Sudden Flood. You're walking in the Run and you hear the onrush of waters, foaming down the gully toward you. You drown, and wake up in the Run on a tree-covered hillock by the East 24th Street Station. 4-point Stability test.

Not the Same River. Looking down at the Cuyahoga, it widens and straightens; the city seems to melt away. A Greek galley (like the one on the Stone) can be seen beating down the river. You feel a horrible sense of anticipation, and slavering hunger. You realize you're watching the boat from six pairs of eyes, and wake up to a roaring sound and Cleveland traffic all around you. 4-point Stability test.

Elder Thing. Looking at the Kingsbury Run, it fills with water, and the plain flattens out around it. **Geology** identifies the weird plants around as Jurassic cycads. There is a strange humming sound as an Elder Thing (see p. 131) glides down the Run on its wings. The sound rises in pitch as the alien is caught in an invisible vortex and pulled apart in stop-motion; its after-images persist in a line, like the rowers on the Stone. Again you wake up to

the roaring sound of Charybdis. 5-point Stability test.

Investigating Scylla and van Schaen

Although the Keeper should stay flexible, this scenario naturally falls into a rhythm, alternating legwork in the Third, bookwork on van Schaen and mythology, and utter weirdness as Charybdis continues to drain through time. This is a good rhythm to shoot for, especially by intercutting between sub-teams of Investigators.

The Painting

Credit Rating/Art (Core clue): Asking around in local art circles, the Investigators can discover that Aioli's *Whirlpool* was bought in Venice in 1928 by one Orem van Schaen at the conclusion of his European tour. There was a great scandal, because van Schaen paid far more than the painting was worth, and possibly more than his family could easily afford. As far as anyone knows, it's still hanging in the van Schaen mansion in Shaker Heights.

If the Investigators did not know the painting's identity yet, **Library Use** can uncover it based on the visible portion in the photograph.

Western Reserve University

Cleveland's finest institution of higher learning has copious archives suitable for academic research. Some likely topics include:

Local Maps

The best map library in the region is the Western Reserve Historical Society Library, but Western Reserve has a good collection too. With **Geology,** an Investigator can realize that all the bodies are dumped either in present-day water (the Cuyahoga, Lake Erie, and Big Creek) or prehistoric water (Kingsbury Run). If the Investigators have already braced Frank Dolezal, they know that he may well have moved the only apparent exception, Flo Polillo's body.

Scylla and Charybdis

These two legendary monsters of Greek lore always appear together. According to some authorities, they are twin daughters of Hecate or of Cetus the sea monster; in other versions, Charybdis is the mother of Scylla. In the *Odyssey*, Circe is able to predict the future, and warns Odysseus to sail closer to Scylla (a demoness with the heads of six dogs at her waist) than to Charybdis (a massive whirlpool that sucks the waters dry thrice

a day and then spits its intake out again). Scylla, after all, will only kill six of his men; Charybdis will destroy everything. Later, when Zeus drives Odysseus back into Charybdis, Odysseus clings to a fig tree growing above her maelstrom and survives until his ship's wreckage resurfaces. This much is available with **Anthropology** or **Occult**, as well as with **Library Use.**

One particularly interesting study of the two appears in *The Odyssey: A Reassessment*, an unpublished doctoral thesis (1923) by Omer H. Van Schaen. Finding this book in the Western Reserve stacks requires a 2-point **Library Use** spend. In this work, van Schaen argues that Odysseus sailed on the Danube River, and that Scylla and Charybdis were not (as is usually assumed) the Straits of Messina between Sicily and Italy, but the Iron Gates, a river pass between Transylvania and Serbia. He likewise argues that the various time dilations and uncertainties of direction experienced by Odysseus in the epic are caused by his close brush with Charybdis, and that Circe, Nausicaa, and Calypso are all alternate versions of Scylla. Reading this work with **Psychoanalysis** in mind, van Schaen seems to alternately hate and worship Scylla and the women of the *Odyssey*.

Orem H. van Schaen

Born in 1904, the youngest son of Cleveland real-estate and rail baron C.F. (Castor Franchot) van Schaen. C.F. and his twin brother P.N. (Pollux Nesbit) are most famous for buying air rights to the Kingsbury Run and the old Nickel Line Railroad in order to build the Cleveland Interurban

line to their brand-new exclusive Shaker Heights suburb. They drowned themselves in 1929 when the Crash wiped out the majority of the van Schaen family holdings.

They left the estate to Orem's twin sisters N.K. and P.J. van Schaen, as Orem had been considered of delicate health. Although educated by private tutors, he proved capable of taking a doctorate in classics from Western Reserve in 1923. This much appears in the public records and biographies, and is available with **Library Use**.

For the gossip, Investigators have to either mingle in Cleveland high society (**Credit Rating** 5+) or talk to reporters (Journalist special abilities, **Flattery**, or **Reassurance** that they won't print anything). Orem left home right after getting his doctorate, and rumor had it that he got mixed up in some trouble in Pennsylvania somewhere. He was committed to a sanitarium "for observation" between 1925 and 1927, but managed to talk his father into letting him go to Europe the next year; he traveled in Greece and along the Danube, buying a painting in Venice and coming home. The argument over the painting was the last straw, and Orem was refused permission to travel or set up his own classical museum with the artifacts he "discovered" on his trip. He hasn't really been seen in polite society since 1930.

The van Schaen Mansion

If the Investigators try to gain admittance to the van Schaen mansion (**Credit Rating, Intimidation**, or even **Locksmith**) they will find N.K. and P.J. eerily detached and unreceptive. They will pay blackmail to suppress the

pictures, if the Investigators are ungentlemanly enough to extort it, but refuse to discuss Orem at all. The Aioli painting, which does indeed look out over an open lawn through a French window, is the only thing in the house free of swirling dust.

If the Investigators have been indiscreetly blackening the good name of van Schaen in polite company, or if they blackmail the sisters, they get a warning to back off delivered by Angelo Lonardo, one of the old-school Mob types under Moe Dalitz. With a 1-point **Streetwise** spend, Lonardo doesn't have his boys beat the offending Investigators to a pulp. Unless they keep bothering the nice ladies. (Use Cleveland's Finest, p. 222, for Mob statistics.)

"Eleven" and "Twelve"

On August 16, 1938, two more bodies are discovered at the E. 9th Street Lakeshore Dump, both dismembered and beheaded. In the chaos of the day-long search for missing parts, Investigators

can get access to the scene with **Cop Talk** and a suitable bribe ($10).

Evidence Collection (Core clue): There are autumn leaves in the severed fist of victim #11. **Biology** identifies them as fig leaves; the fig tree is not native to Ohio.

Forensics: Victim #11, a woman, has been dead for 4 to 6 months; victim #12, a man, for 7 to 9 months. That puts the killings at right around the time of victim #10, or before. The remains of #11 are dried and hardened, almost mummified (similar to the Dried Birds manifestation on p. 222); that of #12 is practically skeletal.

File Spend: Victim #12 resembles the description of a "Greek" friend of Edward Andrassy, seen in his company at Lester's.

Sense Trouble: The Investigator who has had the most time-dilation experiences sees a trail of afterimages from the bodies toward the Terminal Tower, and suddenly sees himself on the CIRR line by Kingsbury Run. With a successful test (Difficulty 5) he can jump off the tracks and avoid the train, which sounds like the onrushing water of Charybdis. If he fails, the train hits him like a wall of water, he feels himself disintegrate utterly – and he awakens again at the Dump. He must make a 5-point Stability test for his deathly hallucination.

Fear Death By Water

Solving this mystery should be fairly simple – van Schaen, driven mad by his studies and by the Stone, has become the Butcher. Finding his lair is more difficult, but there are a number of clues to put together:

Eliot Ness' Last Raid

Just after midnight on the morning of August 18, 1938, frustrated beyond patience at the depredations of the Butcher and the political backstabbing he faced over the case, Eliot Ness led 35 lawmen on one last raid. Backed by 11 squad cars, two paddy wagons, and three fire trucks, his posse descended into the Flats with spotlights blazing and weapons drawn. They razed the shanties and shacks they found, and arrested anyone they could reach. Fire, yowling sirens, and howling mongrels were everywhere. Ness' squads drove deep into the Run as far as 37th Street, overturning tents and kicking in crate walls, and rounding up the slow and luckless.

If at all possible, this should be the only glimpse the Investigators get of Eliot Ness, clutching an axe-handle and squinting against smoke and filth as he rounds up the desperate and the lost, lit by flarelight and police flashers. It's worth moving the raid up or down a day off its historical track to have it happen at the same time the Investigators move against the Butcher at the 24th Street Station, just for drama's sake.

That morning, Ness' men took 63 hoboes back to Central Station, and handed 11 men with criminal records over to the FBI. For the rest, it was the workhouse. At dawn, Ness and his posse searched the ruins for any clue to the Butcher or his whereabouts, but found nothing. They burned the ruins of the three huge hobo jungles they had invaded. This last gamble didn't pay off; Ness uncovered no more leads, and his strongarm tactics alienated the city.

Van Schaen's father and uncle built the CIRR line through Kingsbury Run.

CIRR stations are built of prestressed concrete, like van Schaen's love nest from the photograph. (**Architecture**)

A stand of leafy trees in the Run beside the tracks at the East 24th Street Station includes a fig tree. (**Biology**)

Evidence Collection can spot extra weathering on the East 24th Street Station, as if it's been swung through the cycle of the years more often than the rest of the line.

And finally, the Keeper can feed visions and time-slips that increasingly focus on the Run, the CIRR line, and the East 24th Street Station until the players catch on.

Confronting van Schaen

Discovering the secret entrance to van Schaen's hidden room inside the Station is a matter of **Architecture** or **Evidence Collection** (dust patterns on the floor swirling toward a seemingly blank tiled wall). Levering it open is a Mechanical Repair test against a Difficulty of 5. If it's failed, the door still opens, but with a horrid groan, alerting the Butcher to their presence.

The chamber is a kind of Art Deco combination of museum and operating theater; there are body parts sitting in zinc tubs of chemicals next to Greek and Illyrian statuary, Homeric helmets on top of partially flensed skulls, and razor-sharp antique swords buried in detached human shoulder hanks. Orem is either waiting to spring on them with a sword, or working on the pile of heads and embalmed limbs in the center of the room.

Orem van Schaen, the Butcher

Athletics 9, Health 8, Scuffling 9, Weapons 7

Hit Threshold: 4

Alertness Modifier: +2 (expanded time senses)

Weapon: +1 (broadsword)

Armor: None

Instead of any given round of combat, Orem can expend 1 Health to shift himself in time, allowing him to appear anywhere in the room with a fully refreshed Health pool.

Scylla

Athletics 4, Health 18, Scuffling 10

Hit Threshold: 3 (mostly sessile)

Alertness Modifier: +2 (expanded time senses)

Weapon: +0 (bite); Scylla can bite with up to six heads at a time; if two bite attacks in a row succeed against the same target, Scylla can worry her victim with her canine jaws, and the second attack thus does double damage.

Armor: firearms and projectiles do only half damage; refresh 1

Health per round.

Stability Loss: +2

Scylla's six heads extend on quasi-material tendrils out from her midsection, which resembles a great fish body made of sewn-together human skin and limbs. They are the severed heads of six Butcher victims, but when they open their jaws to yelp or bite, they take on a hideously elongated canine aspect, as though some external force were deforming them out of shape while wielding them like finger puppets.

Charybdis

The onset of Charybdis carries all before it. It must be prevented. The simplest way to thwart Charybdis is Odysseus' method; feed six lives to Scylla in one round. Investigators can sacrifice themselves or hurl convenient hoboes into the waiting maws (and make the 5-point Stability test resulting from such action).

Dynamiting the Station might also work, at the Keeper's discretion. If so, make sure to note the symmetrical spiral patterns in the tile work, to give the players the insight that the Station serves as Charybdis' physical containment field (or summoning tower, if Charybdis is Yog-Sothoth).

But the easiest way is to destroy the Red Stone. Although the Stone is bulletproof diorite, there are a lot of very caustic chemicals littering the chamber. (**Chemistry** to find good, horrible ones. If an Investigator somehow gets past both Scylla and Orem to the chemical tables, they will damage Scylla as strong acid (+0).) The onrush of Charybdis is echoed on the Stone, the bas-relief changing

to show the whirlpool surging up from below. This, combined with the Charybdis water noise coming from the Stone, should tip off the players.

The Red Stone

A red diorite slab about 50 inches wide by 18 inches tall by 6 inches thick, carved in a raised relief that resembles Hittite almost as much as it does Mycenaean Greek (**Art History, Archaeology**). Its description is given on p. 219. However, looking at the Stone, no two observers can agree whether the horrified captain is on the bow or the stern of the ship.

Loose Ends And Further Trails

The Investigators, if they think to bring evidence back to O'Donnell, will get his grudging thanks – he can't very well embarrass Ness any more than the midnight raid already has, and he can't prosecute the weak-minded scion of the van Schaen dynasty even if he survived the confrontation. But O'Donnell is large-minded enough to recognize a job well done (albeit petty enough to let Merylo keep chasing phantoms well into the 1940s), and will be a useful contact in the future.

Van Schaen's lab may contain a Mythos tome or diary salvaged from the ruins of Ferenczy Castle in Rumania in 1928, which may lead to other Yog-Sothoth (or Hastur, or Zhar-Lloigor) cultists. The sidebar box for the cult of Coatlicue (p. 219) offers more possible leads.

Downtown Terminal

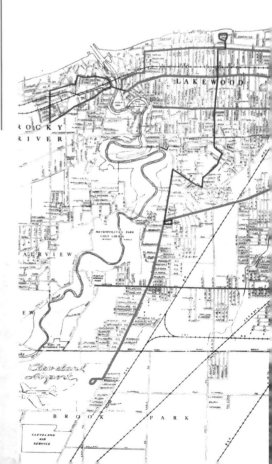

A high resolution version of this map can be found on www.pelgranepress.com

GREATER CLEVELAND

showing

CLEVELAND RAILWAY

Street Car and Motor Coach Routes

Key

Street Car Routes

Motor Coach Routes

Appendices

APPENDIX 1: BASIC ROLE-PLAYING AND GUMSHOE

GUMSHOE-style play using BRP rules

It should be fairly simple to convert the GUMSHOE experience and investigative philosophy to the *Basic Role-Playing* engine at the heart of *Call of Cthulhu*. Any skill roll made to gain a clue, advance the plot, or obtain information automatically succeeds. If you want to incorporate spends as well, allow them in 20-point increments – a character with an Anthropology of 45% can make two spends, or one big dramatic spend. You might require a minimum of 20% in any investigative ability before the player is entitled to clues.

Any skill roll made for dramatic purposes, including all SAN rolls, POW contests, and combat rolls, proceeds as normal. Although the Keeper may want to tweak this model for her own particular flavor, we recommend leaving Conceal, Disguise, Drive Auto, Electrical Repair, First Aid, Hypnosis, Pilot, Psychoanalysis, and Ride as normal rolls. Some skills will vary: a Navigate roll to realize that the dolmen actually points north should automatically succeed, for instance, while a Navigate roll to find your way out of a fog-bound patch of sea

while the Deep Ones are attacking should be a dramatic roll.

Converting BRP to GUMSHOE

The following guidelines enable you to convert existing *Call of Cthulhu* scenarios (either your own, or published ones) and Investigators for *Trail of Cthulhu*. No game conversion is perfect, however, and if you run into something that your game should handle differently, feel free to tinker with it.

Round fractions up.

Investigator Characteristics:

- Ignore STR, CON, SIZ, INT, POW, DEX, APP, and EDU.

- Divide SAN by 10 to derive value of both Sanity and Stability.

- Divide HP by 2 to derive Health.

- Divide Idea Roll by 12 to derive Sense Trouble.

- Divide Luck Roll by 12 to derive Preparedness.

- Ignore Know Roll and Magic Points.

Investigator Skills:

- Reduce all skills below 6% to 0%.

- Divide the following skills by

20 to derive the corresponding ability ratings: Accounting, Anthropology, Archaeology, Art, Astronomy, Bargain, Biology, Chemistry, Craft, Geology, History, Law, Library Use, Locksmith, Medicine, Occult, Pharmacy, Photography, Physics, Psychology (becomes Assess Honesty), and Spot Hidden (becomes Evidence Collection).

- Divide the following skills by 12 to derive the corresponding ability ratings: Conceal, Disguise, Drive Auto (becomes Driving), Electrical Repair, First Aid, Hypnosis, Pilot (becomes Piloting), Psychoanalysis, and Ride (becomes Riding).

- Subtract 10% from Credit Rating skill and divide the remainder by 10, *rounding down in this instance,* to derive Credit Rating ability rating. (Negative results produce a Credit Rating 0.) If your derived Credit Rating is lower than the lowest rating in your Occupation band (see p. 9), raise it to that level.

- Divide Cthulhu Mythos skill by 20 to derive the Cthulhu Mythos ability rating. Subtract this number from 10 and lower Sanity if necessary to match the cap.

- Add Fast Talk and Persuade together; divide the result by 20. Split these rating points between Bureaucracy, Flattery, and Reassurance as you wish. If any of those three abilities are listed as your Occupational abilities, add 1 rating point to that ability.

- For each other language skill, add 1 to your Languages ability rating. If you have a foreign language at 90%+, add 1 rating point. If you have three or more foreign languages at 90%+, add 2 rating points.

- Take the highest of Natural History, Navigate, and Track; divide that skill by 20 to derive Outdoorsman. For each of the lower skills at 90%+, add 1 rating point.

- Take the highest of Climb, Jump, Swim, and Throw; divide that skill by 12 to derive Athletics. For each of the lower skills at 70%+, add 1 rating point.

- Divide Dodge by 10 to derive Fleeing.

- Take the highest of Fist/Punch, Grapple, Head Butt, and Kick; divide that skill by 12 to derive Scuffling. For each of the lower skills at 90%+, add 1 rating point. Add 1 rating point for Martial Arts at 50%+.

- If Damage Bonus is +1D4, add 1 rating point to Scuffling.

- If Damage Bonus is +1d6, add 1 rating point to Scuffling and 1 rating point to Intimidation.

- Take the highest of Handgun, Machine Gun, Rifle, and Submachine Gun; divide that skill by 12 to derive Firearms. For each of the lower skills at 90%+, add 1 rating point. Add 1 rating point for Shotgun at 80%+.

- Take your highest hand-to-hand weapon skill; divide that skill by 12 to derive Weapons. Add 1 rating point if you have two other hand-to-hand weapon skills at 80%+.

- Take the highest of Mechanical Repair and Operate Heavy Machinery; divide that skill by 12 to derive Mechanical Repair. If the lower of those two skills is 70%-89%, add 1 rating point; if the lower of those two skills is 90%+, add 2 rating points.

- Take the highest of Hide, Listen, and Sneak, and divide it by 12 to derive Stealth. For each of the lower skills at 70%+, add 1 rating point.

- If you have any of the following abilities as Occupational abilities, add 1 rating point to them: Cryptography, Forensics, Interrogation, Intimidation, Oral History.

- If you have any of the following abilities as Occupational abilities, add 2 rating points to them: Art History, Cop Talk, Streetwise, Theology.

- If you have any of the following abilities as Occupational abilities, add 3 rating points to them: Filch, Shadowing.

Creatures:
- The creature's Move is its Athletics.

- Divide the creature's average HP by 2; add 1 to the quotient to derive its Health.

- Divide the creature's highest

native attack skill by 3 to derive its Scuffling.

- Divide the creature's highest weapon skill by 4 to derive its Weapons (or Firearms as the case may be).

- Make sure to split scores for different environments if necessary. You may adjust these derived scores up or down by 1 or 2 points if necessary to clearly differentiate the various creatures from each other.

- Hit Threshold is 4 unless special circumstances obtain (creature is slow, creature has native advantages).

- Extrapolate Alertness and Stealth modifiers, if any, from the examples.

- Damage can be extrapolated from the following table, but remember that damage is compressed. Damage in *Trail of Cthulhu* should only go above +1 if the attack does over 2D6+3 damage in *Call of Cthulhu*. Remember to include Damage Bonuses when calculating creature damage!

Call of Cthulhu damage	Trail of Cthulhu damage
1D3, 1D4	-2
1D6	-1
1D8	+0
1D8+1, 1D10, 2D6	+1
3D6, 4D6	+2
5D6	+3
6D6	+5
10D6	+12

- Use the following table for Armor conversions:

Call of Cthulhu points of Armor	Trail of Cthulhu Armor statistic
1	-1
2	-2
3-4	-3
5-7	-4
8-11	-5
12-16	-6
17-22	-7

- If minimum SAN Loss for seeing the creature is 0, additional Stability Loss is +0 (+1 if the creature is clearly non-humanoid); if minimum SAN Loss is 1, additional Stability Loss is +1; if minimum SAN Loss is a die roll, additional Stability Loss is +2; additional Stability Loss is +3 or higher for gods or titans.

Tomes:

Only the *Al Azif* grants +4 Cthulhu Mythos; only the *Necronomicon* grants +3 Cthulhu Mythos. Major tomes grant +2 and minor tomes +1. Differences come from the various topics or eerie side-effects of each tome.

Spells:

Convert spells based on the examples given in this book. Extrapolate Stability costs from these listings and from the Stability Loss table on p. 71, but in general, each 2-3 Magic Points or SAN points should translate to 1 Stability pool point. Only spells that cost permanent POW should cost Stability rating points, and not many of them. Keep in mind

that *Trail of Cthulhu* compresses SAN, Magic Point, and POW scores into ability pools that will likely top out around 10-12 points. Derive Inertia pools for rituals from the resisting POW or Magic Points of the creature or god summoned.

APPENDIX 2: SOURCES AND RESOURCES

"...A VAST, HIGH-CEILED LIBRARY WHOSE WALLS WERE SOLIDLY PACKED WITH TATTERED BOOKS OF PONDEROUS, ARCHAIC, AND VAGUELY REPELLENT ASPECT."

— "THE HORROR AT RED HOOK"

HP LOVECRAFT

If for whatever reason you haven't read the works of **HP Lovecraft** yet, you can rectify that omission speedily and at little cost. Penguin Classics has three volumes in print containing all his adult solo fiction, edited by the redoubtable ST Joshi.

Begin with *The Call of Cthulhu*, and then read, in any order you like:

The Case of Charles Dexter Ward

The Dunwich Horror

At the Mountains of Madness

The Shadow Over Innsmouth

The Dreams in the Witch-House

The Colour Out of Space

The Haunter of the Dark

The Whisperer in Darkness

The Shunned House

The Shadow Out of Time

Pickman's Model

The Rats in the Walls

The Music of Erich Zann

From Beyond

The Thing on the Doorstep

If you've read any five of these tales, that gives you a good start at being the Keeper. Players unfamiliar with the Mythos should ideally read at least *The Call of Cthulhu* or *The Dunwich Horror* to get an idea of what the genre entails.

Howard and Derleth

There are two other authors who, in addition to Lovecraft, directly inspired this book. The Cthulhu Mythos tales of **Robert E Howard** have been collected in *Nameless Cults*. I favor the novel *Skull-Face* (in that collection), but understand that mine is a minority viewpoint. More universally praised Howard stories of the Mythos include *Dig Me No Grave*, *The Thing on the Roof*, and *The Fire of Asshurbanipal*, but really, they're all savagely good.

The solo Mythos tales of **August Derleth** are collected in *The Cthulhu Mythos*. His "posthumous collaborations" with Lovecraft are not recommended, except as a mine for proper names – they are tiresome reworkings of themes Lovecraft did better the first time. Derleth's solo tales, on the other hand, are surprisingly effective and often good fun, especially *The*

Thing That Walked On the Wind, *Ithaqua*, *The Return of Hastur*, and *The Lair of the Star-Spawn* (with Mark R Schorer). His novel *The Trail of Cthulhu* is really a collection of over-obvious short stories, but it has an undeniable thrill and verve, and makes a terrific game background.

Other Mythos Authors

There are hundreds of authors who have touched, for better or worse, on the Cthulhu Mythos, some unwittingly. It's worth reading the writers who influenced Lovecraft, especially **Algernon Blackwood** (*The Willows* and *The Wendigo* for atmosphere, the John Silence occult detective stories for structure), **Arthur Machen** (*The Novel of the Black Seal* and *The Red Hand* are first-rate horror mysteries, and *The Great God Pan* is Dunwich in ovo), and **Robert W Chambers** (his collection *The King in Yellow* gave August Derleth his best idea ever about Hastur).

During his lifetime, Lovecraft freely shared the Mythos with his colleagues and correspondents, primary among them **Clark Ashton Smith,** who was his superior as a prose stylist, but less concerned with structure. Smith preferred to drop Mythos names into strange, far places such as primordial Hyperborea, medieval Averoigne, Mars, and far-future Xothique, all featured in the anthology *A Rendezvous In Averoigne*. Smith also wrote a few much-underrated contemporary Mythos-style horrors, such as *The Return of the Sorcerer, The Treader of the Dust*, and *The Hunters From Beyond*.

Two of Lovecraft's younger correspondents, **Robert Bloch**

and **Henry Kuttner,** have admirably complete anthologies of their Mythos stories available: *Mysteries of the Worm* and *The Book of Iod*, respectively. (Bloch's novel *Strange Eons* is essentially a vastly superior rewrite of Derleth's *Trail of Cthulhu*.) The Mythos story *The Terror From the Depths* by **Fritz Leiber** is good fun, but his excellent novels *Conjure Wife* (about a conspiracy of witches on a New England campus) and *Our Lady of Darkness* (about urban sorcery and Clark Ashton Smith) both possess a strongly Lovecraftian flavor without touching on the Mythos per se.

As an editor, Derleth recruited his own younger generation of writers: **Ramsey Campbell** produced some excellent regional Mythos horror set in England's Severn Valley (collected in *Cold Print*), while the critic **Colin Wilson** produced a surprisingly good Mythos tale with a psychological kick in *The Return of the Lloigor*. Other anthologists stepped up: *Than Curse the Darkness* by **David Drake** (in *New Tales of the Cthulhu Mythos*) is practically mandatory reading on the interaction of political evil and the Mythos, and "Sticks" by **Karl Edward Wagner** (in the 1989 edition of *Tales of the Cthulhu Mythos*) may be the finest Mythos story of the last 40 years, rivaled only by "Details" by **China Mieville** (in *The Children of Cthulhu*).

In the postmodern era, Lovecraft even became the subject of Mythos tales, including *Black Man With A Horn* by the incredibly gifted horrorist **TED Klein,** and of non-Mythos adventures such as *Lovecraft's Book* by **Richard A Lupoff,** in

which HPL gets tangled up with Nazi spies in America. Speaking of Nazis, *Denied to the Enemy* by **Dennis Detwiller** is a mind-twisting novel of Mythos action in WWII. *Delta Green: The Rules of Engagement* by **John Tynes** brings the Mythos into a collision with the 1990s espionage action thriller, while *The Atrocity Archive* by **Charles Stross** blends Lovecraft and Le Carré.

Other Horrorists

The Silver John tales of **Manly Wade Wellman** have a Lovecraft-like relationship with regional feel and folklore (in this case, Appalachia), and his John Thunstone is an occult investigator worthy of emulation. A similarly investigative horror, told at full tilt, is the superb werewolf conspiracy novel *Darker Than You Think* by **Jack Williamson**. The young-adult horror novels by **John Bellairs** (especially *The Dark Secret of Weatherend* and *The Figure in the Shadows*) likewise meld formula and feel surprisingly effectively.

The Fu Manchu novels of **Sax Rohmer** quite obviously influenced Derleth's *Trail of Cthulhu*, but they're a great deal of lurid fun in their own right and show their investigative structure to good advantage. The seven Fu Manchu novels written between 1931 and 1940 (*Daughter, Mask, Bride, Trail, Drums,* and *Island of Fu Manchu,* plus *President Fu Manchu*) are also excellent windows into period paranoia, sadly including period racism.

The "Black Magic" novels **Dennis Wheatley** banged out in the 1930s and 1940s are, if anything, more lurid (and almost as racist), but present a strong dramatic case for the notion that political evil (Nazism in *Strange Conflict* and *They Used Dark Forces*, Communism in *The Devil Rides Out* and *The Haunting of Toby Jugg*) will resort to supernatural evil (Satanism). The Cold War occult espionage novel *Declare*, by **Tim Powers,** makes much the same argument, albeit with vastly more subtlety and a far more Lovecraftian feel. In *The Keep*, **F. Paul Wilson** argues the opposite case, with a rabbi and an SS commandant joining forces against a monster, while *The Tomb* updates Sax Rohmer-style "Oriental menace" for the modern thriller era.

In the realm of pure feel, meanwhile, the ghost stories of **MR James** (*Casting the Runes*, *Count Magnus*, and *Canon Alberic's Scrapbook* seem most relevant to our purpose, but they're all great) have never been surpassed. **Thomas Ligotti** is likely the single best horrorist working today in short fiction; *The Nightmare Factory* is an omnibus collection of his mad, oneiric gems. In *The Perseids and Other Stories*, **Robert Charles Wilson** manages the difficult task of writing superb Lovecraftian tales without ever overtly referencing the Mythos.

Other Fiction

Hitting the investigation side of the 1930s, meanwhile, the detective novels of **Raymond Chandler** (*The Big Sleep*, *Farewell My Lovely*) and **Dashiell Hammett** (*The Dain Curse*, *The Maltese Falcon*) surely need no recommendation. At least tell me you've seen the movies.

On that visual note, the comics *Terry and the Pirates* (1934-1946) by **Milton Caniff** and *The Adventures of Tintin* (1929-1976) by **Hergé** have crystalline storytelling, intricate research, globe-trotting settings, and damn fine period art in common.

Non-Fiction

Since Yesterday, by **Frederick Lewis Allen**, is a popular history of the 1930s in America written in 1941, which makes it even more useful for Thirties storytelling. More conventional, more global, and far more depressing, is *The Dark Valley: A Panorama of the 1930s*, by **Piers Brendon**. The quad-fecta of depressing are *Berlin Diary* by **William L Shirer**, *The Great Terror* by **Robert Conquest**, *The Rape of Nanking* by **Iris Chang**, and *Homage to Catalonia* by **George Orwell**, which are respectively: a first-person reminiscence of Hitler's Germany, historical unveilings of Stalin's purges and Japanese atrocities, and a savage memoir by the Thirties' greatest writer of the waste that was the Spanish Civil War. After all that, it's almost refreshing to read *Unholy Alliance* by **Peter Levenda**, a crackling blend of foaming madness and fair-to-middling research on the "occult front" in the 1930s and beyond, including thrilling tales of the Ahnenerbe.

Should this book have failed to sate your urge for 1930s RPG material, seek ye the exhaustively comprehensive *Pulp Hero* by **Steven S Long** and the delightfully breezy *GURPS Cliffhangers* by **Brian J Underhill**. Finally, this book would have been a wan and anemic shadow of itself without **Daniel Harms'**

magisterial *Encyclopedia Cthulhiana*, at this writing soon to be published in an extended, improved version, *The Cthulhu Mythos Encyclopedia*.

APPENDIX 3: USEFUL DOCUMENTS

These documents are all available for download from the Pelgrane Press Ltd website

www.pelgranepress.com

They may be reproduced for personal use.

The website has other useful resources including, articles maps, documents and links to useful sources.

TRAIL OF CTHULHU
BY KENNETH HITE

Player Name:

Sanity[1]

0	1	2	3
4	5	6	7
8	9	10	11
12	13	14	15

Hit Threshold[3]

Stability

-12	-11	-10	-9
-8	-7	-6	-5
-4	-3	-2	-1
0	1	2	3
4	5	6	7
8	9	10	11
12	13	14	15

Health

-12	-11	-10	-9
-8	-7	-6	-5
-4	-3	-2	-1
0	1	2	3
4	5	6	7
8	9	10	11
12	13	14	15

Investigator Name:

Drive:

Occupation:[2]
Occupational benefits:

Pillars of Sanity:

Build Points:

Academic Abilities	Interpersonal Abilities	General Abilities
Accounting		
Anthropology	Assess Honesty	Athletics
Archaeology	Bargain	Conceal
Architecture	Bureaucracy	Disguise (I)
Art History	Cop Talk	Driving
Biology	Credit Rating	Electrical Repair(I)
Cthulhu Mythos[4]	Flattery	Explosives(I)
Cryptography	Interrogation	Filch
Geology	Intimidation	Firearms[5]
History	Oral History	First Aid
Languages[6]	Reassurance	Fleeing[7]
	Streetwise	Health[9]
		Hypnosis[8]
		Mechanical Repair(I)
		Piloting
	Technical Abilities	Preparedness
Law		Psychoanalysis
Library Use	Art	Riding
Medicine	Astronomy	Sanity[9]
Occult	Chemistry	Stability[9]
Physics	Craft	Scuffling
Theology	Evidence Collection	Sense Trouble
	Forensics	Shadowing
	Locksmith	Stealth
	Outdoorsman	Weapons
	Pharmacy	
	Photography	

[1] In a Pulp game where Sanity can be recovered, mark Sanity pool loss with a line, Sanity rating loss with a cross.

[2] Occupational abilities are half price. Mark them with a * before assigning points.

[3] Hit Threshold is 3, 4 if your Athletics is 8 or higher

(I) These General abilities double up as Investigative abilities

[4] Usually, you can't start with Cthulhu Mythos. Sanity is limited to 10-Cthulhu Mythos.

[5] In a Pulp game If your Firearms rating is 5 you can fire two pistols at once (see p. 42)

[6] Assign one language per point, during play. Record them here.

[7] Any Fleeing rating above twice your Athletics rating costs one point for two.

[8] Only Alienists and Parapsycholigists can buy Hypnosis, and only in a Pulp game

[9] You start with 4 free Sanity points, 1 Health and 1 Stability point.

SOURCES OF STABILITY:

CONTACTS AND NOTES

Keeper's Investigator Matrix

Player					
Investigator					
Drive					
Occupation					
Health					
Sanity					
Pillar 1					
Pillar 2					
Pillar 3					
Stability					
Source 1					
Source 2					
Source 3					
Contact 1					
Contact 2					
Contact 3					
Accounting					
Anthropology					
Archaeology					
Architecture					
Art History					
Biology					
Cthulhu Mythos					
Cryptography					
Geology					
History					
Languages					
Law					
Library Use					
Medicine					
Occult					
Physics					
Theology					
Assess Honesty					
Bargain					
Bureaucracy					
Cop Talk					
Credit Rating					
Flattery					
Interrogation					
Intimidation					
Oral History					
Reassurance					
Streetwise					
Art					
Astronomy					
Chemistry					
Craft					
Evidence Collection					
Forensics					
Locksmith					
Outdoorsman					
Pharmacy					
Photography					

Investigative Ability Checklist

When creating an adventure, use this table to record which abilities are essential to the adventure, which are optional, and which are not used at all. Let your players know which not to take. If you are using pre-existing characters, tick them on the left column table, then build your adventure around them.

Investigative Abilities	Core Clue Tally	Total In Adventure
Academic Abilities		
Accounting		
Anthropology		
Archaeology		
Architecture		
Art History		
Biology		
Cthulhu Mythos		
Cryptography		
Geology		
History		
Languages		
Law		
Library Use		
Medicine		
Occult		
Physics		
Theology		
Interpersonal		
Assess Honesty		
Bargain		
Bureaucracy		
Cop Talk		
Credit Rating		
Disguise (G)		
Flattery		
Interrogation		
Intimidation		
Oral History		
Reassurance		
Streetwise		
Technical		
Art		
Astronomy		
Chemistry		
Craft		
Electrical Repair (G)		
Explosives (G)		
Evidence Collection		
Forensics		
Locksmith		
Mechanical Repair (G)		
Outdoorsman		
Pharmacy		
Photography		

Total Investigative Points

(G) Indicates a General ability which doubles up as an Investigative one

Campaign Frame Notes

Title

Pitch

It's like Blah vs Blah, X meets Y, etc.

Setting

Where is it set? One location, multiple locations? What languages might be used?

Style

Purist or Pulp, or a mixture? Dread or Gore? Are laws enforced? Can firearms be used? Race, gender or politics: an important element?

Mythos

How all pervasive is the Mythos? How much do the general public and the authorities know? Which gods exist? Are important? Just Lovecraft or other authors?

Investigators

Why are they together? What do they have in common? What skills must they have? In what way are they restricted?

Campaign Frame Notes

Continuing NPCs

Rivals, contacts, villains, cultists, friends and colleagues.

Name	Location	Relationship to PCs	Notes

Rules Variants

What caps on abilities? What new abilities are there? Which optional rules to use? Add page references.

Physical Injury and Death

Unlike most abilities, your Health pool can drop below 0.

When it does this, you must make a Consciousness Roll. Roll a die with the absolute value of your current Health pool as your Difficulty. You may deliberately strain yourself to remain conscious, voluntarily reducing your Health pool by an amount of your choice. (You may not voluntarily reduce your Health pool below -11.) For each point you reduce it, add 1 to your die result. The Difficulty of the Consciousness roll is based on your Health pool before you make this reduction.

Father Micah is being chased by Y'golonac cultists through what he initially thought was a convent. A cultist hits him with an antique spiked morning-star, dropping his Health pool to -2. He really wants to get away from them, lest they force him to celebrate their vile fleshly rituals. Thus he must remain conscious. The absolute value of -2 is 2, so this is the Difficulty of his Consciousness roll. He chooses to expend another 2 Health points he doesn't have, pushing himself onward toward the ornately – and obscenely — carven doors. That gives him a bonus of 2 to his roll. He rolls a 6, for a final result of 8. Father Micah gets away, but now his Health pool is down to -4.

If your pool is anywhere from 0 to –5, you are hurt, but have suffered no permanent injury beyond a few superficial cuts and bruises. However, the pain of your injuries makes it impossible to spend points on Investigative abilities, and increases the Difficulty Numbers of all tests and contests, including opponents' Hit Thresholds, by 1.

First Aid: A character with the First Aid ability can improve your condition by spending First Aid points. For every First Aid point spent, you regain 2 Health points — unless you are healing yourself, in which case you gain only 1 Health point for every First Aid point spent.

A character giving First Aid must be in a position to devote all of his attention to directly tending to your wounds.

First Aid can only refill your pool to where you were before the scene in which you received this latest injury. For example, if you get shot and then someone punches you during the same fight, you can repair both. If you get shot, run away, get into another fight, and then somebody punches you, you can heal the punch.

 First Aid can only ever bring you back to one third of your maximum Health points. All other increases must be gained using the Refreshing Health rules (see p. 81). This option makes hurt Investigators very fragile.

If your pool is between –6 and –11, you have been seriously wounded. You must make a Consciousness roll.

Whether or not you maintain consciousness, you are no longer able to fight. Until you receive first aid, you will lose an additional Health point every half hour.

First Aid and serious wounds: A character with the First Aid ability can stabilize your condition by spending 2 First Aid points. However, he can't restore your Health points.

Even after you receive first aid, you must convalesce in a hospital or similar setting for a period of days. Your period of forced inactivity is a number of days equal to the positive value of your lowest Health pool score. (So if you were reduced to -8 Health, you are hospitalized for 8 days.) On the day of your discharge, your Health pool increases to half its maximum value. On the next day, it refreshes fully.

When your pool dips to –12 or below, you are dead. Time to activate your replacement Investigator.

Health Loss For NPCs

 In a Purist game, the Investigators are no different from anyone else. All humans lose Health mechanically in the same way.

 In the Pulp mode, the Investigators are a cut above the rest of the herd. Normal people, both mooks and bystanders, simply (or dramatically, or messily) die when their Health is reduced below 0. Using this rule does make combats much faster, so even Purist Keepers may want to sneak it into battles against cultists, etc. The Keeper may, if she thinks it dramatically appropriate, decide that certain NPCs use the Investigators' Health loss rules.

Weapon Type	Damage Modifier
Fist, kick	–2
Small improvised weapon, blackjack, bullwhip, nightstick, knife	–1
Big improvised weapon, machete, heavy club, fireplace poker, light firearm	0
Sword, heavy firearm	+1

Stability Loss Table

Incident	Stability Loss
You see a fresh corpse; you witness a killing	1
A human opponent attacks you with evident intent to do serious harm	2
You are in a car or other vehicle accident serious enough to pose a risk of injury	2
You experience a strong unnatural sensation such as intense déjà vu, "missing time", or hallucinations	2
You witness acts of torture	2
A human opponent attacks you with evident intent to kill	3
You kill someone in a fight	3
You see a particularly grisly murder or accident scene	3
You see a supernatural creature from a distance	3
You witness an obviously unnatural, but not necessarily threatening, omen or magical effect – a wall covered in horrible insects, a talking cat, or a bleeding window	3
You see hundreds of corpses; you witness a large battle	4
You see a supernatural creature up close	4
You spend a week in solitary confinement	4
You learn that a friend, loved one, or Source of Stability has been violently killed	4
You discover the corpse of a friend, loved one, or Source of Stability	5
You are attacked by a supernatural creature, or by a friend, loved one, or Source of Stability	5
You witness a clearly supernatural or impossible killing	5
You witness or experience an obviously unnatural, and threatenting, omen or magical effect – a cold hand clutches your heart, a swarm of bees pours out of your mouth	5
You kill someone in cold blood; you torture someone	5
You see a friend, loved one, or Source of Stability killed	6
You are tortured for an hour or longer	6
You discover that you have committed cannibalism	6
You are possessed by some outside force, but conscious while it operates your body unspeakably	7
You speak with someone you know well who you know to be dead	7
You are attacked by a single gigantic supernatural creature or by a horde of supernatural creatures	7
You see a friend, loved one, or Source of Stability killed in a particularly gruesome manner or in a way you are helpless to avert	8
You kill a friend, loved one, or Source of Stability	8

Cthulhu Mythos Stability and Sanity Loss Table

Revelation or Intuition	Stability Pool Loss	Sanity Pool Loss
Some aspect of the Mythos is behind this mystery; any specifics are either comfortably distant in space or time, or not immediately relevant to your larger concerns	2	0
This Mythos truth poses a clear and present danger to innocents; this truth goes deeper, reaches back farther, or has wider implications, than you previously believed	3	1
This Mythos truth poses a clear and present danger to you or your loved ones; this truth is global or epochal in scope	4	1
This Mythos truth shatters one of your Pillars of Sanity	6	2
This Mythos truth could destroy the world or is doing so right now, probably inevitably; this truth proves your Drive to be meaningless or doomed	8	3

APPENDIX 4: CONTRIBUTORS

KENNETH HITE

Kenneth Hite claims to have bought the first copy of Call of Cthulhu sold in Oklahoma City, in August of 1981. Since then, he has moved to dread and night-haunted Chicago, written all or part of seventy or so roleplaying game books (including *Nightmares of Mine, Dubious Shards,* and *Adventures Into Darkness*), and acquired the requisite Lovecraftian cat. His "Tour de Lovecraft: The Settings" column appears in *Weird Tales* magazine; his *Suppressed Transmission* column explores the Higher Strangeness in *Pyramid*. His wife Sheila knits.

ROBIN D LAWS

Robin D Laws is a writer and game designer. His roleplaying game designs for Pelgrane Press are The Dying Earth, The Esoterrorists, Fear Itself and the upcoming Mutant City Blues.

Robin's other roleplaying games include Feng Shui , Rune, HeroQuest and Og: Unearthed Editions. Among Robin's six novels are Pierced Heart, The Rough and the Smooth, and Freedom Phalanx, a book set in the universe of the City Of Heroes computer game.

2007 saw the publication of 40 Years Of Gen Con, an oral history of the hobby games industry's biggest convention. Always ready to take an intriguing career detour, his various past projects include collectible card games, computer games, and comic books.

JÉRÔME HUGUENIN

Jérome is a French freelance illustrator and graphic designer born in 1975. He is married with one little girl.
He first worked with Pelgrane Press on the Dying Earth RPG, (top rated in his game collection) and designed all the previous GUMSHOE books.
He will provide art for the up coming GUMSHOE books, including *Mutant City Blues* and *Trail of Cthulhu* supplements.
He also work for French publishers and a local magazine.

When not working he is usually playing bass or trying to grow fruits and vegetables. The rotten one usually end up in his photo collection for his creations – perfect for a monster skin !

SIMON ROGERS

Simon Rogers is the managing director and co-owner of Pelgrane Press Ltd, publishers of the Dying Earth RPG and GUMSHOE system. He also runs ProFantasy Software Ltd, makers of Campaign Cartographer 3 and its add-ons. His job consists primarily of asking other people to do things for him with varying degrees of success.

INDICES

Alien Races

Beasts and Monsters

Gods and Titans

Spells

INDEX

JÉRÔME 07